Medical Aspects
of Claims

Medical Aspects of Claims

Edited by

JAMES J. MARKHAM, J.D., CPCU, AIC, AIAF

Director of Curriculum
General Counsel and Ethics Counsel
Insurance Institute of America

First Edition • 1991

INSURANCE INSTITUTE OF AMERICA
720 Providence Road, Malvern, Pennsylvania 19355-0770

© 1991
INSURANCE INSTITUTE OF AMERICA
All rights reserved. This book or any part thereof may not be reproduced without the written permission of the publisher.

First Edition • 1991

Library of Congress Catalog Number 90-86334
International Standard Book Number 0-89462-060-6

Printed in the United States of America

Foreword

The American Institute for Property and Liability Underwriters and the Insurance Institute of America are independent, nonprofit, educational organizations serving the needs of the property and liability insurance business. The Institutes develop a wide range of programs—curricula, study materials, and examinations—in response to the educational requirements of various elements of the business.

The American Institute confers the Chartered Property Casualty Underwriter (CPCU®) professional designation on those who meet the Institute's experience, ethics, and examination requirements.

The Insurance Institute of America offers associate designations and certificate programs in the following technical and managerial disciplines:

Accredited Adviser in Insurance (AAI®)
Associate in Claims (AIC)
Associate in Underwriting (AU)
Associate in Risk Management (ARM)
Associate in Loss Control Management (ALCM®)
Associate in Premium Auditing (APA®)
Associate in Management (AIM)
Associate in Research and Planning (ARP®)
Associate in Insurance Accounting and Finance (AIAF)
Associate in Automation Management (AAM®)
Associate in Marine Insurance Management (AMIM®)
Associate in Reinsurance (ARe®)
Associate in Fidelity and Surety Bonding (AFSB)
Certificate in General Insurance
Certificate in Supervisory Management
Certificate in Introduction to Claims
Certificate in Introduction to Property and Liability Insurance

vi—Foreword

The Institutes began publishing textbooks in 1976 to help students meet the national examination standards. Since that time, we have produced more than seventy individual textbook volumes. Despite the vast differences in the subjects and purposes of these volumes, they all have much in common. First, each book is specifically designed to increase knowledge and develop skills that can improve job performance and help students achieve the educational objectives of the course for which it is assigned. Second, all of the manuscripts of our texts are widely reviewed prior to publication by both insurance business practitioners and members of the academic community. In addition, all of our texts and course guides reflect the work of Institute staff members. These writing or editing duties are seen as an integral part of their professional responsibilities, and no one earns a royalty based on the sale of our texts. We have proceeded in this way to avoid even the appearance of any conflict of interests. Finally, the revisions of our texts often incorporate improvements suggested by students and course leaders.

We welcome criticisms of and suggestions for improving our publications. It is only with such constructive comments that we can hope to improve the quality of our study materials. Please direct any comments you may have on this text to the Curriculum Department of the Institutes.

Norman A. Baglini, Ph.D., CPCU, CLU
President and Chief Executive Officer

Preface

It is often said that claims work consists of determining coverage, liability, and damages. If so, the determination of damages is at the heart of good claims work, especially for the many cases in which coverage and liability are clear. For injury claims, the determination of damages depends almost entirely on medical issues. Thus, claim representatives should be able to address medical issues. Those who cannot, fail to perform an essential part of claims work.

Historically, claim representatives have had little formal education in medical issues. They have relied on on-the-job training and self-education through standard reference works, or they have simply neglected education in medical issues. Since lines of business written to cover injury claims now represent over half the premium volume of the property and liability insurance industry, claim representatives with a commitment to professionalism cannot ignore their medical education. Furthermore, insurers, regulators, and society at large have become increasingly intolerant of misspent money in claims.

This text was developed to provide claim representatives with a fundamental education in the medical aspects of claims. It addresses both pure medicine, such as anatomy, as well as medical practices, such as billing procedures. It was designed for use in the Insurance Institute of America's Associate in Claims (AIC) 34 course, which as of the fall of 1991, concerns workers compensation and medical aspects of claims. Although the AIC 34 program combines workers compensation topics with this text, this particular text is not limited in application to compensation claims. It applies to any type of injury claim. At several points, this text refers to "casualty" insurance or "casualty" claims. Although these terms are somewhat imprecise, they should be understood to mean any type of injury claim covered by insurance written by the property and liability insurance industry.

viii—Preface

The Institute hopes students of this course are convinced that their medical education must continue. Full-time claims personnel cannot become physicians, but there is literally no limit to what can be learned about medicine and medical practices. For this reason, perhaps the most valuable part of this text is the Appendix to Chapter 1, which provides a list of references. These reference works are essential tools for claim representatives who handle injury claims.

The Institute is deeply indebted to the contributing authors of this text. All are experienced claims personnel who believe strongly in the need for medical education for claim representatives. Each of the contributing authors also served as a constructive and compassionate reviewer of another author's manuscript. I designed the contents of this text and, along with other Institute staff, edited the entire work. The original drawings of human anatomy by Ira Grunther, Grunther Associates, will greatly enhance the students' understanding of the material.

The Institute also deeply appreciates the work of the following people who reviewed portions of this text and made valuable suggestions for improvement: Diane V. Bistany, General Reinsurance Company; David W. Clifton, P.T., Physical Therapy Review Services, Inc.; John Cross, CPCU, State Farm Mutual Automobile Insurance Company; William W. Davis, American Re-Insurance Company; Marletta England, CPCU, Farmers Insurance Companies; William R. Gawne, CPCU, CIGNA; Nadine J. Kaslow, Ph.D., Emory University; David Kendrick, GAB Business Services Inc.; Eric P. Larson, CPCU, St. Paul Insurance Companies; Samuel M. Meeks, CPCU, AIC, Associated Risk Services, Inc.; E. E. Morgan, CPCU, Surplus Lines Stamping Office of Texas; Booth J. Muller, CPCU, State Auto Insurance Company; Louis A. Papastrat, American Re-Insurance Company; Kevin M. Quinley, CPCU, AIC, ARM, Medmarc-Hamilton Resources Corporation; and Thomas P. Vaughn, Ph.D. Robert J. Gibbons, Ph.D., CPCU, CLU, of the Insurance Institute of America reviewed the entire text.

While the above individuals made valuable contributions to the text, the responsibility for the final product rests with the Insurance Institute of America. We welcome corrections and suggestions for improvements—especially from AIC students and course leaders.

James J. Markham, J.D., CPCU, AIC

Contributing Authors

The Insurance Institute of America acknowledges with deep appreciation the work of the following contributing authors:

Beth Brown, R.N.
State Farm Mutual Automobile Insurance Company

Francis X. Comella, Jr., CPCU, CLU, ChFC
State Farm Mutual Automobile Insurance Company

Jonathan H. Gice, CPCU, CRC, CIRS
EBI Companies

Cathy Y. Hamby
Seibels Bruce Insurance Companies

Lee M. Levin, R.N., CRC
Insurance Medical Careers

James J. Markham, J.D., CPCU, AIC, AIAF
Insurance Institute of America

Suzanne M. Switzer, R.N.
Nationwide Mutual Insurance Company

Minh D. Vu, CPCU
The Wyatt Company

Table of Contents

Chapter 1—Anatomy and Medical Terminology 1

Anatomy ~ *Positional Terms; The Human Skeleton; Soft Tissues; The Nervous System; Organs and Systems*

Diagnostic Testing ~ *Sampling Tests; Tests of Function or Performance; Radiographic Tests; Scopes and Fiber Optics; Psychological Tests*

Summary

Glossary

Appendix

Chapter 2—Trauma and Other Injuries 61

Skin Injuries ~ *Superficial Wounds; Lacerations; Scars; Burns*

Injuries to Muscles and Joints ~ *Sprains and Strains; Joint Problems; Carpal Tunnel Syndrome; Temporomandibular Joint Syndrome*

Fractures and Head Injuries ~ *Fractures and Resulting Problems; Head Injuries*

Internal Injuries ~ *Injuries to the Thorax; Injuries to the Abdomen*

Spinal Problems ~ *Sprain and Strain; Spinal Fractures; Disc Bulging and Herniation; Congenital Problems; Degenerative Disorders; Neck Problems; Diagnosis of Spinal Problems*

Summary

xii—Contents

Chapter 3—Psychological Injuries and Conditions 105

Psychological Response to Physical Injury ~ *Common Psychological Responses; Evaluation of Psychological Symptoms*

Diagnosis of Distinct Psychological Disorders ~ *The Diagnostic and Statistical Manual of Mental Disorders; Major Categories of Mental Disorders; Personality Disorders*

Problem Psychological Conditions in Claims ~ *Stress Disorders; Somotoform Disorders; Intentionally Created Symptoms*

Evaluation of Claims for Psychological Conditions ~ *Existence of a Psychological Disorder; Causation; Treatment of Psychological Disorders*

Summary

Chapter 4—Disability 155

The Nature of Disability ~ *Definitions; Effect of Disability on the Value of Claims; Attitudes Toward and Myths About the Disabled; Effects of Disabilities on the Disabled Person; Effects of Disability on the Employer of the Disabled*

Determination of Disability ~ *AMA Guide to the Evaluation of Permanent Impairment; Determining Job Demands; Determining Temporary Disability*

Overcoming Disability ~ *Factors Affecting the Length of Temporary Disability; Overcoming Permanent Impairment*

Summary

Chapter 5—Rehabilitation 189

The Nature of Rehabilitation ~ *Definition; The Need for Rehabilitation; Costs/Benefits of Rehabilitation*

Parties to the Rehabilitation Process ~ *The Professional Rehabilitation Provider; Other Rehabilitation Professionals; Other Key Parties; Quality Assurance*

The Rehabilitation Process ~ *Identification of the Rehabilitation Candidate; Medical Management; Vocational Rehabilitation; Psychosocial Rehabilitation; Forensic Rehabilitation*

Summary

Chapter 6—Evaluation of Medical Treatment 225

Issues on Medical Treatment ~ *Verification of Cause; Necessity of Treatment; Further Treatment; Problems of Controlling Treatment*

The Claim Representative's Role ~ *Identification of Serious Cases; Cases Handled by the Claim Representative*

Medical Records ~ *Purpose of and Standards for Medical Records; Types of Medical Records; Obtaining Medical Records*

Expert Assistance ~ *Retrospective Review; Independent Medical Examination; Problems With Expert Reviews and Examinations*

Summary

Chapter 7—Medical Cost Control 261

The Escalating Cost of Medical Treatment ~ *Historical Perspective; Causes of the Rise in Medical Costs; Effect on Casualty Claim Costs*

Medical Cost Containment Methods ~ *Importance of Cost Containment Methods; Cost Shifting; Fee Audits; Alternative Fee Arrangements; Utilization Review; Guidelines for the Use of Chiropractic Treatments; Guidelines for the Use of Physical Therapy; Effectiveness of Cost Containment*

Summary

Bibliography 295

Index 299

CHAPTER 1

Anatomy and Medical Terminology

Claim representatives must regularly settle claims involving injuries to a claimant. These claims may be medical payments claims, no-fault claims, workers compensation claims, or liability claims. In every such case, claimants must be compensated for the injury or for the treatment of the injury. However, even in a liability claim in which the scope of compensation is the broadest, there are limitations on the amounts to which claimants are entitled. Compensation is only appropriate when (1) the claimant's injury or condition was caused by the insured/compensable event; (2) the claimant's treatment is necessary for, and related to, the injury or condition caused by the insured/compensable event; and (3) the amount of and charges for the claimant's treatment are reasonable. All three of these parameters may involve complex medical, factual, and legal issues. The purpose of this text is to enable claim representatives to evaluate as accurately as possible the medical aspects of their injury cases—that is, to evaluate them *critically*.

Being critical is not necessarily the same as being negative or adversarial. Being critical involves a careful and knowledgeable analysis of the claimant's medical history and condition in light of the three parameters stated above: causation, necessity, and reasonableness. In any case, a claim representative must first *understand* a medical case before he or she can analyze it critically. A great deal of this text is devoted to developing this understanding by defining medical terminology, typical injuries and recovery periods, medical records, and procedures, and practices in the health professions. While some of the material in this text is only relevant to serious injury cases, most of it is important to any injury case.

Understanding a medical case requires a familiarity with medical

2—Medical Aspects of Claims

terminology, human anatomy, and medical tests. The Glossary at the end of this chapter lists some common roots of words that help to understand medical terminology. The rest of the chapter provides information about anatomy and medical testing at a level that may seem extensive to those who are not familiar with medicine. In fact, this chapter is merely a sample of medical information. All claim representatives who handle injury cases should make a career-long effort to expand their medical knowledge. The best way to do so is to read and understand all medical records and reports received on any claim. A good medical dictionary or compact encyclopedia is essential for this task. The Appendix to this chapter includes several standard medical references. For a claim representative who handles injury claims, one or more of these references is as essential an adjusting tool as the recorder or statement pad used to take witness' statements.

ANATOMY

To evaluate injuries and their effect on the normal functions of the human body, the claims professional must develop a good working knowledge of human anatomy. The positional terms defined below and the illustrations in the discussion that follows should help in understanding the human skeleton, the soft tissues of the body, the nervous system, and the organ systems that can sustain trauma.

Positional Terms

The following positional terms identify both areas of the body and the position of injury, disease, or one body part in relation to another body part.
- *Superior* refers to a position which is nearest to the head or the highest place on the body. For example, *superior vena cava* is the great vein that delivers blood from the head, neck, and upper extremities to the heart.
- *Inferior* refers to a position which is farther from the head or lower on the body. For example, *inferior vena cava* is the great vein that receives blood from the body below the level of the diaphragm and returns it to the heart.
- *Anterior* refers to a position nearer to the front of the body. For example, the kneecap is located on the anterior surface of the leg.
- *Posterior* refers to a position nearer to the back of the body. For example, the shoulder blades are located on the posterior body surface.

- *Medial* identifies a position nearer to the midline of the body. For example, the breastbone is in the medial portion of the chest.
- *Lateral* identifies a position that is away from the midline of the body or alongside some other part of the body. For example, the eyes are lateral to the nose.
- *Internal* means within the body. For example, an internal hemorrhage is bleeding on the inside.
- *External* means the outside of the body. For example, the external surface of the body is covered with skin.
- *Proximal* identifies a location closer to the torso of the body. For example, an upper arm fracture that is close to the shoulder area would be called a proximal fracture of the humerus. (The humerus is the bone of the upper arm.)
- *Distal* refers to a location that is away from the torso of the body. For example, an upper arm fracture located closer to the elbow than to the shoulder would be called a distal fracture of the humerus.
- *Central* means at the center. For example, the brain and spinal column make up the central nervous system.
- *Peripheral* identifies a location away from the center. For example, peripheral vascular problems are circulatory problems that occur in the extremities.
- *Visceral* refers to organs within the body. For example, visceral blood vessels supply blood to the stomach wall.

The Human Skeleton

The human skeleton is made up of over 200 bones; however, it is relatively easy to remember them by organizing them by part of the body.

The Cranium. The skull or cranium consists of one frontal bone, two parietal bones, two temporal bones, one occipital bone, one sphenoid bone, and one ethmoid bone. Exhibit 1-1 shows the bones of the cranium.

The *frontal bone* covers the anterior roof of the skull, extends out to form the forehead, and assists in forming the roof of the eye and nasal cavities. Within the frontal bone are air-filled cavities called *frontal sinuses*. Two *parietal bones* help form the sides of the skull. Two *temporal bones* form the lower sides of the skull and extend down to help form the base of the skull. The lower jaw articulates with (that is, is connected by joints) the temporal bones on each side. (A joint is the place where any two bones come together.) The *occipital bone* forms the back of the head as well as a good portion of the base of the skull.

4—Medical Aspects of Claims

Exhibit 1-1
Bones of the Cranium

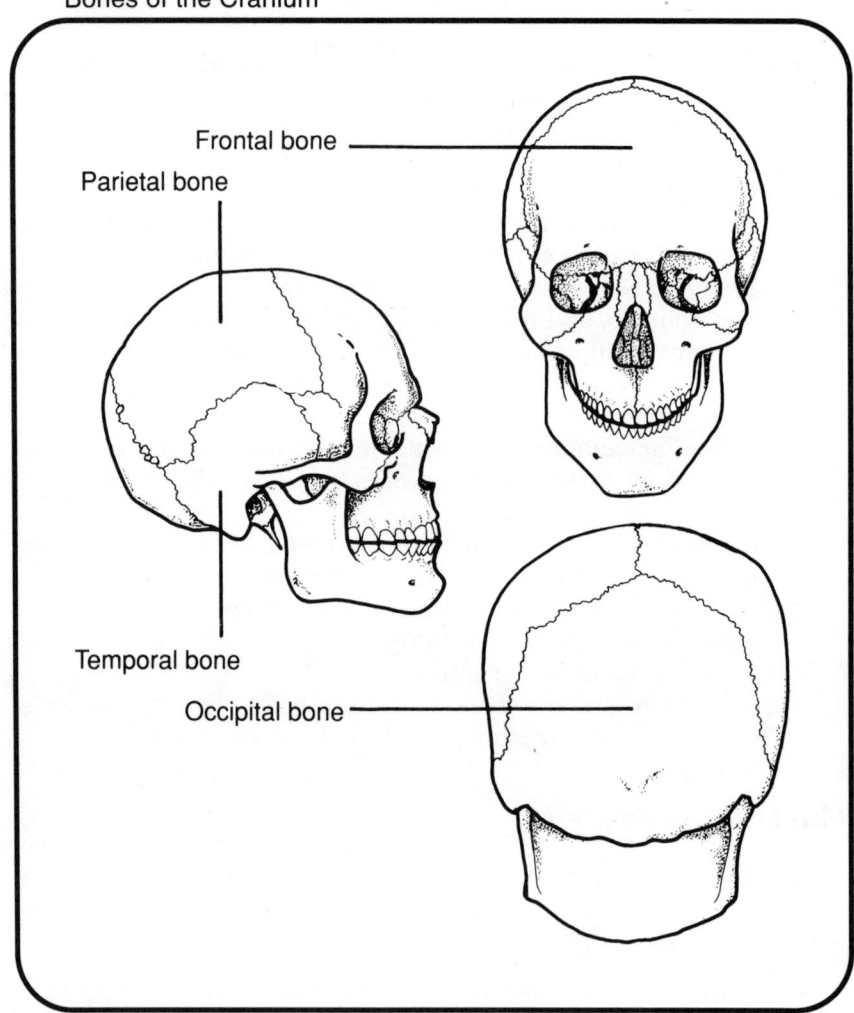

As the spinal cord leaves the brain area, it travels through a large hole in the bottom of the occipital bone called the *foramen magnum*. The first bone of the spine, the *atlas*, supports the skull as it moves forward and backward. On each side of the foramen magnum there are two smooth *condyles* (slightly rounded projections) that articulate with the atlas.

The *sphenoid bone* provides support for the brain from beneath the front part of the brain. The *ethmoid bone*, a light bone located between the eye cavities, helps form the upper part of the nasal septum. Exhibit 1-2 shows the sphenoid and ethmoid bones.

Exhibit 1-2
Sphenoid and Ethmoid Bones

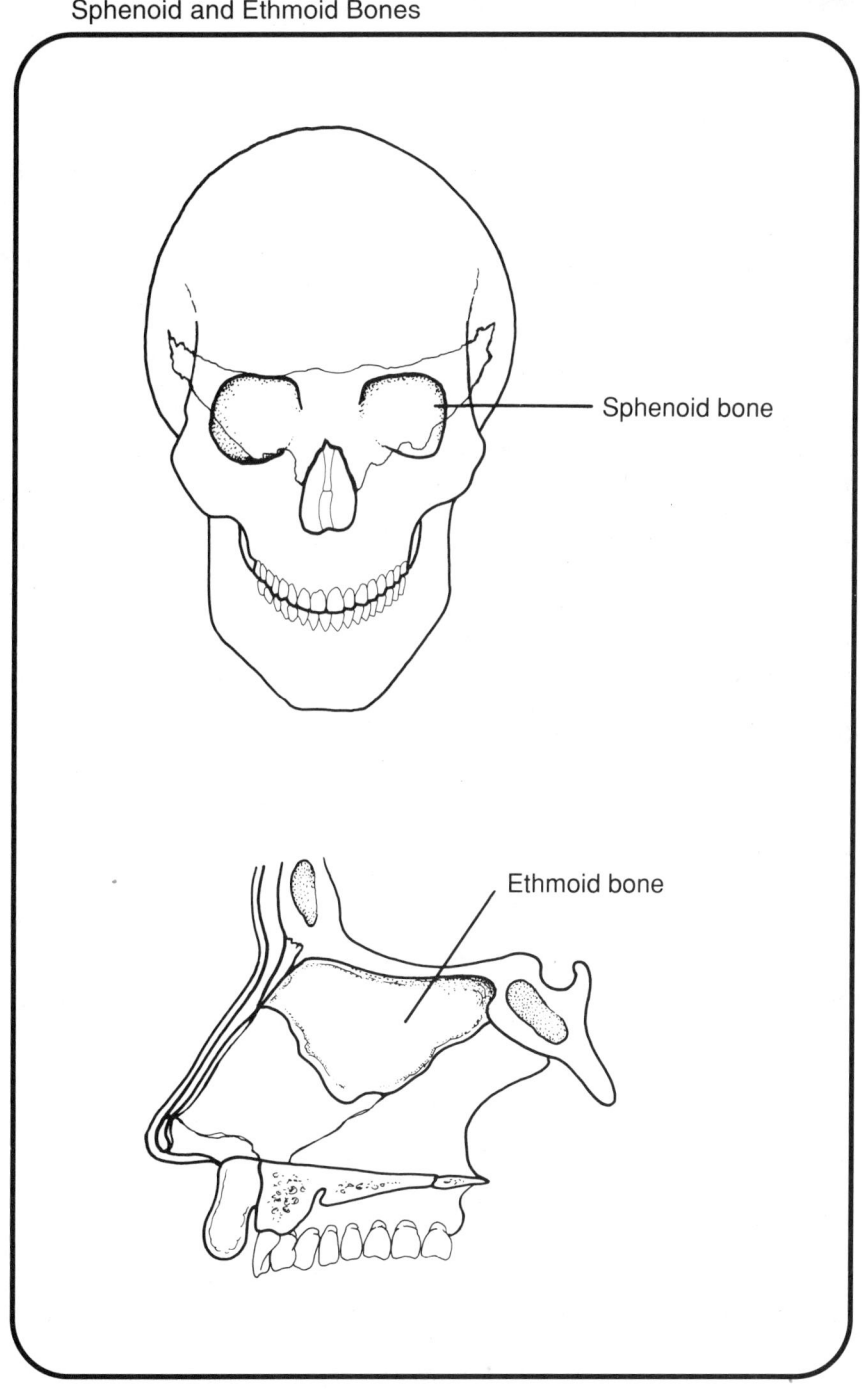

6—Medical Aspects of Claims

The Face. The bones of the face are shown in Exhibit 1-3. Two *nasal bones* lie side by side to form the bridge of the nose. The anterior portion of the nose is composed of cartilage and skin. The *zygomatic* bones form the cheeks and part of the sides and floor of the eye cavities.

The two *lacrimal bones* in the face are about the size of a fingernail. They lie to the front of the medial wall of the orbital cavity, lateral and posterior to the nasal bones. Each bone contains a groove through which the tear duct passes.

The *vomer bone* forms the lower back part of the nasal septum. It lies between the perpendicular plate of the ethmoid bone and the maxillae and the palate of the mouth.

The *palatine bones* are located to the back of the nasal cavities. They form part of the floor of the orbital cavity, part of the lateral wall of the nasal cavity, part of the floor of the nasal cavity, and part of the hard palate of the mouth.

The *interior conchae*, or turbinate bones, extend along the lateral walls of the nasal cavities.

The *maxilla* is the upper jaw bone. This is actually made up of two maxillae, which are fused together at the midline. The maxillae form part of the floor of the eye cavities as well as the hard palate of the inside of the mouth.

The lower jaw is the *mandible*. The two ends of the lower jaw are called rami (plural of ramus). The condyloid processes on the ends of the rami articulate with the temporal bones to form the *temporomandibular joint*, the only movable joint in the skull. A disc separates the condylar process of the mandible and the temporal bone. Ligaments hold the mandible in place and keep it from dislocating.

When the jaw is dislocated by pressure or trauma, the condylar process slides forward over the articular surface and into an indented area in the temporal bone. The jaw is rather easily dislocated, sometimes merely from a yawn or a slight blow. After the ligaments have been stressed by a dislocation, they do not hold the jaw as firmly in place. Repeated dislocations are possible. Backward dislocations are far more rare and can result in fractures to the bone that supports the hearing canal.

The Spine. The *vertebral column* (backbone or spine) is made up of seven *cervical vertebrae* in the neck area, twelve *thoracic vertebrae* in the middle of the back, five *lumbar vertebrae* in the small of the back, the *sacrum* formed by the fusion of five smaller vertebrae, and the *coccyx* formed by the fusion of four or five small vertebrae. A lumbar vertebra is shown in Exhibit 1-4. The vertebrae are linked together by a series of ligaments. In addition to protecting the spinal cord, the vertebral column also provides protection for thirty-one pairs of spinal nerves.

Each vertebra, with the exception of the first two cervical vertebrae, has a drum-shaped body located anteriorly. The body of the

Exhibit 1-3
Bones of the Face

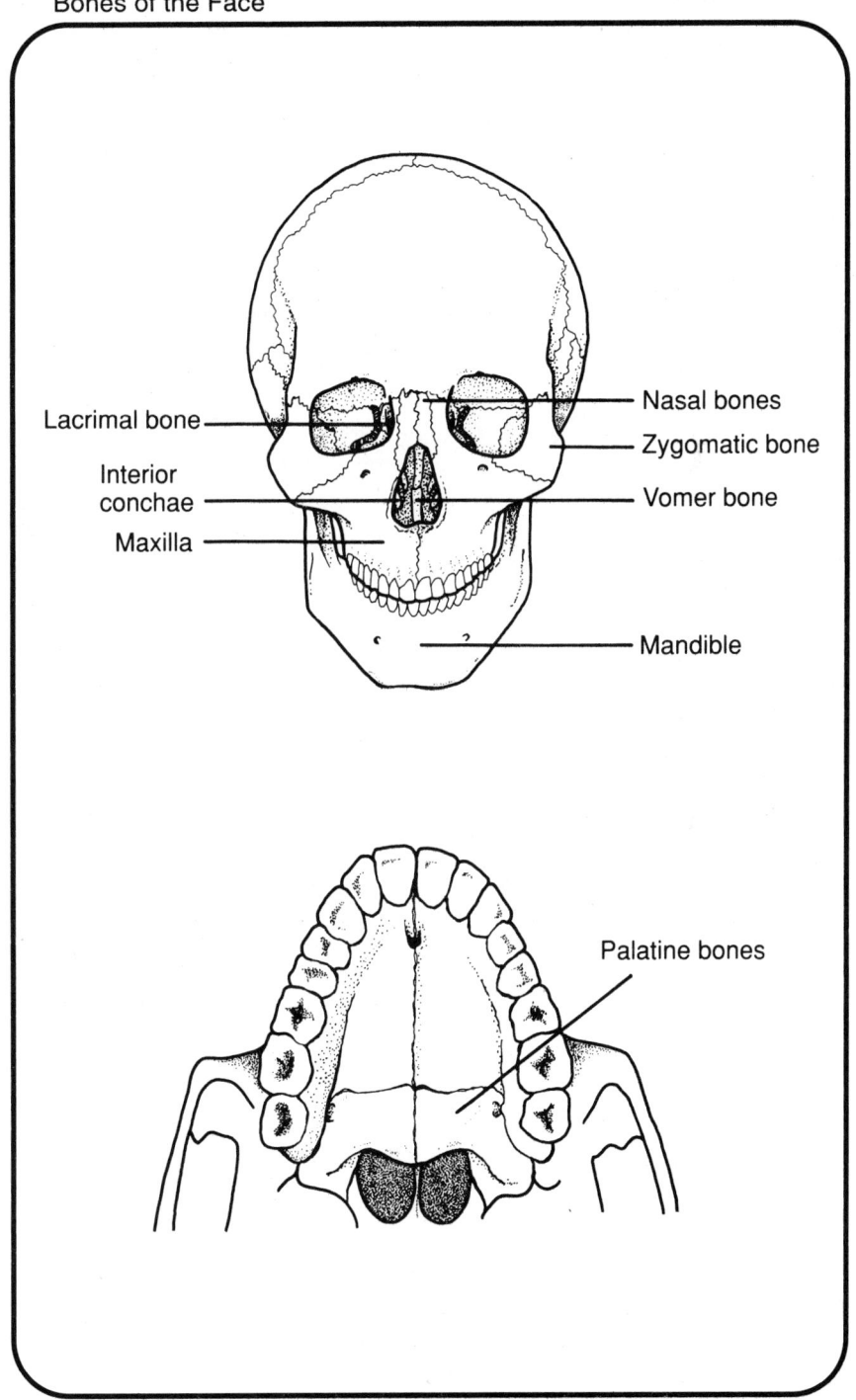

Exhibit 1-4
Lumbar Vertebra

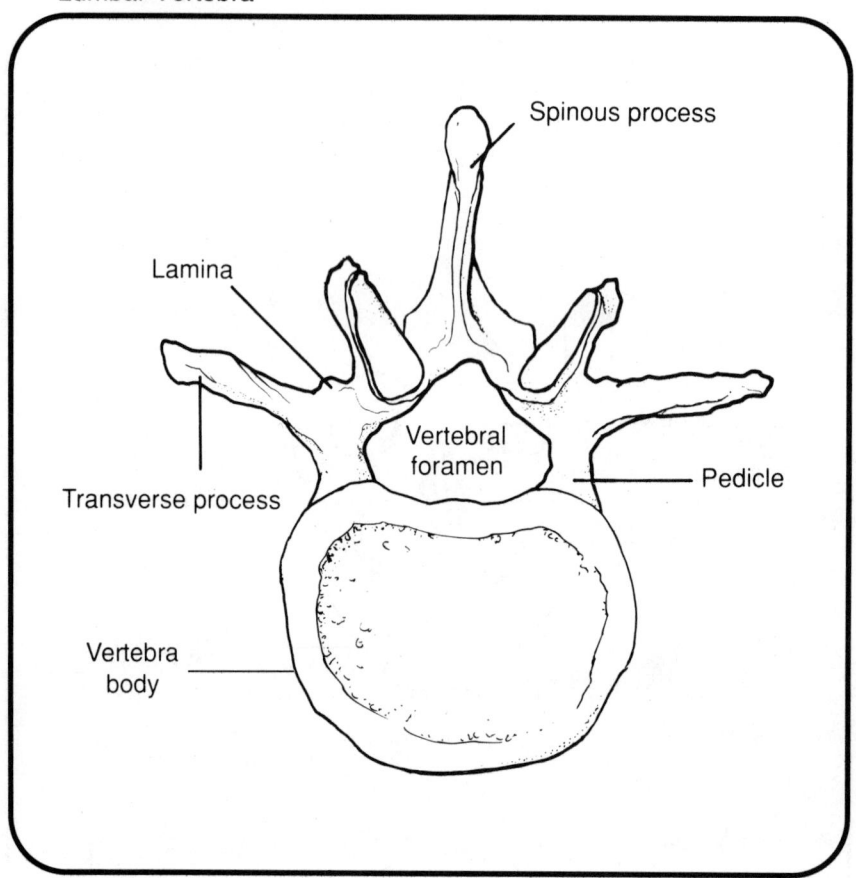

vertebra is the weight-bearing portion of the bone. An *intervertebral disc* of compressible cartilage acts as a shock absorber between the vertebrae.

Extending posteriorly from the body of the vertebrae are two short projections called *pedicles*. Arising from the pedicles are a pair of bony plates that meet and fuse in the midline posteriorly. These plates are known as the *laminae*. (When the laminae fail to fuse during fetal development, the condition is called *spina bifida*.)

The two laminae meet and project downward and backward creating the *spinous processes*, which can be felt under the surface of the skin of the back. *Transverse processes* extend laterally from the junction of the pedicle and the lamina on either side of the vertebra. These processes serve as bony attachments for the muscles and ligaments.

The opening in the center of each vertebra is called the *vertebral foramen*. The spinal cord passes through this protective space. The inferior processes of one vertebra articulate with the superior processes of the vertebra below it. Thus, each vertebra has three joints with both the vertebra above and the vertebra below. The three joints are where the vertebral bodies come together and where the two processes articulate.

Exhibit 1-5 shows the vertebral column. Located at the top of the vertebral column in the neck are the *cervical vertebrae*. They are very flexible, allowing for a wide range of motion in the neck. One feature that distinguishes the cervical vertebrae from the other vertebrae is the presence of three laminae instead of one. In addition to the vertebral foramen through which the spinal cord passes, there are two transverse foramina through which the vertebral arteries pass on their way to the brain.

The *atlas*, the first cervical vertebra, supports the head. The atlas has no real body and no spinous process. It is merely a ring of bone on which the condyles of the occipital bone can rest.

The second cervical vertebra is called the *axis*. A toothlike projection, known as the *odontoid process*, rises up from the body of the axis. This projection fits into the anterior portion of the atlas. When the head is turned from side to side, the atlas stays in place, and the skull and the atlas pivot around the odontoid process.

The *thoracic vertebrae* become progressively larger from the upper to the lower portion of the spinal column. They have distinctive smooth areas on the body and on the transverse processes for articulation with the ribs. These smooth areas are referred to as *facets*.

The *sacrum* is formed by the fusion of five sacral vertebrae. It is concave, curving toward the front of the body. The sacrum fills the back portion of the pelvis. The *coccyx* is often referred to as the tailbone. It is formed by fused vertebrae and attaches to the bottom of the sacrum.

A newborn's spine is concave forward. When the child begins to walk, secondary curves begin to develop in the spine. Some exaggerated curves may result from disease, injury, or postural problems. An increase in the thoracic curve is known as "humpback" or *kyphosis*. An increase in the lumbar curve is referred to as "swayback" or *lordosis*. A lateral curvature is referred to as *scoliosis*, and is present to some degree in almost all people.

The Thorax. The *thorax* is a bony cage formed by twelve pairs of ribs. It is narrow at the top and broader at the bottom. The spaces between the ribs are called *intercostal spaces*. The *sternum* (breastbone) lies in the middle front of the thorax. The *clavicle* (collar bone) and the first rib cartilage articulate with the upper portion of this bone. The next six pairs of ribs connect to the sides of the sternum, separated only by the articulating cartilage. The next three pairs are called false ribs

10—Medical Aspects of Claims

Exhibit 1-5
Vertebral Column

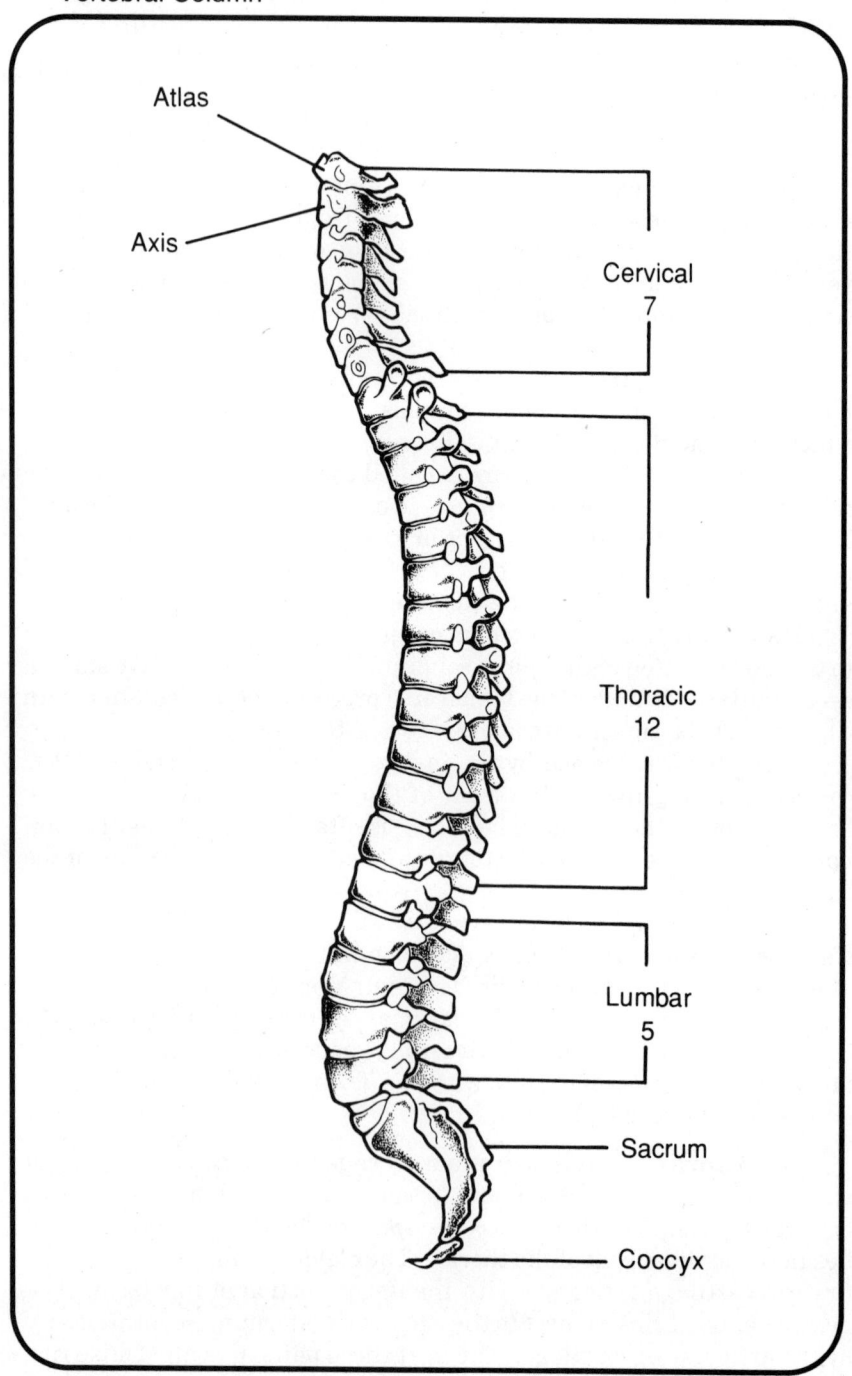

Exhibit 1-6
Thorax

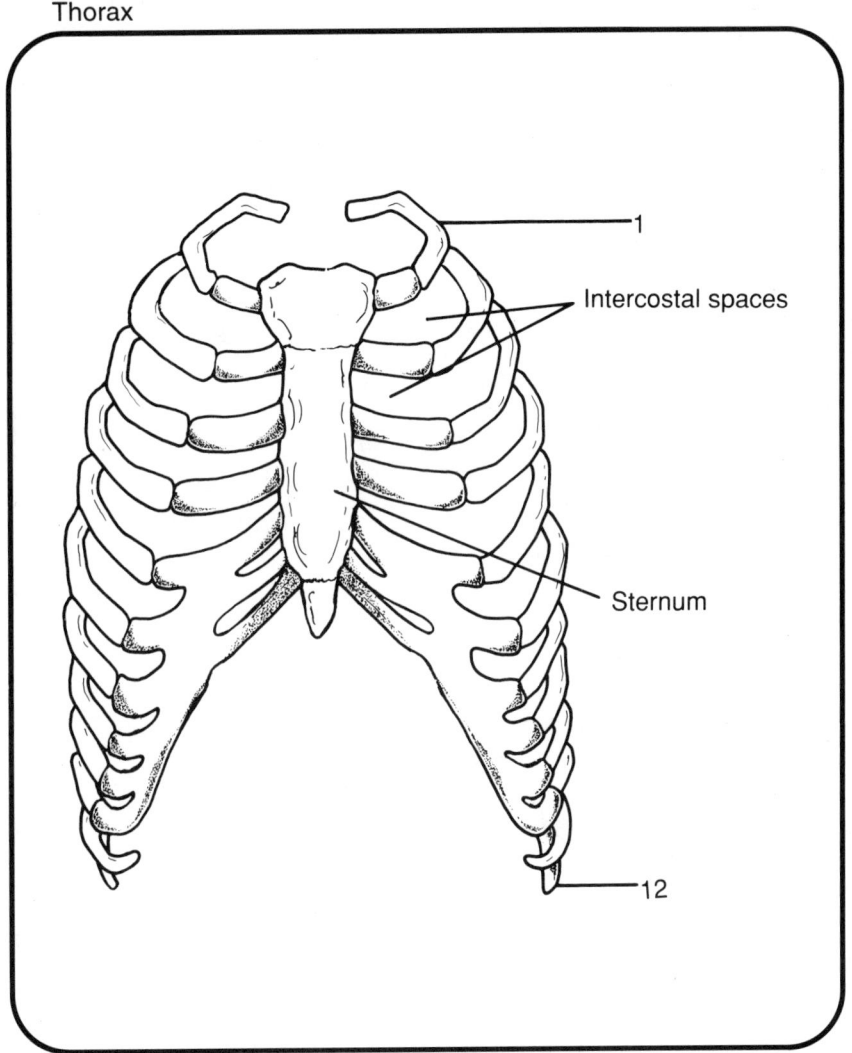

since their cartilage does not connect directly with the sternum. Instead, these ribs turn upward to join the cartilage of the rib above. The last two pair of ribs are called floating ribs since they do not join either the sternum or the cartilage of the rib above. Exhibit 1-6 shows the thorax.

The *clavicle* is also known as the collarbone. It lies in a horizontal position just above the first rib. The medial portion of the clavicle articulates with the sternum, creating the sternoclavicular joint. Laterally, the clavicle articulates with the *acromion process* of the shoulder blade, or *scapula*. The joint between the clavicle and the shoulder blade is called the *acromioclavicular joint*. The clavicle braces the

Exhibit 1-7
Bones of the Shoulder

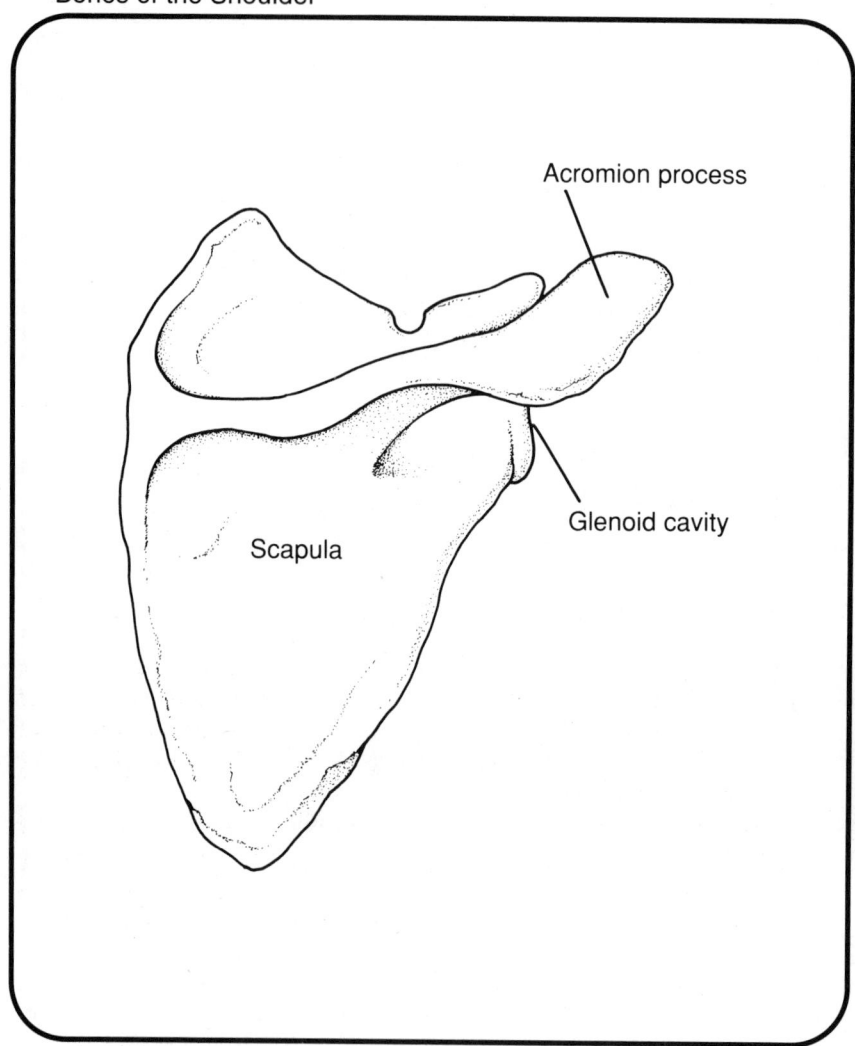

shoulder. Fractures of this long thin bone are fairly common when it is stressed in the middle.

The *scapula*, or shoulder blade, is located in the upper back part of the thorax. While the acromion process articulates with the clavicle, the *glenoid cavity* receives the head of the humerus, or upper arm. Exhibit 1-7 shows the bones of the shoulder.

The Upper Extremities. Extending from the glenoid process of the scapula downward is the long bone of the upper arm, the *humerus*. The rounded upper end of the humerus, which fits into the glenoid cavity, is referred to as the head of the humerus. The head is joined to the shaft of the bone by a constricted area of bone called the neck. Near that neck are two bony prominences onto which the muscles attach. The *greater tubercle* is found on the lateral side, and the *lesser tubercle* is found on the anterior surface.

The portion of the humerus just below the tubercles is often referred to as the surgical neck and is frequently the site of fractures of this bone. At the lower or distal end of the humerus there are smooth surfaces that articulate with the *radius* and *ulna* of the lower arm. The *olecranon process* of the ulna fits into an indentation of the humerus, called the olecranon fossa, when the arm is extended.

The projections on the distal end of the humerus are referred to as the *lateral* and *medial epicondyles*. The medial epicondyle is the bony prominence that can be felt on the inner aspect of the elbow.

The ulna lies on the little finger side of the forearm. It is a slender bone that fits into the olecranon fossa of the humerus. The distal portion of the ulna does not directly articulate with the wrist bones. A disc of fibrous cartilage cushions the space between the wrist and the ulna.

The radius lies on the thumb side of the forearm. Proximally, the head of the radius articulates with the distal portion of the humerus and with the side of the ulna. A break in the lower third of the radius is referred to as a *Colles fracture*. It is a common occurrence when one extends an arm to brace a fall. The *styloid process* at the distal end of the ulna can also be broken off at the same time because of tension of the ligament pulling on that portion of the bone. Exhibit 1-8 shows the bones of the arm.

The wrist is made up of eight small *carpal bones* in two rows of four bones each. The carpal bones are firmly tied together by ligaments. Five *metacarpal bones* form the body of the hand. Their rounded distal ends form the knuckles. Proximally, the metacarpals articulate with the carpals and with each other. Distally, the metacarpals articulate with the *phalanges* or bones of the fingers. Each hand has fourteen phalanges. There are two in the thumb and three in each finger. To distinguish the phalanges from each other, the first set closest to the wrist is referred to as the *proximal phalanges*, the second set is referred to as *middle phalanges*, and the third set farthest from the wrist is called the *distal phalanges*. The thumb has only a proximal and a distal phalanx. Exhibit 1-9 shows the bones of the hands.

The Pelvis. The pelvis consists of two hipbones, each of which includes a ball and socket joint. The ball is the head of the thighbone, or *femur*, and the socket is the cup in the hipbone, known as the *acetabulum*, into which the head of the femur fits. Friction in this as in any joint is reduced by a coating of cartilage and a lubricating agent called *synovial fluid*.

14—Medical Aspects of Claims

Exhibit 1-8
Bones of the Arm

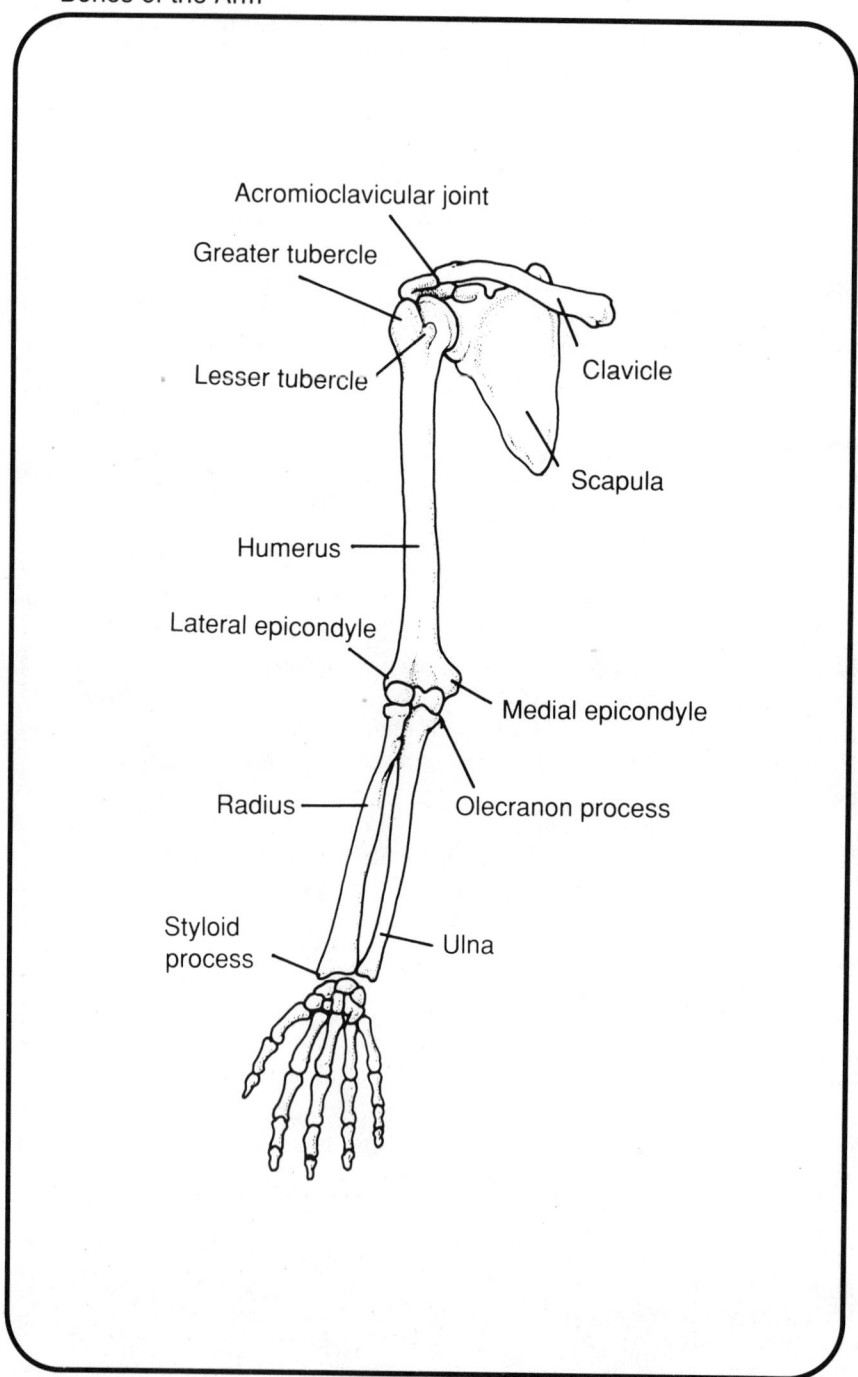

Exhibit 1-9
Bones of the Hand

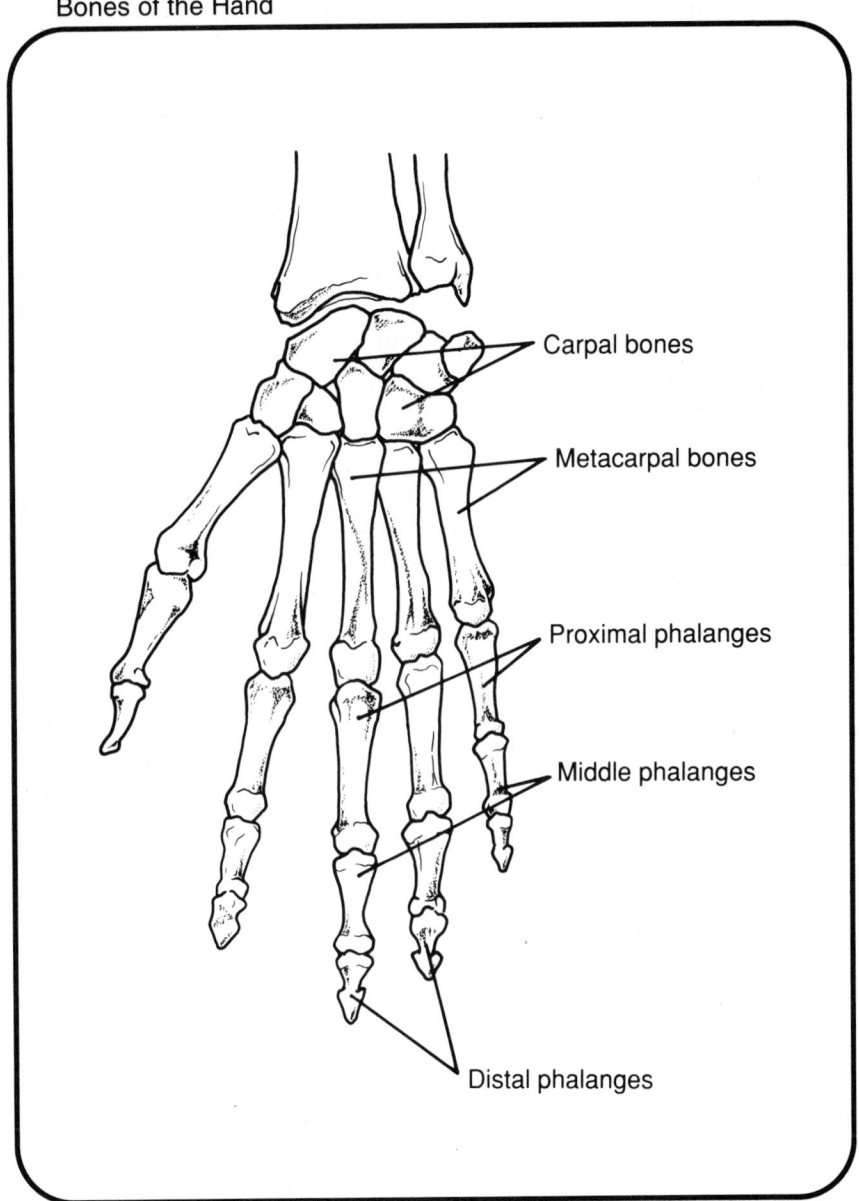

The flared upper portion of each hipbone is called the *ilium*. A wedge of this portion of the hipbone is sometimes amputated for use as a bone graft in spinal vertebrae fusions. The bottom portion of each hipbone is called the *ischium*. This is the area of the pelvis on which we sit. The anterior portion of each hip is called the *pubis*, which is made up of two bars of bone that meet in a flat body to the front. This area is called the *symphysis pubis*. The bars themselves, referred to as *rami*, are frequent sites of pelvic fractures.

The ilium articulates posteriorly with the sacrum at the *sacro-iliac joint*. Improper lifting posture and trauma can result in torn ligaments in this joint. Exhibit 1-10 shows the bones of the pelvis.

The Lower Extremities. The lower extremities include the legs, feet, and toes. Exhibit 1-11 shows the bones of the leg. The thigh bone, called the *femur*, is one of the strongest bones in the body, bearing the weight of the entire upper body. The upper or proximal end has a rounded head supported by a constricted neck. The head fits into the hip acetabulum. When the neck of the femur is fractured, the injury is often generically referred to as a "broken hip."

At the top of the shaft of the femur on the lateral surface is a large protuberance called the *greater trochanter*. A *lesser* or *smaller trochanter* is located on the medial portion of the bone below the neck.

At the lower end of the femur there are two bulges of bone that articulate with the tibia. These two bulges are referred to as the *medial* and *lateral condyles*. On the anterior surface of the distal portion of the femur is a smooth surface for articulation with the *patella*, or kneecap.

The patella forms the cap at the front of the knee. The bone is actually embedded into the principal muscle of the anterior thigh, the quadriceps femoris. The posterior surface of the patella is smooth to articulate with the femur. It is lined with a cartilaginous layer and is lubricated by synovial fluid. The knee cap helps to protect the knee joint from trauma.

The tip at the bottom of the patella is joined to the ligamentum patella, a tendon that attaches to the center of the upper shin bone. The knee joint also contains two discs of articular cartilage, the *medial* and *lateral menisci*. Sudden twisting or wrenching of the knee joint may cause the detachment of one or both of these cartilages.

The *tibia*, or shin bone, is the largest of the two bones of the lower leg. The upper or proximal end branches out into two masses of bone called the medial and lateral condyles. The anterior portion of the tibia is close to the surface of the leg. The lower end of the tibia widens at the base and has a smooth surface for articulation with the talus bone of the ankle and the fibula to the side. The prominence that can be felt on the inner aspect of the ankle is the *medial malleolus*.

The long and slender bone on the lateral aspect of the lower leg is the *fibula*. The head of the fibula articulates with the femur, but not with the tibia. The fibula does not bear the weight of the body and does not enter into the formation of the knee joint.

A projection on the distal end of the fibula, called the *lateral*

1 • Anatomy and Medical Terminology—17

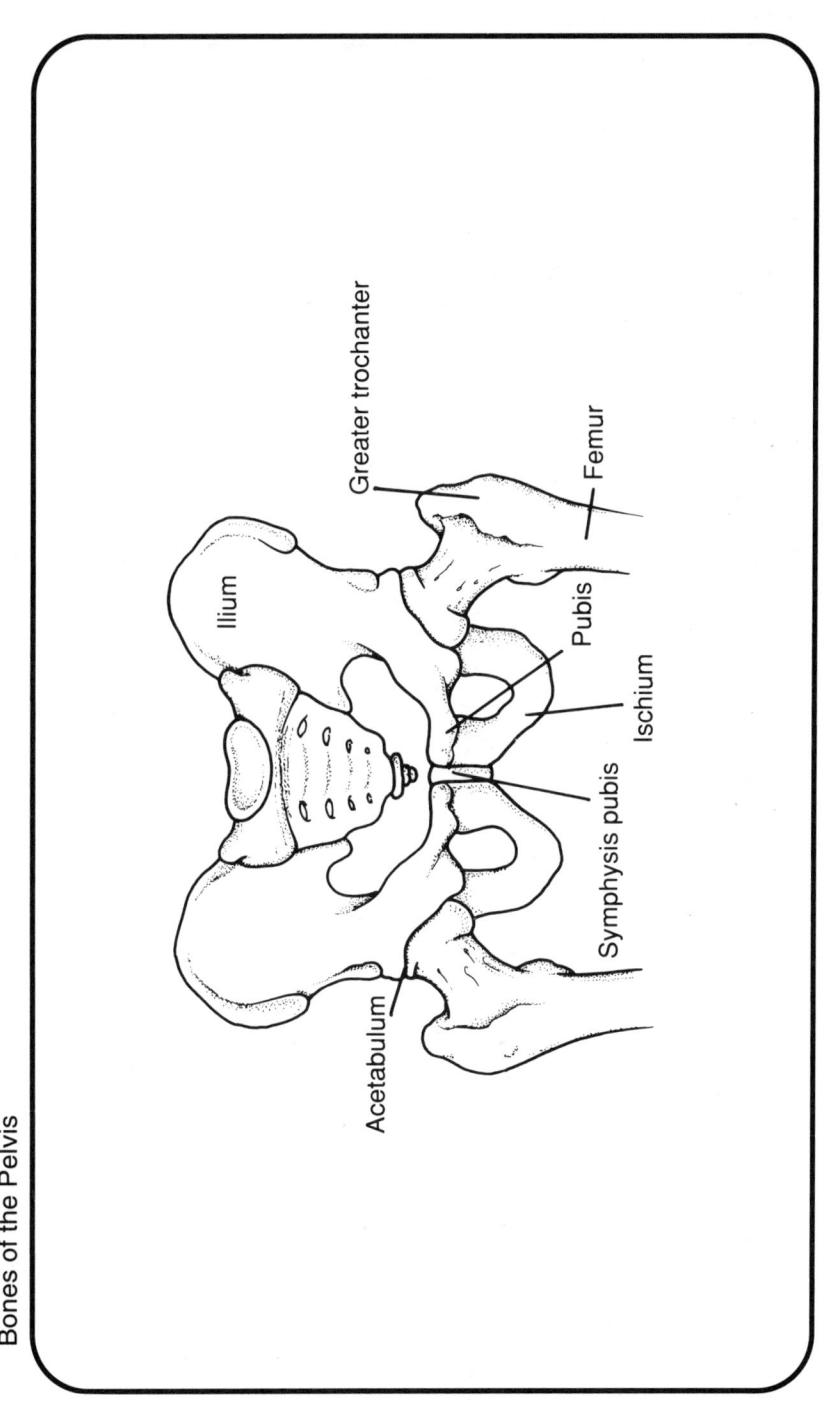

Exhibit 1-10
Bones of the Pelvis

18—Medical Aspects of Claims

Exhibit 1-11
Bones of the Leg

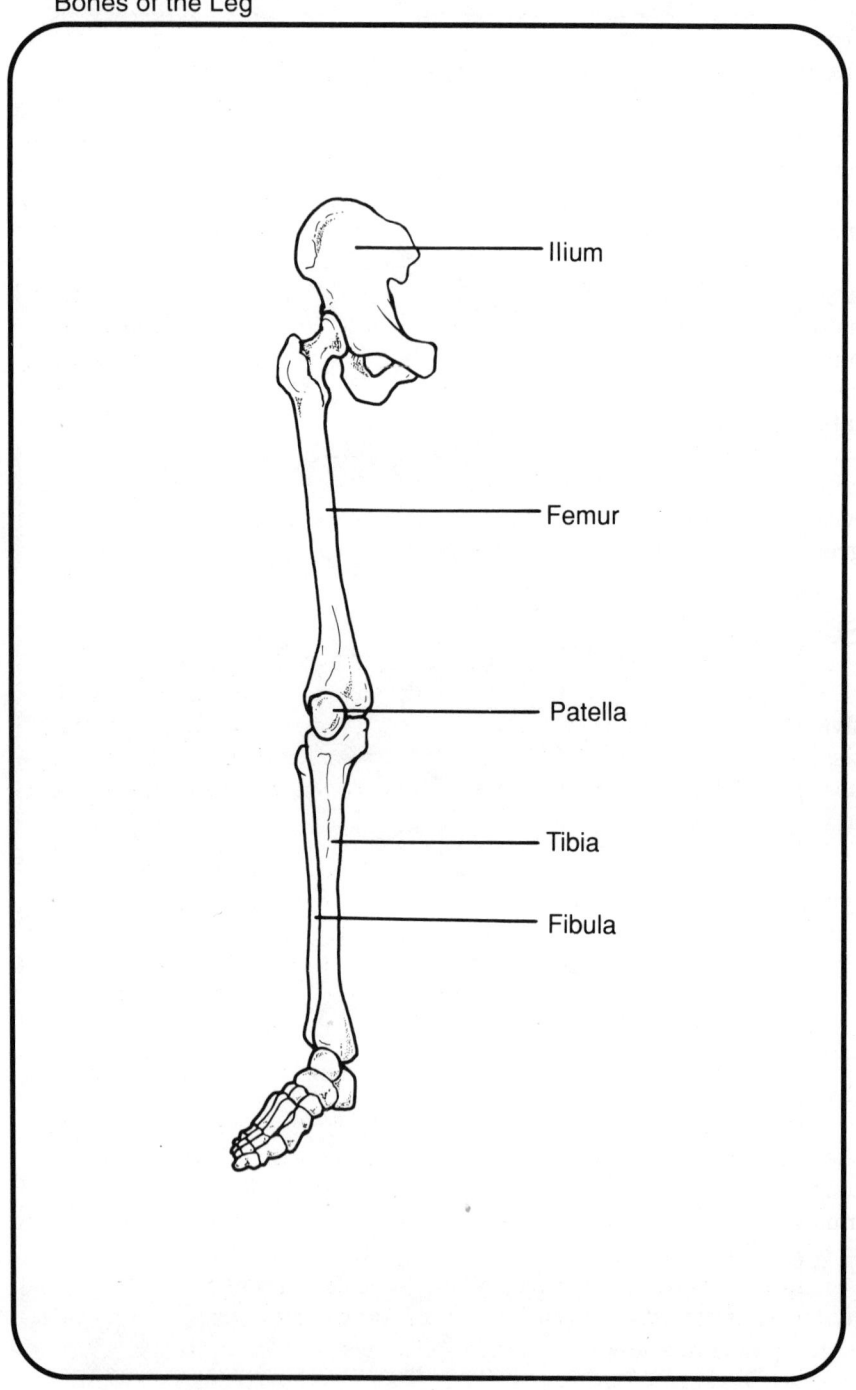

malleolus, forms the bumpy area you can feel on the outer aspect of the ankle. A sudden turn of the ankle can result in a *Pott's fracture*, a fracture of the fibula a few inches above the ankle coupled with a fracture that splits the medial malleolus away from the tibia.

The structures of the foot, shown in Exhibit 1-12, closely resemble those of the hand. Powerful muscles, ligaments, and tendons hold the bones of the foot in place and help to form the arches of the foot. The *longitudinal* arch extends from heel to toe and the *transverse*, or *metatarsal, arch* extends crosswise in the foot.

The uppermost of the seven tarsal bones is the *talus*. The talus articulates with both the tibia and the fibula. The heel bone is known as the *calcaneus*. It lies below and behind the talus. The *cuboid bone*, on the lateral aspect of the foot, articulates with the anterior end of the calcaneus. The *navicular bone*, which lies to the medial side, articulates with the three small cuneiform bones.

There are five *metatarsal bones* in each foot. The first three articulate with the cuneiform bones, while the other two articulate with the cuboid. There are fourteen *phalanges* in each foot, two in the great toe and three in each of the other toes.

Soft Tissues

The nonbony organs and systems of the body are frequently collectively known as *soft tissue*. For purposes of this chapter, the term soft tissue refers to the muscles and skin, which reflects how the term is used in claims. The other organ systems of the body are discussed later in this section.

Muscles. Muscles are classified on the basis of structure. The two types of muscles in the body are striated and smooth. Striated muscles are the voluntary muscles and mostly attach to the bones of the skeleton. Smooth muscles are the involuntary muscles that are found in the walls of all the organs and the blood vessels. A special kind of striated muscle (often considered a separate type of muscle) is the cardiac muscle. This muscle is involuntary and is found in the walls of the heart.

The muscles that are most often injured are those attached to the skeleton. Each one has a protective outer coating. Little partitions of connective tissue divide the muscle into bundles of fibers. When the muscle is pulled beyond its ability to stretch, the bundles of fibers begin to tear. Bleeding and swelling occurs in the area of the tear.

A *spasm* is an involuntary contraction of a striated muscle. If the contraction persists, it is called a *tonic spasm* or a cramp. If the spasm is intermittent, allowing the muscle to relax, the condition is referred to as a *clonic spasm* or clonus.

20—Medical Aspects of Claims

Exhibit 1-12
Bones of the Foot

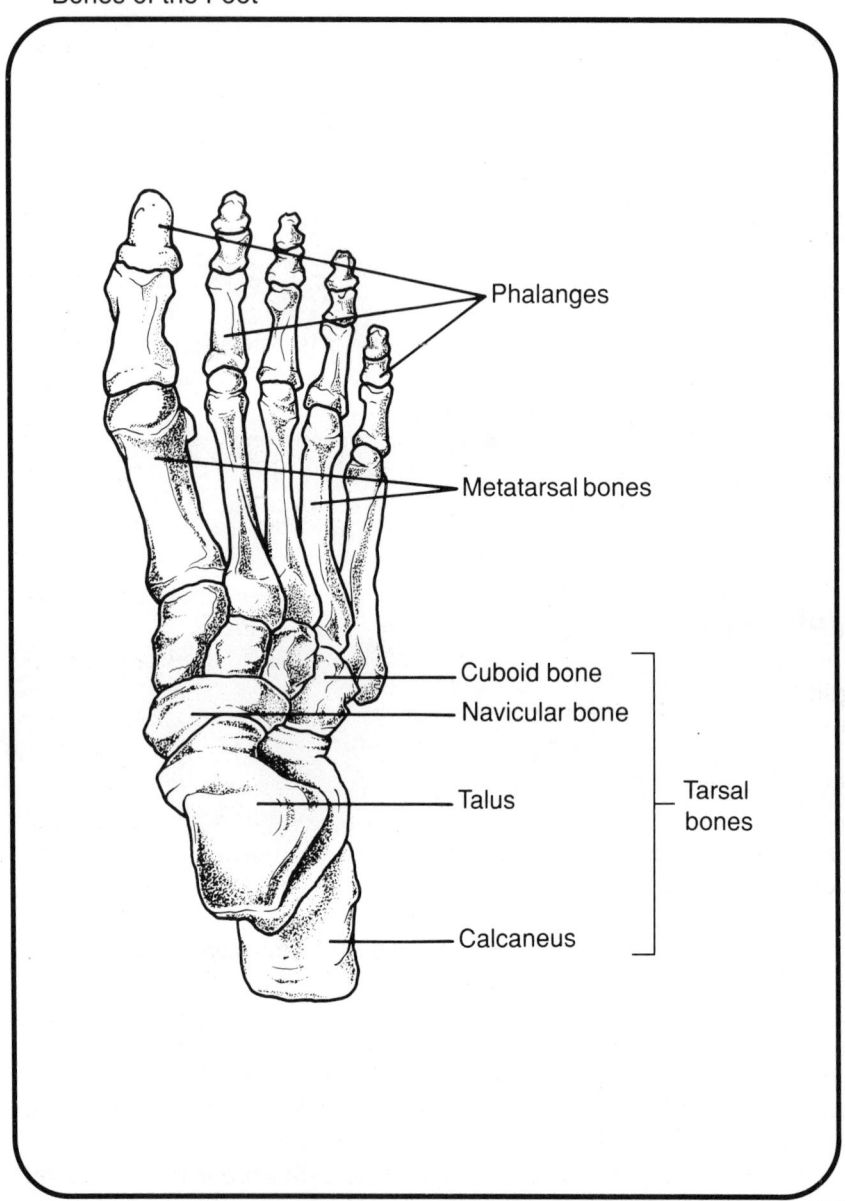

Hypertrophy is an increase in muscle size that comes from repeated use. This condition is typically observable in athletes. *Atrophy* is the shrinking of the muscle from lack of use. When an extremity is casted so that a broken bone heals properly, the surrounding muscles often atrophy.

Each of the more than 600 muscles connected to the skeleton are named by combining two or more of the following classifications.

1. *Location.* Intercostal muscles are located between the ribs; the tibialis posterior muscle is located behind the tibia.
2. *Direction of fibers.* Rectus means that muscle fibers run straight from head to toe; transverse means that the fibers run across the body; obliquus means that the fibers run in an oblique direction.
3. *Function.* Adductors bring a body part in toward the body; abductors draw a body part away from the body; flexors bend a body part, and levators lift a body part.
4. *Shape or Size.* The trapezius is shaped like a trapeze; minimus means that the muscle is small, and maximus means that the muscle is large.
5. *Number of Points of Origin.* The biceps have two points of origin, while the triceps have three, and the quadriceps have four.
6. *Points of Attachment.* The sternocleidomastoid muscle attaches to the sternum, clavicle, and the mastoid process.

The tough connective tissue that separates one muscle from another is called *fascia*. *Fascitis* is inflammation of these fibers.

Bursae are closed sacs of fluid that reduce friction where there is gliding movement between muscles and other surrounding parts. They are found in the elbow, shoulder, hip, and the knee.

Ligaments connect bone to bone and help to hold bones in their proper position. These bands of connective tissue can be torn when overly stretched. Weakening of the ligaments can allow underlying tissues to move out of normal position, causing herniations or dislocations.

Muscles are attached to bones by *tendons*. When a muscle is severely stretched, the tendon sometimes tears away from its attachment to the bone. It may be necessary to surgically reattach the tendon to restore proper skeletal motion. The pulling action of the tendons can also impede the healing of bone fractures. The tension on the tendon can pull apart the fragments of the fractured bone. Fractures of the heel are particularly difficult to heal because of tension from the strongest tendon in the body, the *Achilles tendon*.

Trauma to soft tissues causes localized hemorrhage or swelling during the first several days post injury. Rest and the application of ice are often prescribed to minimize swelling and to prevent further injury. Repeated aggravation can lead to a chronic inflammation. After several days, it is usually recommended that heat be applied to dissipate the tissue fluid and to ease the pain of using the part again. Failure to use the injured body part can cause muscle weakness and increase the possibility of reinjury. Rest and use must be balanced to return the injured part to full function and sensation.

Skin. Skin covers the outer surface of the body. It is made up of two layers, the epidermis and the dermis. The subcutaneous tissue, located under the dermis, is not considered part of the skin.

The *epidermis* is the thin upper layer of skin made up of several layers of cells. These cells have no blood vessels, but they do get some nourishment from the fluid leaking from the capillaries in the dermis. New cells are constantly forming and pushing toward the surface. The outermost cells die, but they continue to serve the useful purpose of protecting the underlying tissues from drying out.

The *dermis* is the inner layer of the skin. It is extremely elastic and can stretch considerably when underlying injury causes fluid to build up under the dermal layer. The fluid buildup can be so great that the skin is in danger of tearing apart. To prevent ragged rips in the skin, a procedure called decompression is used in which the skin is surgically cut to let the fluids escape.

The arteries of the skin are located just below the dermal layer. Capillary beds in the dermis drain waste products from the skin and feed back into the venous system.

Pressure on the skin over a bony part can cause failure of the blood supply. The tissue ultimately dies leaving an ulcerated area called a *decubitus*. Decubitus ulcers are very difficult to heal because they are located over a bony prominence and because of a lack of nutrition to the tissues. Bedsores are a common type of decubitus ulcer found on patients who are bedridden for long periods of time.

A first degree burn to the skin involves only the surface of the skin. It is characterized by redness only. A second degree burn is characterized by blistering. A third degree burn destroys the cell-producing layer of the skin and causes charring of the tissues.

The Nervous System

The nervous system is made up of the *brain*, the *cranial nerves*, the *spinal cord*, and the *spinal nerves*, which branch out to various parts of the body.

The Brain. Exhibit 1-13 shows the parts of the brain. The brain almost completely fills the skull. It is bathed in and protected by *cerebrospinal fluid*, which fills the remainder of the space in the skull. The *cerebrum* is the large part of the brain, which fills the entire upper cavity of the skull. It consists of two halves, or hemispheres. Each hemisphere is divided into four lobes named according to the bones beneath which they lie: the frontal lobe, the parietal lobe, the temporal lobe, and the occipital lobe.

Exhibit 1-13
Parts of the Brain

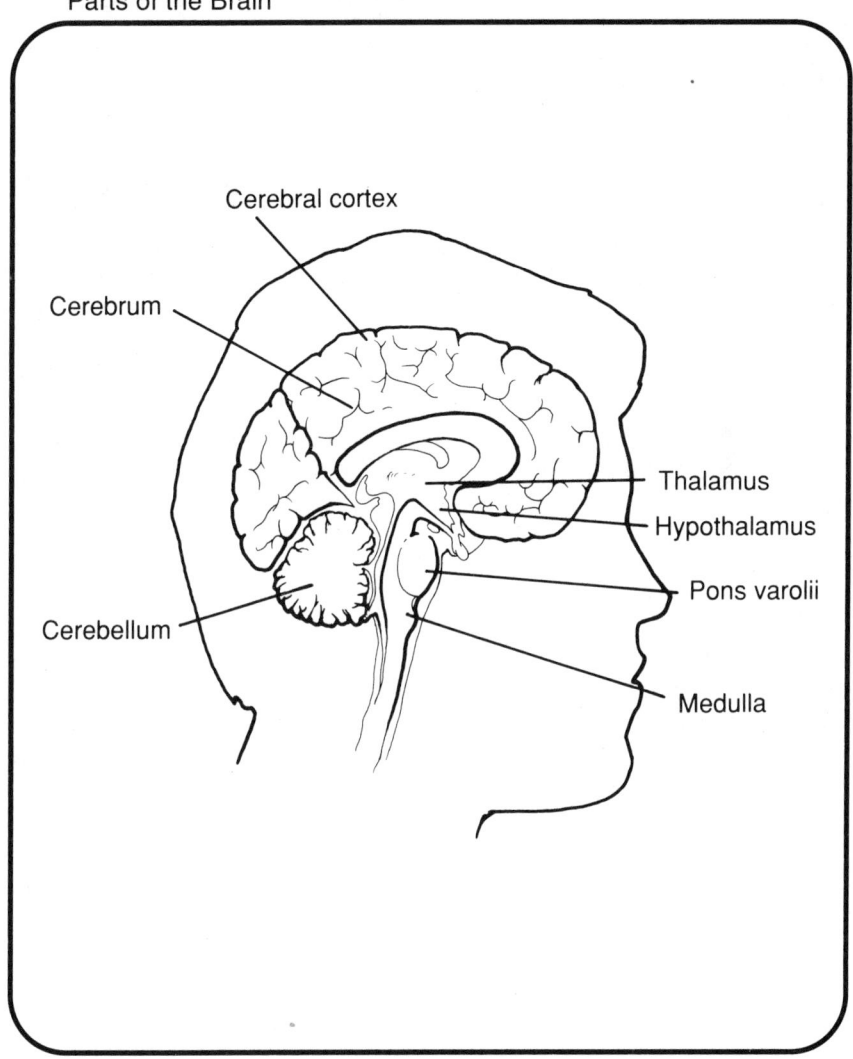

Labels: Cerebral cortex, Cerebrum, Cerebellum, Thalamus, Hypothalamus, Pons varolii, Medulla

    The outermost layer of the cerebrum is known as the *cerebral cortex*, a layered sheet of nerve cells. The cortex is the center of human intelligence and reasoning. The cortex dips down into the underlying regions of the brain in a series of folds and ridges. The folds are called *convolutions*. Between the two hemispheres is a deep groove called the *longitudinal fissure*. In the middle of the fissure is a massive band of fibers called the *corpus callosum*, which connects the two hemispheres of the brain.

    Motor skills are controlled primarily in the frontal lobe. Electrical impulses processed in this area help us to move the muscles of the body.

24—Medical Aspects of Claims

When one chooses to walk about, impulses are sent from the motor cortex to the spinal cord. The spinal cord then relays the impulses or message out to the appropriate skeletal muscles of the lower extremities.

Also in the frontal lobe is the area for motor speech. This area, called *Broca's area*, provides the ability to form spoken words and to understand written words. The motor speech area is located in the left hemisphere in right-handed people and in the right hemisphere in left-handed people.

The most anterior portion of the frontal lobe contains the centers of emotions and capability for abstract thought. Injuries to this area of the brain cause poor judgment and a lack of concern about oneself and one's responsibilities.

Pain and temperature are sensed by sensory nerves of the body, which send a message to the parietal lobe of the brain, where these sensations are interpreted. This section of the brain also helps us to recognize size, shape, and texture. The left hemisphere receives impulses from the right side of the body, and the right hemisphere receives impulses from the left side of the body.

The auditory area lies in the superior portion of the temporal lobe of the brain. The visual area lies in the occipital lobe.

The remaining areas of the cerebral cortex are referred to as the association areas. Impulses must be relayed back and forth through a series of association areas before they can be fully interpreted and a response prepared.

Covered by the hemispheres of the cerebrum is a portion of the brain referred to as the *interbrain* or *dicephalon*. It consists of the thalamus and the hypothalamus. The *thalamus* receives nerve impulses from all over the body by way of sensory nerves. Impulses are channeled through the thalamus, sorted out, and rearranged for relay to specific areas of the cortex. The *hypothalamus* regulates water balance, the metabolism of fat and sugar, normal sleep patterns, and body temperature.

The *midbrain* serves as a conduction pathway and a reflex center. The midbrain controls the movement of the eyeballs in response to changes in the position of the head, turning of the head in response to sound, position of the head in relation to the trunk of the body, and adjustments in the extremities in relation to the position of the head.

The *pons varolii* is the conductive pathway connecting the medulla with the cerebrum. It also connects the two halves of the cerebellum. The *medulla* or *medulla oblongata* is an extension of the spinal cord into the brain. It extends from the level of the foramen magnum of the skull to the pons. In addition to conducting impulses to other centers of the brain, the medulla affects a number of vital functions. It controls the speed of the heart. It also constricts or dilates the blood vessels and

1 • Anatomy and Medical Terminology—25

changes the rate or depth of breathing. Injuries to the medulla, such as those that occur in basal skull fractures, frequently prove fatal because of the resulting interruption of vital bodily functions.

The *cerebellum* lies in the lower back part of the cranium and is made up of two hemispheres. Three paired bundles of fibers connect the cerebellum with the medulla and the spinal cord. The cerebellum is primarily associated with the coordination of muscular activity, but it does not initiate voluntary acts as the cerebrum does. It regulates muscle tone, posture, the maintenance of equilibrium, and the smooth performance of voluntary movements. Injury to the cerebellum can result in loss of equilibrium, reduced muscle tone, or tremors in muscles when activity is attempted.

The *meninges,* shown in section in Exhibit 1-14, are fibrous coverings that protect the brain and the spinal cord. The *dura mater* consists of two layers. It covers the brain and lines the interior of the skull. In some places the two layers of the dura are in contact with each other, but in other places the layers separate as the dura dips down to cover indentations in the brain. Where the two layers separate, the resulting pocket is filled with blood. These blood-filled pockets are known as *cranial venous sinuses*.

The *arachnoid membrane* lies beneath the dura. It has tuft-like extensions that enter into the cranial venous sinuses. These extensions help to return cerebrospinal fluid to the blood stream.

The inner layer of the meninges is referred to as the *pia mater*, or pia for short. The pia covers all of the hills and valleys of the brain surface. Very fine threadlike structures bind the pia with the overlying arachnoid layer.

The *cerebrospinal fluid* is a clear liquid that bathes the cavities and spaces around the structures of the central nervous system. It serves as a shock absorber as well as an exchange medium for nutrients and wastes passing between the bloodstream and the cells. Since the venous pressure is lower than the pressure of cerebrospinal fluid, it is thought that the drainage of the fluid out of the cerebrospinal cavities occurs by the process of filtration. Within the brain are four ventricles or cerebrospinal fluid-filled cavities. They help to circulate the fluid around the tissues to protect them from trauma.

The Cranial Nerves. There are twelve pairs of *cranial nerves* that originate on the under surface of the brain. These nerves control the motor and sensory functions of the organs of the head and neck. They pass through small holes in the skull called foramina on their way to their destinations.

1. The *olfactory nerves* control the sense of smell. The olfactory nerves begin in the nasal passage and travel upward through the ethmoid bone to the brain. Injury to the olfactory nerves

Exhibit 1-14
Meninges of the Brain

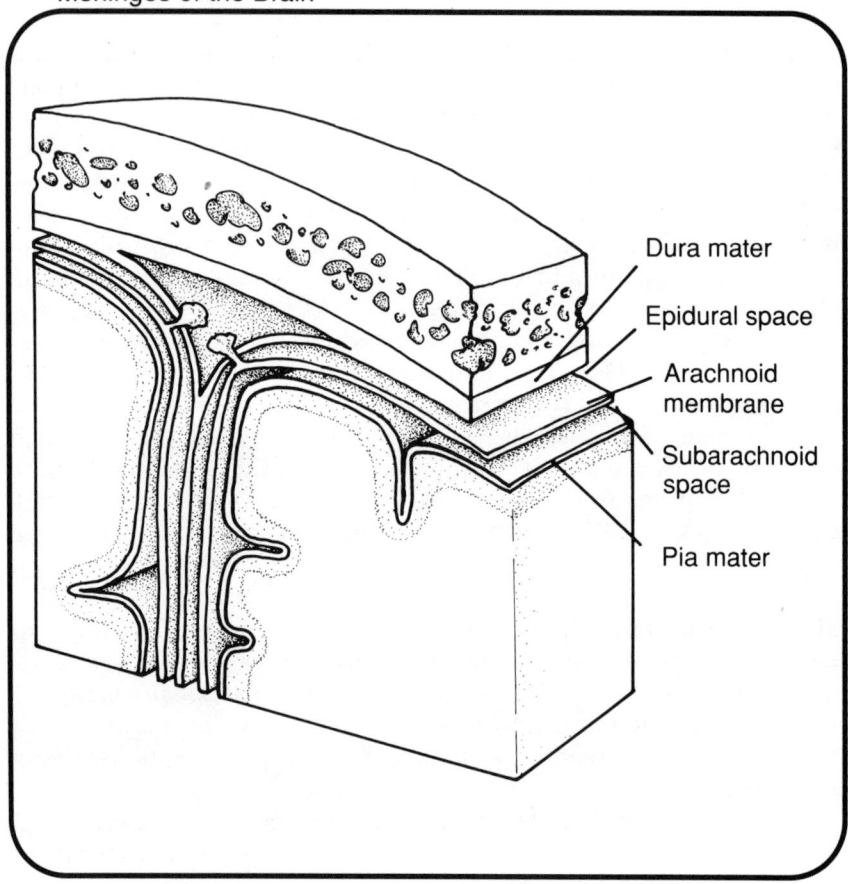

        results in the loss of the sense of smell. This condition is referred to as *anosmia*.
2. The *optic nerves* transmit the images of vision. The nerves originate in the tissues of the retina of the eye and travel to the receptive centers of the brain. Injury to the optic nerves results in blindness.
3. The *oculomotor nerves* control the movement of the eyes. These nerves originate in the midbrain area and regulate most of the muscles of the eye except the superior oblique and the lateral rectus. The nerves send a motor message to the muscle, which contracts both the iris and the muscle for accommodation of the lens. When the oculomotor nerve is damaged, there can be drooping (ptosis) of the upper lid, turning of the eyeball downward and outward, and dilation of the pupil.

1 • Anatomy and Medical Terminology—27

4. The *trochlear nerves* control the movement of the superior oblique muscles of the eye and control sensory ability in that area.
5. The *trigeminal nerves* originate in the pons of the brain. These nerves control the sensory ability of the front part of the head, the face, the nose, the mouth and teeth, and the upper part of the throat (nasopharynx). They also control the movement of the muscles used for chewing.
6. The *abducens nerves* arise in the pons of the brain. They control the sensory and motor function of the lateral rectus muscles of the eyes. Injury to these nerves makes the eyeball turn inward.
7. The *facial nerves* are the motor nerves of the face. They are also involved in the sense of taste on the anterior two-thirds of the tongue. Injury to the facial nerves can result in paralysis and interference with the sense of taste or with the secretion of saliva in the mouth.
8. The *vestibulocochlear nerves* are also called the acoustic nerves. They control the sense of hearing and the maintenance of equilibrium. Injury to the acoustic nerves can result in deafness, disorientation, or dizziness.
9. The *glossopharyngeal nerves* originate in the medulla oblongata and extend to the tongue and the throat. They control the action of swallowing and the sense of taste in the posterior third of the tongue. Special fibers conduct impulses from the large arteries in each side of the neck, the carotid arteries. These special fibers keep the brain informed about the pressure of the blood as it passes through the arteries and the amount of oxygen contained in the blood. Some nerve fibers also control the salivary glands. Injury to the glossopharyngeal nerves can cause a loss of the gag reflex and a loss of sensation in the tongue, difficulty in swallowing, and the loss of carotid pressure monitoring.
10. The *vagus nerve* begins in the medulla and travels to the neck, chest, and abdomen. A very important branch supplies the pharynx and assists in controlling speech. Damage to the vagus nerve near its origin can be fatal, but damage to a branch can cause loss of function in that area. One may suffer from difficulty in speaking, problems in swallowing, dilation of the stomach, or a variety of other problems depending on the location of the injury along the nerve.
11. The *accessory nerves* arise from both the medulla and the cervical segments of the spinal cord. They control the movement of the sternocleidomastoid and part of the trapezius muscles. They are also responsible for sensation in these areas. Injury

to the accessory nerves can result in difficulty rotating the head or raising the shoulder on the affected side.
12. The *hypoglossal nerves* control the movement of the muscles of the tongue. They are also responsible for sensation in this area. Injury can cause trouble in speaking, swallowing, and chewing.

The Spinal Cord. The spinal cord begins at the level of the foramen magnum and extends down to the level of the disc between the first and second lumbar vertebrae. The spinal cord is enlarged in two areas: the cervical enlargement and the lumbar enlargement. Each enlargement gives rise to nerves supplying the extremities.

Like the brain, the spinal cord is covered with protective coverings called *meninges,* as shown in Exhibit 1-15. The *dura mater* is the outermost layer. The space between the dura and the walls of the vertebral canal is called the *epidural* or *extradural space*. It contains a network of blood vessels, fat, and connective tissue. The space between the inner surface of the dura and the arachnoid layer of the meninges is called the *subdural space*. It is filled with a small amount of fluid.

The *arachnoid layer* lies under the dura and above the innermost layer of the meninges, the *pia mater*. The pia lies very close to the spinal cord and helps to nourish the cells of the cord. The space between the arachnoid and the pia is called the *subarachnoid space*. It is in this space that the cerebrospinal fluid circulates and bathes the full length of the cord.

The Spinal Nerves. The thirty-one pairs of spinal nerves branching out from the spinal cord are shown in Exhibit 1-16. There are eight pairs of cervical nerves, twelve pairs of thoracic nerves, five pairs of lumbar nerves, five pairs of sacral nerves, and one pair of coccygeal nerves.

Each spinal nerve has two roots, one for transmitting sensory messages and one for transmitting motor messages. The dorsal or posterior root is the sensory root, while the anterior or ventral root is the motor root.

As the spinal nerves leave the intervertebral foramina, they immediately branch into two parts called posterior and anterior rami. The *posterior rami* consist of motor and sensory fibers that supply the skin and muscles of the back. The *anterior rami* consist of motor and sensory fibers that control movement and sense perception in the extremities and the sides and front of the trunk of the body.

The anterior rami do not run directly from their origin to the area they serve. First, they combine in a complicated network called a *plexus*. As they emerge from the plexus, they become far more specialized as they head for the structures they serve.

The anterior rami of the first four cervical spinal nerves combine to

Exhibit 1-15
Meninges of the Spinal Cord

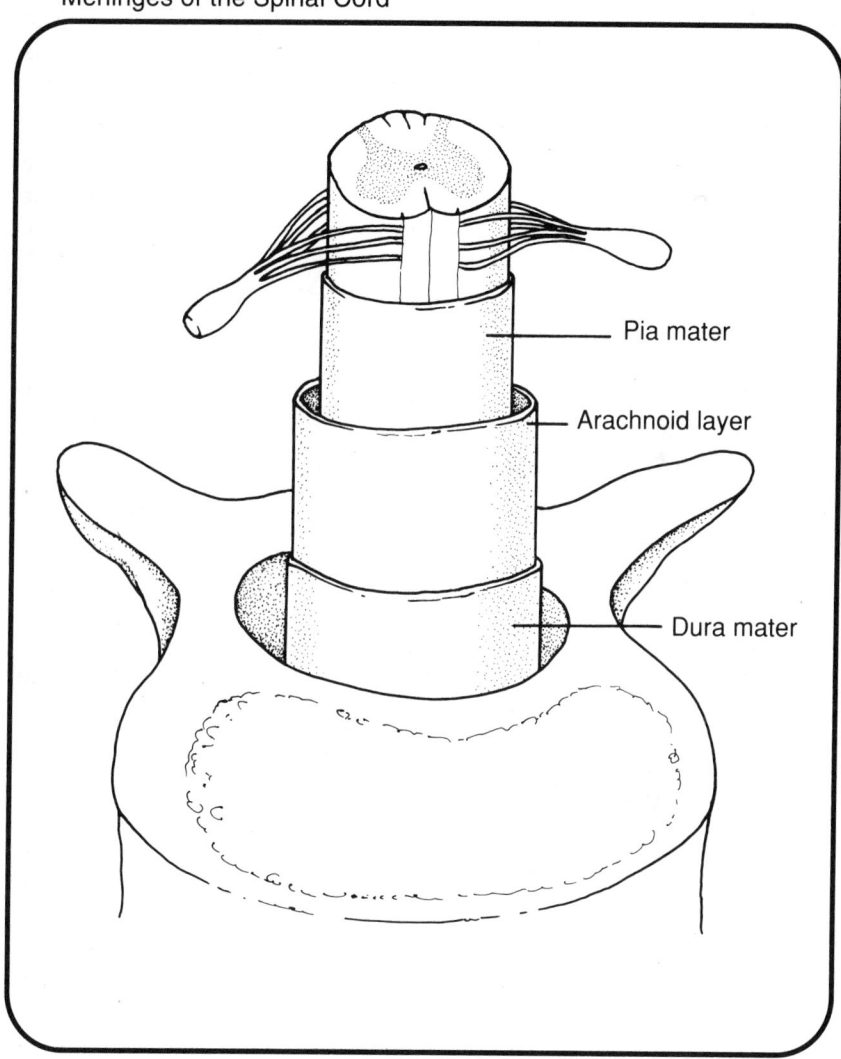

- Pia mater
- Arachnoid layer
- Dura mater

form the *cervical plexus*. The plexus lies deep in each side of the neck. Branches from the plexus go out to the muscles and skin of the neck as well as to the posterior portion of the scalp.

The *phrenic nerve*, made up of fibers from the third, fourth, and fifth cervical spinal nerves, controls movement in the area of the diaphragm. When injury occurs to the spinal cord above the level of the phrenic nerve, the victim suffers from paralysis of the diaphragm and can no longer breathe automatically.

The *brachial plexus* is formed by the anterior rami of the last four

30—Medical Aspects of Claims

Exhibit 1-16
Spinal Nerves

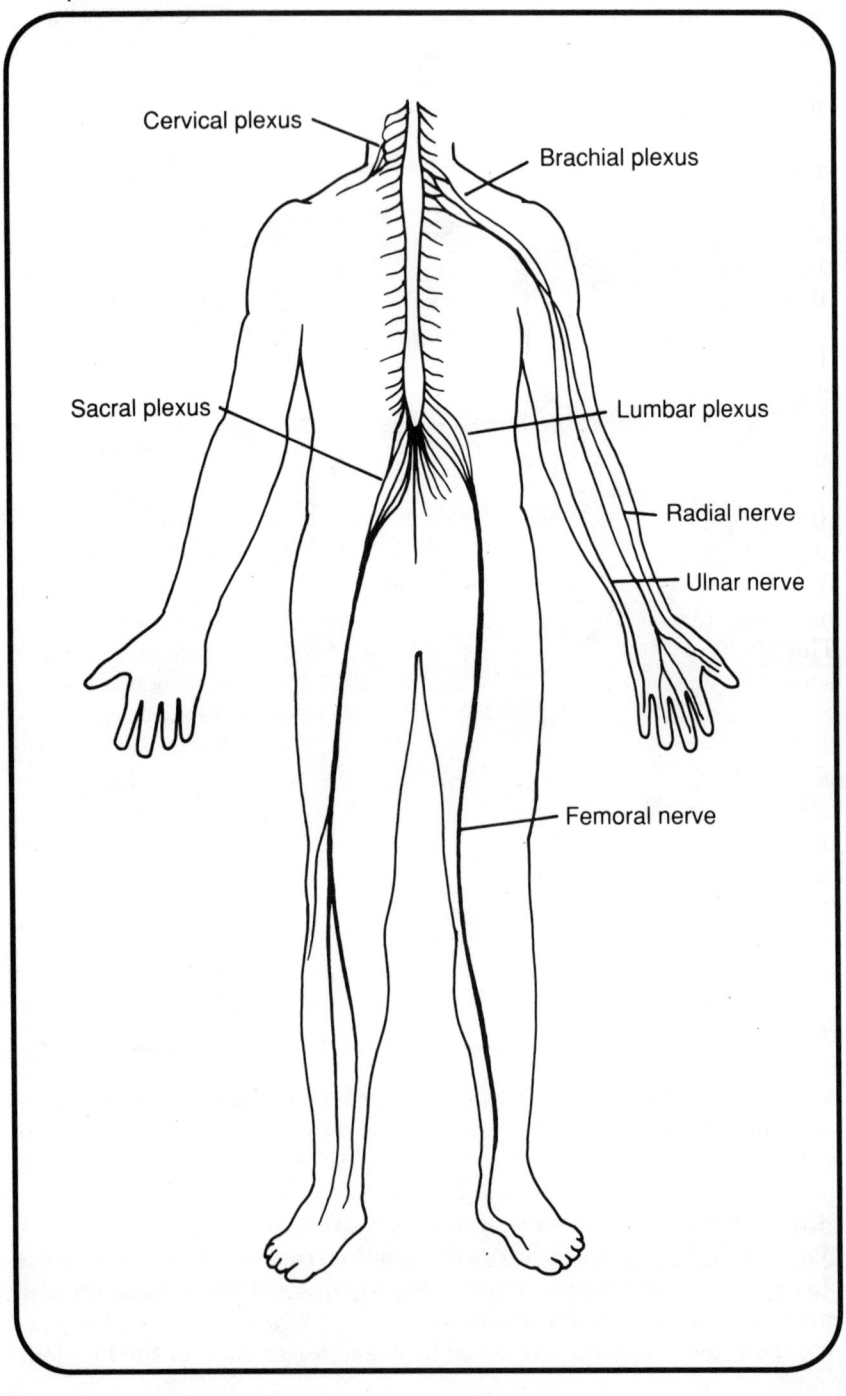

cervical and the first thoracic spinal nerves. Nerves that proceed from the brachial plexus control movement in the anterior arm muscles and are responsible for sensation in the area of the lateral forearm. They also send motor messages to the flexor muscles of the forearm and hand and control sensation in the palm of the hand through the medial nerve.

The *ulnar nerve*, arising from the brachial plexus, controls movement in another portion of the forearm and hand, and is responsible for sensation in the same area.

The *radial nerve* is the largest branch arising from the brachial plexus. It is responsible for sense and motion in the posterior portion of the arm, the forearm, and the hand.

Physicians are able to diagnose the location of a nerve injury by determining what areas are deficient in motor or sensory function. By checking the size and makeup of the affected area, they can often tell whether or not a patient is malingering or perhaps suffering from an emotional-based disorder.

Glove anesthesia is the name of the condition in which the entire hand feels numb. Since the ulnar nerve feeds the little finger and half of the ring finger, and the medial nerve feeds the remainder of the fingers and the other half of the ring finger, both the ulnar and medial nerves would have to be damaged to produce true glove anesthesia. The condition would necessarily be accompanied by widespread loss of sensation or motor function throughout the forearm and upper arm.

The anterior rami of the eleven remaining thoracic spinal nerves do not enter into a plexus. They follow direct paths, segmenting into branches that supply the intercostal muscles, abdominal muscles, and the skin of the chest and abdomen. They are referred to as the intercostal nerves.

The anterior rami of the first four lumbar spinal nerves form the *lumbar plexus*. Nerves leaving this plexus supply motor and/or sensory function to the lower abdominal wall, the external genitalia, and part of the lower extremities. The largest branch leaving the lumbar plexus is the *femoral nerve*, which controls motion and sensation in the thigh area of the leg. Additional branches of the femoral nerve supply the lower leg and foot.

The *sacral plexus* is made up of the anterior rami from the fourth and fifth lumbar and the first three sacral nerves. Branches from the sacral plexus supply motor and sensory function to the buttocks, the genital area, and the lower extremities. The sciatic nerve is the main branch arising out of the sacral plexus. It curves downward through the buttock, across the posterior surface of the ischium, between the greater trochanter of the femur, and then down the thigh before it divides into nerves for the lower foot and leg. Injury to the sciatic nerve can arise from a herniated disc, a dislocated hip, compression from

32—Medical Aspects of Claims

pregnancy, or from intramuscular injections in the area.

The *pudendal plexus* is made up of the anterior rami of the second, third, and fourth sacral nerves. The *pudendal nerve* is the largest branch of this plexus and supplies sense and motor function, respectively, to the skin and muscles of the rectum and genital areas. Anesthesia at the site of this nerve eases the pain of childbirth.

Referred Pain. Medical reports frequently mention the phenomenon of referred pain. Referred pain is pain in a part of the body other than that from which the cause of pain originates. Referred pain is real and indicates some pathology or tissue irritation in one of the organs of the body. The sensation of pain is transmitted from the visceral organs by sensory nerves that are accompanied by sympathetic autonomic fibers. When the message reaches the brain, other messages are passed to the site of pain by the motor nerves. In the case of appendicitis, for example, the sensory messages from the appendix area travel to the brain. The brain sends back a message via motor nerves to the muscles in the area causing them to tighten up. Pain from pneumonia is often referred to the abdomen by the brain. Pain from an inflamed gallbladder is often felt between the shoulder blades. An experienced physician familiar with the common patterns of referred pain can avoid a mistake in diagnosis. However, referred pain can cause a physician to pursue a course of treatment for a disease that is not present.

Injury to Nerves. Back problems are very common in our society. Muscle strains cause swelling in the tissues, which exerts pressure on the nerves if they pass through the affected area. Pressure on a motor nerve can cause weakness in or paralysis of the area. Pressure on a sensory nerve can cause a loss of sensation or altered sensations such as pain, tingling, or "crawling."

Nerve fibers within the brain and spinal column do not have *neurilemma sheaths,* layers of tissue surrounding the nerves. Nerves in the periphery do contain these important sheaths. Because neurilemma is essential to regeneration, it explains why some neurological injuries are reversible, while others are not. If the cut ends of the nerve with a neurilemma sheath are not too widely separated, repair or regeneration is possible. The sheath seems to guide and protect the new nerve sprouts that grow out from the core of the injured nerve. It may take months for the nerve to regenerate and for normal transmission of impulses to be restored.

Organs and Systems

The eye, ear, and the various internal organs and systems are less frequently injured than the soft tissues and nerves. Nevertheless,

Exhibit 1-17
Parts of the Eye

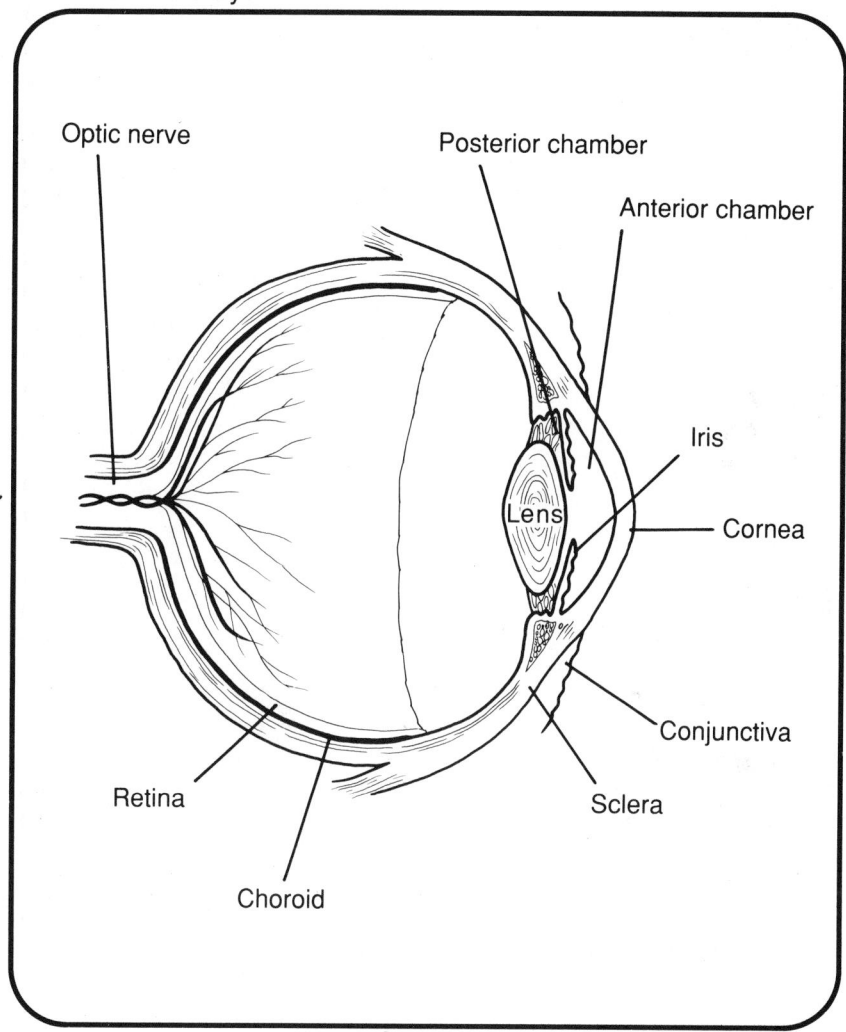

Labels: Optic nerve, Posterior chamber, Anterior chamber, Iris, Cornea, Lens, Conjunctiva, Sclera, Retina, Choroid

when they are, the injury is typically serious. Thus, claim representatives should have a working knowledge of the anatomy of these organs and systems.

The Eye. The parts of the eye are shown in Exhibit 1-17. With six muscles that control the motion of the eye, the eyeball can move in many directions. The eyeball is protected from external debris and from drying by the eyelids. The eyelids regularly spread the tears across the eyes. The mucous membrane that lines each eyelid and reflects down over the front part of the eye is called the *conjunctiva*.

The eyeball itself takes up only a portion of the cavity in which it

34—Medical Aspects of Claims

rests. Behind the eyeball are nerves, blood vessels, the tear gland, and fat tissue. The fat tissue helps to cushion the eyeball in its socket.

The eye has three layers of tissue—an outer fibrous layer, a middle vascular layer, and an inner nerve layer. The fibrous outer layer of the eye consists of the *sclera* and the *cornea*. The sclera is the white of the eye. In the front of the eyeball, the sclera ceases to be opaque and becomes the clear tissue of the cornea. There are no blood vessels in the cornea. The vascular layer of the eye contains many blood vessels that nourish the tissues of the eye. This vascular layer consists of the choroid portion, the ciliary body, and the iris. The *choroid* portion of the vascular layer lies under the sclera. It thickens to form the *ciliary body* and the ciliary muscles that aid in the adjustment of the eye for close vision. The *iris* is the colored portion of the eye, suspended between the cornea and the lens. The hole in its center, called the pupil, expands or contracts to adjust the amount of light entering the eye. The nerve layer of the eye is called the *retina*. Images are projected onto the retina, which flows backward over the back wall of the eye, narrowing into the optic nerve. The optic nerve carries the message from the retina to the sight center in the occipital portion of the brain. It is the brain that "sees" by interpreting the nerve impulses or message.

Suspensory ligaments suspend the lens from the ciliary body. The function of the lens is to bend light rays to focus an image on the retina. Because the lens becomes less elastic with age, eyeglasses become necessary.

The space anterior to the lens and posterior to the cornea is called the *anterior chamber*. The space behind the lens and in front of the retina is called the *posterior chamber*. Each chamber is filled with a substance to keep it inflated. The anterior chamber contains a fluid called the *aqueous humor*, which is constantly being excreted and regenerated. The posterior chamber contains a jelly-like substance known as *vitreous humor*. Unlike the aqueous humor, the vitreous humor cannot be replaced if any is lost through trauma.

The Ear. Exhibit 1-18 shows the parts of the ear. The external portion of the ear receives sound waves and funnels them into the middle ear. Called the *auricle* or *pinna*, the external portion of the ear is composed of cartilage covered with skin.

The *auditory canal*, or external acoustic meatus, extends from the auricle down to the eardrum, or *tympanic membrane*. The external acoustic meatus is formed partly by bone and partly by cartilage. It is lined with skin and protected by ear wax, or *cerumen* as it is sometimes called.

The middle ear, or *tympanic cavity*, transmits the sound waves to the inner ear. The *tympanic membrane* actually separates the external

1 • Anatomy and Medical Terminology—35

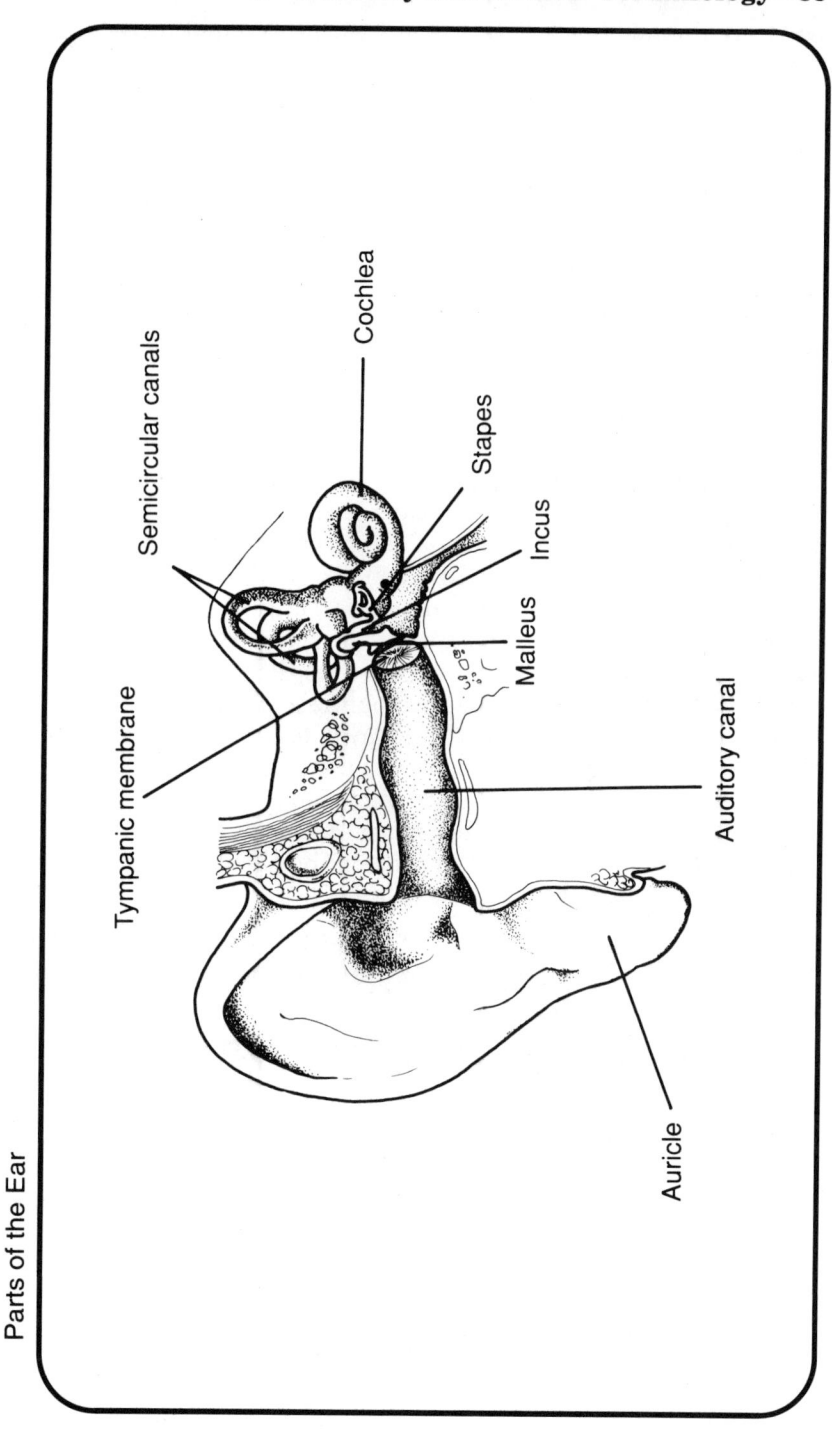

Exhibit 1-18
Parts of the Ear

36—Medical Aspects of Claims

ear from the middle ear. It vibrates with the sound waves that pass down the external canal. The middle ear space is filled with air that reaches it by way of the eustachian tube. This tube opens into the upper back part of the throat and is important in helping to equalize pressure in the middle ear with the atmosphere.

Three small bones extend across the middle ear cavity. They are the *malleus* (hammer), the *incus* (anvil), and the *stapes* (stirrup). They transmit the sound waves from the tympanic membrane to the inner ear. The footpiece-like projection on the bottom of the stirrup fits into the oval-shaped window between the middle and inner ear. The fluid-filled labyrinth, or inner ear, contains the sensors for hearing and body position.

There are three *semicircular canals* in each ear. Each canal contains a patch of hair cells or receptors that pick up changes in body position. Injury can interfere with this sense of balance, or orientation.

The *vestibule* is an internal cave containing sensors that provide information about the position of the head in relation to the ground. The *cochlea*, which is shaped like a snail's shell, picks up sound waves and transmits them to the eighth cranial, or acoustic, nerve.

Conductive deafness arises from the inability of the bones of the middle ear to transmit the sound waves to the inner ear. This occurs when the bones become fused together as a result of aging. Hearing aids can be helpful in conductive hearing loss. They help to transmit the sound waves through the cranial bones rather than through the bones of the middle ear. *Nerve deafness*, on the other hand, occurs either in the acoustic nerve or in the auditory center of the brain. Hearing aids are not helpful in overcoming the deafness that results from nerve-related impairments.

The Circulatory System. The heart, shown in Exhibit 1-19, is the center of the circulatory system. It is well protected by the rib cage and the vertebrae, but trauma is still possible. Gunshot wounds to the heart are often fatal since the victim can rapidly bleed. Fracture fragments from the ribs or the sternum can puncture the heart, also causing rapid death. The heart can be bruised by blows to the chest. An injury of this sort can cause an irregular heartbeat or the buildup of blood in the sac around the heart. Early and appropriate intervention can help to maintain the appropriate heart rate or to drain the excess blood before the heart is literally squeezed to death.

Blood flowing from the heart is carried by the *arteries,* while blood flowing back to the heart travels by way of *veins*. When an artery is cut, the blood flows out in spurts, which correspond to the beats of the ventricles of the heart. Venous injuries result in a steady flow of blood from the injury site.

When part of the structure of the wall of an artery weakens, a

1 • Anatomy and Medical Terminology—37

Exhibit 1-19
Circulation Around the Heart

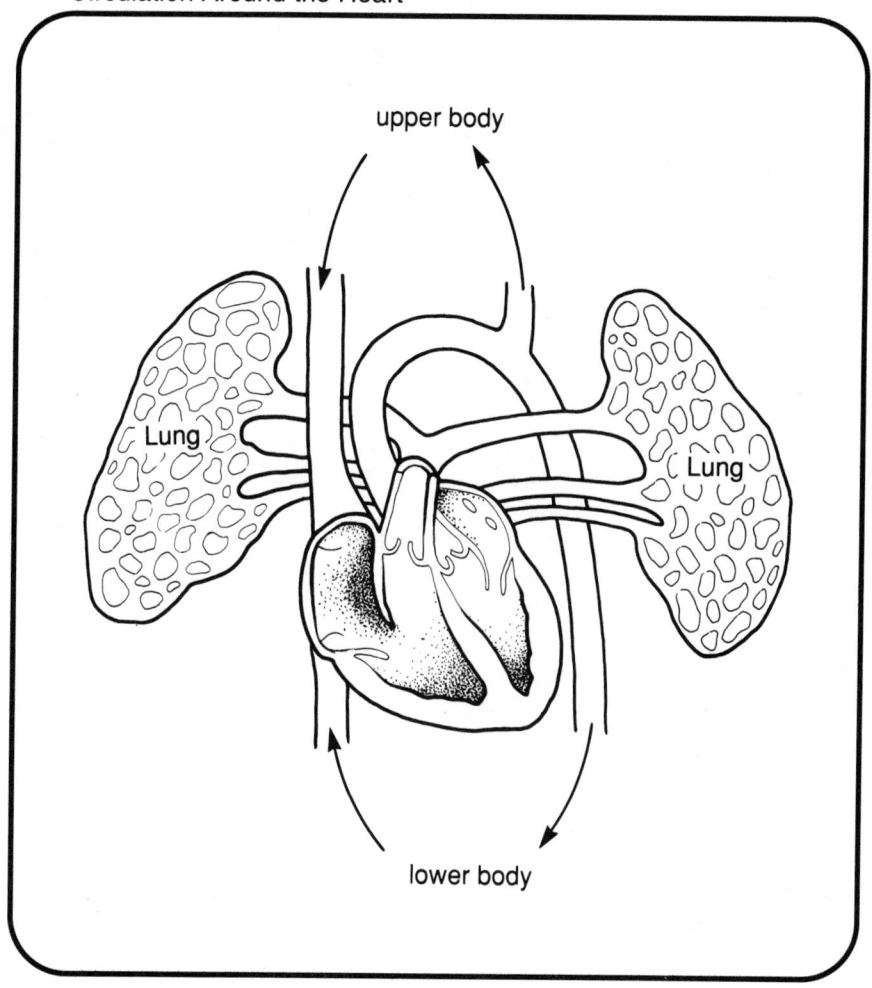

portion of the wall may dilate out. Such a dilation in the wall of an artery is called an *aneurysm*. The weakened area may rupture, causing a fatal or rapid hemorrhage.

Arteriosclerosis, or hardening of the arteries, is a common problem, experienced by most people to some degree as they age. Degenerative changes in the walls of the arteries cause a decrease in elasticity and sometimes excessive deposits of calcium. These changes can be accompanied by atherosclerosis, a fatty degeneration and infiltration in the vessel walls.

Veins generally follow a course parallel to the arteries although there are far more veins than there are arteries. Many veins have valves to prevent the backflow of blood. These valves are more common

38—Medical Aspects of Claims

in the veins of the lower extremities where the return flow must fight against gravity. People who must stand for long periods of time in the course of their work often develop varicose veins, a dilation of the veins that occurs when the veins are no longer able to resist the pressure of the blood and the valves begin to wear out.

Capillaries are the microscopic vessels that connect the tiny ends of the veins and the arteries.

It is not unusual for trauma victims to show some blood in their urine. This is not necessarily indicative of a major hemorrhage. Some bleeding occurs from the disruption of the superficial vessels. After a major trauma, the physician often monitors the red blood cell count. If it is dropping, it is indicative of significant bleeding. Small amounts of blood found in the urine clear within a day or two following trauma.

The Respiratory System. The respiratory system is shown in Exhibit 1-20. The *nasal cavities* open to the outside through the anterior nares, or nostrils. To the rear, they open into the nasopharynx by way of the posterior nares. The vestibule of the nasal cavity is the dilated area just inside each nostril. The *pharynx* (throat) is the passageway that extends downward from the nasal cavities and the mouth. The *larynx* (voice box) passes the air between the pharynx and the trachea. It lies midline in the neck and prevents anything but air from entering the lower air passages. It is composed of nine cartilages joined by ligaments and controlled by the skeletal muscles. The largest of the cartilages is the thyroid cartilage, which forms the Adam's Apple.

The *epiglottis* extends above the thyroid cartilage in front of the entrance into the larynx. This flap of tissue seals off the larynx during the act of swallowing.

The *trachea* (windpipe) is a cartilaginous structure that extends from the larynx downward through the neck and into the thorax. A tracheotomy is a surgical procedure performed to provide free passage of air to the lungs when the air flow is obstructed above the level of the trachea. The trachea ends by dividing into left and right branches known as bronchi. Each *bronchus* enters a lung and then begins to branch out into a series of smaller tubes called *bronchioles*. The right bronchus is more nearly vertical and shorter and wider than the left one. For this reason, it is often into this branch that foreign bodies are inhaled.

The lungs are the primary organs of respiration and are essential for the exchange of gases between the blood and the air. Each lung is covered by a membrane called the *pleura*, which consists of two layers. The space between the layers is called the *pleural cavity*, which is filled with fluid. This fluid lubricates the surfaces as they glide over each other.

The right lung is separated into three lobes, while the left lung is

1 • Anatomy and Medical Terminology—39

Exhibit 1-20
The Respiratory System

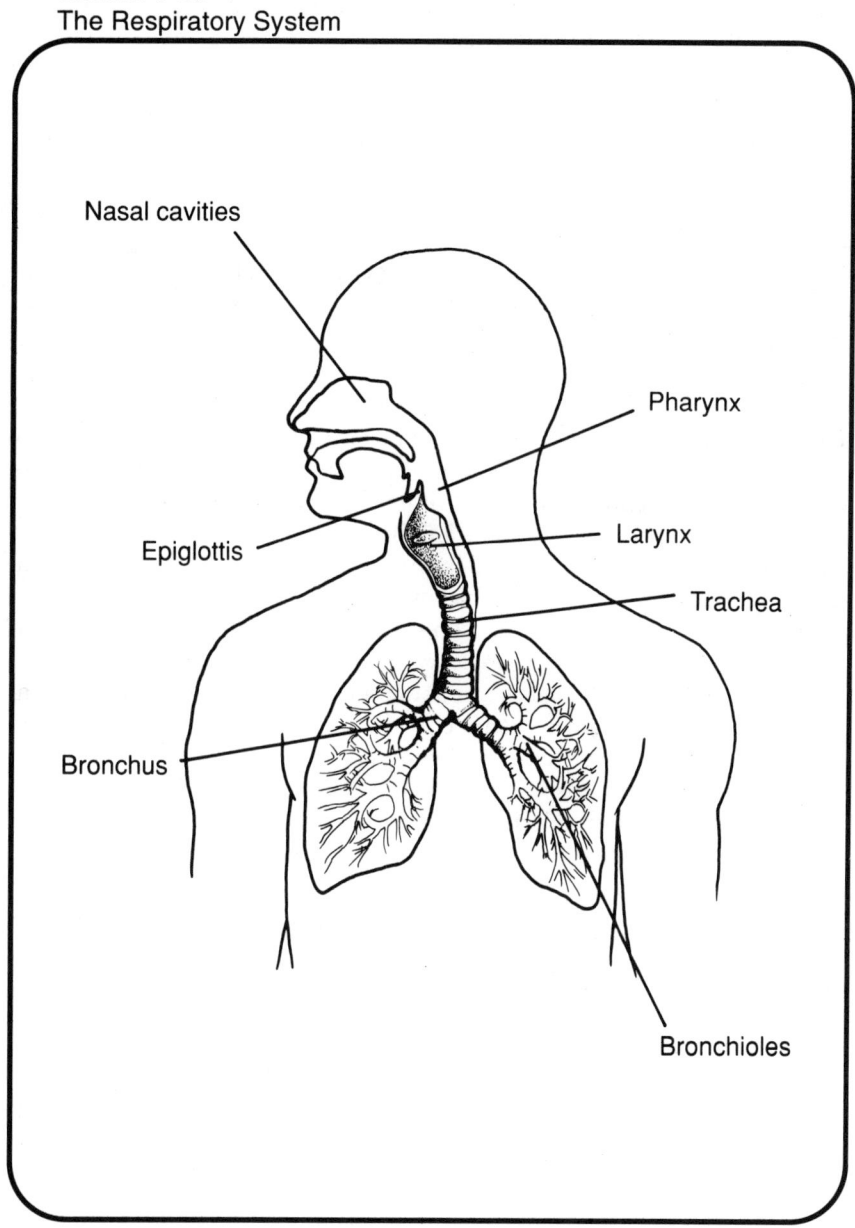

- Nasal cavities
- Pharynx
- Epiglottis
- Larynx
- Trachea
- Bronchus
- Bronchioles

separated into two. Some 700 million *alveoli* (air sacs) diffuse oxygen from the air into the blood supply in the lungs. The oxygen-rich blood then travels to the heart, which pumps it to the parts of the body.

If trauma disrupts the vacuum that surrounds the lungs and keeps

40—Medical Aspects of Claims

them inflated, the lungs will partially or totally collapse. The vacuum must be re-established to help the lungs reinflate. To do this, a surgeon would generally insert tubes through the chest wall. These tubes are then attached to a suction machine that removes excess air, thus re-establishing the vacuum while the hole caused by trauma is sealing itself. The resulting scars on the chest can be rather unsightly because of the size of the tubes.

The Digestive System. Exhibit 1-21 shows the digestive system. Food travels from the mouth and throat down the *esophagus* to the stomach. The cardiac valve at the top of the stomach keeps food within the stomach, preventing it from moving back up into the esophagus.

The *vagus nerve*, stimulated when food is introduced into the stomach, sends a message to the brain. In response, the brain sends a message back to the stomach to produce acids that begin to break down food. The *pyloric valve* at the bottom of the stomach allows partially digested food to travel into the small intestine. Muscular movements called *peristaltic waves* send food along the digestive tract.

The small intestine consists of three divisions: duodenum, jejunum, and ileum. The *duodenum* is wide and about ten inches long. The *jejunum* forms the next two-fifths of the small intestine and connects the duodenum with the ileum. The *ileum* terminates in the cecum of the large intestine at a valve known as the *ileocecal valve*. The large intestine, about five feet long, is attached to the posterior abdominal wall by *mesentery*, a fibrous connective tissue. The appendix is attached to the cecum about an inch below the ileocecal valve.

The cecum continues into the *colon*, which consists of the ascending colon, the transverse colon, the descending colon, and the sigmoid colon. The *ascending colon* extends from the cecum to the underside of the liver where it turns left to form the hepatic flexure. The *transverse colon* crosses the upper part of the abdominal cavity and then turns down to form the splenic flexure. The *descending colon* extends from the splenic flexure to the top of the pelvis where it turns again toward the midline to become the *sigmoid colon*. The sigmoid colon is the s-shaped portion that finally connects with the rectum.

The rectum is about five to six inches long and moves the intestinal contents toward the external sphincter muscles, which hold these contents back until the muscles are voluntarily released. Although the intestines are very resilient, puncture, perforation, hemorrhage, and hematomas can occur.

The Liver and Gallbladder. The *liver*, the largest organ in the body, is critical to survival. It weighs about three pounds and sits in the upper right quadrant of the abdomen. It consists of four lobes of highly vascular tissue. These tissues are fed by the hepatic artery and the portal vein. The liver manufactures a digestive fluid called bile. Bile is

Exhibit 1-21
The Digestive System

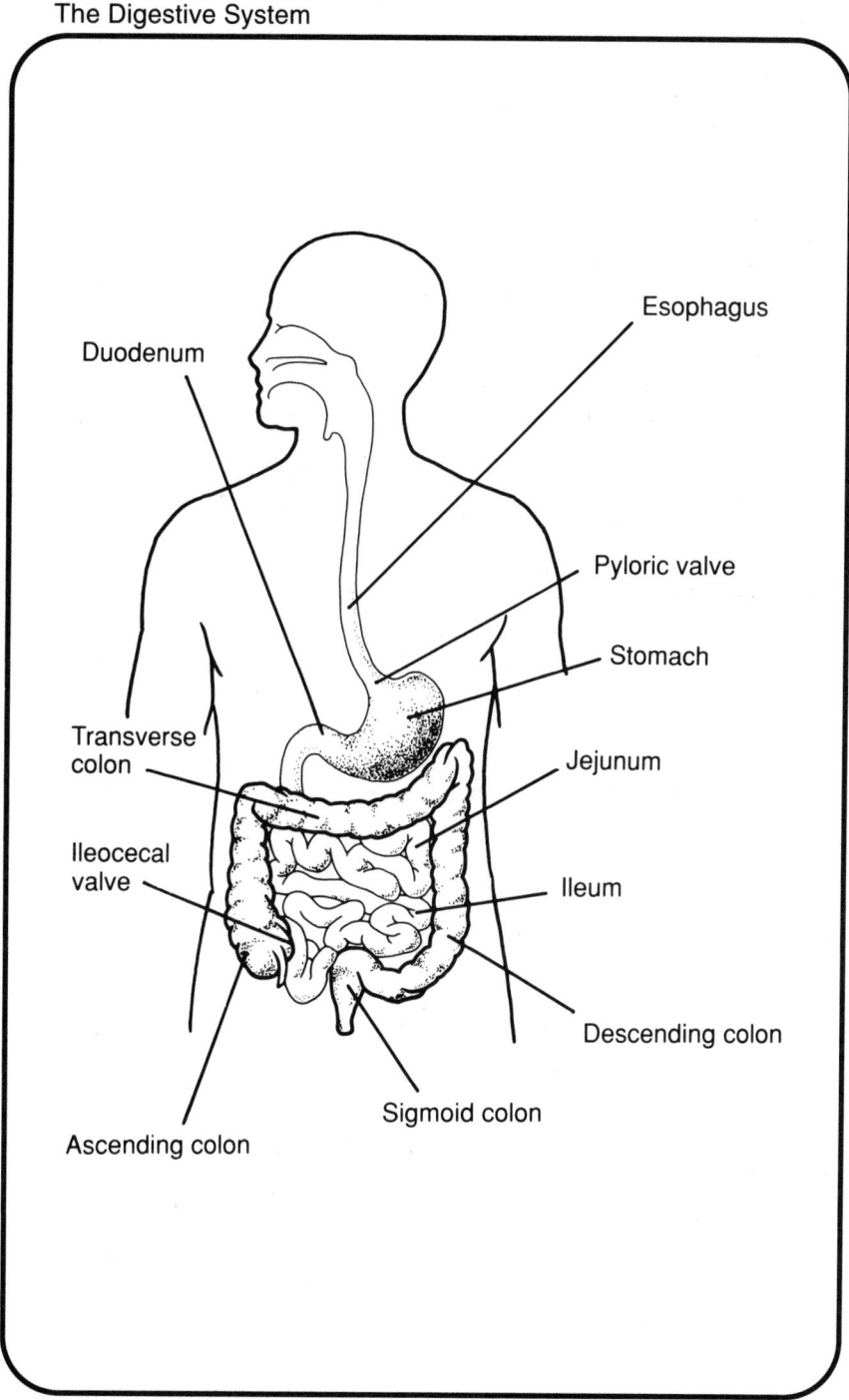

stored in the *gallbladder* and is released into the intestine to aid in the digestion of food.

One of the important functions of the liver is to break down proteins and form urea. The urea is carried to the kidneys by the blood stream and passed out of the body in the form of urine. Old, used-up red blood cells are destroyed and removed from the body by this process. The liver is also important for filtering poisons out of the blood and for storing sugars in the body until needed.

Although death can occur rapidly if the liver ceases to function, the liver does have a remarkable ability to grow new cells when old ones are damaged. When the liver is damaged so severely that it can no longer excrete bile, the pigments from the production of the bile will pass into the bloodstream, causing the skin to turn yellow. This condition is referred to as *jaundice*. The liver, gallbladder, and the other visceral organs are shown in Exhibit 1-22.

The Pancreas. The *pancreas* consists of a body, a tail, and a head. The head rests in the curve of the duodenum, the body extends toward the spleen, and the tail comes into contact with the spleen. Juices manufactured by the pancreas are excreted into the duodenum through pancreatic ducts. These juices assist in the digestion of food as it passes through the intestine.

Scattered throughout the pancreas are special cells called *Islands of Langerhans*, which make *insulin*. Insulin helps the tissues of the body to metabolize sugars. Poor or inadequate functioning of these cells leads to a condition known as *diabetes mellitis*, commonly known as sugar diabetes. When too much sugar circulates in the blood because it is not adequately metabolized, the affected person is sluggish, and healing is greatly slowed. Inadequate control of diabetes following trauma can create numerous complications.

The Spleen. The *spleen* is an organ of the lymphatic system. It lies in the left upper part of the abdomen below the diaphragm and behind the stomach.

The spleen, a highly vascular organ, has a tendency to hemorrhage when a blow is directed to the abdomen. It is fortunate, however, that the functions of the spleen can be assumed by other parts of the body, and surgical removal leaves no lasting effects.

The spleen helps to produce *lymphocytes* (white blood cells). Lymphocytes carry the immune substances, or antibodies, which help to protect the body from disease. When the spleen is surgically removed, other lymphatic tissues produce enough lymphocytes for the body's defensive needs.

The Urinary Tract. Exhibit 1-23 shows the urinary tract. The *kidneys* lie in the posterior portion of the abdominal cavity to either side

Exhibit 1-22
Visceral Organs

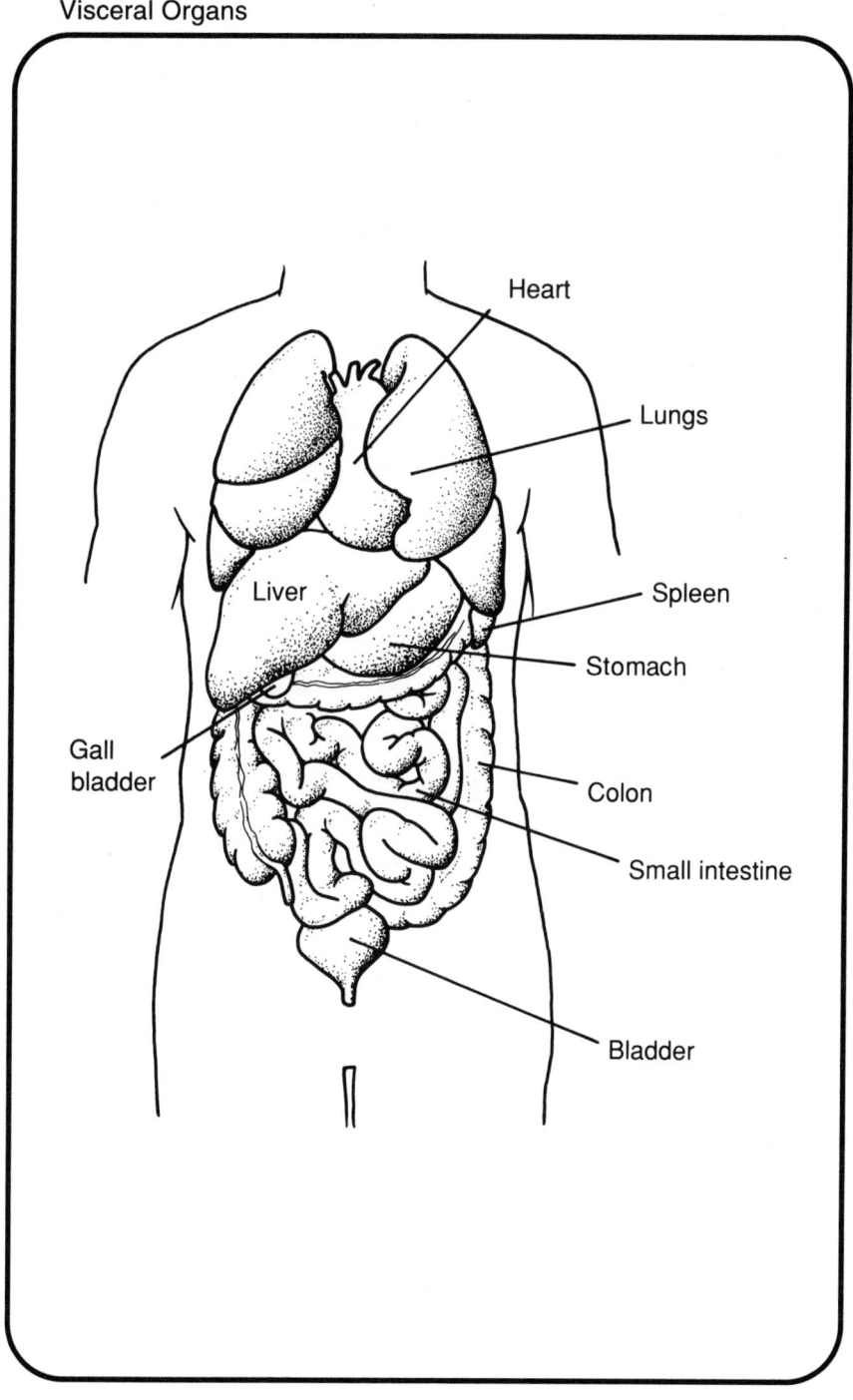

Exhibit 1-23
The Urinary Tract

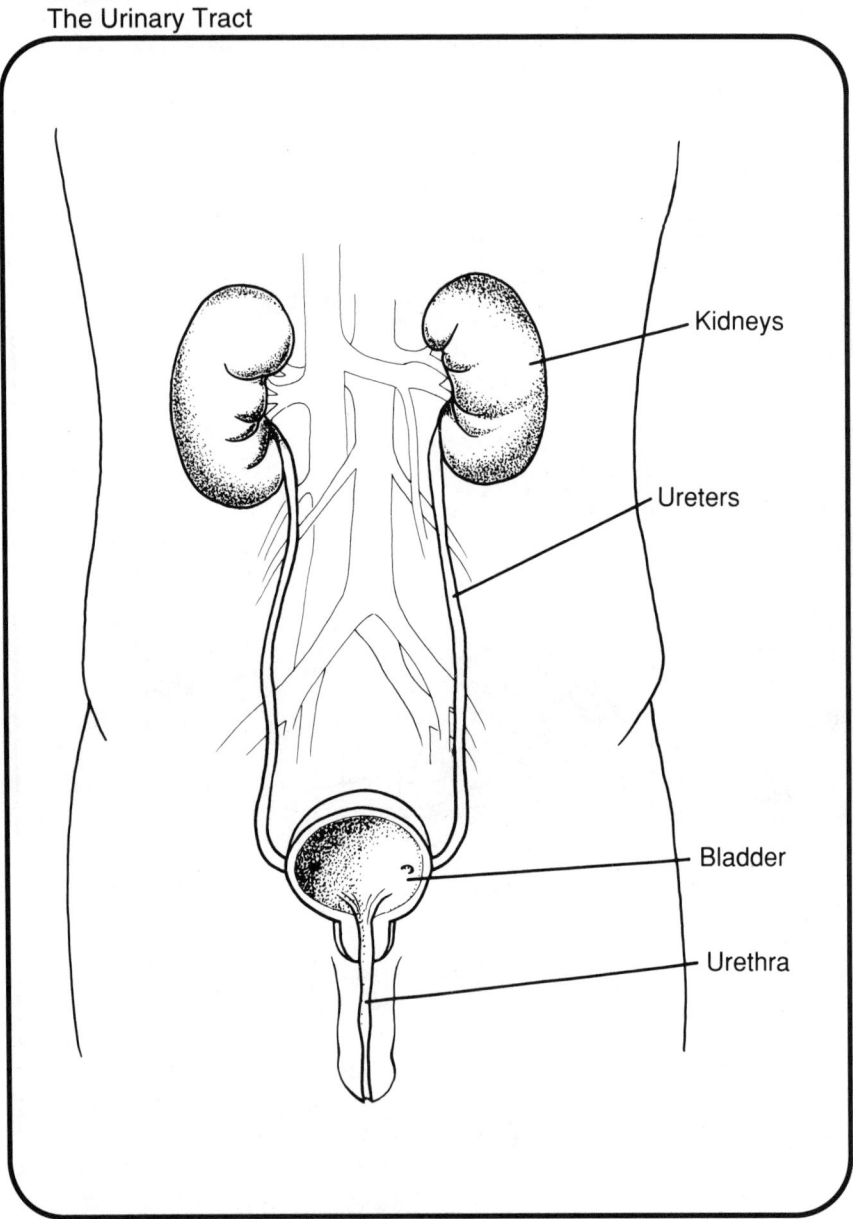

- Kidneys
- Ureters
- Bladder
- Urethra

of the vertebral column. They are protected from trauma by masses of fat and connective tissue. They are not fixed, but actually move up and down with the diaphragm during breathing.

Blood containing waste products enters the kidneys by way of the renal arteries. The kidney tissues filter the blood and send it on its way by means of the renal veins. Waste products are concentrated in the kidneys and flushed out from the kidneys by way of the ureters. The *ureters*, which are about ten to twelve inches long in the adult, pass the waste products in the form of urine to the bladder. Peristaltic waves help to ensure that the urine travels down to the bladder rather than back up to the kidneys, particularly when one is lying down.

The *bladder* is a muscular sac that lies behind the pubis. It stores the urine until it is released voluntarily. About 300 cc of urine can accumulate in the bladder before nerves in the bladder begin to signal the brain that there is a need for release. An average of about 1½ liters of urine are passed during the day.

The urine leaves the bladder by way of the urethra. The urethra in a woman is only about 1 to 1½ inches long, while the urethra in a man is much longer.

As mentioned, some microscopic blood in the urine is not unusual following a trauma. Such bleeding may result from the disruption of superficial vessels. More severe bleeding occurs when the urinary tract structures have been punctured, lacerated, or ruptured. Surgical intervention may be necessary in such cases.

Male Reproductive System. The male reproductive system, shown in Exhibit 1-24, consists of a pair of gonads, or *testes*, and a system of excretory ducts. The *ducts* are the epididymis, the ductus deferens, and the ejaculatory ducts. The accessory structures are the *seminal vesicles*, the *prostate gland*, the *bulbo-urethral glands*, and the *penis*.

The two testes, which produce sperm, are suspended outside the body in a sac called the *scrotum*. The epididymis, attached to the top of each testis, carries the sperm away from the testis.

The *ductus deferens* (vas deferens) carries the sperm from the epididymis to the ejaculatory duct. It passes from the scrotum through the muscles and fascia of the abdominal wall by way of the inguinal canal. The ductus deferens passes in front of the ureter and then turns down into the space between the bladder and the rectum. The ductus deferens eventually joins the duct of the seminal vesicle to form the *ejaculatory duct*. The two ejaculatory ducts enter the prostate gland on the posterior surface and continue through the gland before they end up in the urethra.

The *seminal vesicles* are the sacs that lie behind the bladder and in front of the rectum. They secrete semen, a substance that is important in helping the sperm move about. The duct from the seminal vesicles joins with the ductus deferens to form the ejaculatory duct.

The *prostate gland* surrounds the urethra as it comes out of the bladder. It is composed of muscle and serves as a sphincter for the urinary bladder. It also supplies part of the force for ejaculation.

The *bulbo-urethral glands (Cowper's Glands)* are two glands that

46—Medical Aspects of Claims

Exhibit 1-24
The Male Reproductive System

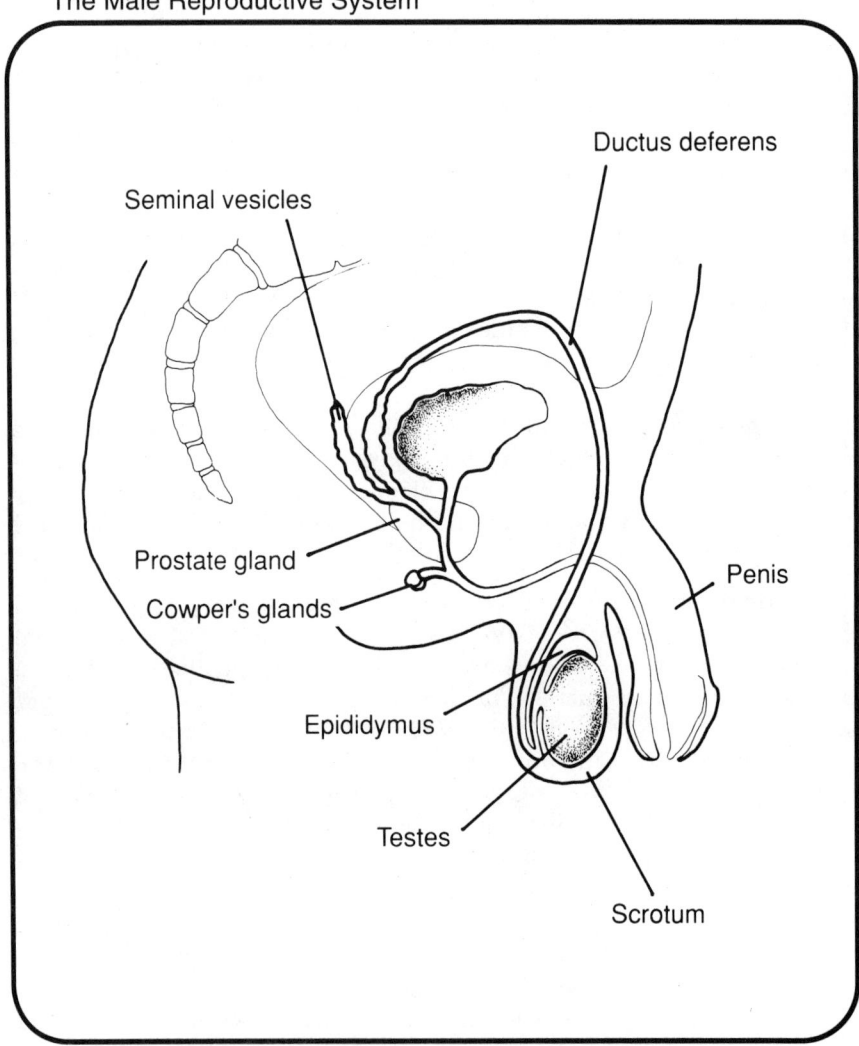

Diagram labels: Seminal vesicles, Ductus deferens, Prostate gland, Cowper's glands, Penis, Epididymus, Testes, Scrotum

lie on either side of the urethra. They produce a substance that helps to neutralize the acidity of the urine and helps to provide a healthy environment for the passage of the sperm. The *penis* is the external organ through which the urethra passes to the exterior of the body.

Female Reproductive System. The female reproductive system, shown in Exhibit 1-25, consists of paired gonads called ovaries, the uterine (fallopian) tubes, the uterus, and the vagina. The associated structures are the external genitalia and the mammary glands.

The *ovaries* are located on either side of the uterus and are at-

Exhibit 1-25
The Female Reproductive System

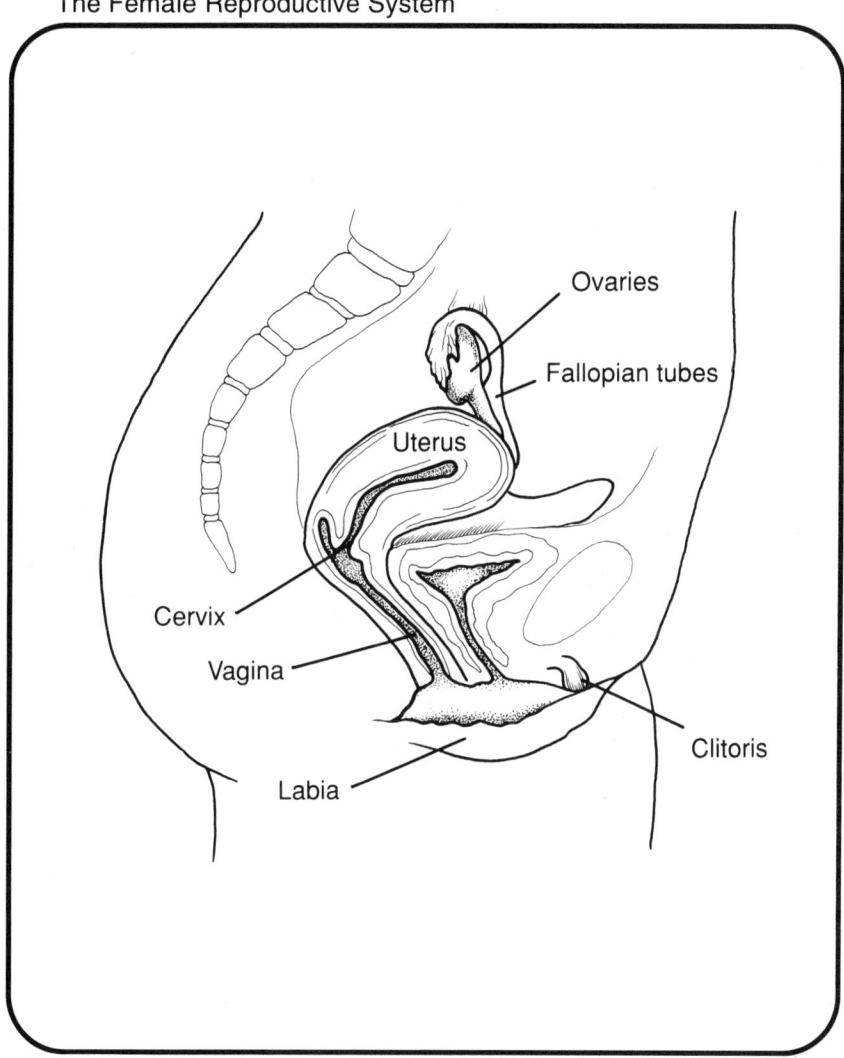

tached to the posterior surface of the uterus by the broad ligament. As the egg cells mature in the ovaries, they are released into the *fallopian tubes*. The ovum travels down the tubes into the body of the *uterus*, where it may become implanted if fertilized.

The upper portion of the uterus is referred to as the body of the uterus. The lower end funnels down to a narrow opening known as the *cervix*. The fundus of the uterus is the portion at the very top of the uterus where the fallopian tubes attach.

The *vagina* is the tube that opens from the external labia up to the cervix of the uterus. The *labia* are folds of skin that protect the vaginal opening. The clitoris is a small structure of erectile tissue that lies anterior to the vaginal opening and plays a role in the arousal process.

The breasts, or mammary glands, are considered to be part of the reproductive system. Each breast consists of about fifteen to twenty lobes, each with a lactiferous duct. These ducts channel toward the nipple where milk is secreted after the birth of a child. The milk production can be suppressed by drugs in the event of a stillbirth or when a woman chooses not to breast-feed.

Trauma to the reproductive areas produces anxiety relating to sexual performance and fertility. The reproductive organs are located such that they are rarely traumatized, but when injury does occur, it often has a devastating effect on the person's sense of well-being or self-esteem.

Medical reports often include the terms *gravida*, *para*, and *abortus*. These terms clarify how many children a woman has carried, how many live births have occurred, and how many fetuses have been spontaneously or surgically aborted. For example, a woman described as Gravida III, Para II, Abortus I has been pregnant three times, has carried two fetuses to full term, and has had one abortion.

DIAGNOSTIC TESTING

The claims representative must have a working knowledge of diagnostic tests to be able to recognize the need for and potential benefit of each test. Tests are frequently administered for medical conditions unrelated to the claim. The claim representative should be able to identify the need for such tests so that payments are appropriately made. There are four typical kinds of diagnostic tests for physical conditions: (1) sampling tests, (2) performance tests, (3) x-ray or sonic wave tests, and (4) scopes or fiber optics tests to visualize the inside of the body. Tests for psychological conditions are also discussed at the end of this section.

Sampling Tests

The following is a list of sampling tests with a brief description of the purpose of the test.

CBC (complete blood count). Blood elements including red and white blood cell counts and the hemoglobin concentration are analyzed. The CBC often helps to clarify the need for other tests.

CBC with differential. In addition to analyzing the blood elements, this test also analyzes the type of white cells, which helps in the diagnosis of specific infections or diseases.

T3–T4. This blood test helps to analyze how well the thyroid gland is functioning.

Culture. Blood samples are placed in culture dishes to identify the presence of bacteria.

Thrombin time. This test is used to diagnose liver disease or blood clotting deficiencies.

Prothrombin time or Pro time. Blood is drawn to monitor the effect of anticoagulating drugs.

BUN (blood urea nitrogen). Blood is analyzed to help determine how well the kidneys are functioning.

Creatinine. Test for this blood element also helps to clarify how well the kidneys are functioning.

Glucose. Blood is analyzed to determine the amount of sugar. This measures how well the pancreas is producing insulin to metabolize the sugar.

Calcium and phosphorus. These elements reflect the condition of the kidneys and the general nutritional state.

Bilirubin. An elevated bilirubin level in the blood suggests problems with liver function.

Transaminase enzymes. Elevations in these enzyme levels in the blood suggest injury to liver, muscles, or heart. They may also suggest the presence of hepatitis.

Alkaline phosphates. Elevations of this substance in the blood suggest liver, bone, or gallbladder disease.

GGTP (gamma glutamyl transpeptadise). Elevations of this substance in the blood suggest liver disease or excessive use of alcohol.

Total protein and albumin. Abnormal levels of these elements in the blood may point to poor water balance, less-than-adequate nutrition, or liver disease.

Uric acid. Elevated uric acid levels in the blood would suggest gout or kidney disease.

Urine tests can also suggest the need for further testing or indicate specific conditions requiring treatment.

Blood in the urine may indicate kidney stones, infection in the urinary tract, or the presence of a tumor. Blood can be found in the urine following fairly minor trauma because capillaries may be broken, which causes a small amount of blood to be released into the urine. Gross observable blood in the urine is a much greater cause for concern than microscopic blood.

White blood cells in the urine suggest infection in the urinary tract.

Glucose in the urine suggests that the body is not secreting enough insulin to metabolize the sugar, an indication of diabetes mellitis.

Ketones in the urine suggest that the body has had to resort to breaking down body protein because of insufficient sugar metabolism. This may result from poor nutrition or diabetes.

Bile elevation in the urine suggests liver disease.

Protein in the urine suggests impaired kidney function.

Biopsy. Small pieces of tissue can be surgically obtained, or hollow needles may be inserted into the tissue from which a specimen is drawn.

Tests of Function or Performance

These tests are typically performed as part of a physical exam. In one performance test, reflex reactions are analyzed to determine how well the muscles and nerves are functioning. The following are the most common reflex tests:

1. *Ankle jerk.* The tendon at the back of the foot is struck to test for possible diseases of the cord, nerves, or intervertebral discs.
2. *Patellar or knee jerk.* The area near the knee cap is tapped with the reflex hammer.
3. *Triceps.* This tests arm reflexes.
4. *Biceps.* Reflexes in the upper arm are tested.
5. *Pupillary* (contraction of the pupil of the eye).

In addition to various reflex tests, the physician will attempt to elicit other physical responses to measure the health of the body and especially the nervous system.

Romberg's sign. Inability to maintain balance when the eyes are shut and the feet put close together. This indicates serious generalized nerve impairments.

Babinski's sign. The great toe extends when the sole of the foot is stroked. If the toe flexes backward, it can indicate a lesion in the nervous system.

Lasegue's sign. The physician raises the straightened leg of the patient. This puts pressure on the sciatic nerve, and pain can indicate the presence of a herniated disc.

Eli's test. The patient lies face down while the physician raises the knee. This can suggest a herniated disc in the lower spinal column.

Percussion testing. This is the act of thumping on a portion of the body to determine if pain is produced as a result.

Dermatome testing. Sensations can be tracked along specific nerve routes. The areas that receive sensations are called dermatomes. Injury to nerves can result in strange sensations in the dermatome of that nerve or in the absence of sensation.

The following tests measure physical performance through sophisticated equipment.

Audiograms measure the hearing ability.

The Caloric test is performed by introducing cold or hot fluid into the ear canal. When there is disease or dysfunction in the inner ear, there will be unusual eye movements as a result of the test.

Echograms, or ultrasound, are the use of sound waves to identify the size or location of body structures.

EEG (electroencephalogram) measures the electrical activity in the brain and can be helpful in diagnosing seizure-related disorders.

ECG or EKG (electrocardiogram) measures the electrical activity within the heart muscle.

EST (exercise stress test) measures the body's response to vigorous exercise.

Holter monitor. A monitor is attached to the patient for twenty-four to forty-eight hours to continuously record the heart rate.

Pulmonary function tests measure lung capacity during inspiration and exhalation.

Thermography. A special camera is used to measure the surface temperatures of the skin. These readings can be used to determine the presence of inflammation, to assess the depth of burns, or to measure the circulation. However, any changes in the temperature in the examination room or any movement of the patient's muscles can produce false results. It has been noted that the presence of cigarette smoke in the room can cause thermographic changes. Although once considered to have great potential for diagnosis and assessment of pain and inflammation, thermography has fallen out of favor because of its relatively low validity.

Radiographic Tests

X-ray films are sometimes called radiographs or roentgenograms. They are pictures of the comparative densities of the areas of the body through which x-rays have been passed. It is important to remember that if the examination reveals no injury and x-rays show no abnormality, it does not necessarily mean that no abnormality is present. It only means that the films did not show the abnormality. The position of the patient, the position of the abnormality, and the quality of the x-ray may make it impossible to be seen.

Myelogram. Air or contrast medium is introduced into the subarachnoid space surrounding the spinal cord and nerve roots. It is used to diagnose ruptured discs, space-occupying lesions, or pressure from bone fragments or overgrowth.

Cerebral angiogram. Contrast medium is injected into cerebral blood vessels, and x-rays are then taken to diagnose obstructions or outpouchings in the vessels.

Pneumoencephalography. Air is injected in the lumbar subarachnoid space. It flows up to the ventricles of the brain, allowing the ventricle size and shape to be analyzed.

Ventriculography. A needle is passed directly into the ventricles of the brain to permit the injection of air for contrast.

Brain scan. Radioactive material is injected into the blood stream. The material concentrates in defective areas, allowing them to be identified.

CT scan (computerized transaxial tomography). A pinpoint x-ray beam is directed on horizontal or vertical planes of the brain. These slices are then fed into a computer, which analyzes and displays them for diagnostic purposes.

Echoencephalography. Pulses of ultrasonic waves are beamed through the head and graphically recorded to identify shifts in midline structures as a result of space-taking lesions.

Bronchogram. Contrast solution is introduced into the trachea, permitting the occlusions or dilations in the bronchial passages to be outlined.

Barium enema. Barium is introduced into the colon through the rectum. The barium creates a sharp outline for x-rays of the wall of the colon.

Cholecystogram. Special salts that are ingested concentrate in the gallbladder so it is visible on x-ray. Gallstones or obstructions can be identified.

Artereogram. Contrast medium is injected into the artery to be x-rayed.

IVP (intravenous pyelogram). Dye injected into a vein concentrates in the urinary tract allowing it to be x-rayed along its length.

Arthrography. X-ray of a joint.

Cardiac catheterization. A catheter is snaked up through a blood vessel and into the heart. Dye is then released, allowing the heart to be viewed on a special device.

Scopes and Fiber Optics

Tubes can be introduced through incisions or through normal body openings to enable the physician to observe the body interior. The *bronchoscope* is used to look down the throat and into the bronchial area. The *ophthalmoscope* is used to look into the eye to observe the retina and internal structures of the eye.

Psychological Tests

In addition to physical tests, psychological tests may be used to diagnose a patient's or claimant's condition. The psychologist or psychiatrist often tests a person's awareness of the environment and reality by asking questions about commonly known subjects such as who the president is, the date, month, and year, and where they are physically located at the time and the like. Serial sevens testing requires the patient to count back from 100 by increments of seven. Psychological testing can be critical in determining whether symptoms are of a psychological or physical origin or both.

Interest Tests. These tests measure vocational or avocational interests and preferences. Interest tests are frequently used to help identify new job options for a disabled worker.

Intelligence Tests. These tests measure the ability to learn, understand, recall, and reason. Although there are many forms of intelligence, most intelligence tests depend heavily on verbal skills. Performance on intelligence tests and scholarly achievement correspond. Thus, intelligence tests are important tools in predicting the ability to succeed in academic pursuits.

Achievement and Aptitude Tests. These tests measure specific skills and bodies of knowledge. They are useful in screening people for skills such as typing or mechanics.

Reading Tests. Reading tests measure the ability to understand written sentences and passages of text. Deficiencies in reading skills can cause poor performance on intelligence and aptitude tests and may require special treatment.

Personality Tests. Personality tests identify characteristic behavior and response patterns. Personality reflects attitudes, experiences, and is influenced by physical well-being and makeup; it is not easily changed after reaching adulthood. Personality tests are useful tools in job placement because every personality is more suited to some occupations than others.

Manual Dexterity and Mechanical Tests. These tests measure the ability to perform manual tasks. They measure speed and accuracy for various levels of detail and complexity. These tests are important in screening for jobs that require high levels of mechanical skill or rapid and accurate performance of mechanical tasks.

SUMMARY

An understanding of medical terminology and human anatomy is essential for any claim representative handling injury claims. Because both areas are so vast, the claim representative who studies them diligently can always add to his or her body of knowledge. This chapter introduced the basics of these subjects and defined numerous medical tests that the claim representative is likely to encounter. The Appendix to this chapter contains various references that would enable an interested claim representative to learn more about the medical field.

GLOSSARY

Roots in Medical Terminology

The roots listed in this Glossary are commonly found in medical terms. Some typically come at the beginning of a word; others, at the end. Each root always has the same meaning. Also included are examples of words in which the roots are a part and definitions of those words.

The following roots are typically found at the beginning of words.

Root	Definition	Example	Definition
A-, Ab-	Away from, lack of	Abduction	Movement away from the body
A-, An-	Absence of	Asepsis	Absence of infection
Ad-	To, toward, near	Adrenal	Near the kidney
Ambi-	Both	Ambidextrous	Having dexterity in both hands
Ante-	Before	Antenatal	Before birth
Anti-	Against	Antiseptic	Against infection
Arth-	Joint	Arthritis	Inflammation in a joint
Auto-	Self	Autolesion	Self-inflicted injury
Bi-, Bin-	Two	Binocular	Pertaining to both eyes
Brachi-	Arm	Brachialis	A muscle of the forearm
Brachy-	Short	Brachydactylia	Having short fingers or toes
Bronch-	Windpipe	Bronchiectasis	Dilation of the bronchial tubes
Carcin-	Cancer	Carcinogenic	Causing cancer

56—Medical Aspects of Claims

Cardio-	Heart	Cardiologist	A heart specialist
Cephal-	Head	Cephalgia	Headache
Chondr-	Cartilage	Chondritis	Inflammation of the cartilage
Circum-	Around	Circumocular	Around the eyes
Contra-	Against	Contra-indication	Any condition making the use of a remedy inadvisable
Costa-	Rib	Costal	Relating to ribs
Cranio-	Skull	Craniotomy	A hole cut into the skull
Crypto-	Hidden	Cryptogenic	Of unknown origin
Cut-	Skin	Cutaneous	Relating to the skin
Cysto-	Sac or bladder	Cystitis	Inflammation of the bladder
Cyto-	Cell	Cytology	Study of the cell
Derma-	Skin	Dermabrasion	Abrading of the skin to reduce scars
Di-	Two	Diplopia	Double vision
Dis-	Apart	Disarticulation	Taking a joint apart
Dys-	Impaired	Dyspepsia	Difficulty in digestion
Em, En-	In	Encapsulated	Inside a capsule
Encephalo-	Of the brain	Encephalitis	Inflammation of the brain
Endo-	Within	Endothelium	Layer of cells inside the heart and blood vessels
Entero-	Intestine	Enteritis	Inflammation of the intestine
Epi-	Over or upon	Epidermis	Top layer of skin
Eu-	Well	Euphoria	Feeling of well-being
Ex, E-	Out	Excretion	Waste products leaving the body
Exo-	Outside	Exocrine	Excreting outward
Extra-	Outside	Extramural	Outside of a wall
Febri-	Fever	Febrile	Having a fever
Gastr-	Stomach	Gastritis	Inflammation of the stomach
Glyco-	Sugar	Glycosuria	Sugar in the urine
Gyneco-	Woman	Gynecologist	Physician specializing in the care of women
Hem-,	Blood	Hematuria	Blood in the urine
Hemi-	Half	Hemisphere	Half of a sphere
Hepat-	Liver	Hepatitis	Inflammation in the liver
Hetero-	Other	Heterosexual	Pertaining to the opposite sex
Hist-	Tissue	Histology	The study of tissue
Homo-	Same	Homosexual	Pertaining to the same sex
Hydr-	Water	Hydrocephalic	Having water accumulated around the brain
Hyper-	Above, excess, elevated	Hyperactive	Overactive

1 • Anatomy and Medical Terminology—57

Hypo-	Deficiency of	Hypoglycemia	Low blood sugar
Hyster-	Uterus	Hysterectomy	Removal of the uterus
Idio-	Self	Idiopathic	Disease of unknown origin
Im-	Not	Immature	Not mature
In-	In	Innate	Occurring within
Infra-	Below	Infraorbital	Below the orbit
Inter-	Between	Intermuscular	Between the muscles
Intra-	Within	Intramuscular	Within the muscle
Leuko-	White	Leukemia	An excess of white blood cells
Macro-	Large	Macroblast	Abnormally large red cell
Mast-	Breast	Mastectomy	Removal of a breast
Micro-	Small	Microbiology	Study of small organisms
My-	Muscle	Myalgia	Pain in a muscle
Necro-	Dead	Necrosis	Death of tissue
Neo-	New	Neonatal	Newly born
Nephro-	Kidney	Nephritis	Inflammation of a kidney
Neuro-	Nerve	Neuron	Nerve cell
Ophthalmo-	Eye	Ophthalmometer	Instrument to measure the eye
Ortho-	Straight	Orthograde	Walking straight
Oss-, Osteo-	Bone	Osseous	Pertaining to bone
Ot-	Ear	Otorrhea	Discharge from the ear
Para-	Around	Paradenitis	Inflammation of the tissues around or adjacent to a gland
Patho-	Disease	Pathology	The study of disease
Pedo-	Child	Pediatrics	Child specialist
Ped-	Foot	Pedograph	Imprint of the foot
Per-	Through	Percutaneous	Through the skin
Peri-	Around	Periapical	Surrounding the root of a tooth
Phleb-	Vein	Phlebitis	Inflammation of a vein
Poly-	Many	Polyarthritis	Arthritis in many joints
Pre-	Before	Prenatal	Before birth
Post-	After	Postpartum	After birth
Procto-	Rectum	Proctology	Study of the rectum
Pseudo-	False	Pseudoangina	False angina
Pyo-	Pus	Pyorrhea	Discharge of pus
Retro-	Backward	Retroversion	Turning backward
Rhin-	Nose	Rhinorrhea	Discharge from the nose
Steno-	Narrow	Stenosis	In a narrowed state
Super-	Above	Superacute	Excessively acute
Supra-	Above, upon	Suprarenal	Above the kidney
Sym, Syn-	With, together	Symphysis	Growing together
Tachy-	Fast	Tachycardia	Fast heart rate
Uni-	One	Unilateral	Affecting one side
Vaso-	Vessel	Vasodilator	Something that dilates a vessel

58—Medical Aspects of Claims

The following roots are typically found at the end of words.

Root	Definition	Example	Definition
-algia	Pain	Cephalalgia	Pain in the head
-asis, -osis	Affected with	Leukocytosis	An increase in the number of leukocytes
-asthenia	Weakness	Neurasthenia	Nerve weakness
-cele	Tumor or hernia	Enterocele	Hernia of the intestine
-ectasis	Dilation	Angiectasis	Dilation of a blood vessel
-ectomy	Excision	Appendectomy	Removal of the appendix
-esthesia	Sensation	Anesthesia	Lacking sensation
-itis	Inflammation	Iritis	Inflammation of the iris
-lysis	Loosening, dissolution	Hemolysis	Destruction of red blood cells
-malacia	Softening	Chondromalacia	Softening of cartilage
-oma	Tumor	Neuroma	Tumor on a nerve
-ostomy	Creation of an opening	Colostomy	Opening into the colon
-otomy	Cutting into	Osteotomy	Cutting into bone
-penia	Lack of	Leukopenia	Lack of white blood cells
-pexy	To fix	Proctopexy	Repair of rectum
-phagia	Eating	Polyphagia	Excessive eating
-phasis	Speech	Aphasia	Inability to speak
-ptosis	A falling	Enteroptosis	Falling of the intestine
-rhoia	Flow	Otorrhea	Discharge from the ear
-rhaphe	Seam	Herriorrhaphy	Surgical repair of a hernia
-taxis	Order, coordination	Ataxia	Lack of coordination
-uric	Urine	Hematuria	Blood in the urine

APPENDIX

An adequate library is essential to the claims professional in analyzing complex medical reports and documents. The following references are good sources of information:

Medical terms

Illustrated Stedman's Medical Dictionary. Williams and Wilkins, 428 East Preston Street, Baltimore, Maryland 21202.

Mosby's Medical and Nursing Dictionary, The C.V. Mosby Company, 11830 Westline Industrial Drive, St. Louis, Missouri 63141.

Dorland's Medical Dictionary. W. B. Saunders Company, West Washington Square, Philadelphia, Pennsylvania 19105.

Taber's Cyclopedic Medical Dictionary, F. A. Davis Co., 1915 Arch Street, Philadelphia, Pennsylvania 19103.

Anatomy, physiology, disease processes, or syndromes, as well as accepted modes of treatment

Fishbein's Illustrated Medical and Health Encyclopedia. H. S. Stuttman, Inc., Westport, Connecticut 06889.

Encyclopedia and Dictionary of Medicine, Nursing, and Allied Health. Benjamin F. Miller, M.D., and Claire Keane, RN, BS, MEd. W. B. Saunders Company, West Washington Square, Philadelphia, Pennsylvania 19105.

The Columbia University College of Physicians and Surgeons Complete Home Medical Guide. Crown Publishers, Inc., One Park Avenue, New York, New York 10016.

Lawyers' Medical Cyclopedia of Personal Injuries and Allied Specialties. The Michie Company, Law Publishers, Charlottesville, Virginia.

Merck Manual. Merck, Sharp & Dohme Research Laboratories, A Division of Merck & Company, Inc., Rahway, New Jersey.

Attorney's Textbook of Medicine: Manual of Traumatic Injuries. Matthew Bender and Co., Inc., 1275 Broadway, Albany, New York 12204.

60—Medical Aspects of Claims

Prescription drugs use, generic and trade names, and usual dosage

The Physician's Desk Reference. Medical Economics Company, Inc., Oradell, New Jersey 07649.

The Essential Guide to Prescription Drugs, 1989 Edition. James W. Long, M.D., Harper/Collins, 10 East 53rd Street, New York, New York 10023

How a medical test is administered and what can be learned from the test

The Patient's Guide to Medical Tests. Cathey Pinckney and Edward R. Pinckney, M.D., Facts on File Publications, 460 Park Avenue South, New York, New York 10016.

To match psychiatric diagnosis codes to their corresponding disorder

The Diagnostic and Statistical Manual of Mental Disorders. American Psychiatric Association, 1400 K Street, NW, Washington, DC 20005.

To match physical diagnoses and treatment codes to their corresponding disorders:

International Classification of Disease (ICD.9.CM). Volume 1: Tabular list of codes and corresponding conditions, Volume 2: Tabular and alphabetical list of medical procedures. Commission on Professional and Hospital Activities, P.O. Box 991, Green Road, Ann Arbor, Michigan 48106.

To assess the legitimacy of permanent impairment ratings

Guides to the Evaluation of Permanent Impairment. American Medical Association, Order Department OP-254/8, P.O. Box 10946, Chicago, Illinois 60610.

CHAPTER 2

Trauma and Other Injuries

A claim representative must have a general understanding of human anatomy, the effects of traumatic injuries and congenital/degenerative disorders, and treatments for such injuries and disorders. *Trauma* is an injury to a living tissue caused by an extrinsic agent, that is, an agent that is outside of or is not part of the affected tissue. In accidental injuries, the extrinsic agent is usually some object that strikes, or is struck by, the victim. In the accidental injury cases that are most common in claims, trauma is probably the most frequent cause of injury and pain. Hundreds of thousands of people injure themselves everyday through inappropriate lifting, falling, or suffering an athletic injury. The purpose of this chapter is to describe both trauma and other causes of injury and to help the claim representative recognize appropriate treatment for such injuries.

The chapter begins by identifying the parts of the body most frequently injured—the skin, muscles, and joints. It continues by describing more serious injuries, such as fractures, and head and internal injuries. The chapter concludes with a review of the many causes of spinal problems. Injuries to the back and neck are very common in claims. Claim representatives must understand that spinal problems can arise from many causes in addition to trauma.

SKIN INJURIES

Skin injuries are very common. Not only is the skin alone often injured, but injuries to other structures of the body usually involve the skin as well. The most common skin injuries are superficial contusions and abrasions, lacerations, scars, and burns.

62—Medical Aspects of Claims

The skin covers the entire body; it varies in thickness from 1½ to 5 millimeters. It is thinnest over the eyelids and thickest over the soles, palms, and the back. Thickness also varies according to age, race, and sex. Exhibit 2-1 shows a cross-section of the skin.

The epidermis is made up of several layers of cells. It is capable of regeneration following injury as long as some of these cells are left undamaged. These cells also extend downward along the hair shafts and can resurface a damaged area. When damage extends below the level of available cells, a scar forms. Normally, the cell layers in the epidermis are constantly replenishing themselves. As the cells mature, they rise to the surface and slough off as dry, flaky skin.

Disability resulting from skin wounds varies not only according to the severity of the wound but also according to location. People who handle food or submerse their hands and arms into liquids may be required to stay out of work for a longer period as a result of skin injuries than people in other occupations. Any procedure involving surgery under general anesthesia will, of course, extend the normal disability period.

Superficial Wounds

Injuries to the skin alone are called superficial wounds because no underlying tissues are involved. The term "superficial" does not mean trivial, but on the surface. However, some superficial wounds may be trivial. They may also be extremely painful and can present a serious risk of infection. Contusions and abrasions are two kinds of superficial wounds.

Contusions. A contusion, or bruise, usually results from trauma caused by coming into contact with a blunt object. There may be no surface skin damage, but there is damage to underlying tissues that results in ruptured blood vessels. There may be simple bruising or the formation of a *hematoma* (pooled blood under the skin's surface). The discoloration that characterizes this injury is called *ecchymosis* and is due to the release of red blood cells into the tissue. As the released blood is reabsorbed, the color lightens until the bruise completely disappears.

If the hematoma does not disappear or continues to increase in size, there is continued bleeding within the tissues. The wound must be incised and the blood removed. Tying or bonding of bleeding vessels, called *ligation*, may be necessary to control the blood loss.

Bacteria can collect in a damaged area and produce an *abscess*, a localized collection of pus, which must be opened and drained. The wound must be carefully cleansed to avoid introducing additional bacteria or spreading any that is already present. Extensively bruised areas without hematoma may be treated conservatively with bed rest

Exhibit 2-1
Cross-Section of Skin

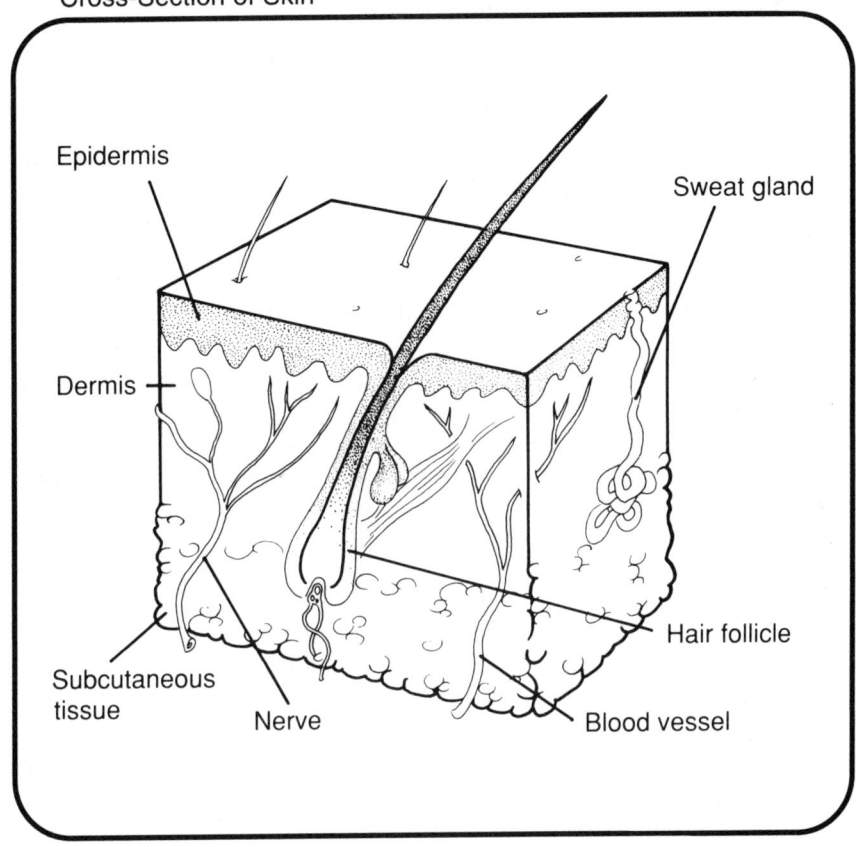

or anti-inflammatory medication. Healing usually occurs completely within about two weeks.

Abrasions. An abrasion is a scrape. Bleeding is usually minimal, but pain can be intense. Foreign matter trapped in the wound can result in permanent disfigurement known as *tattooing*. It is fortunate that as long as skin loss is superficial, most injuries of this type heal without any scarring.

Abrasions are usually treated through routine cleansing and application of a topical antiseptic. A bandage may sometimes be required to prevent irritation, but open-air treatment is generally preferable. Infection is not usually a problem.

When debris is embedded in the wound, the injured person may have to be hospitalized. While the patient is under general anesthesia, the wound is scrubbed with a stiff brush and a detergent until all visible dirt is removed. What cannot be scrubbed away must be trimmed away. Total excision with suture repair or skin graft is sometimes necessary.

Lacerations

A laceration is a tear. Although skin is most frequently involved, other tissues such as fat, muscle, tendon, nerve, bone, and cartilage may also be lacerated. (These other tissues are known as tissues of function.) *Simple lacerations* involve the skin. *Serious lacerations* involve tissues of function.

The severity of a laceration depends both on the depth and location of the wound. A small laceration near the eye can be much more serious than a deep one on the arm. Superficial lacerations generally do not exceed two inches in length and involve only the epidermis. Lacerations that do not penetrate the dermis should heal completely with little or no scarring. Scarring typically accompanies a laceration extending into subcutaneous tissue (tissue beneath the skin).

Skin wounds should be treated in as sterile an environment as possible. In severe cases, prompt sedation is helpful in relieving the victim's pain and anxiety. When repair under local anesthesia is possible, it should be done as soon as possible. Bleeding must sometimes be controlled immediately regardless of an absence of sterile conditions. Antibiotics and a tetanus shot are often used to prevent infection.

The final outcome of a healed laceration depends on many factors including the general body condition. A healthy body will heal itself better than an unhealthy one. For people with diabetes, healing is very poor, infection is common, and the patient's very life may be threatened. Some typical lacerations are discussed below.

Puncture Wounds. A puncture wound is usually caused by a small, sharp object. Infection is a major danger associated with this kind of wound because it is usually deep but small and may drain poorly. A puncture wound should be thoroughly explored to determine the involvement of functional tissue, and the wound should be extensively cleaned. If this is not possible, the wound must be excised and then repaired. A rubber tube must sometimes be inserted into the wound for a 24- to 48-hour period to promote drainage.

Incisions. Incised wounds are generally caused by sharp objects such as a knife. The edges are distinct, and most of the wound is visible. These wounds must be explored to determine the depth of damage or presence of foreign bodies or bacteria.

An incised wound with beveled laceration is the most difficult to heal because the fine edge of tissue is often too thin to survive. A bluish discoloration of the skin means that it will not remain viable. In addition, reattachment and healing to the uninjured tissue can result in excessive scarring as the injured skin contracts. To encourage good healing, it is often necessary to trim the tissue back to a healthy margin, trim the beveled edge to a well-defined one, and reapproximate the tissue.

Avulsion Wounds. In an avulsion laceration the tissue is torn away. Avulsion wounds often occur at the tips of fingers that have been caught in machinery. This kind of wound should be treated as other lacerations, but the lost tissue must also be replaced. Skin grafting is often required. If possible, contiguous tissue may be "stretched" to use as a "flap." Treatment is usually performed in the operating room while the patient is under general anesthesia.

Scars

Scars are visible marks left on the skin where it has healed imperfectly. Scar tissue is visible because it is of different color, texture, and thickness than the surrounding skin and does not have sweat glands or hair. The cosmetic and functional problems created by scars can range from trivial to serious.

Appearance of Scars. Healing generally occurs faster and better when lacerations occur along the existing "lines" of the body. These lines are known as *Langers lines,* which run at right angles to the direction of the muscles as shown in Exhibit 2-2. Nevertheless, because lacerations can occur in any manner, the healing process can be less than perfect. Lacerations occurring around joints can be a problem in that joint function may be impaired.

One of the procedures most frequently used to prevent poor healing is the Z-plasty. This is the incision and suturing of the wound in a zig-zag pattern to promote elasticity at the site. Skin grafting may also be required to prevent unsatisfactory healing.

Two types of scars are most unattractive. The *hypertrophic* scar results when a laceration falls in a direction that was counter to the Langers lines of the skin. This type of scar is composed of dense, fibrous tissue, which is usually elevated and frequently tender. When situated at or near a joint, this scar can result in substantial loss of function of the joint because of an absence of skin elasticity. It is fortunate that the repair of hypertrophic scars is usually quite satisfactory.

The second unattractive kind of scar is the *keloid* scar. This looks much like an exaggerated hypertrophic scar, but it is much more prominent and extends beyond the boundaries of the wound site. It may also itch severely and become progressively larger. The treatment of keloid scars is often unsuccessful because they frequently recur following surgery.

66—Medical Aspects of Claims

Exhibit 2-2
Langers Lines

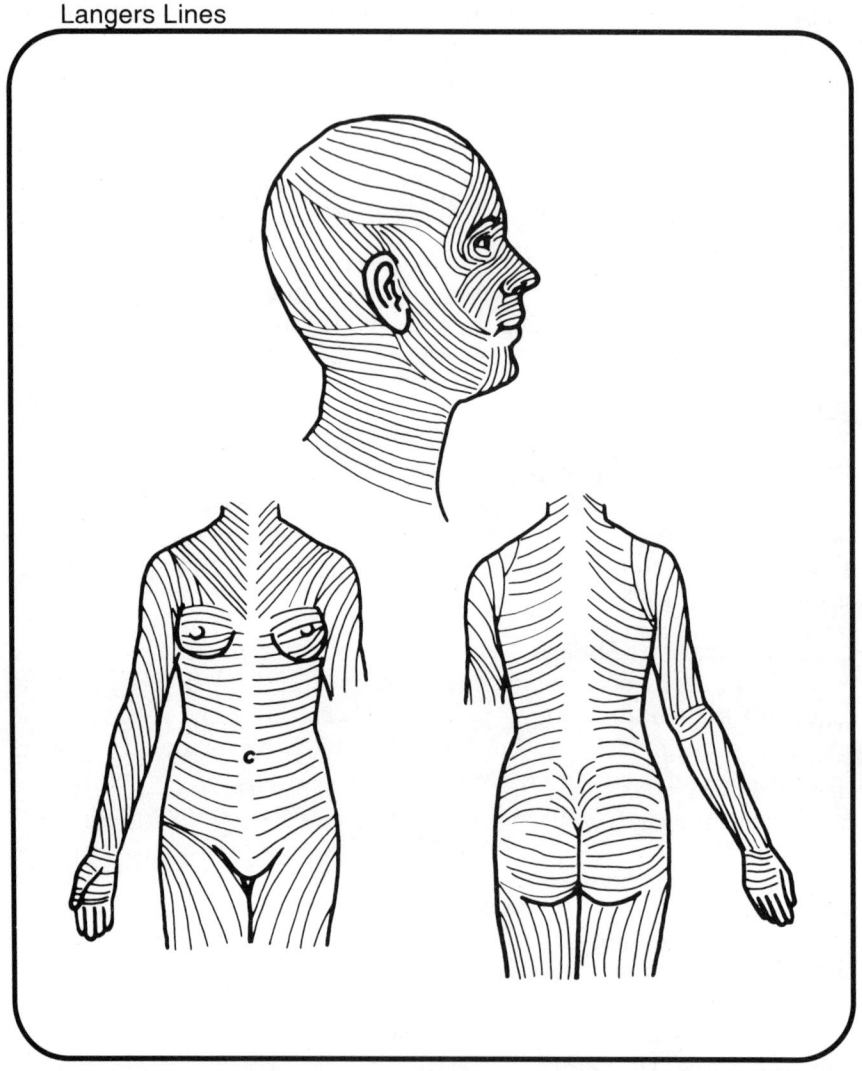

Treatment of Scars. Scars should be repaired and removed such that the skin is incised along the Langers lines. In many cases, the result is excellent, and incisional lines are barely visible. However, in most cases, some evidence of the original scar remains, the extent of which depends on the extent of the injury and the nature of the healing process.

Barring infection or additional trauma, nature takes care of most ordinary skin wounds within a reasonable period of time. A scar will usually begin to subside or blend with the surrounding skin within a three- to five-month period, and appearance typically improves with time. If additional surgery is necessary, time must be allowed between operations so that tissues may fully heal.

Reconstructive surgery is sometimes necessary. Because the goal of reconstructive surgery is to improve or restore function, it is more essential than cosmetic surgery. However, because our society emphasizes physical attractiveness, an individual may suffer mental anguish because of his or her appearance. As a result, cosmetic surgery is sometimes considered as integral a part of a patient's recovery as reconstructive surgery.

Skin grafting is generally performed only if immediate closure of a wound is impossible. Skin for the graft is obtained from the patient's body, usually along the thigh, or from a donor when the patient does not have uninjured skin available, as is the case with severe burn injuries. A graft from the patient is always preferable because it is less likely to be rejected by the body. Depending on the extent of the injury, several grafting procedures may be necessary. Years of surgery may be required before the appearance of the skin becomes acceptable. Grafted skin is extremely sensitive to extremes of temperature, and color matching is a rarity. Grafts are not hair-bearing, do not contain sweat or oil glands, and do not tan as does normal skin.

Dermabrasion and sanding are two similar methods used for scar revision and reduction. *Dermabrasion* involves the surgical removal of skin imperfections through abrasion of the skin surface with stiff brushes. This procedure is most commonly used in the treatment of tattoos and skin discolorations that are not raised. Dermabrasion is also used to decrease the pockmarked scars left by severe acne. Sanding is done with surgical sandpaper and involves a similar abrasive process. It is usually performed to eliminate a scar, such as a keloid, that is elevated above the skin surface.

Burns

Burns can be caused when the skin comes in contact with any hot solid, liquid, or gas, or by radiation exposure. Burns are common in industrial and home accidents. Burns are classified by degrees, as first degree, second degree, or third degree, depending on how deeply the tissue has been affected. The higher the degree, the deeper and more serious is the burn. The severity of burns also depends on the percentage of total skin surface affected. A third degree burn to a very small area can be less severe than a second degree burn over a large area.

First and Second Degree Burns. First degree burns affect only the epidermis. Redness and swelling may occur, and the affected skin peels away without scarring. Second degree burns extend into the dermis, but enough of the dermis survives for the skin to regenerate satisfactorily. Blistering and swelling accompany second degree burns.

Both first and second degree burns can be treated topically for relief from pain and swelling, although recovery from second degree burns is somewhat slower. Both types of burns should leave no visible scars.

Third Degree Burns. Third degree burns extend through the dermis and may involve underlying tissues. These burns are very serious because the skin is killed through its entire thickness and, as a result, cannot serve as a barrier to infections. Unless infection can be controlled with antibiotics, death can result. In addition to the serious risk of infection, healing is very difficult. The skin cannot regenerate itself when the dermis has been destroyed through its entire thickness. Skin grafts are usually needed to repair areas of third degree burns greater than one square inch. Skin grafts and third degree burns heal more rapidly on the torso than on the arms, legs, hands, and feet. Healing is also much better in a patient with good circulation.

INJURIES TO MUSCLES AND JOINTS

The musculoskeletal system includes muscles, nerves, and joints. The most common injuries to these structures are sprains and strains of the muscles and arthritis of the joints. In addition to these two common problems, this section describes two problems often encountered in claims, carpal tunnel syndrome and temporomandibular joint syndrome.

Sprains and Strains

Bones and muscles are joined together by tough bands of dense fibrous connective tissues called ligaments and tendons. Ligaments connect bones to bones at the joint, while tendons connect muscles to bone and transmit the force the muscles exert. Because the blood supply to ligaments and tendons is limited, and because nerve endings in these tissues are limited, injuries to ligaments or tendons are extremely slow to heal. They are also extremely painful since the affected areas generally play such an important part in the movement of the extremities.

When a muscle, tendon, or ligament is forced to move past its normal range of motion, it is stretched and can tear. This is known as a *sprain*. A *strain*, on the other hand, results from working a muscle beyond its normal capacity. Sprains are usually associated with joints and therefore, ligaments, while strains are associated with muscle injuries. For example, in a twisted ankle, the joint is abruptly forced out of place, causing the ligaments that connect the ankle with the lower leg bones to stretch. This is known as a sprained ankle. A strain can occur from the repeated lifting of heavy items for an extended period of time. Ligaments can also be injured through strain.

Sprains are usually treated conservatively with mild pain relievers, wrapping the injured area with an Ace® bandage, bed rest, or elevating the affected area. Since sprains are almost always accompanied by swelling, cold packs may be used to alleviate swelling. Strains are also treated conservatively with mild pain relievers, moist heat, and bed rest.

Unless there are severe complications, disability from a sprain or strain should rarely exceed four weeks and is usually much less. Any diagnosis of strain and/or sprain in which symptoms persist for more than a month should be closely questioned. The affected patient may be suffering from recurring strain or sprain or may have a more serious problem that has not been properly diagnosed or treated.

The term "whiplash" is frequently used to mean strain and sprain of the neck muscles, ligaments, and tendons, but it is most apt as a description of the mechanism causing strain and sprain of the neck. Whiplash of the neck and head can occur in any sudden, violent event such as an automobile accident. Like any other strain and sprain, whiplash should heal within a short period of time.

Joint Problems

Injuries and problems in the joints are especially painful and bothersome because of the integral role of the joints in body movement. The most common joint problem, arthritis, can be minor or very serious. It is usually *not* caused by a single traumatic event. In contrast, dislocations are almost always caused by trauma. In cases of severe joint problems, arthroplasty, or joint replacement, may be necessary.

Arthritis. Arthritis is the inflammation of a joint. Its symptoms are pain, stiffness, and swelling. Arthritis is usually progressive. The two most common forms of arthritis are rheumatoid arthritis and osteoarthritis. *Rheumatoid arthritis* is a disease that causes inflammation of the connective tissue in the joints. It usually appears between the ages of twenty-five and forty-five, three times as often in women as in men. It seriously affects the fingers, wrists, elbows, and knees, is extremely painful, and is often disabling. Rheumatoid arthritis is gradually progressive, but may show great variability of symptoms and periods of improvement. Chronic involvement of the joints can lead to calcification, or freezing of the joints.

Osteoarthritis is the most common form of arthritis, occurring to

70—Medical Aspects of Claims

some extent in most people older than fifty-five. It is more common in women than in men and usually affects weight-bearing joints such as the knee, hip, or spine. In osteoarthritis, the cartilage on the bone ends that smooths and lubricates joint movement degenerates, causing bone-to-bone friction. Osteoarthritis is primarily a degenerative rather than an inflammatory disease, yet its symptoms of pain and swelling are similar to those of rheumatoid arthritis.

Arthritis can also be caused by metabolic problems and infection. As mentioned, trauma may be, but is usually *not* the cause of arthritis, although it may aggravate preexisting symptoms of arthritis.

In cases of alleged traumatically induced arthritis, the claim representative may defend by showing that the arthritis existed before the injury, or would have become just as bad regardless of the injury. Such defenses require careful analysis of a claimant's medical records and involve complex medical issues.

Dislocations. A dislocation is the complete displacement of one or both bones of a joint. A *subluxation* is a partial displacement of bones away from their customary alignment in the joint. Subluxation of the lumbar spine is common. Dislocations are almost always caused by external trauma, although subluxation may be a recurring problem. Although the bones of the affected joint may return to their normal alignment, there can be complications. Surrounding structures may be damaged, chip fractures of the bones may have occurred, and traumatic arthritis may result. Generally, resting the affected joints is sufficient to allow surrounding tissues to heal. With severe dislocations, anesthesia may be necessary before the bones can be realigned, and surgery may be necessary to repair surrounding ligaments.

Bursitis. Bursitis is inflammation of a *bursa*, a small sac located at many joints that assists in joint movement. Bursitis is most common in the shoulder, elbow, and knee. A single traumatic event or repeated trauma is frequently a cause, but bursitis can also develop spontaneously. Bursitis causes considerable pain and limits motion in the affected joint. Acute bursitis will often resolve completely in a few weeks. Chronic bursitis can be treated conservatively with heat, rest, and steroids. Surgery may be necessary if conservative methods fail.

Arthroplasty. The articular (joint) extremities, or bone ends, are covered with a smooth, slightly elastic tissue known as *cartilage*. Cartilage cushions the bone ends so that they can move smoothly against one another. Cartilage has no nerves or blood supply and is thus difficult to heal. If cartilage is damaged by injury, the joint may become stiff and movement limited. Conservative treatment with physical therapy, medication, or cortisone injections are usually unsuccessful if the cartilage has been damaged beyond repair. When this happens, joint replacement, known as joint arthroplasty, may be required.

Arthroplasty is most often performed on the knee and hip. Other joint replacements are less frequent. Because joints move in so many directions, arthroplasty involves more than simply replacing the joint itself. Damaged tendons or ligaments must be carefully repaired to reinstate joint stability and function. Medical researchers continue to develop improved materials for joint replacement. Better surgical techniques also help ensure a return to function that is close to normal. Arthroplasty for small joints has been developing but is usually reserved for the hands and fingers of rheumatoid arthritis sufferers, since this condition is so painful and disabling. Because these joints are so small and close to the skin, precise repair is crucial to function.

Total joint arthroplasty can provide pain relief as well as a return of function. However, even after successful surgery, the affected joint cannot be subjected to the same degree of stress as a normal joint. Man-made devices are not a substitute for the real thing. In successful operations, the patient can usually expect almost two-thirds of normal joint function. A hip replacement typically requires a lengthy rehabilitation period. Most replacement procedures provide function that is adequate for daily living. Someone who has undergone a total knee replacement will not be able to play football or run a marathon, but can certainly perform normal, routine activities.

Carpal Tunnel Syndrome

The carpal tunnel is an anatomical structure formed by bones on three sides of the wrist and ligaments on the palm side. While not itself a joint, the carpal tunnel is adjacent to and defined by the junction of the carpal bones. The median nerve travels through the carpal tunnel along with tendons and blood vessels. Exhibit 2-3 shows the location of the carpal tunnel.

Carpal tunnel syndrome (CTS) is a cumulative trauma disorder involving compression of the median nerve. The compression results from inflammation of the nerve and produces symptoms of numbness, paresthesia, weakness, lack of sensation, and pain in the hands as well as in the thumb, index, middle, and ring finger. The little finger is *not* affected. The pain can radiate into the elbows and shoulders. The hands and arms can cramp, and the hands can also swell. These symptoms are more severe during sleep when the hands are at rest.

The development of CTS stems from the anatomy of the wrist. The flexion action of the fingers is controlled by tendons attached to muscles in the forearm. These tendons pass through a tunnel in the wrist formed by the carpal bones, thus the name carpal tunnel. Any condition that restricts or reduces the size of this tunnel produces pressure

72—Medical Aspects of Claims

Exhibit 2-3
Carpal Tunnel

Carpal bones *Median nerve*

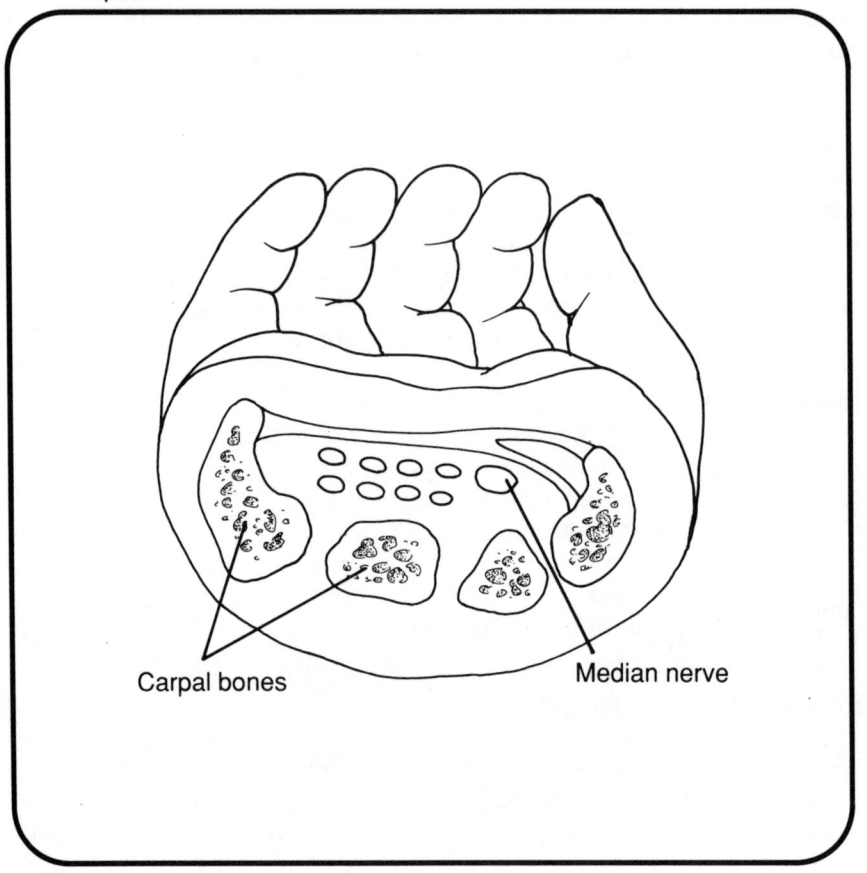

on the median nerve, which produces the symptoms of CTS. These symptoms can result from any number of conditions including tenosynovitis, bursitis, misaligned fractures, rheumatoid arthritis, diabetes, thyroid dysfunction, pregnancy, or repetitive trauma.

Work-related cases of CTS are typically caused by repetitive motion of the hand or wrist that is required in a manual task, such as sewing machine operation, small parts assembly, meat packing, or spray painting. In addition to repetition, excessive use of the hand, use of hand tools, exposure to cold temperatures, or work performed while the wrist is bent in an awkward position can create pressure on the median nerve in the carpal tunnel. Nonoccupational causes of CTS can be aggravated by job-related functions. The disorder occurs most often in persons between the ages of thirty and sixty and is as much as five times more common in women than in men.

The treatment of CTS varies depending on the severity of the disorder. Conservative treatment involves immobilizing the wrist and discontinuing any activities that may be contributing to the problem. Anti-inflammatory medication may also help control the condition. In some cases, surgery may be required to reduce pressure on the median nerve. An incision is made in the palm to release the transverse ligaments. This incision reduces the compression within the carpal tunnel. However, since CTS is a progressive disorder, early treatment can prevent the need for surgery.

The recovery period for carpal tunnel surgery without complications is usually eight to ten weeks. The patient is usually instructed not to engage in activities that caused or aggravated the condition. In many cases, training in proper use of hand tools may reduce the extent to which someone is predisposed to this disorder. If such training is not possible, the patient may have to change to an occupation that does not require repetitive hand movements.

Temporomandibular Joint Syndrome

Temporomandibular joint syndrome (TMJ) is diagnosed more and more frequently. The symptoms of TMJ include pain over the temporomandibular joint and around the ear, a clicking sound when the mouth is open or closed, and locking of the joint, which makes it difficult to open or close the mouth.

The temporomandibular joint is a hinge joint that is formed by the temporal bones, located on either side of the skull just in front of the occipital bone, and the mandible. These bony surfaces are covered with cartilage and cushioned by small membranous sacs that prevent them from rubbing together. The muscles used to open and close the mouth provide stability for this joint. Exhibit 2-4 shows the location of the temporomandibular joint.

In normal jaw function, the left and right joints work together. If the motion of either side is out of balance, dislocation can result. Dislocation can also result from having the mouth forced open rapidly or too far. Grinding of the teeth, other than during eating, and trauma to the side of the face can cause TMJ pain. Inflammation, such as that from osteoarthritis and rheumatoid arthritis, can attack the temporomandibular joint like any other joint in the body.

Disease of the temporomandibular joint may be part of a generalized condition such as arthritis or osteoporosis. Erosion of the lower jaw bone at the joint may exist in patients who have had numerous teeth extracted, knocked out through injury, or who have teeth missing as a result of disease or malnutrition. Injury to the teeth through ulceration, fracture, or decay have also been noted as causes of TMJ

Exhibit 2-4
Temporomandibular Joint

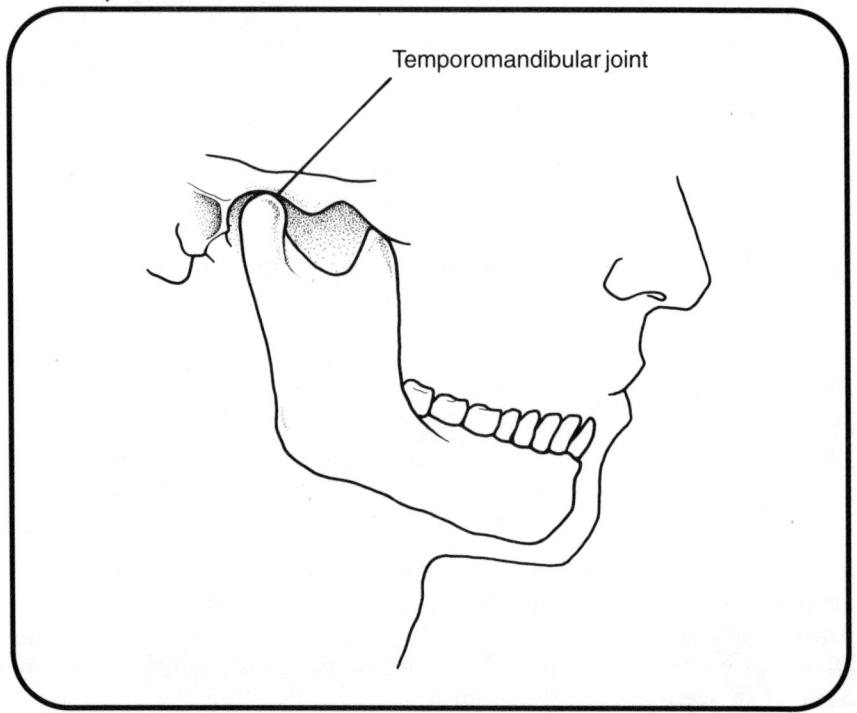

syndrome. The complete absence of teeth causes a severe malocclusion, creating serious pressure on the muscles and nerves in the jaw that can lead to TMJ syndrome.

Psychological factors can also be responsible for TMJ syndrome. Chronic tension and stress may cause repeated clenching of the jaw. Relaxation therapy and biofeedback may be sufficient to relieve these symptoms.

Although many cases of TMJ syndrome result from inflammation, trauma can also be a cause. A direct blow to the jaw or the side of the face can result in injury to or dislocation of the temporomandibular joint. These cases are treated similarly to cases caused by inflammation. Depending on the severity of the disorder, treatment may last anywhere from four to six months.

A complete medical history and examination is important when the joint appears to be the site of a problem. When the diagnosis is not clear after examination, the following additional possibilities should be researched:

1. Glossopharyngeal neuralgia. This is a spasmodic pain brought about by swallowing. While it is felt mostly in the ear and

throat, the pain may radiate into the jaw or even the tongue. A nerve block by local anesthetic may eliminate the pain for several months. However, if the pain continues, section of the involved nerve may be necessary.
2. Temporal arteritis. This is an inflammation of a group of arteries creating severe pain in the temple area.
3. The infra-orbital nerve may be damaged in fractures to the zygoma, the bony arch just below the eye, creating severe spasms during the recovery state. A tumor on this nerve is another possibility to be considered.

Most cases of headache or pain in the face or jaw are not caused by an abnormality of the temporomandibular joint. Most actual cases of TMJ syndrome are caused by inflammation, which can be treated with physical therapy and cortisone-like drugs. A corrective device worn over the teeth during sleep can often help improve or re-establish proper alignment of the jaws. It is rare for surgery to be required in the treatment of TMJ syndrome.

FRACTURES AND HEAD INJURIES

Compared to injuries to the skin, muscles, or joints, bone fractures and head injuries are generally more likely to cause serious and permanent damage. In addition, bone fractures and head injuries are almost always traumatic in origin.

Fractures and Resulting Problems

Broken bones are a common accidental injury. The seriousness of a broken bone depends on which bone is involved, how it is broken, and the age and health of the victim. Forces that are powerful enough to break bones usually also cause damage to the surrounding soft tissues. In addition, improper healing of a broken bone can cause nerve damage and loss of function.

Types of Fractures. Fractures fall into two broad categories:
1. Simple fractures—the bone is broken but there is no external wound
2. Compound fractures—the bone is broken and creates an external wound that reaches the outer layer of skin

Simple and compound fractures are further defined by terms that describe the appearance of the fracture itself. A *linear* fracture is merely a crack in the bone. It appears much like a crack one might see in a china dish. A fracture of this type does not require surgery, since there are no broken pieces to be realigned or joined together. When a bone is broken

76—Medical Aspects of Claims

Exhibit 2-5
Six Kinds of Fractures

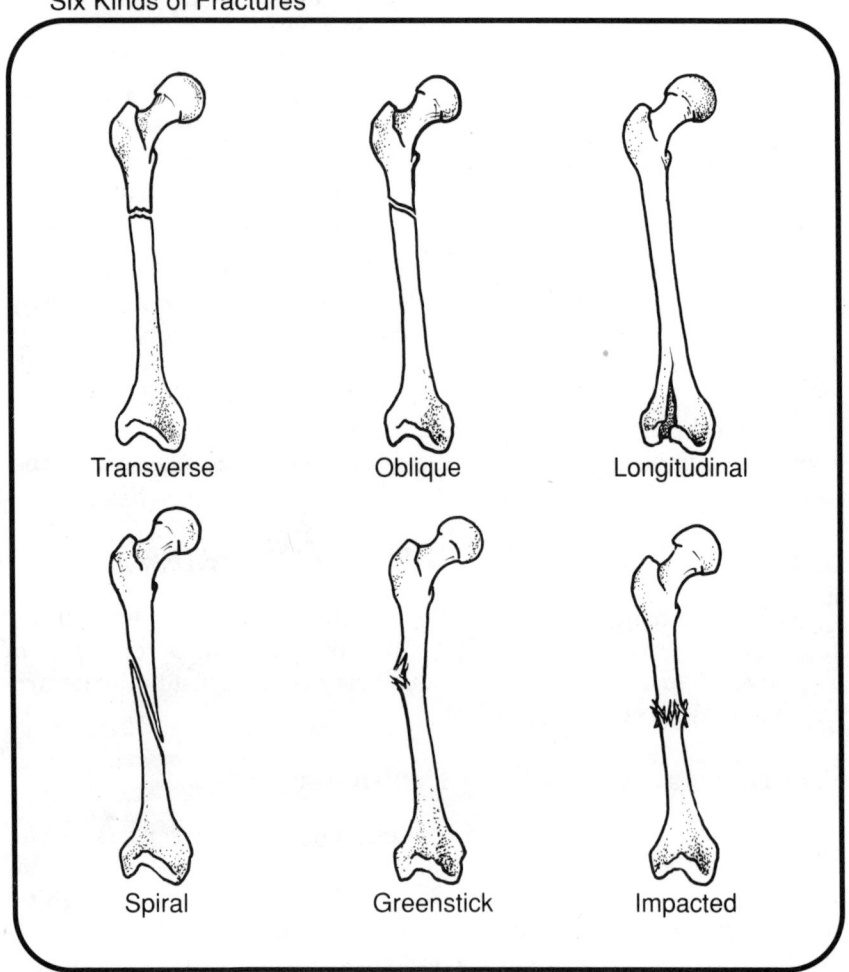

Transverse   Oblique   Longitudinal

Spiral   Greenstick   Impacted

into more than two pieces, the fracture is said to be *comminuted*. This is analogous to a dish broken into several pieces. A comminuted fracture must be surgically repaired. The pieces of the bone must be realigned and joined together until they adhere. Injuries to the bone ends can result in joint stiffness and permanently restricted motion.

There are six major kinds of fractures that fall within the two broad categories, as illustrated in Exhibit 2-5:

1. A *transverse* fracture is a complete break through the midsection of the bone.
2. A *greenstick* fracture looks like a broken green branch; there is no complete break, and one side of the bone appears "torn" or "shredded."

3. An *oblique* fracture is almost identical to the transverse fracture except that the break through the bone is diagonal. Fractures of this kind are most often found in the femur.
4. A *longitudinal* fracture runs along the length of the bone from the joint end of the bone toward the midsection.
5. In an *impacted* fracture, the bone is forced toward its midsection, thereby splintering. These fractures usually occur in the lower leg as a result of landing heavily on the feet.
6. In a *spiral* fracture, the breaks twist around the bone. These fractures most often result when the bone is twisted during injury.

Fractures in which the break is complete are more difficult to heal because there is little or no bone-to-bone contact. Fractures in a long bone are yet more difficult to heal due to the weight of the bone itself and the forces pulling the bones apart.

Healing of Fractures. Bones are surrounded by a membrane containing bone-forming cells that are dormant until a bone has been fractured. When a fracture occurs, these cells are activated to create new bone. Blood vessels are broken and form clots around the fracture site. The bone-forming cells begin to grow in the clot, forming fibrous tissue. Blood vessels surrounding a fracture site feed this tissue and begin to form callus.

Callus is a bony material that hardens into permanent bone. If bone fragments do not align properly, they can heal in a position that results in loss of function. In some cases, fractures to certain bones, such as collarbone or rib, do not require perfect alignment. In bones that are important to everyday activity, proper alignment is of the utmost importance.

When a fracture leaves the fragments out of alignment, it is said to be *displaced*. Displaced fractures are repaired by one of two types of reduction:

1. *Closed reduction* is manipulation through the unbroken skin of the broken bone into proper alignment. Sometimes weights (traction) are used to hold the fragments in place.
2. *Open reduction* involves making a surgical opening over the fracture site and repositioning the bones, possibly using devices such as plates or pins to hold them together.

In some severe cases, a rod may be inserted to take the place of the bone in weightbearing and to provide stability. If this is not possible, the patient may suffer a shortening of the extremity. This can occur when damaged bone must be removed and the remaining pieces attach to each other.

78—Medical Aspects of Claims

Adverse Results. A firm union of a broken bone will usually occur in three to four months following the fracture. However, several adverse results may occur:

1. Partial union. This occurs when the callus does not grow over the entire fractured area, leaving portions of the fragments separated.
2. Fibrous union. This occurs when the callus does not harden.
3. Mal-union. This occurs when the fragments unite in a position that renders the bone far less functional than normal or when the fragments unite with another bone.
4. Non-union. This occurs when the bone does not heal and the fragments are held together only by tissue.

Another problem that may accompany a fracture is nerve damage. Fractures occurring to the middle third of the humerus, for example, may damage the radial nerve, which winds around the humerus and controls sensation and movement in the entire arm. A bone fragment can easily lacerate this nerve, or the nerve can be pinched as the bone heals. If the radial nerve becomes involved with the callus while it is hardening, it may be pinched, resulting in a loss of sensation or movement. In addition, a blow significant enough to fracture the elbow will generally cause the bone to shatter, thereby producing bone fragments that are likely to damage the radial nerve. Other adverse conditions are associated with children, older people, and infection.

Fractures in Children. Children's bones are less likely to break because they are composed of a great deal of cartilage. Cartilage is gradually replaced by hard bone as the child matures. However, a fracture of a child's bone can be a serious problem. At each end of the long bones in children is a growth center that is separated from the remainder of the bone by more cartilage. This area is known as the *epiphysis*. If the epiphysis is damaged by a fracture, the bone may stop growing. This condition may be minor for a sixteen-year-old with little growing left, but is of major importance for a five-year-old.

Osteoporosis. Fractures experienced by the elderly present different problems. Age-related diseases, including osteoporosis, cause the bones to become brittle and extremely susceptible to fractures from trauma or even pressure exerted by the individual's own body weight (stress fractures). Fractures occur more readily in the elderly and are slower to heal. Fractures do *not* cause osteoporosis, but are much more likely to occur in those who have osteoporosis.

Osteoporosis is a decrease in bone density caused by reabsorbtion of the bone's calcium by the bloodstream. Osteoporosis is most common in post menopausal women, but exists asymptomatically in a wider population. Osteoporosis is most often caused by inadequate diet, hormonal changes, and vascular abnormalities (such as those resulting from disease or inflammation).

Since the vertebral bodies are made up mostly of porous bone and have a rich blood supply, they often are the first to reflect osteoporotic changes. The femur is also frequently affected.

Osteomyelitis. Osteomyelitis is an infection of the bone. It can result from a compound fracture, but can also occur independently through infection of the bloodstream. Osteomyelitis causes the buildup of pus around the bone and, in some cases, in surrounding tissues. This pus buildup can cause death of the bone and surrounding tissues, leading to loss of a limb or death if not properly treated.

Osteomyelitis is treated with antibiotics, sometimes on an inpatient basis, and by surgically draining the pus. Osteomyelitis can be acute or chronic. The latter occurs because infections are extremely difficult to eradicate from deep bone tissue.

Head Injuries

Fractures to the skull are very serious because of the skull's role in protecting the brain. Brain injury and damage are the most serious consequences of a fractured skull. However, the brain can also be injured by traumas that do not fracture the skull. This section reviews the most common types of head injuries.

Types of Skull Fractures. Skull fractures fall into the same two broad categories of other bone fractures: simple and compound. Skull fractures can also be comminuted (occurring in several pieces).

The most serious of all skull fractures is a *depressed* fracture, in which a piece of the broken bone is driven inward and presses on the brain. The brain or one of the surrounding membranes may or may not be torn, but the pressure on the brain remains until the bone is returned to its proper position. The location of a skull fracture can be as important as the type in terms of severity.

The *basal skull fracture* occurs to the base, or lower part, of the skull. It is common and potentially the most dangerous location for a skull fracture. This is true because surgery is generally required to realign the bones. However, in and around the basal area of the skull are important nerves, major blood vessels, and nerve centers. The proximity of these vital parts makes surgery extremely delicate, or impossible. A basal skull fracture is the easiest to diagnose, since it is almost always accompanied by bleeding from the ears, mouth, or both. While these symptoms alone do not prove the existence of a basal skull fracture, they can certainly indicate the possibility of one.

Hematomas. Bleeding from skull fractures and other head traumas causes blood clots to form. Because the space in the skull is already filled, there is no room for such clots. The clots cannot exert pressure on the hard skull, but they do press on the soft brain and its coverings. These blood clots are known as *hematomas*. There are two types of hematomas. *Epidural* hematomas occur on or above the dura mater. *Subdural* hematomas occur below the dura mater.

Both types of hematomas cause pressure on the brain, resulting in damaged nerves, thus affecting the five senses. In addition, hematomas may cause death as pressure from the growing hematoma builds. This is especially true of epidural hematomas because such bleeding is from arteries, which spurt blood with great force when torn. This force quickly creates large clots, resulting in great pressure and causing rapid death if not relieved by surgery.

While a subdural hematoma can ultimately have the same effect, it is not as urgent as an epidural hematoma because subdural bleeding comes from veins rather than arteries. Because veins do not spurt blood, but ooze it, it takes longer for a clot to form. Nevertheless, surgery is also required to release the pressure from a subdural hematoma.

Contusions. A contusion to the brain resembles a bruise anywhere else on the body. It does not tear the brain or its coverings and is usually a less serious head injury. Contusions always cause a period of unconsciousness that is usually longer than those from fainting. The length of the period of unconsciousness depends on the severity of the bruise. In most cases, contusions require a relatively short period of recuperation and create no permanent damage. On the other hand, a severe contusion with a lengthy period of unconsciousness and swelling that causes pressure on the brain can temporarily or permanently impair the brain. Swelling usually disappears in about eight weeks, after which the brain again functions normally.

Lacerations. A laceration that may be trivial to a finger can have a serious effect on the brain. In order for the brain to be lacerated, there must be an extremely severe blow to the head. A laceration usually results from a depressed skull fracture. Hemorrhage is inevitable, and contusions to other parts of the brain near the laceration site are highly probable. A laceration is accompanied by all of the symptoms of a contusion. Depending on the location of the laceration, there may be impaired sight, hearing, speech, and motor function.

Concussions. The least complicated and least damaging of head injuries is a concussion. In a concussion the brain is violently shaken about, but no hemorrhaging occurs. There may be a short period of unconsciousness, although in some cases the patient is only momentarily dazed. A concussion may also produce sudden vomiting, dizziness, and temporary loss of sensation or movement in a specific area of the body. These symptoms generally disappear within twenty-four hours. A ringing in the ears is common, but an actual loss of hearing is not the result of a concussion unless there has been an injury to the ear. Blurred vision may also occur, but a permanent change in vision is the result of something other than a simple concussion.

Sometimes, after a patient has apparently recovered, a concussion may again cause symptoms. These episodes may include dull headaches or a sharp stabbing sensation that begins in the area where the blow to the head occurred. These headaches almost always occur when the individual is very tired or emotionally stressed. Another residual symptom of a concussion is dizziness. It is usually described as a sensation of swaying or light-headedness and usually occurs after physical exertion or suddenly shifting position. Neurological tests determine whether residual symptoms are a result of trauma, whether they existed before the injury, or whether the patient may be malingering.

INTERNAL INJURIES

The internal organs are well protected from minor trauma by the musculoskeletal system of the torso. However, sufficiently powerful or penetrating blows can injure these organs. Because of the close proximity of the heart, lungs, liver, stomach, and other internal organs (see Chapter 1, Exhibit 1-22), several organs may be injured by penetrating wounds or blunt trauma to the thorax or abdomen.

There are several factors that influence the severity of internal injuries:

1. Size of the striking object.
2. Site of injury and force of impact.
3. Strength of the abdominal wall (muscle tone).
4. Overall body condition.
5. Level of the patient's consciousness prior to impact.
6. Whether or not the organ is held rigidly in its location by anatomical supports.
7. The more sudden and forceful the blow, the more likely the involvement of an internal organ. Since most of the organs have some degree of mobility, greater force applied slowly is less likely to cause injury than a lesser, but sudden and sharp blow.
8. A person with weak or relaxed muscles in the abdominal area is more likely to suffer internal injury than a person with strong abdominal muscles or a person who is alert to the impending danger and tightens the muscles. The tightening of

the muscles absorbs the force of the impact. However, the resulting muscle injuries may be severe.

The diagnosis of blunt internal trauma can be very difficult. The mental state of the patient may prevent him or her from giving accurate information about the location of the pain. The symptoms resulting from internal bleeding may be delayed by several hours. Patients are often discharged after examination with no objective findings. Such patients may return several hours later, possibly in a state of shock.

Injuries to the Thorax

The organs in the thorax are protected by the rib cage, but can nevertheless be injured by crushing blows or penetrating wounds.

Injuries Caused by Rib Fractures. Blunt trauma that causes a fracture often causes an internal injury when the wound occurs in the thoracic region. Crush injuries may fracture several ribs. If limited to one side, fractures may occur near the rib angles and interiorly, near the costochondral junctions. This produces *flail chest*, in which a segment of the lung is sucked into the wound during inhalation and forced out during exhalation.

A rib fracture may also drive a rib fragment into the lung or out through the skin. Because of the close association of the ribs to the intercostal vessels, overlying skin, and underlying pleurae and lungs, *pneumothorax* (collapsed lung) or *hemothorax* (blood in the lung) are common complications of rib fractures.

In an adult, the middle ribs are most commonly fractured. They are the longest and least protected and are strongly attached at both ends. The first two ribs are protected by the clavicle, and the last two ribs are unattached from the rib cage anteriorly and are freely movable. A major artery that passes over the first rib, lying posterior to the collarbone, is susceptible to compression. It may be constricted by a fractured rib or collarbone, resulting in loss of blood supply to an upper limb. Rib fractures in children are rare because the thoracic wall is elastic.

The lower part of the rib cage protects the upper abdominal organs, the liver, spleen, kidneys, and stomach. If the lower ribs are damaged or if there is a penetrating wound of the lower chest wall, the physician must ascertain whether or not these organs are also damaged.

Aortic Rupture. Rupture of the aorta or damage to its wall may occur in severe automobile or plane accidents. The most common site of rupture is at the attachment of the arterial ligament. The thoracic duct and major veins are rarely damaged because of their protected location adjacent to the vertebral column. However, excessive hyperextension of the vertebral column can cause rupture of the thoracic duct.

Diaphragm Injuries. The diaphragm is the principle muscle of inhalation. Consequently, any injury to it will result in respiratory distress. Injury to the cervical region of the spinal cord or damage to the phrenic nerve can cause paralysis of the diaphragm. Since the diaphragm serves as a partition between the cavities of the thorax and abdomen, weakness or injury may permit abdominal viscera to protrude into the thoracic cavity (diaphragmatic hernia). Exhibit 2-6 shows the positions of the diaphragm during respiration.

Injuries to the Abdomen

Any trauma to the abdomen has far greater significance in its impact on the underlying organs than in the injury to the abdominal wall itself.

Injury may cause digestive juices to leak and bacteria to form, resulting in infection. Tears in the liver and pancreas may release irritating bile or juices. Bleeding in the abdominal cavity may result from tears in the liver or spleen. Injuries caused by blunt trauma to the abdomen are associated with a much higher mortality rate than the rate for penetrating abdominal injuries. Automobile accidents and industrial accidents are leading causes of blunt abdominal injury. Blunt abdominal injuries occur more often in men because men are more frequently in accidents or engaged in violence.

Abdominal injuries are often overlooked because of the existence of a more urgent and obvious injury. Internal bleeding is usually accompanied by widespread abdominal pain. Signs of shock with a drop in blood pressure and systemic evidence of hemorrhage, such as increased pulse rate and gasping for breath, may not initially be present but will generally appear fairly early. The absence of these symptoms, however, does not mean that hemorrhage or peritonitis (infection) will not subsequently occur. Localized abdominal pain and tenderness accompanied by involuntary rigidity of the muscles is evidence of peritoneal irritation. Aspiration (draining with a needle) of the abdominal cavity may reveal the presence of blood or evidence of contamination. Blood passed through the stool or urine may also indicate internal injury.

Liver Injuries. The liver lies under cover of the lower right ribs. It is a soft, pliable structure enclosed in a fibrous capsule. Its proximity to the diaphragm and the lower ribs is important. Fractures of the lower ribs or penetrating wounds of the lower thorax or upper abdomen are common causes of liver injury. Blunt traumatic injuries during automobile accidents are also common. Severe hemorrhage accompanies tears of the liver. Tears occur more frequently in the right lobe than in

84—Medical Aspects of Claims

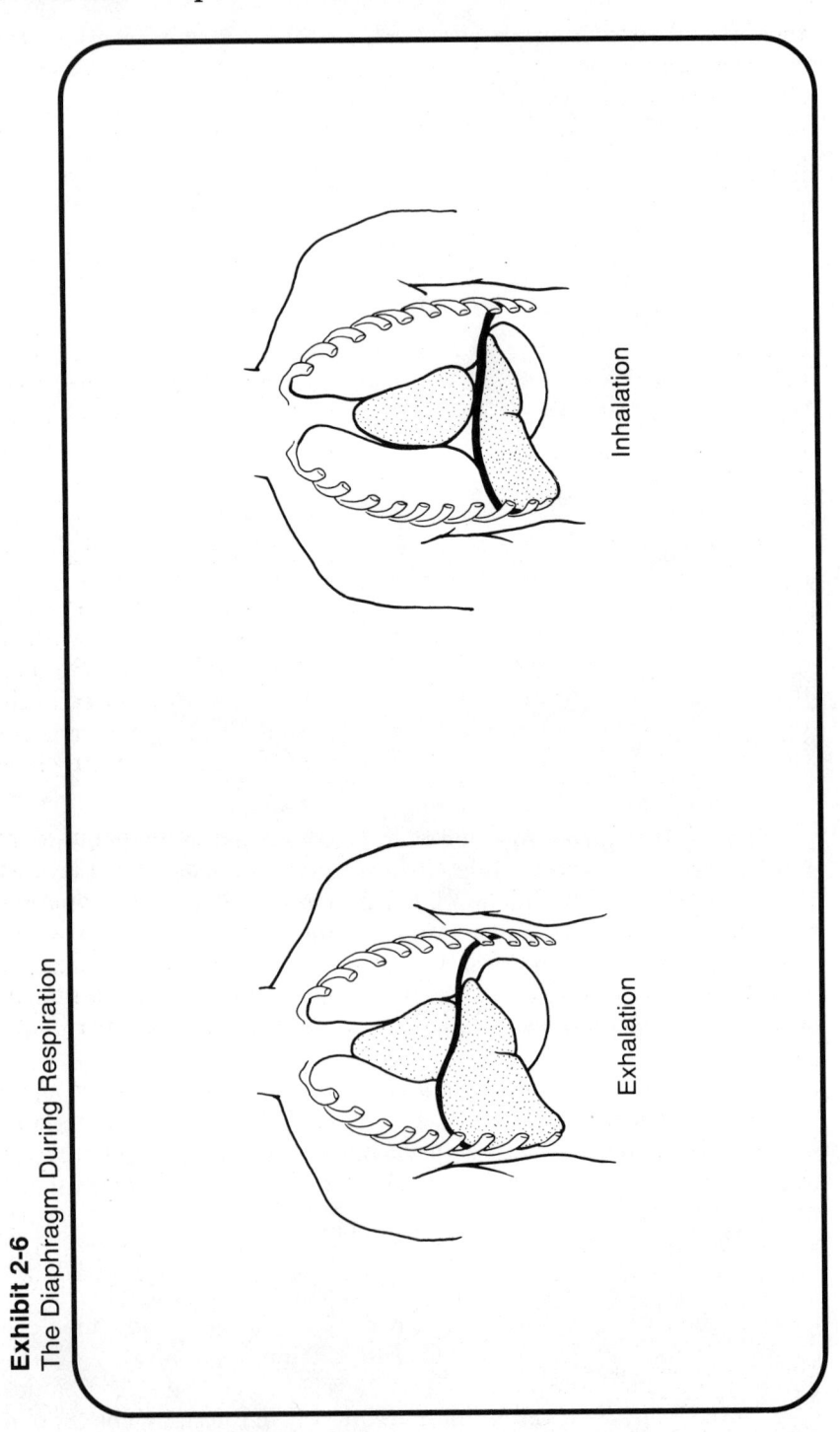

Exhibit 2-6
The Diaphragm During Respiration

the left and on the upper surfaces.

Examination following liver injury usually finds the patient in shock secondary to internal bleeding. Abdominal pain accompanied by tenderness and rigidity in the upper right quadrant of the abdomen are common and may be followed by pain radiating into the shoulder area. The degree of shock is the best indicator of the extent of damage to the liver.

The incoming blood supply to the liver is provided by the hepatic artery, which contributes about 30 percent of the blood flow, and the portal vein, which contributes about 70 percent. When there is severe trauma to the liver region and the hepatic artery is torn, it is possible to ligate (tie or bind) it, providing the patient has a normally functioning liver. Tearing of the portal vein is usually fatal. Exhibit 2-7 shows the structures of the liver. Notice in the lower left portion of the exhibit the juncture of the bile duct and pancreatic duct just below the head of the pancreas in the duodenal wall.

Complications of liver injury are numerous and include infection, malnutrition, vomiting of blood, and the passing of tarry stools. The mortality rate for those suffering a liver injury is extremely high. On the other hand, the liver has amazing regenerative power; once recovered, the patient will not usually suffer additional difficulties. Because the bile ducts, hepatic arteries, and portal veins are distributed in the liver in a segmental manner, large portions of the liver can be removed from patients with severe traumatic lacerations. The remaining liver can continue to function.

Spleen Injuries. The spleen is situated in the left upper quadrant of the abdomen and lies under cover of the ninth, tenth, and eleventh ribs. Normally, the spleen cannot be palpated in an abdominal examination. In healthy individuals, percussion of the area does not produce significant dullness. However, as the spleen enlarges as a result of injury, dullness may be detected along the line of the ninth rib, and a radiograph of the abdomen may reveal damage or an increase in size.

The spleen is the most common organ to be injured from blunt trauma to the abdomen because of its close proximity to the aforementioned ribs. Injury most often occurs during automobile accidents and while playing contact sports. Penetrating wounds of the lower left thorax may also damage the spleen. In most cases of spleen injury, there are associated injuries, including chest trauma. It is possible for the spleen to rupture as much as forty-eight hours following injury.

Pain in the left upper quadrant of the abdomen after injury is often an indication of injury to the spleen. Because of possible irritation of the diaphragm, pain may also be referred to the left shoulder area. If bleeding is of any magnitude, laboratory findings usually show a decreased red blood cell count and an increased white blood cell count.

Exhibit 2-7
Structures of the Liver

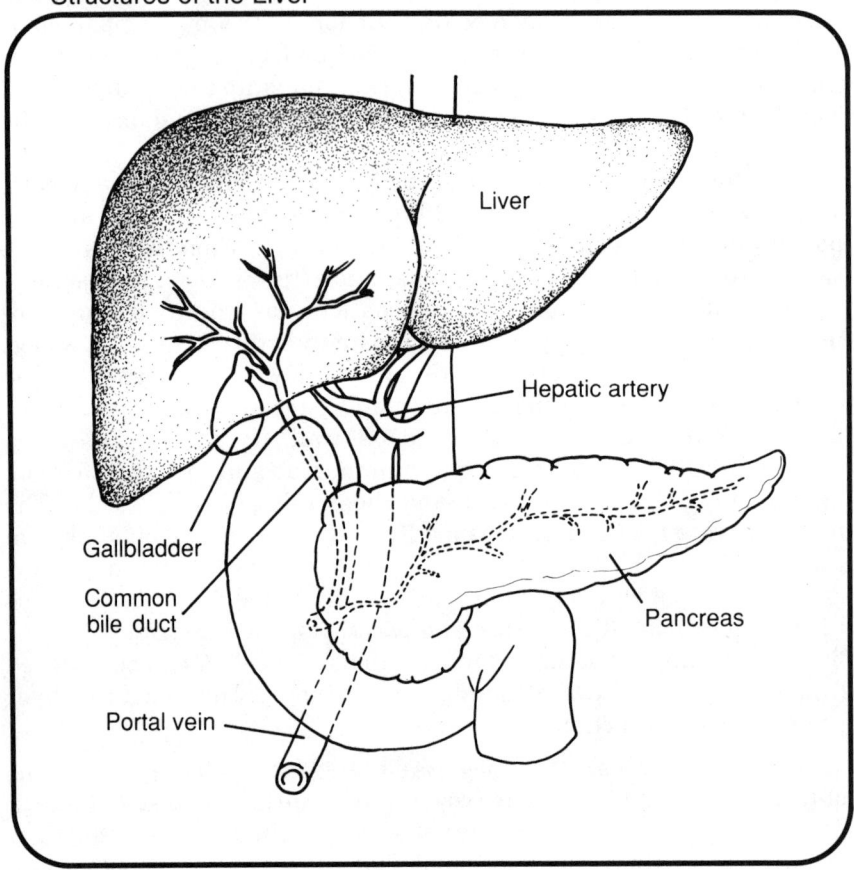

Surgical removal is generally the only acceptable treatment for splenic injury because the spleen contains tiny blood vessels that are too numerous to repair. Since one of the main functions of the spleen is to produce lymphocytes, it might be assumed that the patient who undergoes a splenectomy may be more prone to infections because of a decreased level of immunity. However, there are no conclusive studies to support this assumption.

Pancreas Injuries. The pancreas lies across the upper left quadrant. The relationship of the tail of the pancreas to the spleen sometimes results in damage to the pancreas during splenectomy. The immobility of the pancreas on the rear abdominal wall also makes it vulnerable to blunt trauma. It often "breaks" across the rigid spinal column.

There are no classic symptoms of pancreatic injury. There may be a complete absence of dramatic symptoms even with severe damage. X-rays and other laboratory tests are of little value. A serum test may be used to determine if there has been any elevation of certain enzymes following a suspected pancreatic injury. In the absence of complications, pancreatic injury is best treated conservatively with pain medication and the correction of any fluid deficiency. Severe injuries to the pancreas may require surgical removal.

Complications from severe pancreatic injuries are numerous and sometimes fatal. They may develop early or months or years following the injury. These disorders may range from delayed hemorrhaging to secondary diabetes and pancreatic calcification. Such complications and resulting disorders may necessitate prolonged treatment and numerous surgical procedures.

Kidney Injuries. The kidneys are located behind the thin membrane that lines the abdominal cavity and are surrounded by fat. The right kidney is slightly lower than the left kidney.

Although both kidneys are well protected by the lower part of the thoracic cage and the powerful back muscles, they may be damaged by blunt trauma to the lower sides. An inflamed or damaged kidney will produce tenderness in the mid-back area to one side or the other. Blunt trauma to the lower sides causes injury to the kidney more frequently than to any other abdominal organ. In extreme cases of lateral (side) bending, the kidney can be caught between the twelfth rib and the spinal column.

Pain and tenderness over the area following a history of trauma is usually enough to establish a diagnosis of kidney injury. As with other internal injuries, shock will be present in cases of severe damage. Further confirmation of kidney injury can be established by urinalysis.

Kidney injury is typically treated conservatively if there are no signs of shock or hemorrhage. If blood in the urine persists longer than twenty-four hours, surgical exploration will usually be necessary. If kidney removal is necessary, the proper function of the remaining kidney must first be established. Lumbar nephrectomy (surgical removal of the kidney through the lower back) is a popular method of removing a damaged kidney, since the approach does not require entry into the peritoneal cavity and avoids contamination.

Complications that may follow severe kidney trauma include hypertension, chronic infection, loss of function, cysts, and persistent blood in the urine.

SPINAL PROBLEMS

Chapter 1 described the anatomy of the spinal column. A healthy spine is generally straight, strong, flexible, and pain free. The spine's chief functions are to support the upper body, protect the spinal cord, and allow flexibility of the trunk and head. This section discusses spinal disorders caused by trauma, congenital defects, and progressive/degenerative diseases. It covers the most common problems of the back and neck and the typical treatments for such problems.

Most back problems occur in the lumbar spine, or lower back. This is so because this area is subject to much more movement and bears greater stress than the thoracic spine, or mid-back. The cervical spine, or neck area, is subject to most of the problems of the lumbar spine. Problems special to the cervical spine are described near the end of this section. Sprain and strain, fractures, disc bulging and herniation, congenital abnormalities, and degenerative disorders are described with reference to the lower back.

Sprain and Strain

Poor posture, lack of exercise, and overeating are threats to the back. Poor posture strains the lower back and makes it more vulnerable to injury. A sway back is usually weak. Weak and flabby abdominal muscles deprive the back of its greatest support. Being overweight adds to the strain.

Sprains occur when back muscles or ligaments are stretched or torn. Sprains usually result from improper performance of ordinary activities such as bending, lifting, standing, or sitting. Sprains may also result from the wrenching caused by an accident or injury. Muscle contusions can usually be traced to a definite injury such as a blow to the back.

Strains can have a more subtle history of aggravation from a repetitive activity. One of the most significant findings associated with muscle strains is pain upon palpation of the muscle, but no pain upon palpation of the joint.

Injuries and disorders of the spinal joints are likely to be painful and disabling because of the very close physical and functional relationship between these joints and the nervous system. Normal body mechanics properly align the spinal nerves and skeletal system. Injuries to the spine or elsewhere can alter normal body mechanics. Scar tissue can also develop, hindering joint movement, irritating nerve roots, and causing pain and dysfunction of muscles.

Treatment of low back strain usually begins conservatively with bed rest, muscle relaxants, and cold packs or moist heat. Massages are also helpful but should be replaced by more active physical therapy as the patient progresses.

Spinal Fractures

Fractures of the vertebral bones, commonly called a broken back, can initially require significant care but usually heal without residual problems. In this respect, fractures are less of a problem than many chronic back conditions.

Wedge and Compression Fractures. Fractures of the thoracic and lumbar spine usually result from a fall on the buttocks or feet. These fractures, usually *wedge compression* or *bursting compression* fractures, are stable injuries. Major injuries of the spinal column are generally assessed in terms of their stability, the likelihood that the injury could become worse. Stable injuries, such as compression fractures, are protected from displacement by the rear spinal ligaments. Unstable injuries, such as dislocations, are displaced and may become further so if the ligaments have been torn. More serious fractures and dislocations of the spine can occur in automobile and industrial accidents. These can be unstable, and the spinal cord may be damaged as well. X-rays of the spine in various degrees of flexion and extension may be necessary to determine stability.

When the spine is in a flexed position (bending forward), a force from below or from above can cause the spine to suddenly flex beyond its normal range. In this position, the force is greater on the forward portions of the vertebral bodies. The rear ligaments remain intact causing the vertebral bodies to be crushed in the forward portion, resulting in a wedge compression fracture.

The symptoms of a wedge compression fracture may be mild with only localized tenderness. Since such fractures are stable and the spinal cord is not involved, conservative treatment is usually followed. A short period of bed rest followed by physical therapy may be sufficient treatment. In more severe cases or when patients complain of increased pain, a body cast is sometimes applied. With elderly patients, a brace or corset is often recommended.

If the spine is straight when compression force is applied, a bursting compression fracture results. The intervertebral disc is driven into the porous bone of the vertebral body, and fracture fragments burst outward in all directions. Because the rear spinal ligaments usually remain intact, the spinal column remains stable. Also, it is rare for a fragment to be driven backward far enough to cause spinal cord injury. The symptoms of a bursting compression fracture will be more severe than those of a wedge compression fracture. However, several weeks of bed rest or a fitted body cast for six to eight weeks will usually result in healing with few or no further problems.

Spondylolysis and Spondylolisthesis. Spondylolysis is either a unilateral or bilateral stress fracture in the isthmus of the spinal process with no slippage of the vertebra. This defect may also be congenital. In the majority of cases, there are no symptoms. Following injury, however, fibrous tissue at the fracture site may be stretched, resulting in persistent pain. When spondylolysis is bilateral, the vertebra is basically divided into two parts, the vertebra body and the spinal process surrounding the spinal cord. Under these circumstances, the vertebra body and superior spinal process may slip forward in relation to the inferior spinal process. This advanced stage in which there is evident slippage is called spondylolisthesis. Spondylolisthesis is detectable in about 2 percent of the adult population. Exhibit 2-8 shows these conditions.

Spondylolisthesis is clinically manifested by an increase in lumbar curvature or by chronic low back pain with occasional tightening of the hamstring muscles. Progressive forward slippage may require stabilization of the spinal column. This can be achieved by a local spinal fusion. If there are no complications, mild pain can usually be treated with a lumbosacral support. Patients with severe back pain and nerve root irritation usually require surgical decompression of the nerve roots in addition to a spinal fusion.

Disc Bulging and Herniation

Disc problems are extremely common in adults. In the lumbar region, the L4-L5 and L5-S1 discs are most frequently affected. Degenerative disc disease is very common in the over-thirty population.

Slipped or ruptured discs can cause severe pain and disability. The semisolid center of the disc may shift or bulge and press the nerves. In more severe cases, the disc may rupture (herniate) through its capsule and press against the spinal nerves. On the other hand, discs may bulge or herniate in such a way as to produce minimal symptoms. The vulnerability of the spinal nerves and spinal cord is due to their proximity to the vertebra and intervertebral discs. Exhibit 2-9 shows the relationship of the spinal nerves and cord to the discs. In the drawing of the lumbar vertebrae at the right, three nerve roots are shown at the point where they pass through the intervertebral foramen, the space that forms the nerve root exit.

Types of Disc Bulging and Herniation. There are four types of disc protrusions. A *posterior* protrusion bulges in the direction of the rear of the disc, pressing directly on the spinal column. A *posterolateral* protrusion bulges to the left or right side of the spinal cord. A posterolateral protrusion with a *rupture* of the *annulus fibrosus* involves a tear of the tough membrane containing the gelatin-like material in the center of the disc. This injury allows the semisolid disc center to escape the tough capsular disc. A posterolateral protrusion with rupture of the annulus fibrosus and *fragmentation* of the disc substance involves the breaking into bits of the disc material, which may float away in the spinal canal. Exhibit 2-10 shows top views of these disc protrusions and a healthy disc. In many instances, protrusions falling into the first two

2 • Trauma and Other Injuries—91

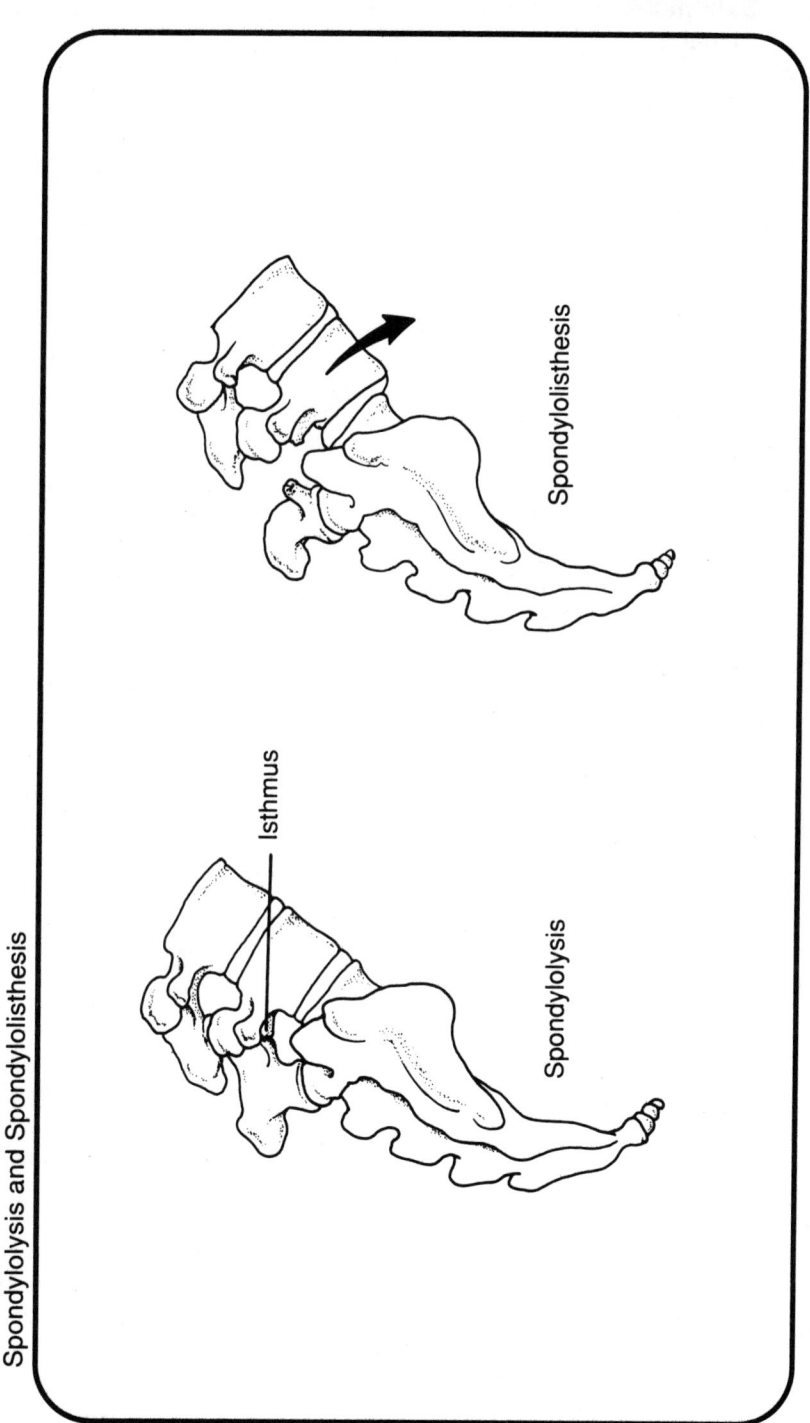

Exhibit 2-8
Spondylolysis and Spondylolisthesis

Exhibit 2-9
Spinal Cord, Discs, and Nerves

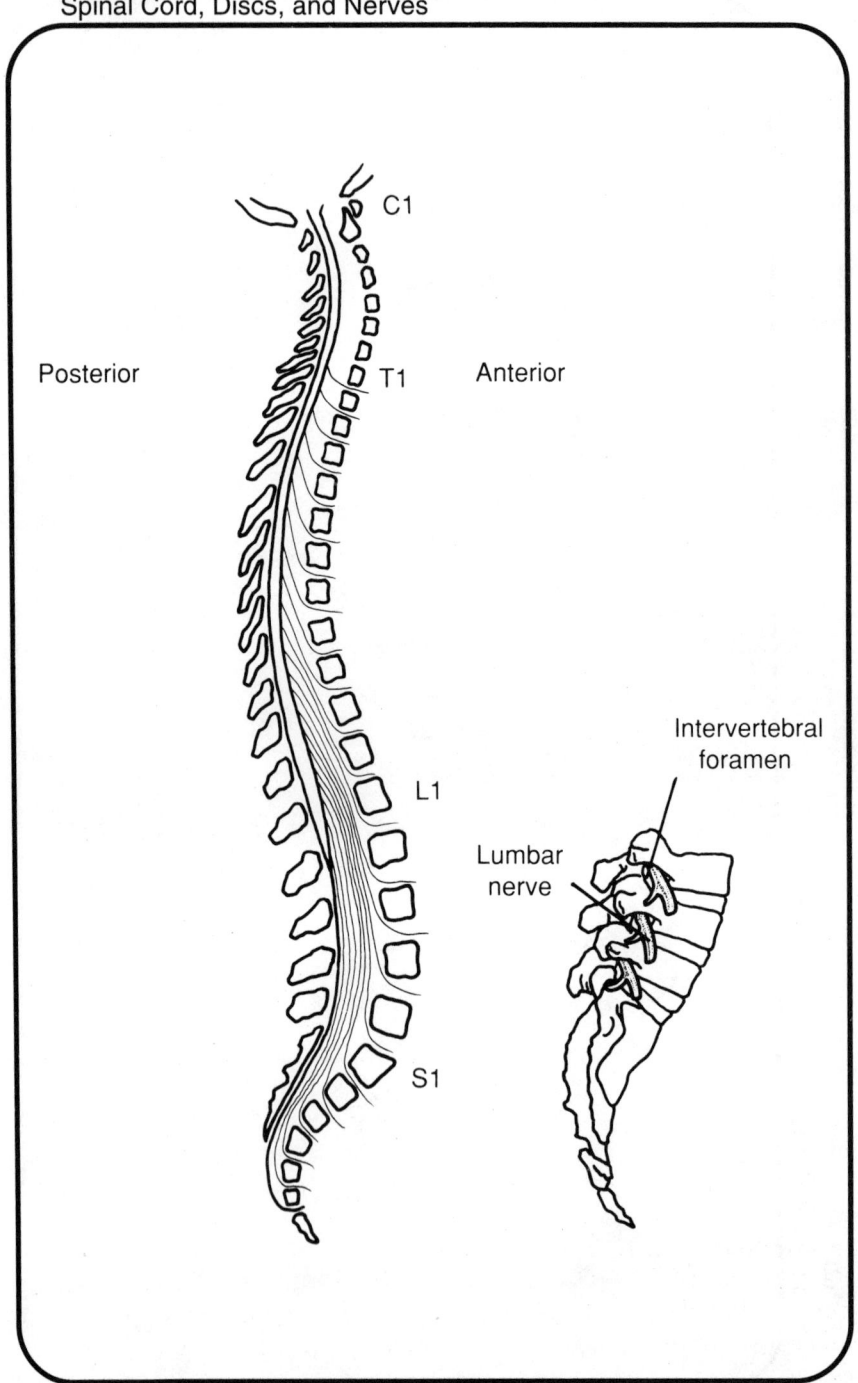

Exhibit 2-10
Healthy Versus Protruding Discs

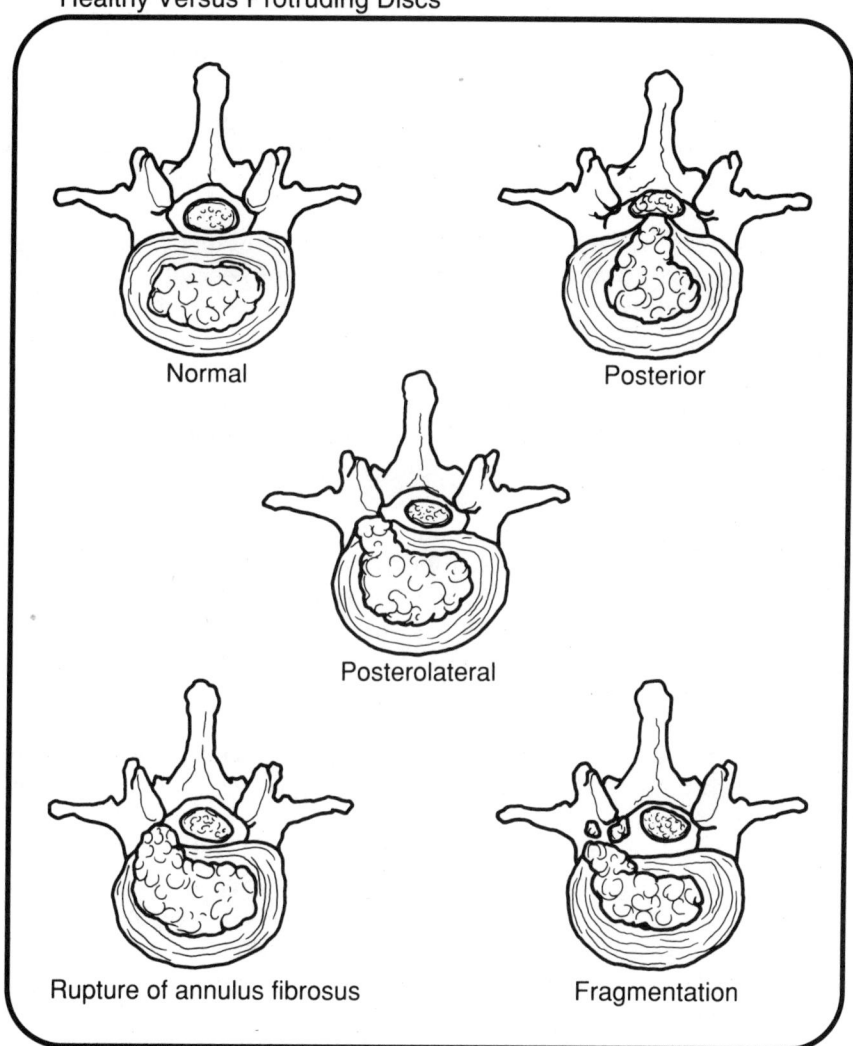

Normal

Posterior

Posterolateral

Rupture of annulus fibrosus

Fragmentation

categories will respond to conservative treatment. While the disc does not reabsorb itself, it does tend to atrophy slightly. The patient is given a series of spinal exercises to strengthen the back muscles and protect against future episodes.

Disc herniation frequently occurs at the level of the sciatic nerve. Pain radiating down the back of the thigh and leg along the sciatic nerve is called *sciatica*. The sciatic nerve is responsible for movement and sensation in the lower extremities. It exits at nerve roots L4, L5, S1, and S2. Sciatica is an extremely uncomfortable condition. Usually described as a dull ache, it can become very sharp and piercing. Pain is usually noticed on one side of the buttocks or the other. The pain can radiate from the buttocks to the thigh, knee, and down to the toes. The pain is usually centralized at the back of the thigh and leg. Pain can occasionally be felt in the front or side of the leg. The pain can be an annoyance, or it can become completely disabling. If pressure or pinching on the spinal nerve continues, actual nerve damage can result, causing either numbness or muscle weakness in the leg.

Treatment of Disc Problems. Treatment of disc herniation is usually directed at pain relief and restoration of normal function. A support such as a corset may be prescribed to reduce or eliminate pain during activity and to reduce pressure on the disc and surrounding nerves. However, with extended use of back supports, there is the risk that the back and abdomen muscles will atrophy. Acute herniation is treated with bed rest, analgesics, and heat. With prolonged bed rest, irritation of the nerve root should be reduced and symptoms should subside.

Surgery is indicated only for patients who do not respond well to conservative treatment or who suffer repeated severe sciatica. During surgery, the disc material is excised, the space explored, and any disc fragments are removed. A laminectomy is often required in order to gain access to the disc. A laminectomy is the removal of a portion of the bony process of the vertebra.

A *spinal fusion* is the fixing of one vertebra to another with a bone graft. Fusions are most commonly performed at the L4-L5 level, fusing these vertebrae with the sacrum. The sacrum is scraped to prepare it for bone graft material, which is obtained from the ilium. The graft material is packed along the sides of the vertebral bodies. The fusion solidifies during the six months after surgery. Spinal fusions are a controversial issue. Some doctors believe that most cases involving a disc problem require a spinal fusion, while others believe fusions should be used only as a last resort. The patient's life-style, occupation, and personal preference are important considerations. A manual laborer, who depends upon the strength and stability of his spine to perform his daily tasks, may well benefit from a fusion, since it can prevent further degeneration and recurrent nerve root entrapment. In contrast, a patient with a relatively sedentary life-style may not require treatment more serious than disc excision.

Congenital Problems

Congenital problems exist at birth. With trauma superimposed on a pre-existing condition, it is often difficult, if not impossible, to distinguish between the causes of the patient's pain. Minor congenital problems are so common that a variation from normal is detectable in more than half the population.

Facet Tropism. Facet tropism is a common congenital problem. The facet joints on the spine are where the superior spinal process of one vertebra join the inferior spinal process of the vertebra above it. Facet tropism is characterized by misalignment of facets in a specific vertebra. Facet tropism typically occurs in the lumbar spine. A facet on one side is aligned differently than the opposite facet. Because of this oblique alignment, the disorder adds rotational stress to the already strained lumbar vertebra. Exhibit 2-11 shows a vertebra with facet tropism.

Sacralization and Lumbarization. Sacralization of a lumbar vertebra is one of the most significant congenital abnormalities causing low back pain. This condition is also known as Bertolotti's syndrome. Sacralization occurs when the fifth lumbar vertebra is fused into the sacrum. When this happens on just one side of the vertebra, it places unusual stress on the disc above and frequently causes herniation.

Similarly, lumbarization of a sacral vertebra, which results in six rather than five lumbar vertebra, also causes great stress on the L5-S1 joint. If herniation or symptoms of nerve root entrapment occur, surgery to decompress the disc should include fusion to weld the affected vertebra.

Spina Bifida. The most common congenital abnormality of the spine is spina bifida. Spina bifida is the incomplete bony closure of one or more spinal processes leaving the neural arch open. This defect may occur at any level of the spine, but is most often found in the lumbosacral region. This condition is usually accompanied by a neurological deficit and may range from mild muscle weakness to complete paralysis of the lower limbs. The mildest degree of spina bifida is known as spina bifida occulta and occurs without any external manifestation. It is detectable only through x-rays. This common form occurs in about 10 percent of the population.

Scoliosis. Scoliosis, or sideward curvature of the spine, is another common congenital abnormality. This defect results when half of a vertebral body fails to form completely, resulting in a short, usually mild curvature of the spine. Scoliosis can also result from muscular contractions due to disc herniation. The deformity is usually not noticeable, and discovery of the condition is usually made only when x-rays are taken for some other purpose. Severe scoliosis is usually associated with multiple congenital abnormalities of the ribs as well. Severe, progressive scoliosis requires early surgical intervention, including spinal fusion, to prevent extreme deformity.

Exhibit 2-11
Facet Tropism

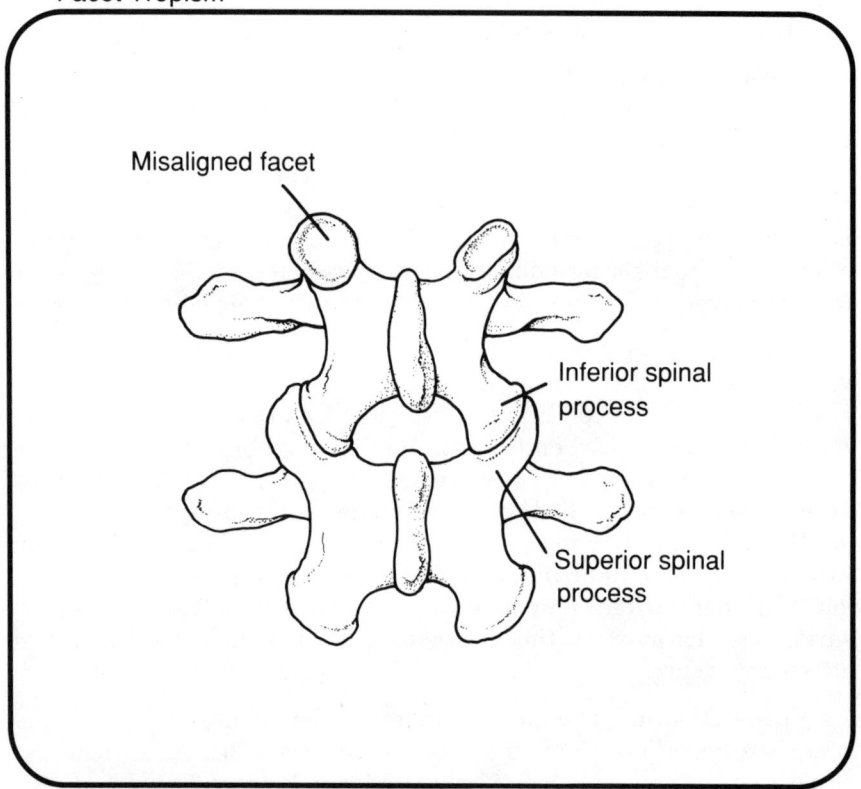

Labels: Misaligned facet; Inferior spinal process; Superior spinal process

Degenerative Disorders

There are four major degenerative disorders. They are spondylosis, osteoarthritis, degenerative disc disease, and spinal stenosis. Although they often occur in combination, each condition alone can lead to spinal nerve root entrapment. Irritation, pinching, and pressing of the spinal nerves can cause severe pain and disability. Unfortunately for those in claims work, traumatic injuries frequently occur in an area already affected by a degenerative disorder. The resulting problems will almost certainly be worse than with a traumatic injury alone, making the claim more difficult to resolve and more expensive.

Spondylosis. As previously described, spondylosis is characterized by degeneration of the disc body. It is most often found in the middle-aged and elderly. The condition is frequently asymptomatic and is discovered by chance on x-rays. Symptoms usually manifest themselves only after fatigue or injury has upset the normal condition of the spine. Thus, a finding of spondylosis as the cause of low back pain should not be considered until all other possibilities have been fully researched and excluded.

Osteoarthritis. Osteoarthritis is often considered a "wear and tear" condition. However, it is more accurately characterized as metabolic and cellular activity within joint cartilage. In the spine, the facet joints are involved. In this condition, the cartilage is invaded by blood vessels from the resident bone. This exposes the normally bloodless cartilage to the circulatory system. The softened cartilage is gradually worn down until there is complete loss of the cartilage space. The cartilage responds to the invasion of the bloodstream by forming a thickened growth known as *chondrophyte*. This growth subsequently undergoes ossification and becomes what is known as an osteophyte or "bony spur." This defect alters the distribution of stresses on the affected joints and can press on the spinal nerves.

Degenerative Disc Disease. Degenerative disc disease is an acceleration of the normal aging process and may be aggravated by trauma. Initial degeneration of the disc occurs in the nucleus pulposus. Degenerative disc disease is characterized by a loss of thickness in the disc space. As the nucleus pulposus resorbs, its gelatinous texture becomes somewhat lumpy. The annulus fibrosus, the tough capsule surrounding the nucleus, loses elasticity, making it more susceptible to separation or tearing. Smooth motion in the spine is replaced by uneven and excessive motion. Because of this instability, the joints may react by forming small osteophytes.

Herniation of a disc is not the same as disc degeneration. Herniation may result from a specific incident, but may also occur as a complication of degeneration.

Spinal Stenosis. Spinal stenosis, shown in Exhibit 2-12, is a disorder characterized by bony narrowing of the central spinal canal or the lateral nerve root exits. Spinal stenosis can be congenital or secondary to advanced stages of degenerative disc disease. It can also result from spinal fusion. The pain from spinal stenosis may be diffuse or radicular (sciatica) depending on whether the location of the disorder is centralized or lateral, respectively. Degenerative disc disease alone does not cause pain. Symptoms result from the narrowing of the spinal canal and nerve root exits caused by disc degeneration and spinal stenosis.

A condition related to spinal stenosis is *facet joint impingement*. This is a chronic degenerative problem in which the nerve root exits become narrowed by osteophytes and subluxation. The nerves, like the central spinal canal in spinal stenosis, become pinched and pressured as a result of this bony narrowing. Facet joint impingement is treated with mobilization. A condition known as *facet joint sprain* can likewise

98—Medical Aspects of Claims

Exhibit 2-12
Spinal Stenosis

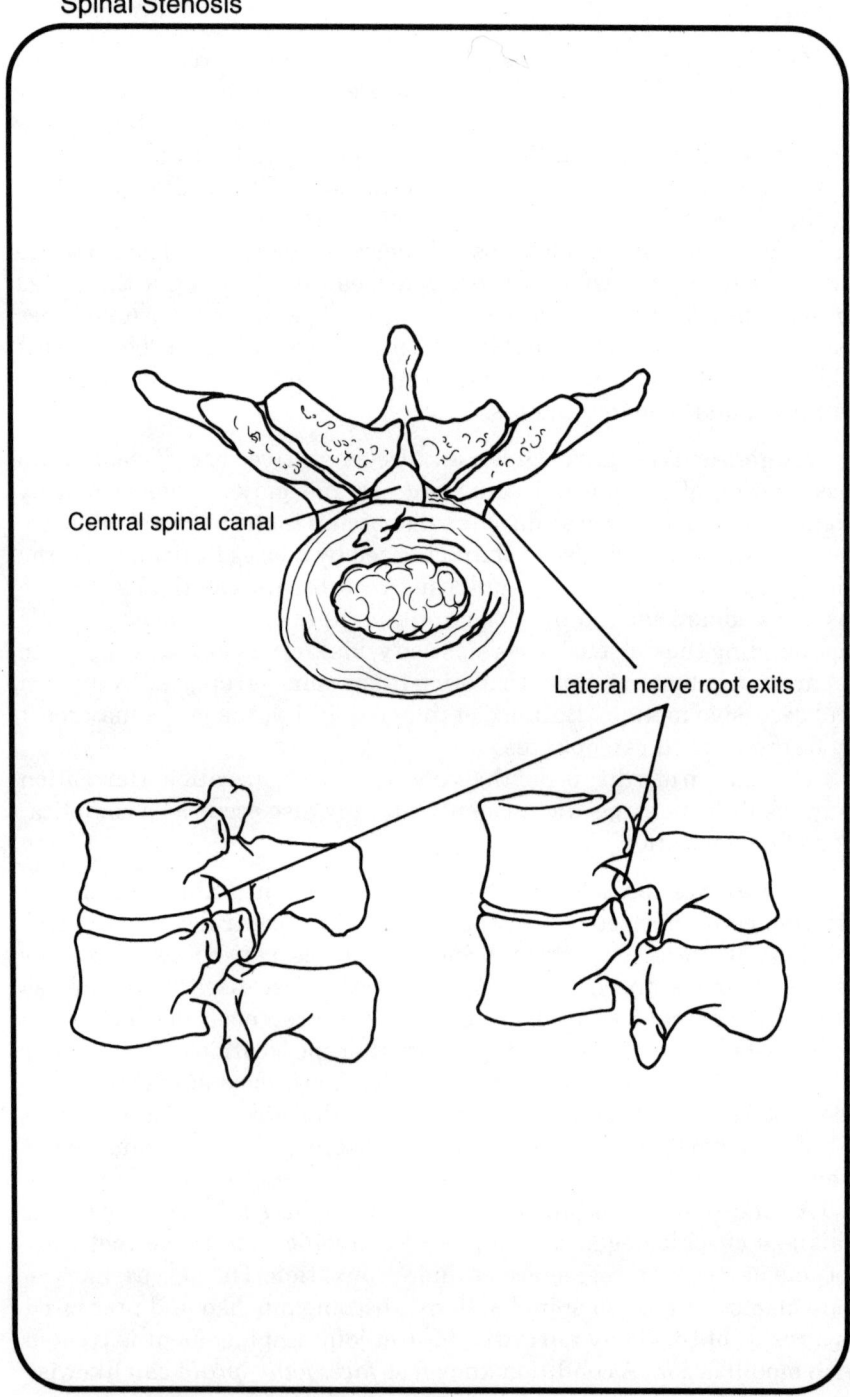

involve subluxation of facet joints, but like any sprain, it is better treated with rest than with mobilization.

Neck Problems

The neck must move more than any other part of the spinal column. Its sturdy, flexible muscle and ligament system continuously holds the head up and allows it to move in countless combinations of three basic movements (rotating left and right, tilting left and right, and tilting front and back). Should something go wrong in the neck, the effects can be far reaching. Pain originating in the neck may be felt in the scalp, face, ears, shoulders, arms, hands, fingers, or occasionally, even in the chest. An examining physician must be aware of these symptom patterns to avoid a misdiagnosis.

Whiplash. Whiplash is the most common cause of pain in the cervical spine. It is caused by the overexertion of the muscles or sudden stretching of the ligaments in the neck. Whiplash commonly results from an automobile accident, but many other incidents can also be responsible. A sudden fall or blow to the head can cause whiplash. Athletic injuries involving rapid movement of the neck can also cause whiplash. Even limited motion can cause a sprain if the neck muscles are already tense. During whiplash, the victim's head snaps backward as the body is propelled in a forward motion. The head may then snap forward in a recoil motion. In an automobile accident, if the vehicle hits a solid object, the reverse can happen. The head continues to move forward as the body suddenly stops. This is known as hyperflexion. When the body moves one way and the head moves the other, as much as 500 to 600 pounds of force falls on the neck.

Generally, there is only slight discomfort at first, but stiffness and pain become more severe after several hours. It is not unusual for someone to report no injury at the scene of an auto accident, but to develop legitimate symptoms of a neck injury later on. The pain generally peaks in several days and usually subsides and is gone within a month. Unless there is an underlying problem with the cervical discs or vertebrae, most victims usually recover, and problems rarely reoccur. Unless there has been severe damage, these tissues will heal themselves without medical intervention. Occasionally, a neck collar, home traction, or muscle relaxants and pain medication will be prescribed.

Degenerative and Traumatic Problems. Degenerative disease in the cervical spine is not quite as common as in the lumbar spine, but many of the problems of the lumbar spine are equally associated with the cervical spine. For instance, herniation of the cervical discs can occur. The most common type of herniation in the cervical spine is the

100—Medical Aspects of Claims

posterolateral protrusion. There is little room in the cervical foraminae for exit of the nerve roots. Thus, dislocation and spur formation of the cervical facet joints easily compress the nerve roots.

The C5-C6 area of the cervical spine is subject to the most movement. These vertebrae and discs normally begin to show the effects of daily wear-and-tear between the ages of forty and sixty. Often when people suffer an injury and indicate they have never had a problem in the past, x-rays reveal that there has been deterioration, caused by aging, underway for some time.

Compression of the sixth cervical nerve root causes weakness in the deltoid and biceps muscles. It can also cause diminished reflex action and sensation in the biceps, thumb, and index finger. Compression of the seventh cervical nerve root causes weakness in the triceps muscle and diminished reflex and skin sensation in the index and middle fingers. Examination may reveal limited motion, but little muscle spasm. When neck pain is present, a complete neurological examination of the upper limbs is almost always indicated.

Treatment of Neck Problems. The treatment for degenerative disease in the cervical spine is similar to that for the lumbar spine. In addition, a cervical "ruff" may be used to rest the neck and relieve pain. A ruff is a series of three rolls of stocking material filled with cotton wool. When symptoms are persistent, a cervical brace or collar may be used. This device is made of sturdier material than a ruff and further restricts motion of the neck. In addition, traction on the cervical spine may also relieve the pain. The majority of patients can be treated effectively without surgery.

Diagnosis of Spinal Problems

An accurate diagnosis of spinal problems requires a physical examination of the patient and various tests.

Physical Exam. To determine the cause of a patient's pain, a physician should obtain a complete medical history and perform a physical examination. X-rays of the affected area will be taken. The doctor should determine when the pain first began, the exact location of the pain, what activities make it worse, and what activities make it better. The patient's hobbies, work, and daily routine should be identified.

Areas of tenderness and muscle spasm, muscular weakness or atrophy, and changes in sensation in the lower extremities should be carefully noted. The doctor should note posture and general physical condition and should have the patient flex, extend, and rotate the body to determine the degree of motion the patient is capable of and to

2 • Trauma and Other Injuries—101

identify movements that produce pain. The doctor may also make pin pricks along the extremities and tap various muscles with a reflex hammer to test nerve function. Laboratory tests are sometimes essential in order to distinguish metabolic or organic causes of symptoms.

Tests. The following procedures are often used to diagnose the origin of back pain.

The *CAT scan* (computerized axial tomography) is a very sophisticated x-ray procedure that provides an image of cross sections of the spine. The information gathered in this process is interpreted by a computer and projected into a picture from which the doctor can distinguish various anatomical structures.

A newer procedure is *magnetic resonance imaging* (MRI), which uses a combination of a huge super-conductive magnet, electromagnetic waves, and a sophisticated computer system to create very detailed images of the body's interior. Unlike conventional x-rays and the CAT scan, the MRI does not use radiation. It is not stopped by dense bone and can image on any plane—vertically, horizontally, and diagonally.

Thermography maps any differences in temperature on the surface of the skin. The skin's dissipation of excessive internal body heat is regulated through the autonomic nervous system. Thermography is based on the presumption that asymmetrical temperature patterns on the skin indicate pathology of an underlying soft tissue. However, physiological studies have shown that the surface temperature of the body is not uniform, symmetrical, or consistent from time to time. It can also be affected by numerous external factors. Thermographic results should *not* be relied on as objective findings because they are not widely accepted in the medical community.

A *myelogram* involves the injection of radio-opaque dye into the spinal column. The dye settles in the spinal column so that x-rays can outline the spinal cord and nerves. This procedure must be done in a hospital because it sometimes produces moderate to severe side effects including nausea, vomiting, and intense headaches.

The *EMG* (electromyogram) is also referred to as a nerve conduction study. It can identify nerve damage.

In addition to these procedures, the following tests and signs help determine the cause of back pain:

1. Ankle Jerk Reflex. The Achilles tendon is struck with a rubber hammer to test the reflex reactions related to L5-S1 nerves. The absence of a reaction is indicative of nerve entrapment.
2. Fabere's Sign (also known as Patrick's Test). With the patient supine, the knee is flexed with the outside of the ankle resting on the knee of the opposite leg and the knee depressed. Pain would indicate arthritis in the hip.
3. The Knee Jerk Reflex. The tendons of the knee are struck for

reflex indications of lesions at the L2-L3-L4 levels.
4. Laseque's Sign. A limited ability to raise a straight leg is usually associated with lumbar nerve root compression. In addition, in sciatica, flexion of the hip is painful with the knee extended but not with the knee flexed.

The following tests are used to determine the cause of cervical pain:
1. Biceps Reflex. In this test, the biceps tendon is tapped. There is normally a contraction of the muscle accompanied by a jerk of the forearm. If the C5-C6 segment of the spinal cord is damaged on the side being tested, the response is depressed or absent.
2. Brachioradialis Reflex. This test determines the existence of lesions at the C5-C6 level. The tendon just above the wrist joint is tapped with a reflex hammer.
3. Finger Jerk Reflex. In this test, the fingers are flexed and tapped in the direction of extension. In cases of corticospinal tract damage between C7-C8-T1, there may be a response of excessive contraction of the fingers.

SUMMARY

Injuries to the skin can be minor contusions or abrasions, or serious burns or wounds. Because the skin protects the body from infection, any injury to the skin is a cause for concern. Cosmetic and reconstructive surgery may be necessary to repair serious burns and scars.

The muscles and joints are frequently injured in accidental traumas, the typical cause of insurance claims. While ordinary muscle strain and sprain should heal quickly and satisfactorily, joint injuries can be more troublesome. This is especially so when the victim suffers from arthritis, a condition that is usually metabolic or degenerative in origin. Carpal tunnel syndrome and temporomandibular joint syndrome are two joint conditions that increasingly appear in claims.

Bone fractures and head injuries can be extremely serious, but can also heal completely. The seriousness of a fracture depends on the nature of the break, the bone involved, and the age, health, and occupation of the victim. Head injuries are serious because of the possibility of brain damage. Prompt and proper treatment of head injuries is critical.

Injuries to the internal organs are less common than those to the musculoskeletal system, but can be harder to detect and potentially fatal if left untreated. Any trauma sufficient to injure the internal organs is likely to have been violent and to have caused conspicuous injury to the musculoskeletal system. Internal injuries should be promptly identified and treated.

Many claims involve alleged injuries to the spine. The spine is a complex mechanism of bones, discs, ligaments, and muscles, all of which can suffer sudden traumatic injury or progressive injury. Because disc problems are common, it is not unusual after an accident to discover a disc problem, but this discovery is not proof that the accident caused the problem. Disc problems, as well as other spinal problems, may result from a number of causes. Accidental trauma is only one of these causes. Claim representatives must understand the many sources of spinal problems in order to assess the validity of a claim and the appropriateness of treatment.

CHAPTER 3

Psychological Injuries and Conditions

Claims for injuries and conditions that are purely psychological in nature are comparatively rare. Yet, psychological injuries and conditions frequently accompany or pre-exist physical injuries, thereby complicating them. The psychological aspect of a case is significant in the investigation, control, and settlement of every claim. Whether they realize it or not, claim representatives must deal with the psychological conditions and problems of claimants. Some cases explicitly involve claims for psychological injury. In other cases, the psychological dimension is important, even if the claim is not explicitly made for a psychological condition.

This chapter begins with descriptions of the usual psychological response to physical injury and of psychological symptoms. All physical injuries cause some psychological response, even if it is only mild and temporary. Psychological symptoms are not as significant as psychological disorders; however, both may require treatment, and both may be the subject of a claim.

The next three sections of the chapter describe psychological disorders. There are comprehensive criteria for diagnosing these disorders. All treatment and discussion of psychological conditions should be based on such standard diagnoses. The diagnostic criteria make clear that judgment and clinical skill play an important part in psychological diagnosis.

Certain psychological disorders are especially important or troublesome in claims either because they appear frequently, preexist a physical injury, or complicate treatment and recovery from physical injury. Claims involving some of these disorders are frequently fraudulent and/or abusive of the insurance system. Claim representatives must therefore develop a working understanding of the behaviors and symptoms of these disorders in order to respond appropriately. The chapter concludes with material concerning the evaluation of psychological conditions.

PSYCHOLOGICAL RESPONSE TO PHYSICAL INJURY

Injuries to the body can create psychological responses that may be weak and transient or profound and permanent. In general, the severity of the psychological response corresponds to the severity of the injury: trivial injuries can be expected to produce trivial responses, and massive injuries are likely to produce massive psychological responses. However, there can be great variability of response to a given injury. Differences in psychological makeup, levels of personal support, and occupational demands affect how people respond to the stress of physical injury.

This section describes certain psychological responses that are commonly associated with physical injury and how such responses should be considered in the evaluation of claims. Beyond the predictable responses described in this section, most psychological conditions are *not* caused by physical injury. Thus, a claim for a psychological condition based on accidental physical injury should be closely scrutinized. Most alleged psychological conditions are found to be the predictable response to injury, conditions that pre-existed the accidental injury, or the result of causes unrelated to the physical injury.

Common Psychological Responses

Injured individuals frequently experience pain, stress, anxiety, and depression in response to a physical injury. They may also exhibit a maladjusted response to the sick role as a result of physical injury. Most individuals also cope with their suffering through defense mechanisms.

Pain. Pain is both physically and psychologically produced. It is directly related to tissue damage and thus serves the important purpose of causing withdrawal or retreat from the cause of harm. However, the reality and extent of pain is related to numerous other factors including personality, expectations, age, and sociocultural background.[1]

Health professionals have observed a wide range of reactions to pain. Some patients are stoic in response to injuries that usually cause great pain; other patients complain loudly, bitterly, or theatrically about injuries that are usually not severely painful. Yet, the subjective reality of their suffering cannot be denied. The presence and extent of pain cannot be objectively proven or disproven.

Pain can cause anxiety and anxiety can increase pain. Likewise, chronic pain can cause depression, and depression can make a patient highly sensitized to pain.[2] This interaction of pain with depression and anxiety shows that psychological reactions to physical injury can reinforce and complicate one another. In addition, while pain, anxiety, and depression serve the useful purpose of leading the victim to seek medical treatment, someone who wishes (either consciously or unconsciously) to prolong treatment will magnify and maximize the symptoms of pain, anxiety, and depression. People with certain psychological disorders or who have secondary motives (such as financial gain) may be found to prolong treatment.

Malingering, factitious disorder, and the various somatoform disorders, discussed later, are recognized psychological diagnoses. Each of these conditions includes the report of physical symptoms for which there is no identifiable organic cause. Pain is a frequently reported physical symptom in these disorders. The presence of physical injury does not preclude the existence of these conditions, which often do coexist with a real physical injury. Thus, pain may be simultaneously "real" and "psychological" at the same time.[3] "Psychological" pain is also referred to as "functional," "psychogenic" or "psychosomatic" pain.

Placebos provide relief from pain in a significant minority of cases. Placebos are agents such as saline solution or sugar pills that have no pharmacological effect. They are inert substances that would be expected to do nothing, yet they have a very real effect. Placebos relieve both "organic" and "psychological" pain.[4] Thus, the effectiveness of a placebo cannot be seen as an indicator that pain is only "psychological."

Pain can usually be effectively managed with medications, although psychological treatment may also be necessary for psychologically caused pain. Properly managed, medications for the relief of pain should not normally result in addiction. Claimants who abuse narcotics are likely to have medical, psychological, or personality problems that complicate settlement of the claim.

Anxiety and Stress. Anxiety is a feeling of apprehension, tension, dread, or uneasiness. It may be caused by specific external threats, such as fear of losing one's job, or from internal psychological conflicts. Anxiety not connected to a specific cause is unfocused and diffuse (sometimes called "free-floating"). Anxiety causes physiological responses including increased blood pressure, heartbeat, and sweating; changes in the rate and depth of breathing; changes in blood chemistry; and suppression of the immune system.[5]

The term "stress" is frequently used synonymously with "anxiety."

108—Medical Aspects of Claims

However, stress also refers to the causes of anxiety. Stresses may be internal or external. The American Psychiatric Association requires that sources and levels of stress be included as part of the information in a complete diagnosis of psychological disorders.[6] Psychosocial stressors are coded from "1" for "none" to "6" for "catastrophic." Examples of the various levels of psychosocial stressors are shown in Exhibit 3-1.

The American Psychiatric Association also suggests that all of the following types of stress be considered: conjugal, parenting, other interpersonal, occupational, living circumstances, financial, legal, developmental, physical injury or illness, and other.[7] An injury that is the subject of an insurance claim or lawsuit creates several of these types of stress including financial, legal, physical, and possibly occupational and conjugal. Thus, because injuries cause stress, and stress causes anxiety, it can be expected that claim-related injuries create a great deal of anxiety.

Anxiety is not considered a psychological disorder unless it is excessive, unrealistic, and irrational. Anxiety disorders such as phobias and panic disorders are described in the following section. Anxiety that is appropriate plays a constructive role. It prepares the body for imminent threats and causes the development and activation of psychological defense mechanisms.

Defense Mechanisms. All defense mechanisms serve the useful purpose of protecting against overwhelming anxiety. Some defense mechanisms, such as humor, are very important social skills. Other defense mechanisms create problems when they become a chronic means of avoiding anxiety-related situations. Some defense mechanisms that may be used to fight the stress of physical injury and illness are as follows:

- *Acting out*—any activity that is pursued to relieve inner tension. The meaning and purpose of the activity may not be recognized by the actor.
- *Constriction of awareness*—a person may focus on one thing to avoid something else. For example, a patient may be focused on the day-to-day quality of hospital care to avoid thinking about the fact that he or she is permanently disabled.
- *Counter-phobic measures*—a person deliberately encounters and tries to master the cause of injury. For example, a person may resume driving a car soon after an auto accident. The anxiety is displaced by a sense of mastery.
- *Denial*—the person does not acknowledge some aspect of reality. Denial is a normal stage in the gradual adjustment to permanent injury, but it is an unhealthy long-term response. Denial can also delay necessary treatment of acute problems.

Exhibit 3-1
Severity of Psychosocial Stressors Scale: Adults

Code	Term	Examples of Stressors	
		Acute events	**Enduring circumstances**
1	None	No acute events that may be relevant to the disorder	No enduring circumstances that may be relevant to the disorder
2	Mild	Broke up with boyfriend or girlfriend; started or graduated from school; child left home	Family arguments; job dissatisfaction; residence in high-crime neighborhood
3	Moderate	Marriage; marital separation; loss of job; retirement; miscarriage	Marital discord; serious financial problems; trouble with boss; being a single parent
4	Severe	Divorce; birth of first child	Unemployment; poverty
5	Extreme	Death of spouse; serious physical illness diagnosed; victim of rape	Serious chronic illness in self or child; ongoing physical or sexual abuse
6	Catastrophic	Death of child; suicide of spouse; devastating natural disaster	Captivity as hostage; concentration camp experience
0	Inadequate information, or no change in condition		

Reprinted with permission from the American Psychiatric Association, DSM-III-R, p. 11.

- *Displacement*—emotionally significant feelings are directed away from their real source or object toward some other object. For example, a claimant may become furious at the doctors or claim representative for not being more helpful, rather than at the person who caused the accident.
- *Fantasy*—daydreams and other fantasies can occupy the mind to the exclusion of anxious thoughts. Unlike other defense mechanisms, fantasies are often consciously controlled.
- *Identification*—adoption of the behavior, thoughts, and perceptions of another person who may be seen as better able to cope with anxiety.
- *Intellectualization*—the unconscious use of reasoning, logic, or attention to intellectual detail to avoid confronting feelings or any uncomfortable interpersonal situation.
- *Isolation*—being able to separate thoughts from feelings about an event or situation. Patients who employ this mechanism

110—Medical Aspects of Claims

can give highly detailed accounts of their accidents and injuries without evidence of any feelings on these matters.

- *Projection*—the attribution of one's own thoughts and feelings to another. For example, someone who has suffered a disfiguring injury might insist that his family members find him repulsive to look at.
- *Rationalization*—the creation of often incorrect explanations for anxiety-producing events or situations. Although reassuring, these explanations may further distort one's perception of reality.
- *Reaction formation*—the creation of the opposite feeling or behavior from that which is causing anxiety. For example, a disabled person might display great bravado about using an artificial limb when he is actually terrified.
- *Repression*—the forgetting of an unpleasant, anxiety-producing event or emotion. Repression of accidents is very common. Many victims of accidental injuries are completely unable to give an account of their accident, even though they were conscious throughout the incident.
- *Undoing*—behavior that symbolically makes amends for previous feelings or behavior. For example, in addition to the obvious financial motive, the filing of lawsuits and insurance claims for accidental injuries between spouses may be caused by this mechanism.

Depression. Depression is both a diagnosis (strictly speaking, major depressive disorder, dysthymia, or adjustment disorder with depressed mood are diagnoses) and a symptom. As a diagnosis, it is addressed in the following section of this chapter. As a symptom and in its mild form, it is as nearly universal a human experience as anxiety.

Mild forms of depression are described as sadness and grief. More serious and lasting forms of depression are described as a loss of pleasure and interest in life, and feelings of complete hopelessness, helplessness, and emptiness. Depression may be accompanied by weight loss or gain, change in appetite, insomnia or excessive sleepiness, decreased energy, psychomotor agitation or retardation, poor concentration, indecisiveness, feelings of worthlessness, and suicidal thoughts.[8]

Physical injury can readily cause symptoms of depression since it results in loss, loss of control, and helplessness. Frustration with recovery and the social isolation and insecurity accompanying injury can worsen symptoms of depression.

Because symptoms of depression are frequently not recognized by physicians, recovery from the physical injury and the depression can be delayed.

3 • Psychological Injuries and Conditions—111

Maladjustment to the Sick Role. The sick role is the set of behaviors and attitudes that a sick person has towards being sick and toward obtaining help from the medical professions. The prevailing beliefs about this role throughout society and the medical professions are (1) the sick person should be exempt from normal responsibilities; (2) the sick person cannot be expected to get well on his own; (3) the sick person will find being sick undesirable; and (4) the sick person will seek competent help to get better.[9]

Some sick individuals do not share the prevailing view of sickness and thus do not behave as expected. Some individuals have great difficulty relinquishing their daily responsibilities. They need to feel important, in control, powerful, competent, self-sufficient, or perfect and have great difficulty in acknowledging weakness, vulnerability, or need for help. Such individuals are likely to delay treatment as long as possible. While such individuals cause difficulty for the medical community, they are less likely to appear as claimants in insurance claims.

In contrast, other individuals may almost "enjoy" being sick. Such individuals may claim to want to get well, but actually thrive on the attention and freedom from daily responsibilities that the sick role affords them. Physicians tend to be uncritical of such patients because it does not occur to them that someone would not want to get well. With such individuals, the receipt of monetary compensation for being sick is a great incentive to prolong the sick role. Claim representatives should be alert to a history of job dissatisfaction or the presence of a personality disorder in claimants. Personality disorders are discussed in the next section of this chapter. Fortunately for claim representatives, most claimants are eager to get well.

Evaluation of Psychological Symptoms

Claim representatives are often unsure about how to handle ordinary psychological responses to physical injury. Should they ignore them? automatically pay for any treatment of them? resist payment for their treatment? No single answer fits all cases. The appropriateness of payment depends on several factors.

Causation in Fact. To be compensable, treatment of any kind must be for an injury or condition that was actually caused by the compensable accident. Although simple to state, this rule is difficult to apply in some cases. For example, while anxiety and depression may be normal responses to physical injury, a person who has suffered a physical injury may also be going through a divorce, may have elderly parents who are dying, and may have difficult teenage children. If this person is found to be anxious or depressed following a physical injury, should the insurer that is only responsible for the physical injury also be responsible for psychological treatment if the psychological response is created by factors unrelated to the injury?

Resolving such problems depends on complex factual medical issues that claim representatives are not competent to address. Yet, a claim representative may be the only one involved in a claim who asks critical questions about alternative causes. While physicians generally try to be conscientious in their observations and conclusions, they will often base their conclusions on information from the claimant that they have accepted at face value. Claim representatives should investigate alternative causes for claimants' symptoms

Focus of Treatment. Assuming that causation is established, there should be no problem in providing compensation for treatment of the ordinary psychological responses to physical injury. The symptoms are very real, and their treatment can generally be effective and appropriate. Nevertheless, if the symptoms are ordinary responses to physical injury, the focus of treatment should be on healing the physical injury. Under this assumption, recovery from physical injuries should simultaneously relieve the accompanying psychological problems.

If treatment focuses primarily or solely on the psychological problems, the claim representative must assume that (1) the claimant is being treated inappropriately or (2) the claimant suffers from a distinct psychological disorder, the cause of which cannot be assumed to be the accidental physical injury. The identification and description of distinct psychological disorders is the subject of the next section of this chapter.

General Damages. Treatment for psychological problems that are normal responses to physical injury should not be regarded as a separate injury in a liability claim. Such psychological problems are part of general damages, which are damages for all intangible losses such as pain and suffering. The ordinary psychological responses to physical injury are exactly what general damages are designed to compensate.

While treatment of the ordinary psychological responses to physical injury may be perfectly appropriate, such treatment does not increase the value of general damages in liability claims. Attorneys for claimants will argue that the fact of treatment provides strong proof of the existence of general damages and thus, the award for general damages should be higher. The appropriate response to this argument is that the existence of general damages is taken for granted. Further proof is unnecessary and does not increase the value of general damages. Indeed, it can be argued that treatment for psychological problems should make the value of general damages less, as the treatment should have relieved the problems.

DIAGNOSIS OF DISTINCT PSYCHOLOGICAL DISORDERS

In addition to the usual psychological responses to physical injury, claim representatives see psychological conditions that are independent problems. These psychological conditions may co-exist with or pre-exist a physical injury. They may also be independent of any physical injury. Their presence complicates the settlement of a claim involving accidental bodily injury. Many of these conditions interfere with obtaining and complying with appropriate medical care. Although these conditions are rarely, if ever, caused by accidental physical injury, their severity may be increased by the stress of a physical injury.

The identification, diagnosis, and description of psychological disorders is based on the *Diagnostic and Statistical Manual of Mental Disorders* (DSM) of the American Psychiatric Association. This section describes both how the DSM works and its major categories of disorders.

The Diagnostic and Statistical Manual of Mental Disorders

The American Psychiatric Association published its first *Diagnostic and Statistical Manual* in 1952 (DSM-I). The manual was revised in 1968 (DSM-II) and again in 1974 (DSM-III). In 1987, DSM-III-R was published as a bridge to DSM-IV, which is expected in 1992. The American Psychiatric Association is constantly refining its manual as research evidence and clinical experience changes.

The DSM provides descriptions of and diagnostic criteria for over two hundred mental disorders. The DSM neither explains the causes of mental disorders, nor does it prescribe types of treatment.

Status of the DSM. The DSM is recognized throughout the psychiatric and psychological professions as providing the standard language for discussion, research, teaching, and treatment of mental disorders. Whenever a psychiatrist or psychologist refers to a particular mental disorder, it is assumed and understood that he or she means the disorder as it is defined in the DSM. Any other usage would have to be explained and justified. Nevertheless, the DSM criteria are relatively recent. Those in the psychiatry and psychology professions use terminology that predates the DSM, which is still considered appropriate. For example, the term "neurosis" is as old as psychiatry itself, yet it has been eliminated from the DSM. Outside of the context of making diagnoses, psychiatrists and psychologists may use terminology in a way that is broader or less defined than the DSM criteria. Such usage is not a rejection of the DSM, but a continuation of professional practices

114—Medical Aspects of Claims

that predate the DSM. In making diagnoses, the DSM criteria should be used.

Any practitioner who asserts that he is not bound by the criteria of the DSM would have to explain himself. While there are possible scientific and philosophical objections to the DSM that are beyond the scope of this text, the DSM represents the consensus of professionals in the field. Testimony or reports from a practitioner who asserts that the DSM is irrelevant or optional would be subject to serious impeachment at a trial or hearing, if not excluded from evidence altogether. Claim representatives should not accept any report or bill from such a practitioner.

Mental Disorders. In order to decide what to include in the DSM, the American Psychiatric Association defined "mental disorder" as follows:

> In DSM-III-R each of the mental disorders is conceptualized as a clinically significant behavioral or psychological syndrome or pattern that occurs in a person and that is associated with present distress (a painful symptom) or disability (impairment in one or more important areas of functioning) or with a significantly increased risk of suffering death, pain, disability, or an important loss of freedom. In addition, this syndrome or pattern must not be merely an expectable response to a particular event, e.g., the death of a loved one. Whatever its original cause, it must currently be considered a manifestation of a behavioral, psychological, or biological dysfunction in the person. Neither deviant behavior, e.g., political, religious, or sexual, nor conflicts that are primarily between the individual and society are mental disorders unless the deviance or conflict is a symptom of a dysfunction in the person, as described above.[10]

This definition makes clear that mental disorders are not simply an isolated response to an incident, but a syndrome or pattern of behavior that is a manifestation of some psychological dysfunction. In addition, the mental disorders are not necessarily sharply distinguished from one another. Numerous disorders share many common symptoms or behaviors. While some diagnoses are mutually exclusive, most are not. Thus, a patient may be diagnosed with two or more disorders if all criteria are met.

Cautionary Statement. The introduction to DSM-III-R concludes with the following cautionary statement:

> The specified diagnostic criteria for each mental disorder are offered as guidelines for making diagnoses, since it has been demonstrated that the use of such criteria enhances agreement among clinicians and investigators. The proper use of these criteria requires specialized clinical training that provides both a body of knowledge and clinical skills.

3 • Psychological Injuries and Conditions—115

These diagnostic criteria and the DSM-III-R classification of mental disorders reflect a consensus of current formulations of evolving knowledge in our field but do not encompass all the conditions that may be legitimate objects of treatment or research efforts.

The purpose of DSM-III-R is to provide clear descriptions of diagnostic categories in order to enable clinicians and investigators to diagnose, communicate about, study, and treat the various mental disorders. It is to be understood that inclusion here, for clinical and research purposes, of a diagnostic category such as Pathological Gambling or Pedophilia does not imply that the condition meets legal or other nonmedical criteria for what constitutes mental disease, mental disorder, or mental disability. The clinical and scientific considerations involved in categorization of these conditions as mental disorders may not be wholly relevant to legal judgments, for example, that take into account such issues as individual responsibility, disability determination, and competency.[11]

This statement makes three important points:

1. The proper application and use of the diagnostic criteria requires clinical experience. Claim representatives or others who might use the DSM as a reference should never consider substituting their judgment for that of an experienced clinician.
2. The disorders identified in the DSM are not the only legitimate subjects of treatment. However, any clinician treating a disorder that is allegedly outside the DSM should explain why DSM criteria cannot be applied.
3. DSM criteria do not necessarily determine legal matters. For example, the criteria for insanity in a criminal matter are established by court cases. However, the fact that the DSM does not determine legal matters does not mean it is irrelevant to legal matters. The DSM establishes standards for practice in psychiatry and psychology and is essential to the resolution of factual medical issues that may arise in legal and claims matters.

Multi-Axial System. The DSM employs a multi-axial system for diagnosis. This means that several types of information are contained in a complete diagnosis. There are five "axes," and each "axis" contains a different type of information. Only the first two describe mental disorders:[12]

- Axis I—Clinical syndromes and V codes. This axis is used to identify most of the mental disorders set forth in the DSM. The V codes identify problems such as marital problems and uncomplicated bereavement that may be the subject of treatment, but are not considered mental disorders.
- Axis II—Developmental disorders and personality disorders.

116—Medical Aspects of Claims

These are special types of mental disorders that are given special emphasis. Personality disorders are discussed later in the chapter.

- Axis III—Physical conditions that are relevant to management of the case. This axis indicates the presence of any injuries or organic problems affecting the patient's mental health.

- Axis IV—Severity of psychosocial stressors. The codes in this axis represent the degree of external stress in a person's life as previously shown in Exhibit 3-1.

- Axis V—Global assessment of functioning. Included in this axis are numbers from 0 to 100 that reflect the clinician's judgment of the patient's overall functioning during the past week. The criteria used to select such numbers are set forth in Exhibit 3-2.

A complete multi-axial diagnosis might appear as shown in Exhibit 3-3.

Organization of Material. For each disorder, the DSM provides the following information when available:

General description. Each entry begins with a general description of the syndrome, including the most prominent symptoms and behaviors.

Associated features. These are features of a syndrome that are often, though not always, present.

Age at onset. Any characteristic pattern or the absence of a pattern is identified.

Course. The usual progression and resolution of symptoms, if any, is described.

Impairment. The usual occupational and social impairments that result from the disorder are identified.

Complications. Problems that may arise as a result of or in the course of the disorder are identified.

Predisposing factors. Characteristics of a person that may precede the disorder and make that person more vulnerable to the disorder are given.

Prevalence. The percentage of the population that at some time in their lives suffer from the disorder is noted.

Sex ratio. The frequency with which the disorder is diagnosed in men and women is identified.

Familial pattern. This is the frequency with which the disorder is found in close relatives versus the general population.

Exhibit 3-2
DSM Global Assessment of Functioning Scale (GAF Scale)

Consider psychological, social, and occupational functioning on a hypothetical continuum of mental health-illness. Do not include impairment in functioning due to physical (or environmental) limitations.

Note: Use intermediate codes when appropriate, e.g., 45, 68, 72.

Code

90–81 **Absent or minimal symptoms** (e.g., mild anxiety before an exam), **good functioning in all areas, interested and involved in a wide range of activities, socially effective, generally satisfied with life, no more than everyday problems or concerns** (e.g., an occasional argument with family members).

80–71 **If symptoms are present, they are transient and expectable reactions to psychosocial stressors** (e.g., difficulty concentrating after family argument); **no more than slight impairment in social, occupational, or school functioning** (e.g., temporarily falling behind in school work).

70–61 **Some mild symptoms** (e.g., depressed mood and mild insomnia) **OR some difficulty in social, occupational, or school functioning** (e.g., occasional truancy, or theft within the household), **but generally functioning pretty well, has some meaningful interpersonal relationships.**

60–51 **Moderate symptoms** (e.g., flat affect and circumstantial speech, occasional panic attacks) **OR moderate difficulty in social, occupational, or school functioning** (e.g., no friends, unable to keep a job).

50–41 **Serious symptoms** (e.g., suicidal ideation, severe obsessional rituals, frequent shoplifting) **OR any serious impairment in social, occupational, or school functioning** (e.g., no friends, unable to keep a job).

40–31 **Some impairment in reality testing or communication** (e.g., speech is at times illogical, obscure, or irrelevant) **OR major impairment in several areas, such as work or school, family relations, judgment, thinking, or mood** (e.g., depressed man avoids friends, neglects family, and is unable to work; child frequently beats up younger children, is defiant at home, and is failing at school).

30–21 **Behavior is considerably influenced by delusions or hallucinations OR serious impairment in communication or judgment** (e.g., sometimes incoherent, acts grossly inappropriately, suicidal preoccupation) **OR inability to function in almost all areas** (e.g., stays in bed all day; no job, home, or friends).

20–11 **Some danger of hurting self or others** (e.g., suicide attempts without clear expectation of death, frequently violent, manic excitement) **OR occasionally fails to maintain minimal personal hygiene** (e.g., smears feces) **OR gross impairment in communication** (e.g., largely incoherent or mute).

10–1 **Persistent danger of severely hurting self or others** (e.g., recurrent violence) **OR persistent inability to maintain minimal personal hygiene OR serious suicidal act with clear expectation of death.**

Reprinted with permission from the American Psychiatric Association, DSM-III-R, p. 12.

Exhibit 3-3
Example of How to Record a Multi-Axial Evaluation

Axis I: 296.23   Major Depression, Single Episode, Severe without Psychotic Features
             303.90   Alcohol Dependence
Axis II: 301.60   Dependent Personality Disorder (Provisional, rule out Borderline Personality Disorder)
Axis III: Alcoholic cirrhosis of liver
Axis IV: Psychosocial stressors: anticipated retirement and change in residence, with loss of contact with friends
             Severity: 4—Moderate (predominantly enduring circumstances)
Axis V: Current GAF: 44
            Highest GAF past year: 55

Reprinted with permission from the American Psychiatric Association, DSM-III-R, p. 21

Differential diagnosis. Disorders that should be distinguished from the disorder in question are identified. Differential diagnoses generally share many of the same symptoms and behaviors as the disorder in question.

Diagnostic criteria. These are the criteria that must be met for the diagnosis to be made. In many instances, a certain number of criteria from a longer list is sufficient to make the diagnosis.

Major Categories of Mental Disorders

The DSM categorizes mental disorders according to common symptoms or patterns of behavior. It is possible for a patient to display symptoms from more than one category of disorders. Within a given category of disorders, most of the diagnoses are exclusive of one another, so multiple diagnoses within a category are uncommon. Nevertheless, a diagnosis may change throughout the clinical course of an illness.

Organic Mental Syndromes and Disorders.[13] All organic mental disorders are characterized by a temporary or permanent disturbance of brain function. They can be caused by a specific illness or injury that has affected the brain, by a systemic illness that secondarily affects the brain, or by the introduction of a psychoactive substance or toxin. Otherwise, organic mental disorders are a diverse group of conditions with different courses and different effects on mental function and behavior.

Delirium. Delirium is an inability to focus on the outside world, or difficulty in appropriately shifting focus from internal to external reality. Speech is incoherent, an indication that the thought process is disturbed. Also common are disturbed sleep cycles; periods of semi-consciousness; hallucinations; disorientation in terms of time, place, or person; and impaired memory. Delirium usually develops quickly (within hours or less) and resolves quickly (a week, or less). Delirium is usually caused by infections, diseases, metabolic disorders, or brain injuries. The young and the old are more susceptible to delirium than are adults.[14]

Dementia. Dementia is characterized by loss of short-term and long-term memory to an extent such that social or occupational activities are impaired. Associated features may include impaired judgment and thought processes; language, motor, or sensory deficits; and personality changes. Even moderate dementia can make independent living impossible. Dementia usually affects the elderly, but can occur at any age. It can be caused by a number of factors: vascular disease; infections of the central nervous system; encephalitis; meningitis; AIDS; brain trauma; toxins; metabolic disturbances; or neurological diseases. Although dementia is usually progressive, it can be stable for long periods.[15]

Amnestic Syndrome. Amnestic syndrome is similar to dementia with respect to memory loss, but lacks the associated features (impaired judgment, cognitive deficits, personality changes) and does not necessarily cause social and occupational problems.[16]

Other Organic Syndromes. Several organic syndromes may occur during but not exclusively with delirium, and can be proven through history, physical exam, or laboratory tests that provide evidence of an organic causal factor. *Organic delusional syndrome* is characterized by prominent delusions, which may vary in nature but are frequently paranoid. *Organic hallucinosis* is characterized by prominent, persistent, or recurrent hallucinations. In *organic mood syndrome* and *organic anxiety syndrome* the symptoms and behaviors are similar to mood disorders and anxiety disorders (discussed subsequently), but the suspected cause is an organic factor. Similarly, the *organic personality syndrome* is a disorder with marked personality disturbances or changes that are believed to be organically caused.[17]

Organic Psychoactive Substance Disorders. These organic disorders are caused by numerous psychoactive substances. Among the disorders are intoxication, withdrawal, delirium, hallucinosis, amnestic disorder, dementia, delusional disorders, and mood disorders. The psychoactive substances include alcohol, amphetamines, caffeine, cannabis, cocaine, hallucinogens, inhalants, nicotine, opium, phencyclidine (PCP), and barbiturates. Not every substance is associated with all of the disorders. For example, caffeine is associated with an intoxication disorder only, and nicotine is associated with a withdrawal disorder only. Other than as associated with caffeine, intoxication is considered a mental disorder only when it results in "maladaptive behavioral changes." It follows that intoxication that does not bother the person or anyone else around him is not considered a mental disorder.

Dependence on and Abuse of Psychoactive Substances.[18] The use of psychoactive substances is not considered a mental disorder. However, dependency on or abuse of these substances that continues despite adverse consequences is recognized as a psychological problem.

Continued use alone is not considered dependence. Clinical *dependence* means that the user consumes increasing amounts of a substance over a longer period of time than he or she had intended; that the user wishes to but has not reduced, or has unsuccessfully tried to reduce usage; that an increasing amount of the user's time is devoted to obtaining and using the substance; that the user's social, occupational, or recreational activities are impaired as a result of use; that the user has developed a physical tolerance for the substance; that the user is experiencing a characteristic withdrawal from the substance; or that the user takes more of the substance to relieve withdrawal symptoms.[19]

Substance abuse is diagnosed whenever the user continues to consume the substance knowing that social, occupational, psychological, or physical problems will result; or when the user knows that use is physically hazardous when driving or operating machinery. Substance abuse may be diagnosed when not all of the criteria for dependence are present.[20]

Any psychoactive substance may become the object of dependence or abuse except for nicotine, which may only be the object of dependence, and caffeine, which may not be the object of either.

Schizophrenia.[21] Schizophrenia is one of the major psychotic disorders. Psychotic disorders are characterized by an inability to recognize or respond to external reality; instead, the patient creates and responds to a "separate" psychological (or internal) reality. The disorder may have an early phase and residual phases characterized by social isolation or withdrawal, impaired functioning, peculiar behavior, a lack of personal hygiene, a blunted or inappropriate affect, incoherent speech, odd or magical beliefs, unusual perceptions, or lack of initiative. During the course of the illness, the ability to perform social, occupational, and personal tasks becomes seriously impaired.

Schizophrenia is marked by such characteristic psychotic features as delusions (false beliefs) and hallucinations (inaccurate perceptions). Bizarre delusions, such as the belief that one's thoughts are being broadcast to the world, and auditory hallucinations are characteristic symptoms. Other symptoms include incoherent speech, dissociation, and a flat or grossly inappropriate affect. (Affect is the external manifestation of emotional "tone" or mood, usually as associated with a thought.) *Catatonic behavior*, also characteristic of schizophrenia, is a psychomotor disturbance such as excitement, posturing, rigidity, or stupor without an organic basis. In making a diagnosis during an acute psychotic episode, the clinician must be careful to distinguish schizophrenia from organic brain disorders and substance abuse problems. Schizophrenia is not diagnosed if symptoms have only been present for less than six months or if the predominant aspect of the problem is a mood disturbance. Mood disturbances with psychotic features are subsequently described.

Delusional Disorder.[22] This disorder is characterized by non-bizarre delusions not caused by any other mental disorder. A non-bizarre delusion is one in which the content is meaningful but has no basis in fact. For example, a non-bizarre delusion is a belief that one is loved by a famous movie star who has never been met. Other delusions might be that one has enormous unrecognized talents, that one has made a major discovery, that one's spouse or lover is unfaithful, or that one is suffering from a physical disorder. Paranoid delusions are common. Examples include feeling that one has been conspired against, spied upon, cheated, followed, poisoned, harassed, or obstructed.

Mood Disorders.[23] A *mood* is a pervasive and sustained emotion that in the extreme can affect one's perception of reality.[24] The manic-depressive (or bipolar) mood is a typical disorder. Both manic and depressive episodes are classified by their severity, the presence of psychotic features (delusions and hallucinations), and the affected person's extent of remission (full or partial). Neither the manic nor the depressive mood is diagnosed if the symptoms can be accounted for by organic mood disorders or schizophrenia.

Manic Episode.[25] A manic episode is characterized by unusually and persistently elevated, expansive, or irritable mood. When the mood is positive, it may seem cheerfully infectious to those who do not know the person. Yet manic episodes are genuine disorders that interfere with the person's occupational or social functioning and may even require hospitalization. Manic episodes may be accompanied by an inflated sense of self-esteem (even to the point of grandiose delusions), decreased need for sleep, loquaciousness, flights of ideas, distractibility, increased activity or agitation, and involvement in pleasurable but dangerous activities such as buying sprees, reckless sexual behavior, or foolish investments.

Depressive Episode.[26] Depression is characterized by persistent

122—Medical Aspects of Claims

and pervasive despair often manifested as a lack of interest in life. It may be accompanied by weight gain or loss, insomnia or hypersomnia, psychomotor retardation, fatigue and loss of energy (not resulting from any exertion), feelings of worthlessness or guilt, diminished ability to think or concentrate, and recurrent thoughts of suicide. A mood disturbance meeting some, but not all, of the symptoms of a depressive episode is diagnosed as *dysthymia*.

Anxiety Disorders. This category of disorders includes panic disorders, phobias, obsessions, compulsions, post-traumatic stress disorder, and generalized anxiety disorder. These disorders all include symptoms of anxiety or behaviors performed to relieve anxiety.

Panic Disorder. Panic disorders are characterized by a sudden onset of fear or insecurity that is unexpected and unrelated to any specific external stimulus. These attacks are characterized by shortness of breath or a smothering sensation, dizziness or faintness, heart palpitations, trembling, sweating, choking, nausea or abdominal distress, an alteration in the perception of one's self or external reality, numbness or tingling sensations, hot flashes or chills, chest pain or discomfort, or fears of dying, going crazy, or losing control.[27]

Agoraphobia. Panic disorders are frequently accompanied by agoraphobia, the fear of being in places from which escape might be difficult or embarrassing. As a result, the person avoids travel or leaving home, or can only do so with a companion. Intense anxiety typically accompanies the "journey." Agoraphobia is sometimes seen without a history of panic disorders.[28]

Social Phobia. Social phobia is a persistent fear of being scrutinized by others, the result being humiliation or embarrassment. This phobia may be manifested by an inability to speak or respond appropriately in social situations, fear of choking while eating, and hand- trembling. While some amount of social discomfort is probably a universal human experience, social phobias are different because they cause remarkable fear or avoidance behavior and can interfere with the person's social or occupational functioning. The victim of a social phobia recognizes that his or her fear is excessive.[29]

Phobias. Phobias are exaggerated responses to objects or situations. The object or situation causes remarkable distress and anxiety, is often avoided, and the victim recognizes that his or her reaction is excessive and unreasonable. The most common simple phobias are to dogs, snakes, insects, mice, blood or injury, closed spaces, heights, and air travel.[30]

Obsessive Compulsive Disorder. This disorder is characterized by obsessions and compulsions severe enough to interfere with daily life or to cause distress. *Obsessions* are persistent thoughts that are intrusive in the sense that they cause distress, are excessively time consuming, and interfere with social or occupational functioning. *Compulsions* are repetitive behaviors performed to relieve the anxiety caused by an obsession. Like obsessive thoughts, compulsive behavior interferes with the normal activities and functions of life. Common compulsive behaviors are hand washing, counting, checking, and touching.[31]

Dissociative Disorders. This category of disorders is characterized by a disturbance in one's sense of identity or memory not caused by organic mental disorders or schizophrenia.

Multiple Personality Disorder. This condition is characterized by the manifestation of two or more distinct personalities by one person. Only one personality is present at a given time. Each personality is a unique and relatively enduring pattern of perceiving, processing, and relating to external reality. Each personality may have its own unique set of memories, behaviors, and social relationships or may share certain memories, behaviors, and relationships. As many as ten or more personalities may coexist. The various personalities may or may not have some awareness of each other. This disorder is generally considered to be the result of severe abuse during childhood.[32]

Amnesia and Fugue. Following severe psychosocial stress, a person may develop *psychogenic amnesia*. This disorder is characterized by a sudden inability to recall important personal information to an extent far beyond ordinary forgetfulness. Such amnesia may be tied to a certain period of time, may be selective to certain events, or, less commonly, may be generalized to a person's entire life. Continuous amnesia includes the inability to remember events up to the present.[33] A psychogenic fugue is a condition in which a person suddenly assumes a new identity, life-style, and often moves to a new location. When the episode ends, the individual claims to have no memory of events that occurred during the episode.[34]

Depersonalization Disorder. Depersonalization is the experience of being detached from, outside of, or out of touch with one's body or mental processes. One may feel like an automaton or as if one is in a dream. It is thought that severe stress may predispose a person to depersonalization disorder. The condition is not caused by schizophrenia, mood disorders, organic mental disorders (especially intoxication and withdrawal), anxiety disorders, or epilepsy.[35]

Sexual Disorders. Sexual disorders include paraphilias (also known as sexual deviations) and sexual dysfunctions.

Paraphilias. Paraphilias are characterized by sexual arousal or

124—Medical Aspects of Claims

urges involving objects, suffering or humiliation of oneself or a partner, or children. Paraphiliacs may feel no distress about their behavior, or they may feel intense guilt and shame. Certain paraphiliac behavior can lead to arrest and incarceration, social alienation, and occupational failure.

Paraphilias include *exhibitionism*, exposing oneself to strangers; *fetishism*, sexual arousal caused by objects; *frotteurism*, the touching, rubbing, or fondling of a non-consenting stranger; *pedophilia*, sexual activity with a child; *masochism*, sexual arousal from being humiliated or made to suffer; *sadism*, sexual arousal from humiliating or inflicting suffering on one's partner; *transvestic fetishism*, dressing in women's clothing by a heterosexual male; and *voyeurism*, observing another who is naked, undressing, or engaged in sexual activity.[36]

Sexual Dysfunctions. Sexual dysfunctions include absent or inadequate sexual interest, inability to feel or sustain arousal, inability to engage in sexual relations, and inability to feel satisfaction from sexual relations. These problems can occur in men and women. None of these problems are regarded as dysfunctions unless they are persistent or recurrent.[37] Occasional sexual problems are common throughout the population and for all age groups.

Sleep Disorders. Sleep disorders include *dyssomnias* (disturbance in the amount, quality, or timing of sleep) and *parasomnias* (abnormal events occurring during sleep). A sleep problem is considered a disorder only if it occurs chronically for at least a month. Transient sleep disorders are common.

Dyssomnias. Dyssomnias may be diagnosed even when the cause is another mental or physical disorder. *Insomnia* is the inability to initiate or maintain sleep, or the failure of sleep to be properly restorative. *Hypersomnia* is a feeling of excessive sleepiness during the day, sleep attacks, or a prolonged transition period from sleep to full wakefulness (sleep drunkenness). *Sleep-wake schedule disorder* is a mismatch between the sleep-wake schedule demanded by a person's daily routine and that person's biological sleep-wake schedule. Sleep-wake schedule disorders can occur after flying through several time zones, or when working different shifts.[38]

Parasomnias. Parasomnias include *dream anxiety disorder*, repeated awakening and detailed nightmares from which the person rapidly becomes reoriented and alert; *sleep terror disorder*, recurrent disturbance of sleep by screams, intense anxiety, rapid heartbeat and breathing, and sweating from which the person only recovers after several minutes of confusion and agitation; and *sleepwalking disorder*, repeated episodes of leaving bed and wandering around with a blank and unresponsive demeanor, none of which is remembered upon waking.[39]

Impulse Control Disorders.[40] These disorders are problems of impulse control that are not elsewhere classified. They involve the performance of an act that is harmful to that person or to others. Such acts are preceded by increasing tension or urge to perform the act. The performance of the act is immediately gratifying, but may be followed by guilt and self-recrimination.

Among the impulse control disorders are *intermittent explosive disorder*, sudden loss of control accompanied by anger and aggression, resulting in assaults and harm to others; *kleptomania*, recurrent stealing of objects that are needed neither personally nor for their monetary value; *pathological gambling*, gambling behavior that compromises or disrupts the person's family or occupation; *pyromania*, setting fires for pleasure and gratification, not for financial gain, to conceal a crime, or out of anger; and *trichotillomania*, pulling out of one's hair for gratification not in response to skin disease or in response to a delusion or hallucination.

Personality Disorders

Personality refers to a person's enduring patterns of perceiving, processing, and relating to external reality and the perception of oneself. Personality traits that cause significant functional impairment or personal distress are maladaptive responses to reality. When these responses or behaviors become patterns or chronic, they are known as *personality disorders*.[41] Personality disorders are so significant that they are separately noted on Axis II of a standard psychological diagnosis.

Personality disorders develop over a lifetime of attempts to adapt to reality. Personality and personality disorders are substantially unchangeable by adulthood. A personality disordered individual may learn additional adaptive and masking behaviors by old age, but is never likely to be completely free of his or her disorder. Many of those with personality disorders do not see themselves as a problem. Instead, they see the world as the source of their problems. Others are distressed by their problems, but are incapable of changing.

This section explains the significance of personality disorders in claims handling, the difficulty in diagnosing personality disorders, and describes the essential characteristics of the various personality disorders.

The Significance of Personality Disorders. Because personality disorders develop over a lifetime, they cannot be attributed to a single accidental injury, the usual subject of insurance claims. Claim representatives should *never* accept a diagnosis of a personality disorder or its treatment as the result of an accidental injury. It is likely that the disorder existed before the injury. It has been estimated that approximately 6 to 10 percent of the general population could be diagnosed with a personality disorder.[42] It is therefore inevitable that personality disordered individuals will be in the population of claimants. Indeed, it is estimated that a much higher percentage of workers compensation claimants are personality disordered than is the general population. It is also estimated that among claimants with purely psychological injuries, the incidence of personality disorders may be approximately 50 percent.[43] These findings are not surprising in that personality disordered individuals tend to be inflexible, less able to cope with stress, and often tend to blame others for their problems.[44]

Those with personality disorders make difficult and dangerous claimants. The physical, emotional, financial, occupational, and legal stress of making an insurance claim and/or pursuing a lawsuit brings out the worst of these individuals. By definition, these individuals chronically display maladaptive behavior towards the external environment. Added stress causes even more pronounced maladaptive behavior.

Most personality disorders feature clinical symptoms that also appear in Axis I disorders. Neither claim representatives nor clinical professionals should confuse the exacerbation of a personality disorder with a separate Axis I disorder. The indicated treatment of and the legal compensability for personality disorders differ from the Axis I disorders. The treatment of personality disorders is often unsuccessful. Only with extended psychotherapy and then only with certain personality disorders is there likely to be any hope for change. As noted above, personality disorders are not legally compensable since they are not caused by accidental injuries. Therefore, the existence of a personality disorder and its role must be established in every case. The failure to note the presence of a personality disorder constitutes an inadequate diagnosis. An inadequate diagnosis cannot serve as a basis for treatment. Claim representatives should not pay for a course of treatment based on such a diagnosis.

Diagnosis of Personality Disorders. Personality disorders are diagnosed only when the person in question shows a pervasive pattern of a certain behavior as well as numerous characteristics of the prototype. Many people show some characteristics of a prototypical personality disorder, but would not be diagnosed with the disorder because they do not share enough of the characteristics or their behavior is not pervasive enough for the diagnosis. Personality disorders are among the most difficult of mental disorders to diagnose; even when a personality disorder is diagnosed, that diagnosis is among the most unreliable of the various mental disorders.[45]

Because they represent a lifetime of maladaptive behavior, personality disorders can only be properly identified with a thorough and accurate history. Such histories are often unavailable. The person in question may be unwilling or unable to cooperate in giving a history. Records from school, military service, and work can be helpful and should be investigated in any claim involving a substantial psychological injury.

Because personality disorders share many symptoms with Axis I disorders, a differential diagnosis can often only be made by a clinician who obtains a careful and accurate account of the course and patterns of symptoms. If the clinician fails to do so, the claim is open to criticism.

Paranoid Personality Disorder. People with paranoid personality disorder chronically interpret the actions of others as deliberately demeaning or threatening. They expect to be exploited and harmed, and continually question, without justification, the loyalty of friends, associates, spouse, or lover. They distort the meaning of innocent remarks and events, are easily slighted or enraged, and bear grudges. They characteristically engage in projection as a defense mechanism. People with paranoid personality disorder appear cold and serious. They are very apt to begin litigation.[46]

Schizoid Personality Disorder. Schizoid personality disorder is characterized by a pervasive pattern of restricted emotions and expressions and indifference to social relationships. The schizoid person has few, if any, close relationships and lacks any desire for close friends or sexual relations. This sort of person seems aloof and indifferent and will choose solitary activities. The affect of someone with a schizoid disorder may seem like that of someone with a paranoid disorder, but the schizoid disorder does not include paranoid thoughts.[47]

Schizotypal Personality Disorder. The schizotypal personality disorder is characterized by a pervasive pattern of peculiar ideas, behavior, and appearance not severe enough to be diagnosed as schizophrenia. However, the oddities of belief and perception characteristic of schizophrenics are also characteristic of the schizotypal disorder, such as a belief in magical influences or that objects in the environment have a special meaning. The person with schizotypal disorder is likely to have inappropriate affect, great social anxiety, and few friends. Such individuals may also meet the criteria for borderline personality disorder (discussed below).[48]

Antisocial Personality Disorder. The antisocial personality disorder is characterized by a pattern of socially irresponsible, truant, cruel, and often deviant behavior for which the person generally feels no remorse. The diagnostic criteria for this disorder are shown in Exhibit 3-4. This disorder is especially noteworthy in claims as an indicator of malingering. The presence of an antisocial personality disorder plus the legal context of a claim are two indicators of malingering.[49] The presence of this disorder is usually fairly easy to spot from the patterns of personal, occupational, and legal problems in the person's life.

Borderline Personality Disorder.[50] This disorder is characterized by a pervasive pattern of instability of self-image, mood, and interpersonal relations. Identity problems may be related to issues of career choice, long-term goals, sexual orientation, types of friends, or values. Relationships tend to be unstable and intense as the person exhibits mood swings, inappropriate anger, chronic feelings of emptiness, and impulsiveness. The person may threaten suicide and engage in self-mutilation.

Histrionic Personality Disorder. This disorder is characterized by a pervasive pattern of excessive emotionality and attention-seeking behavior. This person insists on being the center of attention; is constantly seeking praise, admiration, and approval; and expresses emotions with great exaggeration. This person is likely to be preoccupied with physical attractiveness and will be inappropriately seductive.[51]

Narcissistic Personality Disorder. This disorder is characterized by simultaneous feelings of grandiosity and hypersensitivity; there is also a lack of empathy. The affected person believes he or she is special and feels entitled to the attentions of, and special treatment from, others. Narcissistic individuals also exploit other people and are preoccupied with fantasies of unlimited success, power, brilliance, and beauty; yet they also envy others. They are typically less dramatic than the histrionic personalities, are better integrated than the borderline personality, and are not as irresponsible as individuals with the antisocial personality; yet each of these disorders can coexist with narcissism.[52]

Avoidant Personality Disorder. This disorder is characterized by a pervasive pattern of fear of rejection, social discomfort, and shyness. A person with this disorder is easily hurt by criticism and devastated by social slights. As a result, the individual withdraws from social situations and occupations requiring social skills. This disorder is different from the schizoid personality disorder in that the avoidant individual wants affection and acceptance, but is incapable of seeking it.[53]

Dependent Personality Disorder. This disorder is characterized by submissive behavior and reliance on others for almost everything. Affected persons allow others to make important decisions for them and are unable to perform ordinary tasks without reassurance and encouragement. These people usually cannot initiate tasks, but agree to perform unpleasant tasks to get others to like them. They dislike being alone and have an exaggerated fear of abandonment.[54]

Obsessive Compulsive Personality Disorder. This disorder is characterized by perfectionism and inflexibility, but not necessarily by the more obvious obsessions and compulsions of the obsessive compulsive disorder discussed earlier. A person with an obsessive compulsive personality disorder is preoccupied by details and procedures and rigidly expects things to be done "his or her way." He or she is devoted to work to the exclusion of leisure, yet an excessive focus on details and procedures interferes with task completion. This sort of person appears stiff and rigid, is usually stingy with gifts or compliments, and is overly scrupulous about matters of morality.[55]

Passive Aggressive Personality Disorder. The passive aggressive personality disorder is characterized by anger that is expressed indirectly by resisting expected social and occupational performance. For instance, instead of saying, "I am angry with you," or "I am unhappy about this," the passive aggressive individual will express dissatisfaction by sulking, dawdling, forgetting, or by being intentionally incompetent. The person with this disorder believes that the demands on him or her are unreasonable and that his or her performance is better than others judge it to be. He or she resents suggestions and refuses to do his or her share of a task.[56]

PROBLEM PSYCHOLOGICAL CONDITIONS IN CLAIMS

For the psychologically disturbed person, the condition is always a problem. This section addresses psychological conditions that present problems in claims handling. The conditions here described are especially likely to appear in cases of accidental physical injury and may complicate the recovery in such cases.

Stress disorders may result from an accidental injury, may precede an accidental injury, or may be the only subject of a claim. In the past, legal standards for the successful prosecution of stress claims were so stringent that many cases that were medically valid went uncompensated. These legal standards have been relaxed. Claim representatives must now be able to address the medical merits of stress claims.

Exhibit 3-4
Diagnostic Criteria for 301.70 Antisocial Personality Disorder

A. Current age at least 18.
B. Evidence of Conduct Disorder with onset before age 15, as indicated by a history of *three* or more of the following:
   (1) was often truant
   (2) ran away from home overnight at least twice while living in parental or parental surrogate home (or once without returning)
   (3) often initiated physical fights
   (4) used a weapon in more than one fight
   (5) forced someone into sexual activity with him or her
   (6) was physically cruel to animals
   (7) was physically cruel to other people
   (8) deliberately destroyed others' property (other than by fire-setting)
   (9) deliberately engaged in fire-setting
   (10) often lied (other than to avoid physical or sexual abuse)
   (11) has stolen without confrontation of a victim on more than one occasion (including forgery)
   (12) has stolen with confrontation of a victim (e.g., mugging, purse-snatching, extortion, armed robbery)
C. A pattern of irresponsible and antisocial behavior since the age of 15, as indicated by at least *four* of the following:
   (1) is unable to sustain consistent work behavior, as indicated by any of the following (including similar behavior in academic settings if the person is a student):
      (a) Significant unemployment for six months or more within five years when expected to work and work was available
      (b) repeated absences from work unexplained by illness in self or family
      (c) abandonment of several jobs without realistic plans for others
   (2) fails to conform to social norms with respect to lawful behavior, as indicated by repeatedly performing antisocial acts that are grounds for arrest (whether arrested or not), e.g., destroying property, harassing others, stealing, pursuing an illegal occupation
   (3) is irritable and aggressive, as indicated by repeated physical fights or assaults (not required by one's job or to defend someone or oneself), including spouse- or child-beating
   (4) repeatedly fails to honor financial obligations, as indicated by defaulting on debts or failing to provide child support or support for other dependents on a regular basis
   (5) fails to plan ahead, or is impulsive, as indicated by one or both of the following:
      (a) traveling from place to place without a prearranged job or clear goal for the period of travel or clear idea about when the travel will terminate
      (b) lack of a fixed address for a month or more
   (6) has no regard for the truth, as indicated by repeated lying, use of aliases, or "conning" others for personal profit or pleasure

(7) is reckless regarding his or her own or others' personal safety, as indicated by driving while intoxicated, or recurrent speeding
(8) if a parent or guardian, lacks ability to function as a responsible parent, as indicated by one or more of the following:
   (a) malnutrition of child
   (b) child's illness resulting from lack of minimal hygiene
   (c) failure to obtain medical care for a seriously ill child
   (d) child's dependence on neighbors or nonresident relatives for food or shelter
   (e) failure to arrange for a caretaker for young child when parent is away from home
   (f) repeated squandering, on personal items, of money required for household necessities
(9) has never sustained a totally monogamous relationship for more than one year
(10) lacks remorse (feels justified in having hurt, mistreated, or stolen from another)

D. Occurrence of antisocial behavior not exclusively during the course of Schizophrenia or Manic Episodes.

Reprinted with permission from the American Psychiatric Association, DSM-III-R, pp. 344-346.

Somatoform disorders are characterized by physical symptoms for which there is no organic evidence. Because the alleged physical symptoms are not consciously controlled, they are not regarded as indications of malingering or factitious disorder, labels given by the medical community to behaviors in which the claimant intentionally creates symptoms. The legal and claims community calls this behavior fraud. Stress disorders, somatoform disorders, and intentionally created symptoms are discussed in the sections that follow.

Stress Disorders

Although there may be "stress claims," "stress" is not a medical diagnosis. Circumstances that feel stressful create psychophysiological responses. These responses may initiate, prolong, or worsen a physical ailment or may create separate psychological disorders.

Stress may aggravate existing psychological disorders, especially personality disorders. However, this is very different from causing such disorders as evidenced by the fact that with the removal of stress, the disorder may be mitigated, but it does not disappear. Claim representatives should not accept a clinician's report that an accident caused a psychological disorder unless the clinician has ruled out the possibility of a preexisting problem.

A claim representative is most likely to see diagnoses based on stress for post-traumatic stress disorder, generalized anxiety disorder, and adjustment disorder.

Post-Traumatic Stress Disorder. This disorder may follow a stress that is so severe as to be beyond usual human experience. The disorder is characterized by persistent reexperiencing of the event, persistent avoidance of anything associated with the event or a general numbing of responsiveness, and persistent symptoms of arousal.

The DSM acknowledges that "the classification of post-traumatic stress disorder is controversial since the predominant symptom is the reexperiencing of a trauma, not anxiety or avoidance behavior." The DSM further notes, "However, anxiety symptoms and avoidance behavior are extremely common, and symptoms of increased arousal are invariably present."[57] Such arousal would be indicated by irritability, difficulty in sleeping and concentrating, hypervigilance, and an exaggerated startle response. Given that the American Psychiatric Association regards the diagnosis as somewhat controversial, claim representatives should not accept a diagnosis of post-traumatic stress disorder unless all criteria of the disorder have been clearly established.

The event that causes post-traumatic stress disorder must be one that is "outside the range of usual human experience and that would be markedly distressing to almost anyone."[58] Some of the examples given are rape, military combat, floods, earthquakes, airplane crashes, bombings, torture, and death camps. The DSM acknowledges that "car accidents with serious physical injury" may be a cause, but notes that such a cause is likely to "produce it only occasionally."[59] Thus, the usual accidents and injuries that are the subjects of insurance claims are not normally considered "stressful enough" to cause post-traumatic stress disorder. Any allegation that an ordinary accident caused post-traumatic stress disorder would require a great deal of explanation.

Reexperiencing the traumatic event through flashbacks, dreams, or feelings that the event was recurring is essential to a diagnosis of post-traumatic stress disorder. The reexperiencing must be persistent.

The criteria for a diagnosis of post-traumatic stress disorder are shown in Exhibit 3-5. Notice that the required symptoms must persist for more than a month.

Generalized Anxiety Disorder. This disorder is characterized by unrealistic and excessive anxiety manifested by a variety of physical and behavioral symptoms. The criteria for this disorder are shown in Exhibit 3-6.

Notice that anxiety that is realistic and appropriate because it is based on an actual situation is *not* indicative of this disorder. The clinician must carefully assess what anxiety is realistic and appropriate and what is unrealistic and excessive. A claim representative should respect the skill of an experienced clinician who has thoughtfully considered the matter. However, a claim representative need not accept a diagnosis that is implausible because it fails to explain how or

Exhibit 3-5
Diagnostic Criteria for 309.89 Post-traumatic Stress Disorder

---

A. The person has experienced an event that is outside the range of usual human experience and that would be markedly distressing to almost anyone, e.g., serious threat to one's life or physical integrity; serious threat or harm to one's children, spouse, or other close relatives and friends; sudden destruction of one's home or community; or seeing another person who has recently been, or is being, seriously injured or killed as the result of an accident or physical violence.
B. The traumatic event is persistently reexperienced in at least one of the following ways:
   (1) recurrent and intrusive distressing recollections of the event (in young children, repetitive play in which themes or aspects of the trauma are expressed)
   (2) recurrent distressing dreams of the event
   (3) sudden acting or feeling as if the traumatic event were recurring (includes a sense of reliving the experience, illusions, hallucinations, and dissociative [flashback] episodes, even those that occur upon awakening or when intoxicated)
   (4) intense psychological distress at exposure to events that symbolize or resemble an aspect of the traumatic event, including anniversaries of the trauma
C. Persistent avoidance of stimuli associated with the trauma or numbing of general responsiveness (not present before the trauma), as indicated by at least three of the following:
   (1) efforts to avoid thoughts or feelings associated with the trauma
   (2) efforts to avoid activities or situations that arouse recollections of the trauma
   (3) inability to recall an important aspect of the trauma (psychogenic amnesia)
   (4) markedly diminished interest in significant activities (in young children, loss of recently acquired developmental skills such as toilet training or language skills)
   (5) feeling of detachment or estrangement from others
   (6) restricted range of affect, e.g., unable to have loving feelings
   (7) sense of a foreshortened future, e.g., does not expect to have a career, marriage, or children, or a long life
D. Persistent symptoms of increased arousal (not present before the trauma), as indicated by at least two of the following:
   (1) difficulty falling or staying asleep
   (2) irritability or outbursts of anger
   (3) difficulty concentrating
   (4) hypervigilance
   (5) exaggerated startle response
   (6) physiologic reactivity upon exposure to events that symbolize or resemble an aspect of the traumatic event (e.g., a woman who was raped in an elevator breaks out in a sweat when entering any elevator)
E. Duration of the disturbance (symptoms in B, C, and D) of at least one month.

Specify delayed onset if the onset of symptoms was at least six months after the trauma.

Reprinted with permission from the American Psychiatric Association, DSM-III-R, pp. 250-251.

Exhibit 3-6
Diagnostic Criteria for 300.02 Generalized Anxiety Disorder

A. Unrealistic or excessive anxiety and worry (apprehensive expectation) about two or more life circumstances, e.g., worry about possible misfortune to one's child (who is in no danger) and worry about finances (for no good reason), for a period of six months or longer, during which the person has been bothered more days than not by these concerns. In children and adolescents, this may take the form of anxiety and worry about academic, athletic, and social performance.

B. If another Axis I disorder is present, the focus of the anxiety and worry in A is unrelated to it, e.g., the anxiety or worry is not about having a panic attack (as in Panic Disorder), being embarrassed in public (as in Social Phobia), being contaminated (as in Obsessive Compulsive Disorder), or gaining weight (as in Anorexia Nervosa).

C. The disturbance does not occur only during the course of a Mood Disorder or a psychotic disorder.

D. At least 6 of the following 18 symptoms are often present when anxious (do not include symptoms present only during panic attacks).

Motor tension
(1) trembling, twitching, or feeling shake
(2) muscle tension, aches, or soreness
(3) restlessness
(4) easy fatigability

Autonomic hyperactivity
(5) shortness of breath or smothering sensations
(6) palpitations or accelerated heart rate (tachycardia)
(7) sweating, or cold clammy hands
(8) dry mouth
(9) dizziness or light-headedness
(10) nausea, diarrhea, or other abdominal distress
(11) flushes (hot flashes) or chills
(12) frequent urination
(13) trouble swallowing or "lump in throat"

Vigilance and scanning
(14) feeling keyed up or on edge
(15) exaggerated startle response
(16) difficulty concentrating or "mind going blank" because of anxiety
(17) trouble falling or staying asleep
(18) irritability

E. It cannot be established that an organic factor initiated and maintained the disturbance, e.g., hyperthyroidism, Caffeine intoxication.

Reprinted with permission from the American Psychiatric Association, DSM-III-R, pp. 252-253.

why a patient's anxiety is judged to be unrealistic and excessive or that does not identify physical symptoms required to support the diagnosis. In addition, it should be noted that this diagnosis is only made when the anxiety focuses on *two or more* circumstances and when most other possible causes of the symptoms have been ruled out. The claim representative should obtain an explanation of why other causes have been ruled out.

Adjustment Disorder. This disorder is a maladaptive reaction to stress. Maladaptive means that the reaction impairs occupational, academic, or social functioning or that it is judged to be "in excess of a normal and expectable reaction." This disorder can be difficult to diagnose. The critical psychologist will be careful to apply the criteria from the DSM in making a diagnosis. Exhibit 3-7 shows the criteria for this disorder.

Notice that this disorder can only be diagnosed when the disturbance does not meet the criteria for any other mental disorder and is not an exacerbation of an existing mental disorder. Thus, the diagnosing clinician must go through an exhaustive process of elimination before settling on a diagnosis of adjustment disorder. The exacerbation of a preexisting personality disorder does not qualify as adjustment disorder.

When adjustment disorder is diagnosed, it should be identified by its predominant symptoms. The DSM specifies the following possibilities: anxious mood, depressed mood, disturbance of conduct, mixed disturbance of emotions and conduct, mixed emotional features, physical complaints, withdrawal, work or academic inhibition, or symptoms not otherwise specified.

Somatoform Disorders

Somatoform disorders are characterized by the presence of physical symptoms suggesting a physiological disorder for which there is no organic basis. In the absence of physiological evidence and because of usually strong evidence of a psychological cause, these disorders are considered mental disorders. Unlike malingering or factitious disorders, somatoform disorder symptoms are not consciously created.

Somatoform disorders are generally not of delusional intensity. For instance, the person is not likely to believe that his or her symptoms are caused by a spirit or a hex. On the contrary, the person is likely to consider that the problem may be psychological in origin.

People with somatoform disorders do not usually initially consult a psychologist or psychiatrist. They typically go to one or more physicians who treat physical disorders. Because such physicians may not immediately think of somatoform disorders, or because they are reluctant to suggest that the illness is psychologically created, claim representatives who suspect a somatoform disorder should specifically request the doctor to address the possibility before diagnosing a physical disorder. The following are some somatoform disorders.

Exhibit 3-7
Diagnostic Criteria for Adjustment Disorder

A. A reaction to an identifiable psychosocial stressor (or multiple stressors) that occurs within three months of onset of the stressor(s).
B. The maladaptive nature of the reaction is indicated by either of the following:
   (1) impairment in occupational (including school) functioning or in usual social activities or relationships with others
   (2) symptoms that are in excess of a normal and expectable reaction to the stressor(s)
C. The disturbance is not merely one instance of a pattern of overreaction to stress or an exacerbation of one of the mental disorders previously described.
D. The maladaptive reaction has persisted for no longer than six months.
E. The disturbance does not meet the criteria for any specific mental disorder and does not represent Uncomplicated Bereavement.

Reprinted with permission from the American Psychiatric Association, DSM-III-R, p. 330.

Body Dysmorphic Disorder. This disorder involves a preoccupation with an imaginary defect in the body or a grossly excessive concern about a minor defect. The defect is often alleged to be facial, but may be some other part of the body. While most people see their minor flaws as more serious than does the world around them, those with body dysmorphic disorder have a *grossly excessive* concern.[60]

Conversion Disorder. This disorder is comparatively rare. It involves the loss of use or alteration in function of a part of the body. Conversion disorder usually follows an extraordinary stress such as military combat or witnessing a hideous murder. The "impairment" may affect the limbs, eyesight, hearing, sensation, coordination, or any other function. Previous exposure to the physical problem or seeing another exposed to a problem may predispose a person to conversion disorder, as is often the case in histrionic and dependent personality disorders. Conversion disorder is not diagnosed if the symptoms are due to schizophrenia or to somatization disorder.[61]

Hypochondriasis. This disorder is characterized by preoccupation with the fear of, or belief that one has, a serious illness. This fear or belief persists despite an absence of physical evidence and despite medical reassurance to the contrary.[62]

Somatization Disorder. This disorder is characterized by multiple complaints over several years' time for which the person has sought medical attention. The reported symptoms are often vague, complicated, or dramatic and almost always include gastrointestinal problems, pain, cardiopulmonary symptoms, loss of function of a body part, or sexual complaints. This disorder is usually chronic, with symptoms appearing and disappearing. Doctor shopping, anxiety, and depression are often associated with this disorder. Exhibit 3-8 shows the diagnostic criteria for this disorder.

This disorder is almost never found in men and was formally called hysteria. However, *undifferentiated somatoform disorder* is a less developed form of the same problem and is found equally in men and women. Undifferentiated somatoform disorder is diagnosed when the person has some, but not all, of the symptoms of somatization disorder.[63]

Somatoform Pain Disorder. When the dominant presenting complaint is pain, the disorder is diagnosed as *somatoform pain disorder*. This disorder frequently follows an actual physical injury but is diagnosed as a psychological condition because the symptoms follow no known organic pattern, and all other tests are negative. The affected person usually becomes disabled and risks narcotic dependence and unnecessary surgeries. Previous conversion behavior in those with this disorder is not unusual.[64]

Intentionally Created Symptoms

Symptoms of both physical and mental disorders are sometimes fabricated by people who wish to be treated as sick. The different motives for such behavior distinguish between those who suffer from factitious disorder and those who are malingering. In both conditions, the person consciously controls the symptoms.

Factitious Disorder.[65] A person suffering from factitious disorder has a psychological need to assume the sick role. Although the symptoms may be voluntarily created, the motivation to do so is typically rooted in some unconscious need to be sick.

It is thought that a history of true illnesses during childhood or adolescence may predispose a person toward this disorder, as might significant contact with the medical community through employment or a personal relationship with a physician. Substance abuse, especially with analgesics and sedatives, is common, as is a history of abdominal surgeries.

People with factitious disorder often doctor shop from one community to the next as their behavior is discovered. They present their symptoms dramatically, but are vague and inconsistent about details.

A factitious psychological illness is quite difficult to diagnose. A clinician must eliminate all other possibilities, but should note the presence of uneven cooperation from the client. A factitious disorder must often be inferred from the fact that the collection of symptoms reported by the person is clinically meaningless.

138—Medical Aspects of Claims

Exhibit 3-8

Diagnostic Criteria for Somatization Disorder

A. A history of many physical complaints or a belief that one is sickly, beginning before the age of 30 and persisting for several years.
B. At least 13 symptoms from the list below. To count a symptom as significant, the following criteria must be met:
   (1) no organic pathology or pathophysiologic mechanism (e.g., a physical disorder or the effects of injury, medication, drugs, or alcohol) to account for the symptom or, when there is related organic pathology, the complaint or resulting social or occupational impairment is grossly in excess of what would be expected from the physical findings
   (2) has not occurred only during a panic attack
   (3) has caused the person to take medicine (other than over-the-counter pain medication), see a doctor, or alter life-style

Symptom list:

Gastrointestinal symptoms:
   (1) **vomiting (other than during pregnancy)**
   (2) abdominal pain (other than when menstruating)
   (3) nausea (other than motion sickness)
   (4) bloating (gassy)
   (5) diarrhea
   (6) intolerance of (gets sick from) several different foods

Pain symptoms:
   (7) **pain in extremities**
   (8) back pain
   (9) joint pain
   (10) pain during urination
   (11) other pain (excluding headaches)

Cardiopulmonary symptoms:
   (12) **shortness of breath when not exerting oneself**
   (13) palpitations
   (14) chest pain
   (15) dizziness

Conversion of pseudoneurologic symptoms:
   (16) **amnesia**
   (17) **difficulty swallowing**
   (18) loss of voice
   (19) deafness
   (20 double vision
   (21) blurred vision
   (22) blindness
   (23) fainting or loss of consciousness
   (24) seizure or convulsion
   (25) trouble walking
   (26) paralysis or muscle weakness
   (27) urinary retention or difficulty urinating

3 • Psychological Injuries and Conditions—139

Sexual symptoms for the major part of the person's life after opportunities for sexual activity:

(28) **burning sensation in sexual organs or rectum (other than during intercourse)**
(29) sexual indifference
(30) pain during intercourse
(31) impotence

Female reproductive symptoms judged by the person to occur more frequently or severely than in most women:

(32) **painful menstruation**
(33) irregular menstrual periods
(34) excessive menstrual bleeding
(35) vomiting throughout pregnancy

Note: The seven items in boldface may be used to screen for the disorder. The presence of two or more of these items suggests a high likelihood of the disorder.

Reprinted with permission from the American Psychiatric Association, DSM-III-R, pp. 263-264.

Malingering. Malingering differs from factitious disorder in that the motive for creating the symptoms is external, such as impending military service or a criminal trial. The circumstances of insurance claims always present an incentive that might be the cause of malingering. However, the fact that a claimant has symptoms for which there is no organic basis does not necessarily mean that person is malingering. There may be a somatoform or factitious disorder.

The DSM advises that malingering should be strongly suspected if any combination of the following are present:

1. Medicolegal context
2. Marked discrepancy between the person's claims and the objective findings
3. Lack of cooperation during evaluation or treatment
4. Antisocial personality disorder[66]

Insurance claims in which there is no objective evidence of injury automatically meet two of these criteria. However, a claimant should never be accused of malingering unless there is definite evidence that symptoms are voluntarily produced. Such evidence would include surveillance films or eyewitnesses' testimony showing the claimant behaving in ways that would be incompatible with his alleged disorder.

When alert to the possibility of malingering, physicians can usually detect it. Malingering patients do not know as much about disorders as physicians and will tend to overstate or misstate the symptom pattern they are trying to mimic. Most physicians agree that the following six clinical criteria are most useful for detecting malingering:[67]

- Weakness to manual testing not seen in other activities
- Disablement disproportionate to objective findings
- Pain does not follow an organic pattern
- Endorsing suggestions of false symptoms
- Cogwheel weakness (diffuse weakness)
- Overreaction during examination

Malingering of psychological symptoms can usually be detected through clinical assessment and psychological testing. The Minnesota Multiphasic Personality Inventory, the Rorschach Inkblot Test, and the Bender-Gestalt tests are regarded as helpful for this purpose.[68] Malingered intellectual deficits are fairly easy to detect since the person is rarely able to present a consistent and meaningful pattern of intellectual deficit.

EVALUATION OF CLAIMS FOR PSYCHOLOGICAL CONDITIONS

Claim representatives must be able to evaluate claims for psychological conditions. Such claims may result from or accompany physical injuries, or they may be for a purely psychological condition. The evaluation should include a review of three fundamental questions. First, is there a diagnosable psychological disorder? A correct diagnosis is a crucial step in determining causation and treatment. Second, what caused the disorder? The issue of cause is crucial in determining legal liability or compensability under various insurance policies. Finally, what is the appropriate treatment? The fact that a disorder is genuine and was caused by an insured event does not mean that any and all types and amounts of treatment must be uncritically accepted. The issues raised by these questions are discussed below.

Existence of a Psychological Disorder

The first step in the evaluation of any claim for psychological injury or condition is to determine the presence of a diagnosable psychological disorder. Claim representatives cannot diagnose patients or disorders, but they can review a clinician's report to determine how thoroughly and carefully the diagnosis was made.

A good diagnosis should conform to the standards of the DSM. A report explaining a diagnosis should describe all symptoms of the disorder as specified by the DSM and explain how all relevant differential diagnoses have been made. Unless all characteristic symptoms have been identified and all relevant differential diagnoses have been made, a diagnosis cannot be accepted as accurate.

A correct diagnosis is a prerequisite to proper care and should be required by claim representatives before any psychological condition is accepted as compensable. A correct diagnosis prevents improper treatment of symptoms and controls therapist bias. A number of psychological tests can be used to assess a patient and to supplement clinical observation. However, testing can be inaccurate or invalid for a number of reasons. Finally, it must be understood that the diagnosis of an identifiable disorder does not automatically mean the person is disabled.

Treatment of Symptoms. Clinicians should treat disorders, not symptoms. A disorder is one of the conditions documented in the DSM. Unless a disorder has been properly identified, the clinician can only respond to symptoms. Treatment would therefore be inappropriate because a given symptom may be characteristic of a number of disorders, each of which is treated in a different way. For instance, the DSM lists twenty-one disorders with depressed mood as a characteristic, twenty-one disorders with fatigue as a characteristic, and thirty-four disorders with some impairment in occupational functioning as a characteristic. In addition, a symptom such as irritability is frequently attributed to psychological causes, yet it can be caused by any of at least twenty-one medical conditions or any of at least twenty-six medications.[69]

Therapist Bias. The claim representative must consider therapist bias because it can influence the validity and compensability of a claim. Therapist bias is the failure of the therapist to be adequately critical of a patient's statements. That is, the therapist fails to be objective about or to appropriately analyze a patient's statements and behavior, thereby drawing inappropriate conclusions about the patient's state of mind as it relates to a given accident or injury. For instance, if a patient tells a therapist that he or she has been anxious since an automobile accident or if the patient exhibits symptoms of anxiety, the therapist should not assume that the auto accident caused this state of mind.

Therapist bias usually develops out of the therapist's attempt to create an atmosphere of trust. Since trust is essential to successful therapy, the therapist must be able to establish trust by acknowledging the patient's statements while realizing that the patient may be disguising an issue (or his or her feelings), falsifying an issue, avoiding an issue, or acting and speaking in such a way that is clinically significant, but not necessarily "true" in the sense that the words or behavior do not represent reality. A good therapist will distinguish between what is "true" for the patient and what is true in reality.

Careful use of DSM criteria can help a therapist to avoid bias. A therapist who conscientiously applies the DSM criteria must carefully address whether each required characteristic or behavior is present

142—Medical Aspects of Claims

and must rule out every relevant differential diagnosis. Inconsistencies in the patient's statements, behavior, demonstrated moods, and test results would be apparent. Although therapists can be misled by difficult and unusual patients, careful use of diagnostic criteria minimizes the extent to which misinformation from the patient causes such problems.

Psychological Testing and Its Problems. Psychological tests can be invaluable aids in diagnosing mental disorders. A clinical evaluation alone is not nearly as reliable as an evaluation supplemented by testing. Using psychological tests, the clinician can compare a patient to population norms and identify abnormalities. However, psychological tests are not always foolproof. Claim representatives should realize that these tests can be inappropriately and incorrectly applied, administered, and interpreted.

Types of Tests. Tests can be categorized by type and format. The most common types of tests are intelligence, personality, and neuropsychological. The format can be objective, in which the subject can answer in only a few ways, or projective, in which the subject can answer in any manner.

The most common intelligence test is the Wechsler Adult Intelligence Scale-Revised (WAIS-R). The WAIS-R is an objective test containing ten subtests, five verbal subtests and five performance subtests. The WAIS-R yields both verbal and performance IQs and a full-scale IQ. In addition, the results from many of the subtests provide valuable clues about levels of education, neurological problems, cultural and social judgment and background, and ability to concentrate.

The most widely used personality test is the Minnesota Multiphasic Personality Inventory (MMPI). The MMPI is an objective test that yields ten clinical scales and four scales regarding the validity of the testing. The clinical scales measure personality tendencies, such as hypochrondriasis, hysteria, paranoia, and introversion. The scales regarding the validity of the test measure tendencies to lie, exaggerate, or to be defensive. Malingering can often be detected using these scales. These scales must be interpreted in light of one another. The MMPI subscores are not independently meaningful as are the subscores of the WAIS-R.

Two popular projective tests of personality are the Rorschach Inkblot Test and the Thematic Apperception Test (TAT). In the Rorschach, the subject views ten standardized inkblots in sequence and describes what he sees. The test administrator records the subject's responses and the timing and emotion of the responses. In the TAT, the subject views several illustrations of ambiguous scenes and is asked to make up a story about each scene. Although the content of the TAT illustrations is more structured than the Rorschach inkblots, the

3 • Psychological Injuries and Conditions—143

subject is encouraged to personally interpret the scenes. The administration and scoring of these projective tests is more difficult than that for the objective tests. In addition, the emotional stress of taking these tests make them inappropriate for severely disturbed individuals.

A frequently used neuropsychological test is the Halsted-Reitan Battery. This battery includes the WAIS-R, the MMPI, and various other tests designed to detect brain abnormalities. Administering this battery is expensive and time-consuming.

Testing Problems.[70] Although testing can be a valuable supplement to clinical evaluation, it has numerous problems. There are literally hundreds of psychological tests, and the validity and reliability of many have not been established. Test results for the same subject vary from test to test and from examiner to examiner. Claim representatives presented with psychological testing evidence from tests they have never heard of should consult an expert. Many tests are not valid; they have not been shown to measure what they purport to measure.

Aside from problems of validity and reliability, tests may be inappropriately or incorrectly administered. Most psychological tests are "normed" against white, middle-class Americans. Using such a test for someone who is not a white, middle-class American may be inappropriate and meaningless. This problem has been corrected to a great extent in the most recent edition of the MMPI but persists in many other tests.

Some psychological tests are normed such that they yield an unusually high percentage of "false positive" results. This means that the subject is identified as having an abnormality or pathology when neither exists. Tests that tend to yield such results are favorites among plaintiff attorneys.

All valid psychological tests have strict guidelines for administration. An expert hired by a claim representative to review psychological testing should always investigate and critique the circumstances under which the test is administered and scored. Many test results are highly sensitive to environmental factors. Scoring cannot be assumed to be accurate. A defense expert should always obtain the raw data of test administration.

Tests prove nothing about causation. An injury and a mental abnormality shown by testing cannot be connected unless there are both "before" and "after" tests that show a clinically significant difference between pre-accident and post-accident state of mind. Even then, other potential causes would have to be examined and eliminated.

Most important, the majority of psychological tests have been designed under the assumption that test subjects will honestly answer questions on the test and will have no motives other than providing

144—Medical Aspects of Claims

accurate data to the test administrator. Because of the number of false or exaggerated claims, this assumption is often untrue. The claim representative should therefore question the validity of almost all psychological tests of claimants. Although the MMPI has certain internal checks of validity, it is not foolproof, and most other tests have no such safeguards. It is obvious to many claimants how to fake deficits on an intelligence test. Neurological deficits are more difficult to fabricate, but giving answers to create the appearance of being impaired will invalidate all results of a test.

Disability. Many individuals with psychological disorders are working. The existence of a disorder does not automatically result in disability. Total disability caused by psychological problems is generally limited to the most severe cases. However, some degree of occupational impairment is a common characteristic of many disorders.

As explained in the next chapter, disability must be analyzed in terms of the relationip between the impairment and the job requirements. This is also true of alleged psychological disabilities. Because many jobs require minimal social or intellectual skills and involve minimal stress, disability cannot be assumed even in the presence of fairly substantial psychological disorders. Indeed, the experience of regular employment duties and income may have a beneficial effect on many disorders.

Causation

Physical injuries do not normally cause psychological disorders. Purely psychological disorders do not usually have simple causes. These two facts should cause claim representatives to be skeptical and critical of all claims they receive for psychological injury.

A causal relationship between physical injury and psychological disorder is generally limited to cases of head trauma with resulting brain injury and organic brain disorders. A competent neurologist can review and comment on such cases. A neuropsychologist may be needed to explain the functional consequences of specific injuries.

Once a claim representative has determined that an identifiable psychological disorder actually exists, the cause of the disorder should be examined. Potential defenses related to causation include the following: the condition preexisted the injury, the condition is part of the natural progression of, or an aggravated form of, a preexisting condition, or there are other causes of the condition.

Preexisting Conditions. The National Institute of Mental Health estimates that approximately one person in five has a diagnosable mental disorder.[71] Many of these people become claimants. As a matter of probability, a significant minority of claimants can be expected to have mental disorders. This fact does not mean that the injury or event that is the subject of the claim was the cause of the mental disorder. One of the most common failures of psychological experts for the plaintiff is the failure to consider and report preexisting psychological problems.[72]

A preexisting mental disorder can only be detected through a complete history and review of records. A complete history should be taken by an experienced clinician who is aware that there may be motives to misrepresent the facts of a claim. The following topics should be covered:

- Family including infancy and childhood
- Education
- Marital experience
- Sexual experience
- Occupation
- Military service
- Medical records
- Drug and alcohol use
- Psychological treatment

In addition to obtaining a complete history, the clinician should get documentation on the claimant's academic, occupational, medical, legal, and military records. Many emotional difficulties and intellectual deficits that are allegedly recent turn out to have a long history.

Progression or Aggravation of a Preexisting Condition. Many psychological disorders are characterized by periods of exacerbation and remission. An exacerbation of a preexisting psychological disorder that coincides with an accidental physical injury or some other event cannot necessarily be attributed to that injury or event. In addition, some psychological disorders become progressively worse. The occurrence of a physical injury in the course of a psychological illness does not mean that the injury caused the disorder to get worse; it would have done so anyway.

Certain psychological disorders may be aggravated by a physical injury or other event that is the subject of a claim. Such aggravation is usually relieved as soon as the injury heals or the event in question ceases. If there is an event that aggravates a condition, it does not mean that the claimant should be compensated for the entire condition. Once the condition has returned to its preinjury status, the responsible party has no further liability for the future of the condition.

Other Causes. Even when a psychological disorder appears to be a genuine and recent development, the claim representative should not accept a physical injury as the cause for the condition until other potential causes have been considered. Such an analysis means that all other circumstances in the person's life must be reviewed.

Other Stresses. Other causes of stress should be considered. While the extent to which stress is experienced varies from person to person, certain events or circumstances are regarded as "objectively" and universally stressful. These events and the relative degree of stress associated with each are shown in Exhibit 3-9. The value of the death of a spouse is arbitrarily set at 100, and all other events are "valued" in relation to it. Notice that positive events, such as marriage, may also be sources of stress.

A claim representative faced with a claim for a psychological disorder should identify every coexisting event or circumstance in the claimant's life that might be causing stress. An independent examining doctor should question the claimant about such events. For example, while a serious personal injury is regarded as relatively stressful (rated at 53), a divorce is even more so (rated at 73). Thus, a claimant who is going through a divorce is likely to be experiencing more stress from that event than from his injury. However, stresses should be regarded as having a cumulative effect. Thus, a divorce and a serious personal injury together are likely to be more stressful than the death of a spouse.

Medical Causes. The claimant's medical history should be carefully reviewed for possible causes of psychological disorders. Indeed, a thorough medical review should be a precondition to any psychological diagnosis. An enormous number of psychological symptoms and conditions may be caused by physical illnesses and disorders. Before confirming a claim for a serious psychological disorder or disability, a claim representative should consider spending the money necessary for a complete physical exam and tests, including blood work, metabolic studies, and brain scans. A defense psychiatrist attuned to organic causes of psychological problems can provide valuable assistance in identifying cases that need a complete physical workup. The psychiatrist is especially useful in this type of case because he or she is also a medical doctor.

Drug Use. The claim representative should pay attention to the claimant's use of legal and illegal drugs. Many patients abuse prescription drugs either because of lack of supervision by the physician or because the patient consults many different physicians who are unaware of one another or other drug treatments. Even properly administered drugs can cause psychological problems. The possibility of drug-induced symptoms should be considered in every psychological diagnosis. The use of illegal drugs can cause any number of physical and psychological symptoms and may be accompanied by financial, occupational, and legal difficulties or personality disorders.

3 • Psychological Injuries and Conditions—147

Exhibit 3-9
Relative Stress Value of Life Events

Life Event	Mean Value
1. Death of spouse	100
2. Divorce	73
3. Marital separation from mate	65
4. Detention in jail or other institution	63
5. Death of a close family member	63
6. Major personal injury or illness	53
7. Marriage	50
8. Being fired at work	47
9. Marital reconciliation with mate	45
10. Retirement from work	45
11. Major change in the health or behavior of a family member	44
12. Pregnancy	40
13. Sexual difficulties	39
14. Gaining a new family member (e.g., through birth, adoption, oldster moving in, etc.)	39
15. Major business readjustment (e.g., merger, reorganization, bankruptcy, etc.)	39
16. Major change in financial state (e.g., a lot worse off or a lot better off than usual)	38
17. Death of a close friend	37
18. Changing to a different line of work	36
19. Major change in the number of arguments with spouse (e.g., either a lot more or a lot less than usual regarding child-rearing, personal habits, etc.)	35
20. Taking out a mortgage or loan for a major purchase (e.g., for a home, business, etc.)	31
21. Foreclosure on a mortgage or loan	30
22. Major change in responsibilities at work (e.g., promotion, demotion, lateral transfer)	29
23. Son or daughter leaving home (e.g., marriage, attending college, etc.)	29
24. Trouble with in-laws	29
25. Outstanding personal achievement	28
26. Wife beginning or ceasing work outside the home	26
27. Beginning or ceasing formal schooling	26
28. Major change in living conditions (e.g., building a new home, remodeling, deterioration of home or neighborhood)	25
29. Revision of personal habits (dress, manners, association, etc.)	24
30. Trouble with the boss	23
31. Major change in working hours or conditions	20
32. Change in residence	20
33. Changing to a new school	20
34. Major change in usual type and/or amount of recreation	19

148—Medical Aspects of Claims

35. Major change in church activities 19
    (e.g., a lot more or a lot less than usual)
36. Major change in social activities 18
    (e.g., clubs, dancing, movies, visiting, etc.)
37. Taking out a mortgage or loan for a lesser purchase 17
    (e.g., for a car, TV, freezer, etc.)
38. Major change in sleeping habits 16
    (a lot more or a lot less sleep, or change in part of day when asleep)
39. Major change in number of family get-togethers 15
    (e.g., a lot more or a lot less than usual)
40. Major change in eating habits 15
    (a lot more or a lot less food intake, or very different
    meal hours or surroundings)
41. Vacation 13
42. Christmas 12
43. Minor violations of the law 11
    (e.g., traffic tickets, jaywalking, disturbing the peace, etc.)

Adapted from Holmes, T.H. and Rahe, R.H.: **The Social Readjustment Rating Scale,** *Journal of Psychosomatic Research* 1967; 11:213-218, as reprinted in Herbert Lasky, J.D., *Guidelines for Handling Psychiatric Issues in Workers' Compensation Cases* (Ranchos Palos Verdes, CA: Lex-Com Enterprises, 1988), p. 167-168.

Treatment of Psychological Disorders

Even when a psychological disorder is genuine and is caused by an accident or event of a claim, the claim representative does not have to accept treatment that seems to be inappropriate or excessive in duration or cost. Following are brief descriptions of the major forms of treatment and some parameters for proper treatment.

Psychotherapy. Psychotherapy is the treatment of emotional, behavioral, personality, and psychiatric disorders based primarily on verbal and nonverbal interaction between patient and therapist (or clinician), not on the use of chemical and physical treatments. Unlike psychoanalysis, which is based on the Freudian model of treatment and in which the therapist (psychoanalyst) does little interacting, most current psychotherapy involves the therapist to a much greater degree. Psychoanalysis is typically a long-term treatment. Psychotherapy can range anywhere from a few months to a number of years depending on the nature of the disorder, the goals of the patient, and the style of the therapist. Each session is typically fifty minutes or one hour long.

Psychotherapy requires a certain level of cooperation from the patient. The patient ordinarily must be functional and have enough psychological strength to endure the sometime stressful nature of treatment. Psychotherapy is not the best choice when immediate symptom relief is required for the well-being of the patient or those around him.

Medications. Psychopharmacology, the use of medication to treat psychological illness, has greatly improved in recent years. A wide range of drugs are available to treat various problems, especially the symptoms of schizophrenia, affective disorders, and anxiety disorders. Symptom relief may range from slight to substantial. The biggest drawback of drug therapy is side effects. They can range from unpleasant to dangerous. Any form of drug therapy should be carefully monitored and preceded by a thorough physical.

Behavior Modification. Behavioral therapists are often at odds with psychotherapists' methods of effecting change. Behavioral therapists emphasize making changes in behaviors and thinking, not the value of insight into emotions. Behavioral therapy is based on conditioning through which new behaviors or responses are learned. Some therapists may use behavioral techniques with disorders such as compulsions or substance abuse or for the relief of depression or anxiety.

Hospitalization. Hospitalization is indicated when the patient is completely out of touch with reality or cannot control behavior to the extent that he is a danger to himself or others. Hospitalization may also be necessary when the patient's entire environment must be controlled, as during the administration of a complex drug regimen or during withdrawal from an addictive substance. Otherwise, hospitalization is probably no more effective than out-patient forms of treatment; it is also much more expensive.

Hospitalization is also necessary during administration of electroconvulsive shock therapy. This therapy involves administration of electric shocks to the body and can be dangerous. Electroconvulsive shock is effective with major depressions and can overcome suicidal episodes.

The American Psychiatric Association's Role. In 1989, the American Psychiatric Association published a four-volume task force report, *Treatment of Psychiatric Disorders*. Although there are no generally accepted treatment guidelines in the field of psychiatry in the sense that any single condition has a single mode of treatment, this work provides a systematic review of the scientific literature regarding what forms of treatment are effective with various disorders.

The *Treatment of Psychiatric Disorders* manual does not dictate what treatments must be used for specific disorders. A psychiatrist could administer treatment not described in the manual and not be guilty of malpractice. Nevertheless, a psychiatrist or psychologist who does not use the manual's treatment modes would have to justify why the described treatments were not tried first.

Undoubtedly, *Treatment of Psychiatric Disorders* will be revised as additional scientific evidence accumulates. Claims personnel are unlikely to use this manual directly, as doing so requires sophisticated evaluation of the quality of scientific evidence. However, claims personnel can expect that psychiatric utilization review services will refer to this manual regularly when formulating their opinions.

Utilization Review Services. Utilization review services are companies that evaluate the appropriateness, duration, and cost of medical services. They typically operate as independent fee-for-services companies, serving insurers that are responsible for health and medical costs. Utilization review has grown enormously in recent years as insurers, employers, and government agencies have grown increasingly conscious of rising health costs.

Utilization review of psychiatric and psychological services is available. The American Psychiatric Association has a division devoted to utilization review and case management. Utilization review services can more expertly than claim representatives analyze psychological conditions.

Claim representatives or their managers should develop guidelines as to when utilization review services should be consulted. Many insurers have utilization review guidelines applicable to claims in general. They should be reviewed to see whether they are appropriate for psychiatric cases. Utilization review should certainly be considered when the cost of psychiatric or psychological treatment exceeds several thousand dollars or when psychological disability is alleged. It should also be considered for certain often abused diagnoses, such as post-traumatic stress disorder, adjustment disorder, and generalized anxiety disorder.

SUMMARY

Psychological injuries and conditions are a significant part of virtually every case of accidental physical injury. In addition, psychological injuries and conditions may alone become the subject of a claim. The claim representative should not be overly concerned with the usual psychological consequences of a physical injury even if they become the subject of treatment. Unless a psychological disorder not related to the physical injury is diagnosed, these symptoms are considered part of the general damages that are expected in the claim. Payment for treatment is appropriate, assuming causation is established, but should not continue past the normal physical healing period.

Diagnosis of a psychological disorder not related to the physical

3 • Psychological Injuries and Conditions—151

injury represents a more serious psychological problem. All diagnoses should be made with reference to the criteria in the DSM. All typical symptoms of a disorder must be identified, and all differential diagnoses must be made. A correct diagnosis is the essential first step in evaluating the validity of a claim for a psychological condition.

Certain psychological disorders are especially troublesome for claim representatives handling bodily injury claims. These disorders are either frequently associated with claims for bodily injury or are likely to be the real cause of alleged bodily injury. They include the stress disorders, somatoform disorders, malingering, and factitious disorder.

The evaluation of claims for psychological disorders is a three-step process. First, it must be determined that a disorder actually exists. Symptoms alone without a meaningful diagnosis should not be the focus of treatment. The usefulness and limitations of psychological testing must be understood. Second, the cause of the disorder must be established. This involves investigating the circumstances of a claimant's life that may have been responsible for the disorder, the possibility of a preexisting disorder, and other possible causes. Finally, the appropriateness, duration, and cost of treatment must be reviewed. This process requires some familiarity with the various modes of psychological treatment and may require the services of a utilization review service.

Chapter Notes

1. Hoyle Leigh, M.D. and Morton F. Reiser, M.D., *The Patient: Biological, Psychological, and Social Dimensions of Medical Practice*, 2nd ed. (New York: Plenum Medical Book Co., 1985), p. 210.
2. Leigh & Reiser, p. 226.
3. Leigh & Reiser, p. 233.
4. Leigh & Reiser, p. 229.
5. Leigh & Reiser, p. 49-50.
6. American Psychiatric Association, *Diagnostic and Statistical Manual of Mental Disorders*, 3rd ed.-Revised (Washington, DC, 1987), pp. 18-20. Hereafter DSM-III-R.
7. DSM-III-R, pp. 19-20.
8. DSM-III-R, pp. 218-223.
9. Leigh & Reiser, pp. 18-19.
10. DSM-III-R, p. xxii.
11. DSM-III-R, p. xxix.
12. DSM-III-R, pp. 15-20.
13. Adapted from DSM-III-R, pp. 97-163.
14. Adapted from DSM-III-R, pp. 100-103.
15. Adapted from DSM-III-R, pp. 103-107.
16. Adapted from DSM-III-R, pp. 108-109.
17. Adapted from DSM-III-R, pp. 109-116.
18. Adapted from DSM-III-R, pp. 165-185.
19. Adapted from DSM-III-R, pp. 166-168.
20. Adapted from DSM-III-R, p. 169.
21. Adapted from DSM-III-R, pp. 187-198.
22. Adapted from DSM-III-R, pp. 199-203.
23. Adapted from DSM-III-R, pp. 213-233.
24. DSM-III-R, p. 401.
25. Adapted from DSM-III-R, pp. 214-218.
26. Adapted from DSM-III-R, pp. 218-224.
27. Adapted from DSM-III-R, pp. 235-238.
28. Adapted from DSM-III-R, pp. 238-241.
29. Adapted from DSM-III-R, pp. 241-243.
30. Adapted from DSM-III-R, pp. 243-245.
31. Adapted from DSM-III-R, pp. 245-247.
32. Adapted from DSM-III-R, pp. 269-272.
33. Adapted from DSM-III-R, pp. 273-275.
34. Adapted from DSM-III-R, pp. 272-273.

3 • Psychological Injuries and Conditions—153

35. Adapted from DSM-III-R, pp. 275-277.
36. Adapted from DSM-III-R, pp. 279-290.
37. Adapted from DSM-III-R, pp. 290-296.
38. Adapted from DSM-III-R, pp. 298-308.
39. Adapted from DSM-III-R, pp. 308-313.
40. Adapted from DSM-III-R, pp. 321-328.
41. DSM-III-R, p. 335.
42. Robert J. Cooper, M.D. and Glen Repko, M.D., *The Disability Due to Personality Disorder*, reprinted in Herbert J. Lasky, *Guidelines for Handling Psychiatric Issues in Workers Compensation Cases* (Rancho Palos Verdes, CA: Lex-Com Enterprises, 1988), p. 278.
43. Cooper and Repko, p. 278.
44. Cooper and Repko, pp. 308-309.
45. Daniel W. Shuman, *Psychiatric and Psychological Evidence* (Colorado Springs, CO: Shepards/McGraw-Hill, 1986), p. 40.
46. Adapted from DSM-III-R, pp. 337-339.
47. Adapted from DSM-III-R, pp. 339-340.
48. Adapted from DSM-III-R, pp. 340-342.
49. DSM-III-R, p. 360.
50. Adapted from DSM-III-R, pp. 346-347.
51. Adapted from DSM-III-R, pp. 348-349.
52. Adapted from DSM-III-R, pp. 349-351.
53. Adapted from DSM-III-R, pp. 351-353.
54. Adapted from DSM-III-R, pp. 353-354.
55. Adapted from DSM-III-R, pp. 354-356.
56. Adapted from DSM-III-R, pp. 356-358.
57. DSM-III-R, p. 235.
58. DSM-III-R, p. 250.
59. DSM-III-R, p. 248.
60. Adapted from DSM-III-R, pp. 255-256.
61. Adapted from DSM-III-R, pp. 257-259.
62. Adapted from DSM-III-R, pp. 259-261.
63. DSM-III-R, pp. 266-267.
64. Adapted from DSM-III-R, pp. 264-266.
65. Adapted from DSM-III-R, pp. 315-319.
66. DSM-III-R, p. 360.
67. F. Leavitt and J.J. Sweet, "Characteristics and Frequency of Malingering Among Patients with Low Back Pain," *Pain*, Vol. 25, 1986, p. 357.
68. David J. Schretlen, "The Use of Psychological Tests to Identify Malingered Symptoms of Mental Disorder," *Clinical Psychology Review*, Vol. 8, 1988, p. 451.
69. *Personal Injury Law Defense Bulletin*, No. 6, May 1989, Germantown, MD: Center for Defense Case Analysis, Inc.

70. Material is adapted from Paul R. Lees-Haley, Ph.D., "Confronting Neuropsychological Testing," *For The Defense*, May 1990, p. 27.
71. As cited in Paul R. Lees-Haley, Ph.D., "A Checklist for Defending Psychological Testing Claims," *Claims*, Dec. 1989, p. 49.
72. *The Personal Injury Law Defense Bulletin*, no. 6, May 1989, The Center for Defense Case Analysis, Inc.

CHAPTER 4

Disability

Disability is the inability to perform one's occupation or other daily activities. Caused by a physiological condition or injury, disability is essentially a medical issue. Nevertheless, disability has causes and effects that extend beyond medical issues. It is a serious psychological, social, and economic problem. It affects the individual, his or her family and employer, the insurance industry, and the economy as a whole. Reducing or overcoming disability likewise benefits all these parties. Claim representatives who handle disability claims have enormous responsibilities toward the disabled person and the insurer. No matter how well compensated, the disabled have suffered and continue to suffer greatly. Nevertheless, insurers that must compensate the disabled are entitled to know that their service is not being abused, especially since disability cases represent the vast majority of money paid out for injury claims. This chapter describes the nature of disability, explains how disability is determined, and how it may be overcome.

THE NATURE OF DISABILITY

Disability is distinct from related conditions of impairment and handicap. Disability substantially affects claim values, the disabled, the nondisabled, and employers of the disabled.

Definitions

Certain key words related to the condition of disability appear often in medical, psychological, and vocational rehabilitation reports.

156—Medical Aspects of Claims

A clear understanding of these definitions is essential to a claim representative's understanding of the subject of disability.

Disability. Disability is an alteration in a person's capacity to meet personal, social, or occupational demands, or to meet statutory or regulatory requirements. Disability is assessed more in terms of performance than in terms of medical criteria. People are disabled in their personal lives if, for example, they cannot feed or bathe themselves. Someone who cannot leave the house or drive might be considered socially disabled. A person who cannot meet the physical demands of a job would be occupationally disabled.

Impairment. Impairment is an alteration in health status and is assessed in a medical context. Impairment refers to specific injuries, illnesses, losses, or deficits of function in the body. An impairment does not automatically result in disability.

For example, an injured worker may have a fracture of the right leg, which is an impairment, but because her job requires telemarketing activities, she is not occupationally disabled. However, since her leg is casted, she is personally and socially disabled because, for example, of her inability to drive her car or shower normally.

Thus, impairment is a function of the health status of an individual, whereas disability is a function of an individual's ability to meet personal, social, or occupational demands or statutory or regulatory requirements.

Handicap. A handicap refers to the degree of functional limitation resulting from an impairment.[1] The existence of a handicap depends on the extent to which an impairment impedes a person's functioning.

The sense of handicap can be illustrated with an extreme example. Suppose a person is born with no arms, but can use feet to perform all activities of daily living (washing, eating, dressing, toileting). Most people believe that someone who has missing limbs or uses crutches or a wheelchair is handicapped. This person would not be considered handicapped because the absence of arms does not impede physical functioning. In contrast, someone with a very minor impairment may be considered to be handicapped if that impairment interferes with normal functions. Who the person with the impairment is and how that person perceives himself or herself influences the effect of the impairment and thus, the nature or existence of a handicap.

Workers Compensation Definitions of Disability. This section defines disability as it applies in the workers compensation system. The determination of disability in this context often depends on statutory definitions. The definition of disability under workers compensation may not match the definition under other systems. Temporary-total and permanent-partial disabilities account for most income benefits paid as reported by the U.S. Chamber of Commerce.

Temporary-Partial. This condition means that an injured worker is temporarily unable to perform some job-related tasks. For example, minor low back strains, superficial cuts, bruises, and burns are often regarded as a temporary-partial disability. An injured worker can receive temporary-partial disability benefits if the disability meets statutory criteria.

Temporary-Total. This term means that the injured employee cannot to any extent perform his or her occupational duties, but that the condition is not permanent. The overwhelming majority of all injuries sustained in the course of employment and involving some disability are in this category.

Permanent-Partial. This kind of disability is caused by an injury that involves the permanent loss of a member of the body, such as an eye, a foot, or a finger, or loss of some body function that interferes with the worker's ability to perform his or her tasks. Under most workers compensation laws, certain scheduled injuries are defined as partial disabilities even if the worker is able to perform his or her job duties.

Permanent-Total. This form of disability means that the injured worker is permanently and totally incapacitated from carrying on gainful work. Blindness in both eyes, double amputations, or a spinal cord injury would be considered a permanent-total disability. As with permanent-partial injuries, workers compensation laws define certain injuries as a total disability regardless of whether or not the injured person is still working.

Effect of Disability on the Value of Claims

The extent and duration of disability are generally the key factors affecting the value of a claim. Disability usually affects the value of a claim even more than the injury itself. A serious injury from which a claimant is disabled for only a short time is likely to cost less than an ordinary injury from which a claimant experiences extended disability. The presence of some disability is a key indication that a case is serious rather than routine, and the presence of *permanent* disability is a key indication that a serious case may be catastrophic. A claim representative must carefully investigate and verify any alleged disability, bringing serious and potentially serious cases to the attention of supervisors and managers.

Workers Compensation Claims. Claims involving medical

payments represent only a small fraction of total workers compensation payments. Indeed, medical-only claims represent a minority of medical benefits. The majority of medical benefits are paid on cases involving some disability.

All indemnity payments are made on claims involving disability. In 1990, indemnity payments represented approximately 60 percent of all compensation benefits. Furthermore, the extent of indemnity benefits paid on a given case is directly tied to the length of disability. The longer the disability, the longer the benefits must continue. Determining when a claimant's disability has ended and terminating disability benefits are among the most important tasks of a compensation claim representative. Compensation cases involving permanent disability are serious and expensive enough to warrant the use of sophisticated claims handling techniques such as vocational rehabilitation and retraining.

Liability Claims. As with workers compensation claims, the value of a liability claim is closely related to the extent and duration of disability. Indeed, in a liability claim, the award of general damages multiplies the financial consequences of disabilities.

In a liability claim, the claimant can recover special and general damages. *Special damages* are compensation for out-of-pocket expenses such as medical bills and lost income. Thus, the extent of special damages that may be collected is directly linked to the amount of lost income as a result of the disability. *General damages* are compensation for the intangible effects of injury such as emotional pain and suffering, inconvenience, and scarring. One widely disparaged but just as widely practiced method for computing general damages is to equate general damages to several multiples of the special damages. Thus, general damages might be regarded as, for example, three times the amount of the special damages. Since lost earnings are already part of special damages, this approach increases the cost of disability well beyond its face value.

Besides formulas used to compute damages, the extent and duration of disability are widely accepted as indicators of general damages. For instance, if a person must be absent from work as a result of suffering caused by disability, it is clear that the disability is bad enough to interfere with normal activities. This kind of disability is adequate evidence for general damages.

Attitudes Toward and Myths About the Disabled

There is a great deal of literature discussing the uneasiness felt by able-bodied persons in the presence of disabled persons.[2] Much of this attitude is the result of how we see ourselves, and to a great extent, this image or our image of what we should be is created by our culture. We are bombarded with images of perfect, young bodies. Anyone who is not young or perfect can be seen as somehow less desirable. This "standard" affects how we view the disabled and how the disabled view themselves. Historically, the segregation of disabled people in special schools, classrooms, or jobs did not allow the able-bodied to overcome their prejudices about the disabled. These biases are slowly dissolving as the disabled are becoming integrated in society.

Acceptance of Disabilities. People have become more tolerant of people with disabilities. In the past, it was common for a family to abandon a deformed baby to die.[3] With improvements in medical technology, however, there are better chances for disabled people to live and to lead a relatively normal life. People with accident-related spinal abnormalities can live somewhat normally. Soldiers who have lost, or lost the use of, limbs have stayed alive and have managed to lead a relatively normal life. As a result, the able-bodied are more exposed to the disabled, and they have begun to rethink their prejudices toward those who are different. Disabled soldiers were among the most prominent groups who benefited from the growing interest in vocational rehabilitation programs. Following World War II, Korea, and Vietnam, the disabled soldier gained unprecedented acceptance in the workplace.

In recent years, numerous programs have specifically targeted the disabled population. Government has become interested in providing opportunities in education and training for individuals who are not able to keep pace in the job market. The disadvantages that disabilities produce can often be overcome with proper education, training, and placement. The government and society have acted, in part, out of self-interest. When the disabled are working, they too are paying taxes, thus helping to support a system from which others can benefit.

Debunking Myths About Disabilities. Emotional maladjustment is not necessarily an offshoot of physical disability. Numerous researchers have concluded that "little support exists to favor nondisabled over disabled groups in terms of level of adjustment."[4] It would seem logical to see the onset of disability as a traumatic experience that affects, at least temporarily, a person's state of mind, and thus, his or her ability to adjust to the disability and to the world. It could also be hypothesized that the individual's predisability personality and state of mind play a large part in determining the extent and duration of adjustment problems.[5] An individual's emotional strengths and ability to cope with adversity play a large part in predicting how that individual will cope with disability after an injury. Coping mechanisms are an individual's typical responses to stress. Some coping mechanisms are healthy—others are not. A healthy individual, or someone who has been successful in coping with stressful events, would be especially good at handling stress without becoming psychologically harmed or incapacitated.

It is also commonly assumed that there is a relationship between the severity of physical disability and the extent of adjustment. However, according to Rubin and Roessler, there is little research to support this assumption. Rather, the extent of the psychological impact experienced by each individual seems to be related to the significance the disability possesses for that individual.[6] Severe behavioral aberrations are not uncommon for a person with an objectively minor impairment. In contrast, another person with a severely debilitating impairment may make an excellent adjustment.

The idea that disabled individuals experience "excessive frustration" is another unfounded assumption. Many nondisabled individuals believe that disability is an insurmountable barrier to the achievement of many goals. The nondisabled cannot imagine how they would cope with disability and assume that the lives of the disabled must be filled with frustration.[7] This response is a projection of the observer's feelings onto the disabled person and has no more foundation than the assumption that the disabled are maladjusted.

The fear or suspicion that disability is punishment for sin is a lingering bias. At the core of this prejudice is the thought that someone or something must be blamed for the disability, rather than a rational understanding of the organic basis of disability.[8]

Effects of Disabilities on the Disabled Person

How a person behaves *before* a disabling injury or illness is usually how that person will behave *after* the injury. Generally, if a person was able to overcome obstacles prior to an injury, he or she will be able to do the same after the injury even though the obstacles may have changed. Personalities do not fundamentally change. Most disabled individuals learn to accept their limitations, although others find that adopting the role of a sick person suits their psychological needs. The nondisabled cannot ever live the life of a disabled person, but they can perform certain exercises, discussed below, to simulate the effects of disability.

Acceptance of Disability. When an individual is injured and especially if the injury is catastrophic, there may be the tendency to ask, "Why me?" Medical professionals who work with the disabled know it is really not helpful to dwell on this question. It is more helpful to concentrate on the present, plan for the future, and to avoid or prevent complications of the injury or disease. This positive approach (or response) develops gradually through a step-by-step process.

A well-known book provides a model that identifies the stages an individual may experience when one's own death is imminent or when a loved-one is about to or has already died. Professionals dealing with those who have suffered a sudden disability have observed disabled individuals experience very similar stages. These stages are denial, rage and anger, bargaining, depression, and acceptance.[9]

Denial. "No, not me." This is a typical reaction when someone learns that he or she is terminally ill. According to Dr. Kubler-Ross, this response helps to cushion the impact of the patient's awareness of death. Denial is also a common reaction among the disabled.

Rage and Anger. "Why me?" The individual resents the fact that he or she has been affected. Likewise, newly disabled individuals are often enraged at what they perceive as the injustice of their disability.

Bargaining. "Yes me, but..." In this stage, people begin to recognize the fact of death, but because they have not totally accepted it, they remain on the edge of denial and feel as if they may still have some control over their circumstances. The state of mind of a disabled person in this stage would be reflected in the thought process, "I will do anything if my disability could be removed." The person is essentially attempting to strike a bargain by offering to do anything in return for his or her "health."

Depression. "Yes, me." The person mourns past losses, things not done, wrongs committed. The disabled faces and feels sad about the reality of what they have lost and the limitations in their lives. When a person has suffered a serious accident, living through the anniversary of the accident is a significant milestone. The disabled person and his or her family often judge the recovery or lack of recovery at this date. Depression or other psychological setbacks are common around anniversary dates.

Acceptance. "My time is very close now and it's all right." For those approaching death, this final stage is "not a happy stage, but neither is it unhappy. It's devoid of feelings, but it's not resignation, it's really a victory."[10] The disabled at a similar stage accept their condition and look forward to dealing with the rest of their lives.

Everyone who suffers a disability neither goes through each stage nor does so in the exact order. Understanding each stage makes it easier to understand what a person goes through after a serious injury or illness. Like the terminally ill person, the fundamental and common experience of the disabled or seriously injured person is loss.

Adopting the Sick Role. Medical doctors have observed that their patients typically adopt a "sick role" that reflects popular attitudes towards sickness and treatment. This role includes being exempt from normal responsibilities and requiring help from others to get well, plus

162—Medical Aspects of Claims

the duties to seek help and to regard the sickness as undesirable. In general, the sick role is a constructive relationship for purposes of treatment.[11] However, some patients indefinitely adopt the sick role. They claim to regard their sickness as undesirable, but may actually enjoy the experience. Such patients make the sick role their vocation unless they come to see the prospect of getting well as attractive as being "sick." The person who has suffered a soft tissue injury of the back, such as lumbar strain and sprain, and has recovered is a common example. This person may have seen that being disabled is not that bad. Household chores, food shopping, and general child care chores may have been assumed by an uninjured mate or family member. In fact, disability may have come to have been seen as a favorable state because of the perceived positive experience created by nurturing. This care may have been lacking before the accident, but forthcoming after it.

In an actual case involving a knee injury on the job, the injured worker required surgery and a long recuperation period. In the interim, the wife of the injured worker returned to the workforce, leaving him responsible for the couple's two small preschoolers. An interesting development in the injured worker's recovery followed. He became "Mr. Mom," and his wife flourished in the workplace. Following recuperation, this man had a difficult time scheduling job interviews because he could not get childcare assistance. His previous employer had eliminated his job and he did not know where to go next. However, he did not seem to mind. Also, he was not very motivated to change the newly established roles and relationships in his family, which had evolved to his liking. This example shows that the effects of disability can permeate all aspects of a disabled person's psyche and can change the nature of the family structure and how it functions.

Simulated Disability. Students in nursing or rehabilitation counseling commonly "try" temporary disability so that the impact of the disability will have personal significance and meaning. This exercise helps the student to empathize with a person who is disabled. The assumption is that empathy and experience will better prepare the student to treat a disabled person. The following are some ways in which one can simulate disability:

- Put petroleum jelly on eyeglass lenses to mimic vision difficulties
- Wear earplugs to create the experience of hearing impairment
- Use crutches or a wheelchair at a mall, shopping center, or food store to appreciate the importance of barrier-free design and to experience being "different" in public

These exercises make it possible to experience the feelings related to being disabled in a functional world.

Effects of Disability on the Employer of the Disabled

Although employers are encouraged to hire the handicapped, there is often not enough information known to employers to quell myths about the disabled. It would be ideal if no group of people were excluded from consideration for hire given that the candidates for any position are suited for the job. However, some employers are not interested in any person for whom the job would have to be modified for them to perform it well. Indeed, not many years ago, candidates were specifically asked on job applications if they had certain health problems because employers viewed such problems as impediments to getting the job done, such as diabetes or epilepsy. Since that time, the understanding of these two diseases has grown to the point that discrimination is relatively uncommon. It is hoped that discrimination against disabled candidates will similarly end. Nevertheless, legislation has been passed to ensure equal treatment for disabled candidates. In addition to legislation, the costs of disability have also affected employers.

The Americans With Disabilities Act. In 1990 the federal government passed the Americans with Disabilities Act. This was a clear statement by Congress that employers must *not* discriminate on the basis of disability.

This act prohibits discrimination on the basis of disability in regard to hiring, compensation, promotion, and other conditions of employment if the candidate is otherwise qualified. A qualified person is one who, with "reasonable accommodation," can perform the "essential functions" of a job. The failure to provide "reasonable accommodation" to a disability is specifically listed as an act of discrimination unless making accommodations would cause undue hardship. It also provides guidelines on the accommodations employers must make for disabled people.

The act defines "reasonable accommodation" as possibly including "making existing facilities used by employees readily accessible to and usable by individuals with disabilities; and...job restructuring, part-time or modified work schedules...acquisition or modification of equipment or devices...the provision of qualified readers or interpreters...."[12]

Thus, federal law makes it mandatory for employers to adjust to the needs of the otherwise qualified disabled. Protected by this law, the disabled who can perform the essential functions of a job can enter the workforce. In addition, prudent employers can be expected to review their hiring practices to be sure they are giving appropriate consideration to the disabled.

The Costs of Disability. The National Safety Council estimates

164—Medical Aspects of Claims

that approximately 75 million work days were lost in 1988 due to work-related accidents, costing $47.1 billion in direct costs plus the value of lost productivity.[13] Lost production time due to off-the-job accidents (mainly auto accidents) was almost twice as great.[14] Among disabling work-related injuries, back injuries were the most common, representing 22 percent of all cases and 32 percent of all compensation paid.[15]

DETERMINATION OF DISABILITY

Making a determination of disability depends on two factors: identifying a person's physical impairments; and describing the physical, intellectual, and social demands of that person's job. Disability cannot be based on physical impairments alone unless such impairments would render *anyone* disabled from *all* occupations. Many individuals with extensive impairments are able to work full time.

Claim representatives have generally left the determination of disability to physicians. Although medical expertise is necessary to determine physical impairment, many physicians know little or nothing about the demands of their patient's jobs when they make a disability determination. Such disability determinations should not be accepted at face value. When the physician does not know or fails to inquire about the demands of the patient's job, a statement about disability is made out of context and is therefore not wholly valid. The patient may in fact be able to work if the job is modified. Also a factor in a physician's determination of disability is that physicians tend to be uncritical of what their patients say and are likely to accept a statement from the patient that he cannot work. When the physician fails to evaluate an injury in the context of occupation, is uncritical of what the patient says, and when the claim representative is uncritical of the physician's report, it is as if the patient/claimant makes the determination of disability.

Claim representatives should be familiar with how physical impairments are evaluated as they relate to job demands. This section describes how physical impairment is determined by physicians and how the demands of various occupations can be determined.

AMA Guide to the Evaluation of Permanent Impairment

Claim representatives regularly review medical reports that document a physician's determination of some percentage of impairment. To determine such percentages, a physician should use the *AMA Guide to the Evaluation of Permanent Impairment*. This book was first published in a single volume in 1971 as a result of many years of ad hoc committee work on behalf of the AMA. The goal of the committee was to create a practical guide for rating physical impairments. The AMA has made a substantial effort to keep the book updated and has published a number of editions since 1971. In 1981 the AMA's Council on Scientific Affairs determined that twelve expert advisory panels were needed to update the clinical information supporting the impairment ratings. Editions of the guide published since 1981 have been improved as a result of the recommendations of such panels.

Purpose and Approach of the Guide. The guide espouses the philosophy that all physical and mental impairments affect the whole person, and therefore, all separate impairment ratings should be combined and expressed as impairment of the whole person.[16] The guide translates medical information and data into a form that can be used by nonmedical personnel in social, administrative, economic, or legal systems.

It is quite common for physicians to be asked about the functional capabilities of an individual who has an impairment. According to the guide, it is not possible for a physician to assess the ability of an individual to perform tasks or to meet functional demands because the physician is relying only on medical information, not on occupational requirements. The physician can, however, assess whether or not a particular medical condition has become stable. When a condition is stable, there is no medical reason to expect that an individual will gain or lose functional ability.[17] An individual should not be identified as being permanently impaired until he or she has been medically rehabilitated to the maximum level and the impairment is well established.

Impairment Criteria. The guide provides a set of medical criteria that form the basis for establishing well-formulated medical ratings of permanent impairment. Most criteria are quantitative, such as range of motion abilities in orthopedics. For instance, *goniometry,* the measurement of joint motion, would be used to establish this kind of criteria. The two arms of a goniometer have a pointer on one end and a protractor scale on the other. In addition to helping a physician diagnose a patient's functional loss, careful examination of joint motion can reveal the progression of a disease and can provide objective data for determining the effect of a treatment program. Exhibit 4-1 shows normal range of motion for different parts of the body. Other criteria are qualitative, providing the basis for assessing nonphysical impairments that are less easily quantified, such as psychiatric problems.[18] Although physical impairment is the usual cause of disability from work, intellectual and social impairments may be obstacles to retraining and obtaining new work. Evaluating intellectual and social impairments is *not* within the ability of most physicians. Such evaluations should be done by psychologists or psychiatrists.

Exhibit 4-1
Normal Range of Motion for Parts of the Body

		Range in Degrees
Neck	Flexion	45
	Extension	55
	Lateral Flexion	40
	Rotation	70
Shoulder	Flexion	180
	Extension	50
	Abduction	180
	Adduction	50
	External rotation	90
	Internal rotation	90
Elbow	Flexion	160
	Extension	0
Wrist	Flexion	90
	Extension	70
	Ulnar deviation	55
	Radial deviation	20
	Pronation	90
	Supination	90
Hip	Flexion	120
	Extension	15
	Abduction	45
	Adduction	45
	External rotation	40
	Internal rotation	40
Knee	Flexion	130
	Extension	0
Ankle	Plantar flexion	45
	Dorsiflexion	20
	Inversion	30
	Eversion	20
Torso	Flexion	75-90
	Extension	30
	Lateral flexion	35
	Rotation	30

There are also medical facilities established for the purpose of helping the physician to obtain information about the patient's physical capability. This information is obtained through standardized evaluations, sophisticated equipment, and computers that accurately measure an individual's abilities. For example, a facility may use Cybex™ equipment to measure how much weight an individual can lift, pull, or push from floor to waist or waist to overhead. Information about functional capacity and complete medical data are essential to nonmedical agencies and people who make determinations of disability.

In determining disability, the physician must include a physical examination, an analysis of the patient's medical history, and diagnostic and laboratory tests. The findings should be analyzed to determine the nature and extent of the loss, and loss of use or derangement of the affected body parts, systems, or functions.[19] The physician must then compare the results of the analysis with medical impairment criteria. The guide states that this comparison need not be performed by the same physician who did the evaluation as long as the medical data is listed using standard notation. Thus, an independent medical examiner can review a disability determination using records only. Finally, the physician must determine the impairment rating taking into account that the final impairment value is applied to the "whole person."

If a patient has several impairments, each must be evaluated separately. For instance, a physician would consider a soft tissue problem of the neck caused by an automobile accident and a low back strain and sprain from a work-related accident by evaluating each impairment separately, providing documentation for each area or body part.

Reports of Impairment. Reports from examining physicians should contain clear, accurate, and objective information. There should be enough data so that a knowledgeable reviewer can understand the rating and assess its validity for its intended use. The following is a comprehensive list of essential information:

- *Medical evaluation*
    1. Narrative history of the medical condition(s) with reference to onset and course, findings from previous examinations, previous treatment, and responses to such treatment.
    2. Results of the most recent clinical evaluation, including all of the following when obtained: physical examination findings, laboratory test results, electrocardiogram, x-ray studies, rehabilitation evaluation, mental status examination and psychological tests, and any other special tests or diagnostic procedures.
    3. Assessment of current clinical status and statement of plans for future treatment, rehabilitation, and reevaluation.
    4. Diagnosis and clinical impressions.
    5. Expected date of full or partial recovery.
- *Analysis of the findings*
    1. Explanation of the impact of the medical condition(s) on daily activities.

2. Explanation of the medical basis for conclusions about the stability of the condition.
3. Explanation of the medical basis for a conclusion that the individual is, or is not, likely to suffer incapacitation as a result of the medical condition.
4. Explanation of the medical basis for any conclusion that the individual is, or is not, likely to suffer injury or risk of further medical impairment by engaging in activities of daily living or any other activity necessary to meet personal, social, and occupational demands.
5. Explanation of any conclusion that restrictions or accommodations are, or are not, needed to perform the daily activities essential to meet personal, social, and occupational demands. If restrictions or accommodations are necessary, there should be an explanation of their therapeutic or risk-avoiding value.

- *Comparison of the data with impairment criteria*
  1. Description of specific clinical findings related to each impairment, with reference to how the findings relate to the criteria described in the guide. Reference to the absence of, or to the examiner's inability to obtain, pertinent data is essential.
  2. Comparison of specific clinical findings with the specific criteria pertaining to the particular body system as listed in the guide.
  3. Explanation of each percent of impairment rating, with reference to the applicable criteria.
  4. Summary statement of all impairment ratings.
  5. Combined or "whole person" rating when more than one impairment is present.[20]

Claim representatives reviewing a physicians report must remember that while permanent medical impairment is related to the health status of the individual, disability can be determined only with reference to the personal, social, or occupational demands, or statutory or regulatory requirements that the individual is unable to meet as a result of the impairment.[21]

Determining Job Demands

The most thorough and reliable way to determine the demands of a job is through a job analysis, described in the final section of this chapter on overcoming disability. However, for cases in which a job analysis is not possible or practical, there are standard references that provide information about thousands of occupations. These references are the *Dictionary of Occupational Titles* and *Selected Characteristics Companion Volume.*

Dictionary of Occupational Titles. Since the first edition was published in 1939, the *Dictionary of Occupational Titles* (DOT) has provided the U.S. Employment Service and others with detailed standard occupational information essential to the effective classification and placement of job seekers. It describes the job duties and requirements for virtually all jobs in the U.S. The fourth edition published in 1977 describes approximately 20,000 jobs.

In addition to job placement, this book is useful for employment counseling, occupational and career guidance, and labor market information services. Originally, the primary use of this book was to match job openings with the qualifications of job applicants at the U.S. Employment Service. The Employment Service needed to standardize all job information and to provide a uniform occupational language for use in all of its offices. Although the book was originally created to meet a need of the Federal-State Employment Service system, it is used today by vocational rehabilitation counselors, rehabilitation nurses, job placement specialists, and others in the private sector of rehabilitation service delivery.

As used in the DOT, "occupation" refers to a collective description of numerous individual job duties performed, possibly with many variations, in many establishments.[22] The DOT organizes occupations in a variety of ways. First, the DOT looks at occupations based on similarities of jobs.

Every occupation has a nine-digit *occupation code*. For example, 241.217-010 is the code for "CLAIM ADJUSTER (bus. ser.; insurance) insurance adjuster; insurance-claim representative; or insurance investigator." This occupation is described as follows:

> Investigates claims against insurance or other companies for personal, casualty, or property loss or damages and attempts to effect out-of-court settlement with claimant: Examines claim form and other records to determine insurance coverage. Interviews, telephones, or corresponds with claimant and witnesses; consults police and hospital records; and inspects property damage to determine extent of company's liability, varying method of investigation according to type of insurance. Prepares report of findings and negotiates settlement with claimant. Recommends litigation by legal department when settlement cannot be negotiated. May attend litigation hearings. May be designated according to type of claim adjusted as AUTOMOBILE-INSURANCE-CLAIM ADJUSTER (bus. ser.; insurance), CASUALTY-INSURANCE-CLAIM ADJUSTER (clerical); FIDELITY-AND-SURETY-BONDS-CLAIM ADJUSTER (bus. ser.; insurance); FIRE-INSURANCE-CLAIM ADJUSTER (bus. ser.; insurance); MARINE-INSURANCE-CLAIM ADJUSTER (bus. ser.; insurance); PROPERTY-LOSS-INSURANCE-CLAIM ADJUSTER (clerical).[23]

170—Medical Aspects of Claims

The first three numbers in an occupation code identify the occupational group. All occupations are grouped into nine broad "categories," identified by the first digit, such as professional, technical, or, in the case of "claim adjuster," *clerical and sales occupations* (2). The second digit refers to a "division" within a category, in this example (24), *miscellaneous clerical occupations*. The third digit specifies the particular occupational group within the division, in this case (241), *investigators, adjusters, and related occupations*.

The *middle three digits* of the code are the worker functions ratings of the tasks performed in the occupation. Every job requires a worker to perform (or to function) in relation to data, people, and things. The worker function rating identifies the difficulty or complexity of the functions of a given job as they relate to data, people, and things. Worker functions that involve more complex responsibility and judgment are assigned lower numbers. Less complicated functions are assigned higher numbers. For example, synthesizing data (0) is a higher level skill than comparing data (6). The listing of all codes is shown in Exhibit 4-2. The coding for claim adjusters (217) indicates the need for a fairly high level of skill handling data (2), an even higher level skill in handling people (1), but little skill in handling things (7).

The *last three digits* in the occupational code indicate the alphabetical order of occupation titles within six-digit code groups if more than one occupation is included within a given six-digit code. These last three digits differentiate a specific occupation from all others. All jobs listed in the DOT have a unique nine-digit code.

The DOT also lists occupational title, industry designation, and alternate titles as part of occupational information and includes a brief description of the tasks performed.

Selected Characteristics Companion Volume. The *Selected Characteristics of Occupations Defined in the DOT* is a companion volume that was developed in response to a need for more detailed information about the occupational characteristics listed in the DOT. The *Selected Characteristics* volume includes information about environmental conditions, mathematical and language development, specific vocational preparation, and physical demands.

Environmental conditions are the physical surroundings for a job. Designations include "I" for inside, "O" for outside, or "B" for both, and exposure to extremes of cold, heat, wetness, or humidity.

Mathematical and language development codes and requirements range from Level 6 to Level 1. Level 6 mathematical development means that advanced calculus, algebra, and statistics are required on a job. Level 6 language development means that the job includes reading and writing novels, technical journals, and manuals; and persuasive speaking. Level 1 math skill requires adding and subtracting

Exhibit 4-2
List of Codes in the *Dictionary of Occupational Titles*

DATA (4th Digit)	PEOPLE (5th Digit)	THINGS (6th Digit)
0 Synthesizing	0 Mentoring	0 Setting up
1 Coordinating	1 Negotiating	1 Precision working
2 Analyzing	2 Instructing	2 Operating-controlling
3 Compiling	3 Supervising	3 Driving-operating
4 Computing	4 Diverting	4 Manipulating
5 Copying	5 Persuading	5 Tending
6 Comparing	6 Speaking-signaling	6 Feeding-offbearing
	7 Serving	7 Handling
	8 Taking instructions-helping	

two-digit numbers. Level 1 language skill requires reading and writing compound and complex sentences.

Specific vocational preparation training time codes and requirements range from Level 1, short demonstration, to Level 9, over 10 years. This information, plus the extent of language and mathematical skill required for a job, is crucial in determining the feasibility of a new career for someone disabled from his or her former job. A job requiring much higher skills than a worker currently possesses is not a likely choice.

The physical demands of a job are expressed in terms of the following factors:

1. Strength
2. Climbing and/or Balancing
3. Stooping, Kneeling, Crouching, and/or Crawling
4. Reaching, Handling, Fingering, and/or Feeling
5. Talking and/or Hearing
6. Seeing

Strength, the first physical demands factor, is expressed in terms of the kind of work required—sedentary, light, medium, heavy, and very heavy. These degrees of strength are stated as follows:

  S - Sedentary Work. Lifting ten pounds maximum and occasionally lifting and/or carrying such articles as dockets, ledgers, and small tools. Although a sedentary job is defined as involving sitting, some walking and standing are often necessary in carrying out job duties. Jobs are sedentary if walking and standing are required only occasionally, and other sedentary criteria are met.

  L - Light Work. Lifting twenty pounds maximum with frequent

lifting and/or carrying of objects weighing up to ten pounds. Even though lifting of weights may be negligible, a job is in this category when it requires walking or standing to a significant degree, or when it involves sitting most of the time with a degree of pushing and pulling of arm and/or leg controls.

M - Medium Work. Lifting fifty pounds maximum with frequent lifting and/or carrying of objects weighing up to twenty-five pounds.

H - Heavy Work. Lifting 100 pounds maximum with frequent lifting and/or carrying of objects weighing up to fifty pounds.

V - Very Heavy Work. Lifting objects in excess of 100 pounds with frequent lifting and/or carrying of objects weighing fifty pounds or more.[24]

The physical demands are described with reference to the worker's position and movements as defined below:

- Worker Position(s)
  — Standing: remaining on one's feet in an upright position at a workstation without moving about
  — Walking: moving about on foot
  — Sitting: remaining in the normal seated position
- Worker Movement of Objects (including extremities used)
  — Lifting: raising or lowering an object from one level to another (includes upward pulling)
  — Carrying: transporting an object, usually holding it in the hands or arms or on the shoulder
  — Pushing: exerting force upon an object so that the object moves away from the force (includes slapping, striking, kicking, and treadle actions)
  — Pulling: exerting force upon an object so that the object moves toward the force (includes jerking)

The following example represents a typical listing for an occupation. The listing for "Claims Adjuster, DOT #241.217-010," would be shown as follows:

- Environment = B (both inside and outside)
- Mathematical = 3 Compute discount, interest, profit, and loss; commission, markups, and selling price; ratio and proportion, and percentages. Calculate surfaces, volumes, weights, and measures.

  Algebra: Calculate variables and formulas, monomials, and polynomials; ratio and proportion variables; and square roots and radicals.

Geometry: Calculate plane and solid figures, circumference, area, and volume. Understand kinds of angles and properties of pairs and angles.
- Language = 5
  Reading: Read literature, book and play reviews, scientific and technical journals, abstracts, financial reports, and legal documents.
  Writing: Write novels, plays, editorials, journals, speeches, manuals, critiques, poetry, and songs.
  Speaking: Conversant in the theory, principles, and methods of effective and persuasive speaking, voice and diction, phonetics, and discussion and debate.
- SVP (specific vocational preparation) = 6 (over one year up to and including two years)
- Physical Demands = 1 = L (Light) and 5 (Talking and Hearing)

Determining Temporary Disability

It would be ideal if temporary disability were determined by the same approach as is permanent disability: the worker's physical impairment would be identified and compared to the physical demands of the job. As the worker's condition improved, this comparison would be made continually to see what aspects of his or her job the worker could reassume. It is unfortunate that temporary disability is rarely determined so thoroughly. In a typical case of temporary disability, the physician states a diagnosis and certifies that the claimant was disabled for exactly the period of time the claimant was actually away from work. The claim representative is in the position of evaluating a period of disability after it has ended.

The Claim Representative's Role. Despite the difficulty in critically analyzing a period of temporary disability, claim representatives do have powers they can use to complete this task. During the period of disability, the claim representative can obtain an independent medical exam. This right is usually available in workers compensation cases and liability claims in suit. In liability claims not yet in suit, the right may not exist, but the request for an independent medical exam is an effective and assertive claims-handling practice. The claimant may cooperate. If the claimant refuses to submit to an IME, this would be a signal to the claim representative that the claimant may have something to hide.

Even after a period of disability has ended, the claim representative can investigate the physical requirements of the claimant's job and

174—Medical Aspects of Claims

insist on an explanation of specifically how the injury in question prevented the claimant from performing his or her job. With a knowledge of the physical demands of the claimant's job, the claim representative may be in a better position to judge disability than a physician who only knows the claimant's medical impairments. This possibility is particularly important in light of the fact that the economy is increasingly dominated by sedentary and light-duty jobs. In such jobs, even a serious injury, such as a broken leg, may not be disabling if the claimant has transportation to and from work and if the job can be modified in minor ways.

It is pointless to contest every case of disability, most of which are legitimate. A claim representative can best guard against disability claims that abuse the system by knowing the typical periods of disability for various injuries. These cases should receive special effort and attention. Typical periods of disability for various injuries are listed in the final section of this chapter.

The Cooperative Physician. Many physicians believe that a return to normal daily activities has a valuable, therapeutic effect on patients. These physicians will eagerly cooperate in an effort to return the patient to work. The vast majority of physicians will cooperate in answering questions from a party with a legitimate interest in the patient's recovery, whether the party is the employer or insurer paying the bills. In any case, the physician cannot be expected to provide information unless the patient has signed a medical authorization.

Assuming the physician is cooperative, the claim representative should obtain a predicted return-to-work date as soon as possible. If the return-to-work date seems unusual, the claim representative should get an explanation. If job modifications are feasible, the physician should be encouraged to consider authorizing the claimant's return to work even before complete recovery. If the claimant is still reported to be disabled on the originally projected return-to-work date, the claim representative should ask the physician for an explanation and a new projected return-to-work date.

OVERCOMING DISABILITY

The claim representative's goal in all cases of disability is to help, encourage, or require the claimant to overcome his or her disability. In cases of temporary disability, the length of disability depends on the various factors explained in this section. The claim representative's goal is to minimize the length of disability in light of the claimant's medical needs. Permanent impairment, by definition, cannot be overcome, but it need not result in permanent disability. The ways in which a permanent impairment is prevented from becoming a permanent disability are also discussed in this section.

Factors Affecting the Length of Temporary Disability

Exhibit 4-3 shows periods of hospitalization, total disability times, and partial disability times for various injuries. Claim representatives must use the information in this exhibit with care. Numerous factors can affect the length of a given disability. The disability periods indicated in this exhibit are average periods. In addition, hospitalization periods have been declining in recent years as hospitals and doctors have more carefully scrutinized hospital use.

The injuries that make up a great percentage of claims normally heal on their own in a short time. Eighty-five percent of patients with acute mechanical low back pain from soft tissue irritation recover within five days to two weeks.[25] Eighty to eighty-five percent of all patients with acute low back pain recover within three days to three weeks regardless of treatment.[26] Claim representatives should not accept a diagnosis of strain or sprain if the condition lasts for months. Simple strains and sprains will resolve much sooner. Strains and sprains outside of the claim context, such as those resulting from sports, housework, or yardwork, always heal quickly. So should strains and sprains involving claims.

Aside from the nature of the injury itself, several factors play an important role in determining the length of temporary disability. These include the claimant's age and occupation, the existence of pre-existing or complicating conditions, and the claimant's motivation.

Age. In general, the older the person is who suffers an injury, the slower they heal. Older people are also more likely to have pre-existing conditions or other frailties.

Injured workers in their late 50s or early 60s may view an accidental injury as justification for early retirement. This is especially common among workers in the construction business. These people may have always worked in carpentry, masonry, or electrical work, but as a result of injury may be restricted to light-duty work. Since most of construction is medium to heavy-duty work, a return to their previous occupation is impossible. In general, most workers are unaware of their transferable skills. As a result, when they are unable to perform their usual work duties, they see their future in other occupations as bleak. Therefore, regular disability payments may act as a disincentive to considering alternative employment, and old people may tend to view this money as the key to retirement.

Exhibit 4-3
Typical Lengths of Disability for Various Injuries

Location & Description of Injury	Hospitalization	Total Disability	Partial Disability
SPRAINS			
Shoulder Joint			
Moderate	0	5 - 7 days	1 - 3 weeks
Severe	0 - 5 days	2 - 4 weeks	1 - 3 weeks
Complications	5 - 6 days	2 - 3 months	1 - 2 months
Hip Joint			
Active	1 - 4 days	2 - 3 weeks	1 - 4 weeks
Inactive	1 - 4 days	7 - 10 days	1 - 4 weeks
Severe	1 - 2 weeks	10 - 12 weeks	1 - 4 weeks
Knee Joint			
Slight-active	0	2 - 3 weeks	2 - 3 weeks
Slight-inactive	0	1 - 2 weeks	2 - 3 weeks
Moderate-active	0	3 - 4 weeks	2 - 3 weeks
Moderate-inactive	0	2 - 3 weeks	2 - 3 weeks
Severe	5 - 10 days	6 - 8 weeks	2 - 3 weeks
Ankle Joint			
Slight-active	0	1 - 2 weeks	1 - 2 weeks
Slight-inactive	0	2 - 7 days	1 - 2 weeks
Severe-active	0	3 - 4 weeks	1 - 2 weeks
Severe-inactive	4 - 7 days	2 - 3 weeks	1 - 2 weeks
LACERATIONS			
Scalp			
1-1/2 - 2"	0 - 2 days	2 - 5 days	2 - 4 days
3" - 6"	0 - 3 days	1 - 2 weeks	2 - 4 weeks
Complications	5 - 10 days	2 - 5 weeks	2 - 4 weeks
Face			
Less than 2" near eyes	0 - 3 days	5 - 7 days	1 - 2 weeks
Severe	0 - 5 days	10 - 14 days	1 - 2 weeks
Chest			
Average	1 - 3 days	2 - 5 days	4 - 6 weeks
Severe	3 - 5 days	2 - 3 weeks	4 - 6 weeks
Penetration Chest	3 - 8 days	4 - 6 weeks	4 - 6 weeks
Shoulder & Arm			
Superficial-more than 2"	1 - 3 days	5 - 10 days	2 - 4 weeks
Involving muscles	3 - 7 days	3 - 4 weeks	2 - 4 weeks
Tendons severed	5 - 7 days	3 - 5 weeks	2 - 4 weeks
Nerves severed	6 - 10 days	6 - 12 months	2 - 4 weeks
Elbows & Forearm			
2" - 5"	2 - 5 days	10 - 21 days	1 - 3 weeks
Muscle	4 - 8 days	4 - 8 weeks	1 - 3 weeks
Thigh			
Deep	2 - 5 days	2 - 4 weeks	1 - 3 weeks
Muscle	7 - 12 days	3 - 6 weeks	1 - 3 weeks
Leg			
Moderate	3 - 5 days	1 - 2 weeks	1 - 3 weeks
Knee	4 - 7 days	4 - 10 weeks	1 - 3 weeks
Achilles tendon	10 - 14 days	4 - 10 weeks	1 - 3 weeks

FRACTURES

Skull

Simple line or linear	5 - 15 days	3 - 5 weeks	3 - 12 weeks
Compound	2 - 6 weeks	6 - 8 weeks	3 - 12 weeks
Compound complication by infection	4 - 12 weeks	10 - 12 weeks	3 - 12 weeks
Depressed	2 - 4 weeks	10 - 15 weeks	3 - 12 weeks

Ribs

Single, simple	1 - 2 days for Observ.	1 - 3 weeks	2 - 4 weeks
Complications	2 - 4 weeks	4 - 6 weeks	2 - 4 weeks

Humerus

Dominant arm (active)	5 - 27 days	8 - 12 weeks	2 - 3 weeks
Non-dominant arm (inactive)	5 - 27 days	5 - 8 weeks	2 - 4 weeks

Ulna & Radius

Dominant arm (active)	2 - 3 days	9 - 12 weeks	2 - 3 weeks
Non-dominant (inactive)	2 - 3 days	6 - 8 weeks	2 - 3 weeks
Surgical pinning	5 - 7 days	10 - 12 weeks	2 - 3 weeks
Both bones	3 - 8 days	6 - 18 weeks	2 - 3 weeks

Pelvis

Without displacement	3 - 10 days	8 - 10 weeks	3 - 6 weeks
Complication	2 - 5 weeks	8 - 16 weeks	3 - 6 weeks

Femur

Head or neck of femur	3 weeks to 3 months	2 - 6 months	4 - 8 weeks
Shaft	3 weeks to 3 months	3 - 6 months	4 - 8 weeks
Lower third	3 weeks to 3 months	3 - 6 months	4 - 8 weeks

Tibia & Fibula

Fibula only	0 - 1 day	5 - 6 weeks	2 - 6 weeks
Upper third	0 - 1 day	12 - 16 weeks	2 - 6 weeks
Tibia only	1 - 4 weeks	8 - 14 weeks	2 - 6 weeks
Both bones	3 - 5 weeks	12 - 18 weeks	2 - 6 weeks
Lower third	2 - 4 weeks	14 - 16 weeks	2 - 6 weeks

SPINAL FRACTURES

Diagnosis		Hospitalization	Disability
Transverse processes	TL	2 - 3 days	4 - 13 weeks
	Cervical	2 - 3 days	4 - 13 weeks
Fracture of spinous process	TL	2 - 3 days	4 - 13 weeks
	Cervical	2 - 3 days	4 - 13 weeks
Fracture of lamina	TL	4 - 6 days	12 - 39 weeks
	Cervical	3 - 4 days	10 - 30 weeks
Sacral region fusion		15 - 28 days	18 - 52 weeks
Body of sacrum		5 - 10 days	9 - 26 weeks
Coccyx		0 - 3 days	6 - 13 weeks

Sacroiliac Sprains	**Total**	**Partial**
Slight	3 - 8 days	3 - 5 days
Severe	3 - 6 weeks	2 - 3 weeks
Spinal Dislocation	6 - 12 weeks	(Highly disabling) 3 - 9 months Usually associated with some cord compression or root injury

178—Medical Aspects of Claims

Location & Description of Injury	Hospitalization	Total Disability	Partial Disability
HEAD INJURIES			
Fracture, Skull			
Simple line or linear	5 - 15 days	3 - 5 weeks	3 - 12 weeks
Compound	2 - 6 weeks	6 - 8 weeks	3 - 12 weeks
Compound w/infect.	4 - 12 weeks	10 - 12 weeks	3 - 12 weeks
Depressed	2 - 4 weeks	10 - 15 weeks	3 - 12 weeks
Fracture, Nasal Bone			
Simple	0 - 2 days	1 - 2 days	
With brain concus.	4 - 8 days	3 - 4 weeks	3 - 5 days
Badly shattered	2 - 7 days	2 - 3 weeks	3 - 5 days
Fracture, Maxillary			
Compound w/surgery	2 - 4 days	5 - 10 weeks	1 - 3 weeks
Fracture, Mandibular			
Usual	3 - 4 days	5 - 6 weeks	1 - 2 weeks
Compound, infection	5 - 7 days	6 - 8 weeks	1 - 3 weeks
Dislocation, Mandibular			
Usual	none	3 - 7 days	none
Puncture of Skull			
Usual	10 - 14 days	8 - 12 weeks	2 - 3 weeks
Contusion of Head			
Temp. unconscious.	1 - 2 days	5 - 7 days	Recovery must be complete
Concussion			
Usual	7 - 10 days	3 - 5 weeks	
Severe	2 - 3 weeks	8 - 12 weeks	

Occupation. Temporary disabilities are more common among blue collar than white collar workers. The incidence of injury is higher in jobs that require lifting or repetitive manual tasks, such as assembly-line work. In addition, an injured worker who must return to manual labor must be in better health and more completely recovered than an injured worker who can return to light or sedentary work.

Attitudes toward returning to work also differ among workers. People who work in factories at repetitive jobs tend to accept continuing workers compensation disability as relief from work that is boring and dull. It is also common for blue collar workers to have an adversarial attitude toward the employer. This less-than-comfortable situation makes the return to work altogether less attractive. In contrast, white collar workers or general office workers usually minimize the seriousness of injuries and may attempt to return to work almost too soon. Of course, individual cases do not always correspond with these generalizations.

Pre-Existing Conditions. Pre-existing conditions such as diabetes, heart disease, or psychiatric problems affect the recovery of an injured worker. Diabetes delays the healing of wounds; as a result, a longer course of antibiotics and a longer healing time may delay the return-to-work date. In addition, blood sugar is more difficult to control after the stress and damage to the body caused by a serious accident. In fact, it is common for the sugar level of diabetics to be uncontrolled for some time after a significant injury. A hospital course followed by treatment at home, sometimes for many years, must often be covered by a compensation insurer when a compensable accident has exacerbated pre-existing diabetes.

Heart disease, another condition that often pre-exists an injury, directly affects an individual's recovery. It is also common for heart disease to go undiagnosed until a heart attack is brought on by stressful conditions.

Stroke, or cerebral vascular accident, is another body weakness that may pre-exist an accident and may cause serious injuries. It can also result from injuries. In any given case, the insurer must determine if the accident caused the stroke or if the stroke occurred first and the accident followed. A physician can review the following pre-existing factors to determine the likelihood of a causal connection between a stroke and accidental injuries:

- Family history of stroke
- Smoking
- History of high blood pressure
- Symptoms of severe headache
- Obvious head injury or trauma

Psychiatric conditions can also precede or result from an injury. Both pre-existing and resulting psychiatric conditions can complicate and delay recovery from physical injuries.

Complications. Complications are secondary diseases, illnesses, or conditions that develop after an initial injury and delay overall recovery. Osteomyelitis (bone infection), for instance, can complicate recovery from a fractured bone. This problem is usually treated with antibiotics and sometimes with surgery to remove dead bone. Recovery time is lengthened greatly when the physician fails to take early, aggressive action or delays referring the case to an appropriate physician with expertise in osteomyelitis. Other types of infections can also make a relatively simple problem much worse.

Sensitivity to medications can also complicate recovery. An individual who must take anti-inflammatory medication for low back sprain, but who has stomach lining sensitivity, can suffer ulcers.

Motivation. The length of disability can vary according to differences in motivation from one person to the next. Individuals who are motivated to work out of commitment or by a desire to return to their normal routine often return to work although still in pain or not fully recovered. These individuals are also likely to be the most scrupulous in following doctors orders and physical therapy routines that will hasten their recovery. In addition, someone who is not receiving any disability compensation may be highly motivated to return to work even before fully recovered.

On the other hand, a common but problematic reaction to physical disability is the injured person who is motivated to stay disabled. Claim representatives often see this condition when the case is in litigation or when the claimant stands to gain something from the injury. The gain might be financial or psychological if, for instance, the injured individual (no matter how slightly injured) receives, as part of complex family dynamics, the attention and love he or she may not have received before the accident. There may be very little motivation to recover from injury when the value of a case depends on the amount of medical bills generated in treatment. This situation is common in liability cases. In temporary disability claims under workers compensation, the motivation to return to work may be low because of factors unrelated to the injury, such as impending layoffs, friction between the supervisor and the "injured" worker, or union rules that state that the worker must be 100 percent recovered before a return to work is permitted.

The phenomenon that people with claims take longer to heal than people without claims is not entirely a result of malingering. Conscious malingering is probably relatively rare. In part, this phenomenon is based in fact. For instance, injuries that are most painful and difficult naturally take the longest to heal and are most likely to generate a claim. So on one hand, there is nothing unusual about the connection between delayed healing and the making of a claim. However, claim representatives and physicians have observed that the act of asserting a claim seems to delay recovery. This delay is not usually a result of malingering or the severity of the injury, but of unconscious motivations. To rationalize or to justify making a claim or suing another person, many claimants magnify their injuries and symptoms. The claimant who seems miraculously to stop ailing once a claim is settled has not necessarily been malingering, but may simply no longer need to justify the act of asserting a claim or maintaining a lawsuit.

Overcoming Permanent Impairment

Many who suffer injuries are left with permanent impairments. However, permanent impairments need not lead to permanent disability. Impaired people may be able to return to a former job if the work can be modified. Otherwise, they may be able to use their remaining abilities in other employment. Both a job analysis and an assessment of physical capabilities and transferable skills will help the injured person to overcome permanent impairment. A vocational rehabilitation counselor can also provide valuable services. Nevertheless, some workers will suffer a permanent loss of earning capacity, which must be properly accounted.

Job Analysis. An on-site job analysis performed by a vocational rehabilitation professional is a powerful tool for the claim representative. Everyone affected by a long-term disability will benefit from a job analysis since the duties are clarified and quantified. The injured worker and his or her family, the employer, attorneys, and the insurance claim representative will better understand how to approach the case and what to expect about the worker's occupational future.

Job analysis is especially important in insurance claims in which a return-to-work is of utmost importance. A return to work is important in workers compensation because many states put the burden of proof on the employer/insurer to show that jobs are available and that the injured worker can physically do the job. Such burden of proof is easily met when an employee has returned to his or her former job.

After an accident that causes orthopedic or neurological injuries, it is of utmost importance that the recovered individual be able to perform all job duties safely. However, despite an injured worker's desire to return to work or an employer's desire to have an employee back on the job, it may be difficult to reinstate the employee unless everyone knows and understands the physical demands of the job.

The purpose of job analysis is to determine what jobs are and to define their limits, that is, to describe where job activities begin and end.[27] It is preferable to perform a job analysis at the job site because the vocational rehabilitation professional can watch the job being performed. As a result, he or she will have a better idea of job requirements than would be provided by a written job description. Written descriptions may enumerate only the nonphysical aspects of the job, such as hours to be worked.

The vocational rehabilitation professional should observe the environment at the job site, making note of any barriers such as stairs or narrow doorways. In watching the job being performed, the vocational rehabilitation specialist should observe the *activities* of the workers, not the characteristics of the individuals doing the job. This will help the analyst include the important physical demands of the job in the analysis, such as standing, walking, sitting, lifting, carrying, pushing, pulling, climbing, balancing, stooping, bending, kneeling, crouching, crawling, reaching, handling, fingering, feeling, talking, hearing, tasting, smelling, and seeing. A job analysis should include the amount of weight the employee must lift, push, pull, or carry, as well as how frequently such work is done. Frequency of work may be expressed in number of times per hour or as a percentage of the workday.

It is also important to inspect any tools, machines, or assisting devices used on the job, and to note the work hours and whether the job is performed indoors or out. Other environmental conditions such as temperature (hot, cold, or alternating), wetness, humidity, noise, vibration, and heights should also be included in the analysis. A sample form for a job analysis is shown in Exhibit 4-4.

Job analysis information is useful not only as it provides an overall picture of the job, but as a means of identifying segments of the job that can be modified to allow a worker to return to work at an earlier date. Ultimately, the employer controls whether the job may be modified or not. Some changes are easy to accomplish, such as allowing a worker to use a stool to sit instead of standing 100 percent of the time or eliminating lifting by switching duties with another worker whose job tasks do not include lifting. However, employers should be encouraged to make substantial changes as well because an injured employee is usually most comfortable and most willing to attempt to return to work when he or she knows the job, the environment, and the employer.

Determining and Restoring Physical Capacities. The physical capacities form is another useful tool for the claims professional. It quantifies what an individual *can* do and is usually completed by a physician or work-hardening/work-tolerance specialist. Exhibit 4-5 shows a sample physical capacities form.

Work tolerance, or *work hardening*, operates on the premise that it is better to prepare a worker for strenuous work *before* he or she returns to work, thus reducing the possibility of injury on the job. The injured worker is most likely to be deconditioned because of the injury and consequent inactivity. Aerobic conditioning (bicycling, walking, swimming) and strength conditioning are part of a work tolerance program.

A work hardening specialist might use special equipment to evaluate an individual's ability to perform certain work-related tasks, such as lifting a pail of processed meat or pushing a dolly loaded with books. The actual activity is broken down into segments. This allows the examiner to test individual muscle groups with specific machines. For example, if an individual must pick up 50-pound bags of potatoes and move them from a skid to a truck, the major muscle groups involved in the action would include the quadriceps (front of thigh), biceps (arms), and abdominals. The injured worker would therefore be tested on equipment that isolates each of these muscle groups. A worker's performance on machines must be greater than, or at least equal to, what would be required on the job.

Both a job analysis and a physical capacities test are important in the recovery process and in resolving claims involving disability because

Exhibit 4-4
Job Analysis Form

Claim # _____
Claimant: _____
Job Title: _____ D.O.T. #: _____
Firm & Address: _____
Union: _____
Person Contacted: _____ Phone No.: _____
Job Summary/Description of Tasks: _____
_____

Work Schedule (hours, days per week): _____ Wage: _____
Education/Training: _____

PHYSICAL DEMANDS:

[ ] Standing _____ Hours/Day
[ ] Sitting _____ Hours/Day
[ ] Walking _____ Hours/Day
[ ] Lifting _____ lbs. – how often/day
[ ] Driving _____
[ ] Carrying _____ lbs. – how often/day

[ ] Pulling _____ lbs. – how often/day
[ ] Climbing _____ Height _____ Frequency _____
[ ] Balancing _____ Height _____ Frequency _____
[ ] Bending/ _____ Body part _____ Frequency _____
    Squatting
[ ] Twisting _____ Body part _____ Degrees _____ Frequency ___
[ ] Rotation _____ Body part _____ Degrees _____ Frequency ___
[ ] Crawling _____ Distance _____ Frequency _____
[ ] Kneeling on _____ Duration _____ Frequency _____
[ ] Reaching _____ Distance _____ Frequency _____

ENVIRONMENTAL CONDITIONS:

Inside _____% Outside _____% Both _____% Temp. extremes _____
Fumes _____ Dust _____ Gases _____ Odors _____ Mist _____
NOISE OR VIBRATION: _____
HAZARDS: _____
MACHINES, TOOLS, EQUIPMENT: _____
GENERAL COMMENTS: _____
_____
_____
_____

PHYSICIAN'S COMMENTS: _____
_____

Analyzed by: _____ Job Approved: _____
                   SIGNATURE
Date: _____ Not Approved: _____

      _____   ___/___/___
         Physician's Signature   Date

184—Medical Aspects of Claims

Exhibit 4-5
Physical Capacities Form

Claimant Name: _____
Claim #: _____ Representative: _____
Insurance Co.: _____ Adjuster: _____

In an 8-hour workday, patient can: (Circle full capacity for each)

Sit	1	2	3	4	5	6	7	8	Hrs/Day
Stand	1	2	3	4	5	6	7	8	Hrs/Day
Walk	1	2	3	4	5	6	7	8	Hrs/Day

Patient can lift/carry: (Please check as appropriate)

	Never		Occasionally		Frequently		No Restriction
	Lift	Carry	Lift	Carry	Lift	Carry	
0-10 lb.	[ ]	[ ]	[ ]	[ ]	[ ]	[ ]	[ ]
11-25 lb.	[ ]	[ ]	[ ]	[ ]	[ ]	[ ]	[ ]
26-50 lb.	[ ]	[ ]	[ ]	[ ]	[ ]	[ ]	[ ]
51-100 lb.	[ ]	[ ]	[ ]	[ ]	[ ]	[ ]	[ ]
100+ lb.	[ ]	[ ]	[ ]	[ ]	[ ]	[ ]	[ ]

Patient can use hand for repetitive: (Please check as appropriate)

	Simple Grasping		Fine Manipulation		Pushing and Pulling	
Right	[N]	[Y]	[N]	[Y]	[N]	[Y]
Left	[N]	[Y]	[N]	[Y]	[N]	[Y]

Patient can use feet for repetitive movement such as foot controls: (Please check as appropriate)

Right   [N]   [Y]   Left   [N]   [Y]

Patient is able to: (Please check as appropriate)

	Not at all	Occasionally	Frequently	No Restriction
Bend	[ ]	[ ]	[ ]	[ ]
Climb	[ ]	[ ]	[ ]	[ ]
Crawl	[ ]	[ ]	[ ]	[ ]
Squat	[ ]	[ ]	[ ]	[ ]
Reach	[ ]	[ ]	[ ]	[ ]
Twist	[ ]	[ ]	[ ]	[ ]

Patient is able to drive: (Please check as appropriate)

	Not at all	Occasionally	Frequently	No Restriction
Car	[ ]	[ ]	[ ]	[ ]
Small Truck	[ ]	[ ]	[ ]	[ ]
Large Truck	[ ]	[ ]	[ ]	[ ]
Automatic Transmission	[ ]	[ ]	[ ]	[ ]
Standard Transmission	[ ]	[ ]	[ ]	[ ]
Heavy Equipment	[ ]	[ ]	[ ]	[ ]

RETURN TO WORK STATEMENT

As a result of this evaluation, patient could perform: (Please check as appropriate)
[ ] No Work
[ ] Part-time   Sedentary work – 10 lbs. maximum lifting or carrying articles.
[ ] Full-time   Walking/standing on occasion.

[ ] Part-time   Light Work – 20 lbs. maximum lifting, carrying 10 lb. articles frequently,
[ ] Full-time   most jobs involving sitting with a degree of pushing and pulling.

[ ] Part-time Medium Work – 50 lbs. maximum lifting with frequent lifting/carrying of
[ ] Full-time   up to 25 lbs., frequent standing and walking.
[ ] Part-time Heavy Work – 100 lbs. maximum lifting with frequent lifting/carrying of
[ ] Full-time   up to 50 lbs. frequent standing and walking.
[ ] Part-time Very Heavy Work – lifting objects over 100 lbs. and frequent lifting/
[ ] Full-time   carrying of 50 lbs. or more, frequent standing/walking.

When will patient be released
        to return to work: [ ] Immediately [ ] _____ (Please specify)
Date: _____ Physician's Signature _____

---

the results of both help to determine a disabled person's potential for future work. That is, once the job requirements and the workers physical capacities are known, there is little conjecture involved in deciding if a recovered worker can return to work and in what job he or she can work.

Transferable Skills. Transferable skills are abilities that can be applied equally from one job to another. For example, speaking to customers on the telephone may be one job requirement. The individual may not be able to perform the other duties of this job because of an inability to lift more than 50 pounds. However, telephone skills can be "transferred" to another job where they are important and where the physical tasks are not as strenuous. The worker might therefore be eligible for a job in telemarketing, for instance, which requires good telephone skills but no heavy lifting.

An understanding of transferable skills is important and useful knowledge when one must locate employment for an individual who does not know where to look. The injured worker ready to return to work should also be encouraged to identify transferable skills so that the job search will be less difficult.

Role of Vocational Rehabilitation and Counseling. Overcoming disability can be difficult for some people. A vocational rehabilitation counselor can make a difference. This type of rehabilitation work is described in the next chapter. The vocational rehabilitation counselor is usually hired by an insurance company or self-insured employer to assist an injured worker through recovery and back to work. An important function of the vocational rehabilitation process is to build a rapport with the injured worker and to develop and demonstrate trust, caring, and sensitivity to the worker's needs. However, the claimant must be aware that the vocational rehabilitation counselor will be communicating with the insurance company. Once this is clarified, there should be no misconception as to what the counselor is to do and to whom the counselor's reports are sent.

Most people have never had any vocational counseling. Family or friends usually influence where and for whom an individual works.

There is often very little thought given to the job search process. A vocational rehabilitation counselor is experienced in assessing an individual's physical ability to work, level of motivation, job skills, educational preparation, and work experience. The vocational rehabilitation counselor can also identify the many industries in which the claimant could return to work.

Job skills counseling, including resume preparation and interviewing skills, is another way in which the vocational rehabilitation counselor can help. Intense preparation in job skills counseling may be necessary if, for example, the injured worker has worked for thirty years in construction as a carpenter and because of a back injury and subsequent surgery is unable to return to carpentry.

Many times an injured worker is fearful about returning to work because of the possibility of reinjury. A rehabilitation counselor fosters confidence that the injury will not recur when proper body mechanics are considered and safety measures are followed. Generally, in this role, the counselor is reinforcing information that the physician or physical therapist has already given to the claimant.

The vocational rehabilitation counselor may also actually search for a job on behalf of the claimant. The counselor will search for job openings that fit the physical capabilities, work experience, and education of the injured worker and then pass on to the injured worker any useful information.

Determination of Loss of Earning Capacity. Determination of loss of earning capacity is important in claims. If an individual is injured and unable to return to his or her job, the claim representative must determine the difference between the salary at the time of the injury and the salary that the individual is now *capable* of earning upon return to work. The worker need not have actually returned to work for the latter to be determined. A claim representative will rely very heavily on a vocational rehabilitation professional for information about available jobs and for job analyses.

The problem of reduced earnings is particularly common among injured construction workers. For example, it is not unusual for workers in construction to earn more than $20 per hour for their work. Should an injury prevent a worker from returning to this work, it is possible that this worker's earning capacity outside of construction may be only $8 to $10 per hour if he or she has only an elementary or high school education.

SUMMARY

Disability, which is different from impairment and handicap, is a major concern of claim representatives who handle injury claims. The extent and duration of disability are probably the key factors affecting the value of injury claims. In addition to its effect on claims, disability has a profound effect on society, the employer, the economy, and, of course, on the disabled themselves.

Disability can only be determined by analyzing an individual's physical impairment, the demands of that individual's job, and then by comparing the two to see if the impairment prevents the individual from meeting job demands. The AMA has standardized the evaluation of physical impairment in its *Guide to the Evaluation of Permanent Impairment*. Job demands can be researched through the *Dictionary of Occupational Titles* and *Selected Characteristics Companion Volume*. Temporary disabilities generally cannot be analyzed as thoroughly as permanent disabilities. Nevertheless, claim representatives should know typical lengths of disability for various injuries so they may concentrate their effort and attention on cases that may be abusive to the system.

Other than the nature of the injury, the length of temporary disabilities depends on the age and occupation of the individual, the presence of pre-existing or complicating conditions, and the individual's level of motivation. Overcoming permanent impairment may require job analysis, assessment of the individual's physical capabilities, services from a vocational rehabilitation counselor, and assessment of transferable skills.

Chapter Notes

1. Stanford E. Rubin and Richard T. Roessler, *Foundations of the Vocational Rehabilitation Process* (Baltimore: University Park Press, 1978), p. 55.
2. Rubin and Roessler, p. 65.
3. Rubin and Roessler, p. 1.
4. Rubin and Roessler, p. 58.
5. Rubin and Roessler, p. 59.
6. Rubin and Roessler, p. 59.
7. Rubin and Roessler, p. 60.
8. Rubin and Roessler, p. 60.
9. Elizabeth Kubler-Ross, *Death: The Final Stage of Growth* (New York: Simon and Schuster, 1986), p. 10.
10. Kubler-Ross, p. 10.
11. Hoyle Leigh, M.D. and Morton F. Reiser, M.D., *The Patient: Biological, Psychological, and Social Dimensions of Medical Practice*, 2d ed. (New York: Plenum Medical Book Co., 1985), pp. 18-23.
12. All quoted language is based on the Senate bill S.933. Final law was enacted July 26, 1990.
13. *Accident Facts 1989 Edition* (Chicago: National Safety Council), p. 34.
14. *Accident Facts*, p. 36.
15. *Accident Facts*, p. 37.
16. *Guide to the Evaluation of Permanent Impairment* (Chicago: American Medical Association, 1984), p. iii.
17. *Guide to the Evaluation of Permanent Impairment*, p. x.
18. *Guide to the Evaluation of Permanent Impairment*, p. vii.
19. *Guide to the Evaluation of Permanent Impairment*, p. viii.
20. *Guide to the Evaluation of Permanent Impairment*, p. 223.
21. *Guide to the Evaluation of Permanent Impairment*, p. x.
22. U.S. Department of Labor, *Dictionary of Occupational Titles*, Employment and Training Administration, 4th ed. (1977), p. xv.
23. *Dictionary of Occupational Titles*, p. 196.
24. U. S. Department of Labor, *Selected Characteristics of Occupations Defined in the Dictionary of Occupational Titles*, Employment and Training Administration (1981), p. 465.
25. Rene Calliet, *Soft Tissue Pain and Disability* (Philadelphia: F.A. Davis Co., 1988), p. 95.
26. Calliet, p. 118.
27. Ralph E. Matkin, *Insurance Rehabilitation: Service Applications in Disability Compensation Systems* (Austin, TX: Pro-Ed, 1985), p. 117.

CHAPTER 5

Rehabilitation

Rehabilitation is a process and a set of services that may be applied to certain claims. It is an alternative to both uncritical payment and thoughtless resistance in claims handling and can be the greatest good resulting from claims handling. Rehabilitation is only appropriate for certain claims, generally the most serious, as it can be expensive. Claim representatives must understand rehabilitation so that they can appropriately use and control it.

This chapter begins with a description of the nature of rehabilitation, including the need for and benefits of rehabilitation. This section makes clear that claim representatives must exercise judgment in the use of rehabilitation. Following is a description of the parties to the rehabilitation process and definitions of their roles. Again, the role of the claim representative in selecting and evaluating rehabilitation services is emphasized. The last section in the chapter describes the rehabilitation process from selection of appropriate cases through various rehabilitation services. Included in this discussion are medical management, vocational rehabilitation, psychosocial rehabilitation, and forensic rehabilitation.

THE NATURE OF REHABILITATION

Rehabilitation offers the possibility of helping injured parties overcome their problems while helping insurers control claim costs. It is a process that includes medical management, vocational rehabilitation, and psychosocial rehabilitation. This section defines rehabilitation, explains the need for rehabilitation, and discusses the costs and benefits of rehabilitation.

Definition

A dictionary defines rehabilitate as "to restore to a former capacity...." This definition has become the principle that underlies rehabilitation in workers compensation. The International Association of Industrial Accident Boards and Commission's (IAIABC) definition of rehabilitation reflects this principle:

> The restoration of an occupationally disabled employee to that person's optimum physical, mental, vocational and economic usefulness.[1]

The physical, mental, vocational, and economic needs of the injured worker are addressed in this definition.

Statutory References. Several states have focused primarily on the vocational component in their definition of rehabilitation. Minnesota, for example, uses the following language in its workers compensation statute:

> Rehabilitation is intended to restore the injured employee...so the employee may return to a job related to the employee's former employment or to a job in another work area which produces an economic status as close as possible to that the employee would have enjoyed without disability.[2]

Notice also that this definition does not reflect the IAIABC's concept of optimum usefulness, but instead focuses on restoration "as close as possible" to pre-injury status.

This definition is based on rehabilitation applied to workers compensation claims. Examples of definitions based on rehabilitation in other lines of casualty insurance are scarce, with the exception of a few auto no-fault statutes. Minnesota, for example, refers to rehabilitation under its automobile insurance law in the following language:

> A reparation obligor is responsible for the cost of a procedure or treatment for rehabilitation or a course of rehabilitative occupational training if the procedure, treatment, or training is reasonable and appropriate for the particular case, its cost is reasonable in relation to its probable rehabilitative effects, and it is likely to contribute substantially to medical or occupation rehabilitation.[3]

The Rehabilitation Process. This chapter uses a more general definition. Rehabilitation as applied to all lines of casualty insurance is a process that diminishes the impact of an accident or illness for the person and his or her family. Completely successful rehabilitation will restore the individual to the highest level of function consistent with the residual disabilities. The rehabilitation process includes, but is not limited to, three major components:

1. *Medical Management*—expediting maximum medical improvement or recovery. This is accomplished through, but not

limited to, services such as the following:
- Selection and use of qualified physicians and medical practitioners
- Selection and use of qualified health care and rehabilitation facilities
- Use of independent medical examinations and consultants
- Use and monitoring of other health care providers (physical therapists, occupational therapists, speech and language therapists, etc.)
- Monitoring of medication usage and ongoing therapy
- Procuring medical equipment, such as prosthetic devices
- Maintaining appropriate levels of care throughout the process while minimizing incurred costs

2. *Vocational Rehabilitation*—expediting the return to employment. This is accomplished through, but not limited to, services such as the following:
   - Job analysis of previous occupation
   - Return to work in the previous occupation
   - Return to work through job modification
   - Return to work in a new job with the most recent previous employer
   - Investigation of all transferable skills through employment history and job reference check
   - Vocational evaluation to identify job goals for job placement
   - Job-seeking skills training and job placement with a new employer
   - On-the-job training
   - Short-term training or formal retraining

3. *Psychosocial Adjustment*—maximizing psychological and social adjustment to the disability. This is accomplished through, but not limited to, services such as the following:
   - Assessment of disabled person, spouse, family support, and financial resources
   - Counseling on adjustment to disability, pain, chemical dependency or vocational change
   - Psychological testing and counseling

A number of the services included in this process overlap claim handling techniques that are not pure rehabilitation. For example, the selection of qualified physicians and medical practitioners is accomplished even if the claim is not for rehabilitation. A claim is considered to be in rehabilitation when it is referred to a rehabilitation provider. These providers are discussed later in the chapter.

The Need for Rehabilitation

Bodily injuries represent a multibillion dollar annual cost to the casualty insurance business. The workers compensation, auto, general liability, medical malpractice, and other coverages protecting against bodily injury are a substantial exposure for this business. While the issues of liability and coverage make some claims questionable, thus somewhat mitigating these exposures, the majority of claims are legitimate liabilities to the insurer. The insurance claim representative is faced with the challenge and responsibility of managing the bodily injury exposure. The challenge and responsibility arise from pressures from outside and within the business.

Pressures From Outside the Industry. The following case illustrates society's and the insurance business' interest in providing more than just financial reimbursement for an injury.

A machinist who worked for his employer for fifteen years took great pride in his work and was considered a valuable employee. One day, he caught his hand in a press, resulting in the amputation of his hand and arm just above the wrist. The workers compensation insurer provided prompt payment of indemnity (lost wages) benefits and paid for the expense of the hospital and follow-up medical care. The machinist was devastated by the loss of his hand. Although fitted with a prosthesis, he considered himself a cripple and refused to wear the prosthesis. His employer hired a replacement because it appeared that the machinist would not return to work.

This case demonstrates that financial reimbursement alone does not always "compensate" an injury. Clearly, the employer would have been better off if he or she did not have to train and hire another worker; society, too, loses a productive member; and the insurance company's payments are probably extended as a result of the worker's disability. A better way to handle the case would have been through rehabilitation. Professor Arthur Larson, a leading authority on workers compensation, has stated:

> It is probably no exaggeration to say that in this field (rehabilitation) lies the greatest single opportunity for significant improvement in the benefits afforded by the workers compensation system.[4]

Rehabilitation offers similar opportunities in other lines of casualty insurance, such as auto and general liability.

Among the outside pressures to manage the bodily injury exposure is the erosion of common-law defenses, such as assumption of risk, that results in insurance benefits for a greater number of persons and fewer legal strategies for mitigating the bodily injury exposure. Another major pressure is brought by the growth of "no-fault" insurance. Workers compensation benefits have existed since the early 1900s, but benefit levels and the numbers of employees covered have increased. A number of states mandate no-fault or first-party medical auto coverage. A third pressure is brought by the potential for high-dollar jury awards for plaintiffs who have suffered, in some instances, relatively minor bodily injuries. Insurance benefits have been provided to an expanding number of persons, while legal defenses are restricted. All of these forces increase the pressure to control the exposure on injury claims.

Support From the Insurance Business. The insurance business itself has set out to meet society's expectations. The Insurance Rehabilitation Study Group is composed of representatives from among the largest casualty insurers in the United States and is influential in the casualty insurance industry generally. In a 1975 report, the Study Group stated the following:

> While insurance losses and benefits are usually stated in monetary terms, the full consequences of human disability cannot be measured by money alone. Earnings lost due to accident or sickness can be replaced and medical expenses can be reimbursed, but there is no meaningful way to financially translate the value of an arm or a leg, or the personal dignity of being able to contribute to society as a useful member rather than merely existing disabled and dependent....If insurance is to protect against these human losses, it must do more than provide financial compensation alone. It must also strive to restore such losses. Insurance should provide the means for disabled workers to return to gainful employment whenever possible, and to regain as much functional independence as they can, even if they cannot return to work. Compensation cannot accomplish these goals without rehabilitation.[5]

The National Commission on State Workers Compensation Laws, a group of representatives from major workers compensation insurers, government, and other experts, made a number of recommendations in the early 1970s to improve the workers compensation system in the U.S., including the following:

- Reduce litigation in all workers compensation claims.
- Increase benefits to equitable levels in all states.
- Provide quality services (including rehabilitation) in a uniform manner in all states.

Costs/Benefits of Rehabilitation

Rehabilitation can be a significant claim expense. Costs can be hundreds or thousands of dollars per case. Claim departments are reluctant to authorize such expenses unless they can foresee substantial savings on the cost of the underlying claim. Studies of rehabilita-

194—Medical Aspects of Claims

tion provide some insight into whether the benefits of rehabilitation justify its cost.

Formal Studies. The benefit of rehabilitation relative to its cost has been questioned. To date, formal studies on the use of rehabilitation in liability claims have been limited to workers compensation. These studies address the cost/benefit of rehabilitation in claims where a return to employment is a primary consideration. The studies provide examples of the average costs and the percentage of cases with a successful outcome (return to work) that can occur through the rehabilitation process. Four studies are summarized below:

State	Sample	Return To Work	Cost Per Case*
California[6]	850 closures in 1982 as reported to the California Worker's Compensation Institute (CWCI)	69%	$4,526
Florida[7]	1,173 closures in 1985 as reported by 7 rehab providers to the Worker's Compensation Research Institute (WCRI)	77%	$2,620
Michigan[8]	1,537 closures in 1986 as reported to the Bureau of Worker's Disability Compensation	40%	$2,303
Minnesota[9]	3,000 closures in 1987 as reported to the Department of Labor and Industry	77%	$3,570

*All costs reflect the rehabilitation professional or provider costs only. Rehabilitation temporary total benefits, tuition, books, and maintenance are not included.

Several points must be noted in comparing these studies. First, sample size varies from 850 cases in California to 3,000 cases in Minnesota. Second, the average cost-per-case figures in the California and Florida studies were based on 1982 and 1985 closures, respectively, and would have to be adjusted to be compared to the 1986 or 1987 closures. Finally, the return to work rates in all but the Michigan study are based on program completers, not on all rehabilitation recipients. For example, the Florida study eliminated cases that involved lack of cooperation, medical instability, settlement, and insurer or attorney termination of the program. Adding noncompleters back into the Florida sample would result in a 50 percent return-to-work rate compared to the reported 77 percent rate.

These studies suggest return-to-work rates of approximately seven of every ten injured persons who receive and complete rehabilitation service (eliminating noncompleters from the Michigan sample results in a 64 percent return to work rate). The average cost per case ranges from $2,300 in Michigan to $4,500 in California.

There is no consensus on what constitutes an acceptable return-to-work rate, and there is no consensus on an average cost per case that defines cost-effective rehabilitation. It is still likely that rehabilitation will continue as a benefit of workers compensation insurance. The studies to date may reaffirm that although rehabilitation is working, there are opportunities that are likely to improve cost effectiveness.

Case Studies. As an alternative to formal study, case studies have frequently been offered as evidence of the cost-effectiveness of rehabilitation. While such studies provide "soft" evidence, they illustrate the application of rehabilitation and imply cost/benefit. Three cases are included here (one workers compensation, one auto liability, and one medical malpractice) to demonstrate the successful application of rehabilitation. In each case, rehabilitation significantly mitigated the exposure for the casualty insurer.

Workers Compensation Case Study. After raising her family, Mary worked at a nursing home for five years as a nurse's aide. She was considered a dedicated employee who was very fond of the patients. She injured her back lifting a patient. Her condition required surgery. Her post-surgical progress was slow, and her treating physician, who felt she would never be capable of returning to nurse's aide work, thought she was likely to be a case of total disability.

The workers compensation insurer reserved the claim in anticipation of several years of wage loss and continued care. The claim representative also referred Mary's case to rehabilitation. Mary needed and received a vocational evaluation. Her employer would not allow her to return to work unless she could perform her prior job. The evaluation revealed that Mary had a strong aptitude for office work. Job placement efforts began, and within weeks Mary was placed as a medical receptionist. The outcome of rehabilitation changed Mary's future and saved the workers compensation insurer thousands of dollars in wage loss benefits.

Auto Liability Case Study. Fred had just turned twenty-one years old when he sustained a severe fracture to his left ankle in an automobile accident. The injury required multiple surgeries. He could not return to his employment as an auto mechanic, had never completed high school, and was engaged to be married. Although his medical bills were paid, he had no clear financial security.

The auto insurer was anticipating an expensive claim. Through rehabilitation, Fred secured a high school equivalency diploma and was successfully employed in a light-duty delivery job. The new employer developed definite career plans for Fred, his fiancee became his wife, and his future turned from bleak to secure and promising.

Medical Malpractice Case Study. Joey was five years old when he had open heart surgery. Because of an anesthesiology accident, he suffered severe brain damage. It appeared that he would be institutionalized for life. His family was devastated.

The insurer was facing a malpractice lawsuit with a $1 million policy limit. Intensive rehabilitation was begun, which helped Joey make a spectacular medical recovery. He was mainstreamed in public school and was able to live at home with his parents. By age eight, Joey walked with a limp and needed continuous tutoring to stay competitive in school, but he could lead a relatively normal life with his family and friends. The case was resolved through an annuity settlement at well under half of the policy limit, largely the result of successful rehabilitation.

The Claim Representative's Responsibility. The claim representative must decide which cases should receive rehabilitation services and what kind of services should be provided. Not every case will benefit from rehabilitation. If the medical management of a case is already appropriate, if the injured person's vocational future is secure, and if that person's psychosocial adjustment is satisfactory, rehabilitation services would be a waste of money.

Yet, the formal studies and case studies demonstrate that some cases clearly benefit from rehabilitation services. In such cases, rehabilitation can provide enormous savings on the claim and an important humanitarian service. With an adequate understanding of the rehabilitation process, claim representatives can ensure that money allocated for rehabilitation is well spent.

PARTIES TO THE REHABILITATION PROCESS

Rehabilitation services are provided by professionals who specialize in rehabilitation. This section describes the rehabilitation provider as well as numerous other professionals who may play a role in the rehabilitation process. Also described are the roles of other key participants, the most important being the injured person. The section concludes with suggested guidelines by which claim representatives can control the rehabilitation process.

The Professional Rehabilitation Provider

Rehabilitation is traditionally thought of as a process that takes place when a person is hospitalized or during outpatient follow-up such as physical therapy. Rehabilitation has also traditionally taken place through public, nonprofit service providers. For example, the earliest providers were veterans' hospitals since the early federal rehabilitation laws focused primarily on veterans injured in the First World War. Over the years, however, there has been a tremendous growth in a private, for-profit rehabilitation service delivery system. There has also been a concurrent demand for qualified professional rehabilitation providers.

Private Rehabilitation Services. The oldest and largest private rehabilitation service (currently employing over 2,500 nurses and counselors) is the firm, Intracorp. Intracorp was established and is still owned by CIGNA (previously INA), one of the largest casualty insurance corporations in the United States. There are currently hundreds of other private rehabilitation firms ranging from national groups to individual sole practitioners. Many large casualty insurers employ their own professional staff in a rehabilitation organization.

Qualifications of the Professional Rehabilitation Provider. The rehabilitation provider is a professional who is directly responsible for the overall development and management of the rehabilitation of an injured insurance claimant. This professional coordinates all rehabilitation efforts and counsels the injured person in moving toward medical improvement and/or a return to employment. Such providers are qualified by their education—many are registered nurses or have master's degrees in rehabilitation counseling—and by experience in the insurance rehabilitation field. Such providers neither provide hands-on therapy nor practice medicine.

There is some controversy about the qualifications required of a rehabilitation provider. Some states have passed licensure laws that require a rehabilitation provider to hold a master's degree and pass a national examination in order to practice. Georgia, for example, requires rehabilitation providers handling workers compensation cases to hold a master's degree and pass the national certification examination that gives the provider the designation of Certified Rehabilitation Counselor (CRC).

Most states do not regulate providers. Thus, persons with or without a bachelor's degree or experience in working with disabled persons may be considered qualified. In response to this absence of regulation, many persons and a growing number of registered nurses have taken the national examination for the designation of Certified Insurance Rehabilitation Specialist (CIRS).

A claims handler will often see rehabilitation providers with the CRC or CIRS designation. The claim representative may also see the credentials M.A., M.S., or R.N. Any of these designations reflect valid and important qualifications. A claim representative should also contact the state licensure board and the state's industrial commission to determine if specific qualifications are required for a rehabilitation provider to practice in that state.

Other Rehabilitation Professionals

Other professionals may become involved in the rehabilitation process by invitation of the rehabilitation provider or through the health care delivery system. These other professionals are identified here to provide a complete list of all who may become involved in the rehabilitation process.

While this list may seem overwhelming, most cases require the services of only a few of these professionals. While rehabilitation may become a lengthy, expensive process for a catastrophic injury (brain injury, for example, that leaves the victim dependent on others to survive), only a minute percentage of all bodily injuries or diseases are catastrophic. The majority of rehabilitation cases require less than six months of service and cost no more than a few thousand dollars in direct payments to the rehabilitation provider.

Attending Physician. An attending physician is the professional initially contacted for treatment by the injured person. He or she is typically a general practitioner or, in some cases, a chiropractor. This physician is not necessarily a specialist in the disabling injury or disease. However, the attending physician is a key person since the injured person will rely on the attending physician's recommendations for medical treatment and rehabilitation.

Physiatrist. A physiatrist is a physician who specializes in physical medicine and rehabilitation. Physiatrists are prominent in the medical management of catastrophic injuries, such as spinal cord injuries. Their specialty is recognized by the American College of Physical Medicine and Rehabilitation and the American Congress of Rehabilitation Medicine.

Consulting Physician. A consulting physician usually specializes in a given area of medicine and helps diagnose or treat an injury or disease. The following are two kinds of consulting physicians frequently involved in cases of accidental injuries:

- *Neurologist*—an expert in the treatment of disorders of the nerves and nervous system, including the central nervous system (brain and spinal cord) and the peripheral nervous system (sensory and motor nerves throughout the body)
- *Orthopedist*—a physician who specializes in the preservation and restoration of the function of the skeletal system (bones),

its articulations (joints), and associated structures (muscles, tendons, and ligaments)

Hospital-Based Nurse. A hospital-based nurse develops the overall hospital-based nursing plan, including basic needs such as bowel and bladder care, skin care, and medications. This nurse may be a motivating force for the individual to progress beyond the initial negative responses to a disability. All *registered nurses* must complete a college degree or three-year hospital training program and pass an examination to acquire a license. A rehabilitation nurse should complete an affiliation in a rehabilitation hospital.

Occupational Therapist. An occupational therapist provides treatment that helps a disabled person relearn and carry out the activities of daily living, such as eating, dressing, and homemaking. An occupational therapist may also provide physical therapy for upper extremity injuries (hands, fingers, arm) through heat, massage, splinting, and supervised exercise. An occupational therapist must complete a bachelor's degree and pass a national examination to become registered and to receive the title of OTR.

Occupational therapy provides group and individual services to maximize independence in individuals with physical, behavioral, and cognitive impairments. Education and treatment services include teaching daily living skills; developing motor skills and sensory functioning; developing prevocational and vocational capacities; designing, fabricating, and applying selected orthotic devices or adapted equipment; administering and interpreting tests, such as manual muscle and range of motion; modifying environments; and driving training.

Physical Therapist. Physical therapists provide treatment to help the injured person achieve maximum physical restoration through "physical agents" such as heat, light, water, electricity, massage, and exercise. An important part of physical therapy in cases in which the lower extremities are affected by injury or disease is helping the injured person relearn ambulation (walking). A physical therapist must complete a bachelor's degree, and often a master's, and pass a state examination in order to receive a license and the title of RPT.

A physical therapist is a licensed medical professional who by means of examination, treatment, or instruction is able to detect, assess, prevent, correct, or limit physical disability, bodily malfunction, or pain. A physical therapist also administers and evaluates tests of bodily function and structures.

A rehabilitation physical therapist evaluates the neuro-musculo-skeletal systems of the patient and sets short- and long-term goals as appropriate. The therapist then develops and implements a treatment program that emphasizes exercises and activities that will lead to the highest level of independence. This treatment program may include the use of adaptive equipment. As appropriate, the therapist will also participate in the discharge plans, including home modifications, and set up a follow-up procedure.

Speech Pathologist. A speech pathologist provides treatment for an injured person in the areas of speech and language. The speech pathologist must complete a master's degree, have one year of work experience, and pass a national examination for registration to practice.

In a rehabilitation setting, the speech pathologist typically evaluates a patient through observation and formal testing to diagnose speech, language, and cognitive/communication deficits. Areas of treatment based on the evaluation and diagnoses may include swallowing therapy to re-establish eating by mouth; oral and language exercises to improve swallowing, voice, or speech intelligibility; and cognitive/communication treatment to improve attention, orientation, memory, speed of processing information, thought organization, and higher level reasoning and problem-solving skills.

Audiologist. An audiologist provides treatment for hearing loss. This treatment may involve the testing and fitting for a hearing aid and training in lip reading and maintaining speech quality. An audiologist must complete a master's degree, have one year of work experience, and pass a national examination for registration to practice.

Prosthetist. A prosthetist designs and fits artificial limbs for individuals who have suffered an amputation. The prosthetist usually completes a one- to two-year technical training program. No registration or licensure is required to practice in most states.

Certified Orthotist. A certified orthotist provides care for patients with disabling conditions of the limbs and spine through the use of devices known as orthoses. The certified orthotist also assists in formulating prescriptions for orthoses and examines and evaluates the patients' orthotic needs. The certified orthotist is responsible for evaluating the patient's orthotic needs, formulating the design of the orthosis, and selecting materials and components; making all casts, measurements, model modifications, and layouts; performing fittings, including static and dynamic alignments; evaluating the orthosis on the patient; instructing the patient in its use; and maintaining patient records. The orthotist not only assists in prescribing the device, but ensures that its implementation conforms to the prescription. The title, Certified Orthotist, is awarded to the practitioner who successfully completes the formal education, experience, and examination requirements in this discipline.

Rehabilitation Engineer. A rehabilitation engineer helps to modify home or work environments in order to maximize the injured person's independence and function. This engineer usually holds a bachelor's degree in engineering. No license or registration is required unless this individual is working in a hospital or health care facility. In the latter case, the individual must pass a national exam for certification.

The engineer designs and builds equipment for therapists and hospital staff to help improve and increase patients' abilities. The engineer also fabricates or adapts equipment that helps to prevent future injuries or subtle deterioration that could lead to loss of function or painful, expensive correction. In creating such equipment, the engineer protects patients and maintains their existing health and abilities. The rehabilitation engineer also provides technical support for creating adaptive equipment, hospital equipment, computers, and environmental control units. In short, rehabilitation engineers conceive and produce devices that help handicapped people to lead more independent and productive lives, increasing the chances that they will return to work.

Recreational Therapist. A recreational therapist assists the injured person in selecting activities, hobbies, sports, and exercises that maximize the injured person's recreational opportunities. A recreational therapist must complete a bachelor's degree. No license or registration is required in most states.

Social Worker. In the hospital setting, the medical social worker does a complete assessment of the claimant and family. In many rehabilitation hospitals, this social worker acts as the case manager, interfacing with the insurance carrier and outside rehabilitation professionals.

Social workers interview the claimant and family to identify psychosocial, financial, and discharge needs. Social workers also provide individual, group, and family counseling, and serve as an advocate and referral agent for continuing care needs. A social worker can earn a degree at the bachelor's, master's, or doctoral level. In jurisdictions that require licensing, a master's degree generally is required.

Psychologist. A psychologist treats an individual through counseling in an attempt to help overcome emotional or psychological reactions to an injury or disease. A psychologist may also administer tests to diagnose an emotional or psychological problem, or to define vocational potential. Most states require a psychologist to have a doctoral degree, two years of experience, and to pass a state or national test to become licensed to practice.

Psychiatrist. A psychiatrist's role is very similar to a psychologist's in regard to treating and evaluating injured persons. A psychiatrist is also a medical doctor and is thus qualified to prescribe medications.

Work Evaluator. A work evaluator administers tests and work assignments to an injured person to formulate a vocational rehabilitation plan if a return to employment is feasible. The work evaluator should hold a bachelor's degree; some hold master's degrees. No licensure or certification is required to practice in most states. A national certification examination is available, however, which gives the title of Certified Vocational Evaluator (CVE).

Job Placement Specialist. A job placement specialist helps the injured person to find appropriate employment. The job placement process includes training the person in job application, interviewing techniques, and contacting prospective employers. A job placement specialist should hold a bachelor's degree or have at least two years' experience in a private employment agency. No licensure or certificate is required to practice in most states.

Other Key Parties

In addition to the rehabilitation provider and other rehabilitation professionals, there are several other key parties in the rehabilitation process. These parties are the injured person, the family, the employer (when relevant—rehabilitation is not limited to employed persons), and the claim representative. There may be other parties not listed here.

For example, a plaintiff attorney can take an adversarial or a supportive role in the rehabilitation process. In addition, not all the parties listed here would necessarily be involved in every rehabilitation case.

The Injured Person. As mentioned in Chapter 4, an individual may react in a number of different ways after a serious injury. *Denial* is one common reaction. The affected person may deny the fact that the injury or disease has occurred, or may believe that recovery will occur. He or she may attempt to continue living as if the disabling condition never occurred. This initially appears to be somewhat healthy, but can lead to significant problems in the long run. For example, while in the hospital, an individual with an amputated hand may indicate a complete acceptance of the loss. Yet, when discharged home and facing the public, this same person may hide the limb or may refuse to use a prosthesis. Denial is obvious in the person with a significant back injury who attempts to return to heavy-duty work and re-injures himself or herself.

An individual may also react with *anger*, thus rejecting attempts by others to help in the rehabilitation process. The person may blame others for the condition. This reaction may be prolonged when someone else is, in fact, to blame, such as in liability claims.

A third reaction is *depression*. The person may experience feelings of helplessness or hopelessness, which work against a return to a productive life-style.

A fourth reaction may be *fear*. The person may be afraid to face his or her spouse, family, employer, or society. The fear of pain may stop the person from attempting therapy or exercise. The fear, not always specific, may be a fear of the unknown.

Finally (and hopefully) the affected person, with adequate resources and support, may come to *accept the disability*. In doing so, the affected person demonstrates an understanding of his or her limitations and does not dwell on the disability. This person may demonstrate his or her acceptance through behavior rather than words by, for example, following medical or vocational rehabilitation recommendations to the best of his or her ability.

The majority of individuals who sustain an injury or disease usually experience some combination of these reactions. The injured person often initially reacts with denial or anger, then gradually moves through a period of depression to acceptance. Very few individuals are able to accept a disability immediately after an injury or illness. However, rehabilitation should not be delayed until the individual gets to the point of accepting a disability. Rehabilitation must begin despite less than optimal reactions. The affected person must be assisted through the rehabilitation process to the point of accepting the disability.

Family. The injured person's family may react to the condition in the same way as the affected person. The spouse and other family members may deny, become angry, depressed, fearful, or may accept the disability. Sometimes the injured person accepts the disability, but the spouse or family does not. The family may see the injured individual as a "different person," a stranger, difficult to accept and love. This would obviously have a negative effect on the injured person. Few injured persons are able to begin to accept their injury without the support of a spouse or family.

Employer. An employer can play a critical role by providing an opportunity for the injured person to return to a productive life by allowing the person to return to work either by modifying the job, transferring the person to a new job that can be performed despite the disability, or developing an entirely new position. This kind of concern and involvement can contribute to the emotional and psychological well-being of the person.

204—Medical Aspects of Claims

Claim Representative. The claim representative's role may vary from company to company, but usually includes identifying the need for rehabilitation, communicating with the rehabilitation provider, establishing the objectives and guidelines for the rehabilitation case, and monitoring the progress of each rehabilitation case. The claim representative must determine the extent of the insurer's financial commitment to the rehabilitation plan (although in certain states, rehabilitation is a *required* part of workers compensation). The claim representative must also maintain communications with the medical practitioners and the employer. Equally important is communication with the injured person in order to clarify the benefits and the goals of the rehabilitation process.

Quality Assurance

Claim representatives must judge the service of the rehabilitation provider. How this is done is questioned not only by casualty insurers but also by state legislators and regulators. Several states, including California, Minnesota, and Georgia, have established extensive rules regarding a rehabilitation provider's conduct in handling workers compensation claims. Yet even in those states, there are no comprehensive service standards against which to measure the service of the rehabilitation provider.

In the absence of clear service standards, a casualty insurer is encouraged to develop its own checklist of expectations by which to monitor a rehabilitation provider. Following are examples of the types of activities that can be included in such a checklist:

- The injured person must be contacted within a few days of referral to minimize any delay in the rehabilitation process.
- The claim representative must be contacted within an additional five days to discuss the preliminary rehabilitation plan and to minimize any rehabilitation activity that has not been authorized by the claim representative.
- An initial written report must be submitted to the claim representative within thirty days of referral, outlining the rehabilitation plan.
- The rehabilitation plan must include ultimate goals, steps to reach such goals, and time and cost estimates.
- The rehabilitation provider should communicate with the claim representative at least every thirty days.
- The claim representative must be contacted immediately by phone when any significant change or deterioration in the progress in the rehabilitation plan develops.

- A formal "case conference" must be held for any case that continues to require rehabilitation service beyond six months or $2,000 in rehabilitation costs.
- A case conference should include the claim representative, the rehabilitation provider, and the injured person. Progress and problems should be reviewed and steps to conclude the rehabilitation plan and terminate service should be determined.

This is certainly not an exhaustive list, but without other standards for quality assurance, it provides the claim representative with an initial basis for monitoring the rehabilitation process.

THE REHABILITATION PROCESS

Rehabilitation has been defined as a "process" that reduces the impact of an accident or disease upon the affected person and family. This section further describes this process. Exhibit 5-1 is a flowchart of the rehabilitation process. Notice that the three major components of the process—medical management, vocational rehabilitation, and psychosocial rehabilitation—occur in parallel. This does not, however, mean that progress will be even in all areas. The following discussion follows the flowchart.

The process of rehabilitation begins with an injury or disease. Once the claim representative receives a notice of loss, he or she must make decisions regarding initiation of rehabilitation. If the injury is identified as severe, the decision is heavily weighted in favor of initiating rehabilitation. If the injury or disease is less severe, the claim representative may use certain formal evaluation tools and exercise good judgment in deciding to begin rehabilitation. Once the claim representative has identified the need for rehabilitation, he or she must determine who will coordinate the rehabilitation services.

The claim representative may select an in-house insurance rehabilitation staff member or an outside rehabilitation provider to coordinate rehabilitation services. An in-house rehabilitation staff member is typically the first choice because it affords advantages of quality control, ease of communication, and reduced expense. If an in-house rehabilitation staff member is not available, an outside rehabilitation provider would be used. In this case, the claim representative must assess the qualifications of the provider. The basic qualifications for licensure of rehabilitation providers have been discussed earlier in this chapter. Beyond these credentials, the claim representative should question the owner or manager of the firm to find out about the education and experience of all staff, the philosophy of the firm, the methods used by the firm to serve the injured person, the experience of the firm with other insurance companies, the cost, and the professional

206—Medical Aspects of Claims

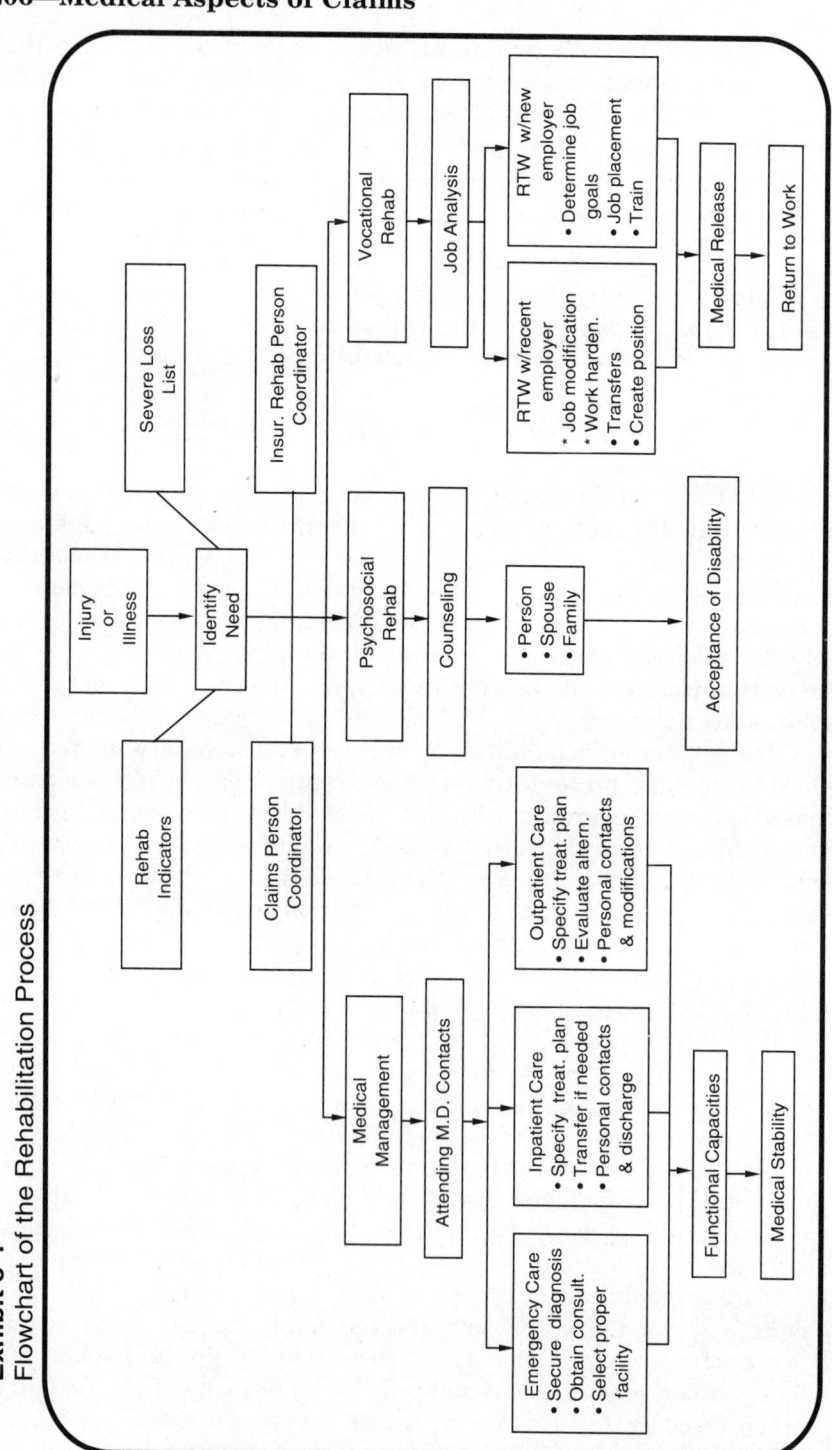

Exhibit 5-1
Flowchart of the Rehabilitation Process

liability insurance coverage of the firm. The rehabilitation provider should be questioned about experience with the specific injury in question. A list of other insurers who have used the firm should be obtained, and several of these insurers should be called for a reference. The claim representative can also contact the state industrial commission to determine whether the firm or individual provider is required to be registered and whether there have been any complaints filed (should a registration and complaint process exist in the particular jurisdiction). The likely personality match between the rehabilitation professional and the injured person is also an important factor to be considered.

Once the need for rehabilitation has been identified and the person who will coordinate rehabilitation services has been selected, the actual rehabilitation begins. The work included in the three major components of the process—medical management, vocational rehabilitation, and psychosocial rehabilitation—is performed. Ideally, the work in these components will be pursued simultaneously since progress in each area contributes to progress in the remaining areas. However, there are exceptions. For example, a return to work may be unfeasible or irrelevant. In this case, vocational rehabilitation would not be pursued. If return to work is feasible, progress in vocational rehabilitation (such as a specific job offer from an employer) may encourage the injured person to return to work on a trial basis rather than to stay away from the work place.

The steps in the rehabilitation process, including the three major components, are described below.

Identification of the Rehabilitation Candidate

The question of who should be involved in rehabilitation is difficult to answer because parties who are appropriate in workers compensation claims may not be so in liability claims. For example, Minnesota mandates the use of a rehabilitation evaluation in workers compensation claims involving forty-five days off from work for any type of back injury or ninety days off from work for all other types of injuries. This requirement would be irrelevant for an infant or a retired person involved in a liability claim, but it may be appropriate in a claim covered by the Longshore and Harbor Workers' Compensation Act or even in an automobile liability bodily injury claim.

Studies of rehabilitation have concluded that the shorter the gap between an injury or onset of disease and the beginning of rehabilitation, the better the outcome. Candidates for rehabilitation should therefore be identified as soon as possible. With this in mind, the claim representative may apply the following rehabilitation referral guidelines in most casualty claims.

208—Medical Aspects of Claims

Identification by Type of Injury. Rehabilitation should be considered *upon first notice of loss* in the following types of injury, assuming coverage and liability exist:

- *Spinal Cord Injury or Suspected Paralysis.* With this injury, the individual depends on a wheelchair and may require home modifications, attendant care, and extensive medical follow-up.
- *Head Injury or Suspected Brain Damage*, including CVA (Cerebral Vascular Accident, or stroke) and post concussion syndrome. With this injury, the individual depends on others for activities of daily living and may require long-term residential care.
- *Myocardial Infarction.* While many persons survive a heart attack, the psychological impact can easily lead to total disability.
- *Moderate or Major Burns.* This injury includes at least second and third degree burns over 15 percent of the total body surface (not including eyes, ears, face, or genitalia) or any second degree or third degree burn of the eyes, ears, face, or genitalia.
- *Amputations Other Than Fingers and Toes.* While many types of prostheses are available, the psychological impact of the loss of a hand or leg may easily lead to total disability.
- *Multiple Fractures or Any Crushing Type Injury.* These injuries may lead to partial or full amputation of an extremity or would at least require repeated surgeries, resulting in less than full function.
- *Injury to Brachial Plexus* (major nerve root in the shoulder). This injury is extremely painful and can easily lead to the complete loss of arm function.
- *Heel Bone Fracture.* These injuries often require multiple surgeries and a year or more of recovery. These fractures often occur bilaterally (both heels are fractured).
- *Vision Loss.* In addition to its enormous practical effect, blindness, whether partial or complete, is psychologically devastating for many persons.
- *Hearing Loss* (over fifty decibels bilaterally). While many types of hearing aids are available, the psychological impact of a hearing loss can lead to total disability.

Identification by Formal Evaluation Tools. Some casualty insurers use evaluation tools rather than specific types of injury criteria to determine the need for rehabilitation. Two examples, shown in

Exhibits 5-2 and 5-3, are for workers compensation and liability, respectively. Even when the actual form is not used, it is likely that the claim representative who is experienced in selecting cases for rehabilitation is mentally reviewing the factors included in the form.

Workers Compensation Cases. The factors listed in Exhibit 5-2 apply to workers compensation claims. A number of studies have investigated sociodemographic variables that can be used to make predictions about the chances of an injured person becoming totally disabled or returning to a productive life. For example, advanced age and lack of medical progress appear to predict total disability.[10] Researchers have found that education,[11] wages compared to the compensation rate,[12] and the physical demands of the work[13] may predict total disability.

The factors included in the sample evaluation tool have been taken from such studies and weighted. Age, for example, is weighted so that a young person (under twenty) would be considered a low risk of total disability compared to an older person (over fifty-five). The person whose time on the job is longer (over ten years) is considered a lower risk than the relatively new employee (less than one year).

The significance of some of these factors may appear to be obvious. A person with good medical progress is obviously a better risk than a person whose condition has worsened. However, in any given case a person who receives wages that are two times as great as his or her compensation rate may or may not be a better risk than one who receives wages equal to or less than compensation. Motivation compared to wages is a complex relationship and is not always a good predictor for a given case. The sample evaluation tool is not infallible. It is a guide to the claim representative in determining the risk of extended disability and identifying the need for rehabilitation in a workers compensation claim.

An "other factors" category is included to leave room for the claim representative's judgment. An example of one "other factor" may be attorney representation, which tends to delay a return to work for people with low back injuries.

Liability Cases. The factors in Exhibit 5-3 apply to liability claims. Some are similar to the workers compensation factors (age and claimant's general health after accident), but there are three key factors relevant to liability cases that are not as critical in workers compensation cases:

- Determination of legal liability
- Policy limits
- Claimant's and his or her family's attitude

Liability claims by definition require a determination of legal

Exhibit 5-2
Evaluation Tool to Identify the Need for Rehabilitation in Workers Compensation Case

FACTORS

RATING

FACTORS				
AGE	Under 20 / 1	20-40 / 2	41-55 / 3	Over 55 / 4
TIME ON JOB	Over 10 yrs / 1	5-10 yrs / 2	1-4 yrs / 3	Less than 1 / 4
TYPE OF WORK	Light / 1	Moderate / 2	Heavy / 3	Extra Heavy / 4
NET WAGES	More than 2X Comp / 1	2X Comp / 2	Equal to Comp / 3	Less than Comp / 4
JOB MARKET	Many / 1	Some / 2	Few / 3	None / 4
EDUCATION	H.S. Grad / 1	Some H.S. / 2	Grade School / 3	Some Grade School / 4
MEDICAL PROGRESS	Improvement Noted / 1	Some Improvement / 2	No Improvement / 3	Condition Worsened / 4
OTHER FACTORS*	1	2	3	4

TOTAL SCORE ▢

*To include current and/or pre-existing problems which may negatively impact the period of time until maximum medical recovery and/or return to work will occur (i.e., current and/or pre-existing medical problems, level of claimant's/insured's cooperation, etc.).

SCORING KEY

25 = Refer to rehabilitation immediately.
20-24 = Strong rehabilitation potential. Monitor closely and refer to rehabilitation if no RTW by 30 days post injury.
15-19 = Claim has rehabilitation potential. Monitor closely and refer if no RTW during next 60 days or 90 days post injury.
0-14 = Claim may have rehabilitation potential. Monitor closely and consider referral to rehabilitation if no RTW during next 60 days or 150 days post injury.

Exhibit 5-3
Evaluation Tool to Identify the Need for Rehabilitation in Liability Case

DETERMINATION OF NEGLIGENCE AGAINST DEFENDANT	Less than 50 / 0	50/50 / 1	60/40 / 2	70/30 / 3	80/20 / 4
POLICY LIMITS	0-$250,000 / 0	$250,000 / 1	$300,000 / 2	$500,000 / 3	More than $500,000 / 4
CLAIMANT'S/FAMILY ATTITUDE	-	Negative / 1	Neutral / 2	Positive / 3	Requests Rehabilitation / 4
CLAIMANT'S AGE	-	More than 55 / 1	41-55 / 2	30-40 / 3	Less than 30 / 4
CLAIMANT'S GENERAL HEALTH AFTER ACCIDENT	-	Good / 1	Fair / 2	Poor / 3	Very Poor / 4
DEGREE TO WHICH IMPAIRMENT BLOCKS EMPLOYMENT	-	No Effect / 1	Mild Effect / 2	Moderate Effect / 3	No Return Possible / 4
ESTIMATED LENGTH OF DIABILITY	Less than 90 Days / 0	3 to 4 Months / 1	5 to 8 Months / 2	9 to 12 Months / 3	More than 12 Months / 4

TOTAL SCORE ☐

SCORING KEY

20+ = Refer to rehabilitation immediately
10-20 = Consider referral to rehabilitation for evaluation
0-10 = Low potential for rehabilitation

liability. For instance, cases in which it is determined that the defendant has a greater than 50 percent chance of a successful defense would likely not be rehabilitation candidates since the primary liability of the defendant is doubtful. On the other hand, if the defendant has an 80 percent or more chance of an unsuccessful defense, negligence is probable, which encourages a strategy like rehabilitation to mitigate damages.

Policy limits also affect the decision to support rehabilitation. A severe injury involving lower policy limits (less than $250,000) would likely exhaust policy limits, so rehabilitation would only represent a cost beyond the policy limit of the insured. On the other hand, with high limits, even severe injuries might be controlled through rehabilitation, resulting in savings to the insured. In this case, rehabilitation is more likely to be supported.

Finally, the claimant's and his or her family's attitude in a liability claim is very important since the provision of rehabilitation is not required in this line of casualty insurance. Workers compensation statutes (in all states but Indiana) mandate some provision for rehabilitation (although the actual provision is only enforced in a small number of states including California, Minnesota, Florida, Oregon, and Georgia). No statute mandates rehabilitation in general or in professional liability cases, and only a handful mandate rehabilitation in auto no-fault cases. Thus, the voluntary acceptance of rehabilitation services is critical in a liability claim. It is most likely that an insurer would have to agree to make advance payments before a liability claimant would be cooperative. Advance payments are payments for medical or other expenses as they are incurred rather than payments made after the final settlement or judgment. An insurer receives credit for the amount of any advance payments in a final settlement or judgment.

Judgment. A final factor used to identify cases for rehabilitation is good judgment. A list of severe injuries and illnesses or a formal evaluation tool to identify the need for rehabilitation cannot substitute for the claim person's judgment. For example, there have been cases in which a relatively minor physical injury has led to total disability because of the injured person's emotional response to the injury. A condition known as "reflex sympathetic dystrophy" is a good example of this phenomenon. The syndrome can start with a simple strain of an extremity (hand, arm, or leg) and progress to the point at which the limb becomes useless as a result of self-inflicted immobility. Although a list of severe injuries and a formal evaluation system will ensure that the majority of persons needing rehabilitation will be identified, this type of condition is neither included in the list of severe injuries nor does it meet the criteria of the formal evaluation tool; yet rehabilitation is needed. Therefore, as in this case, good judgment is required to identify candidates for rehabilitation who do not otherwise meet the selection criteria.

Medical Management

Medical management, the first of the three major components of rehabilitation, occurs over several stages of treatment. Its purpose is to help optimize and expedite the healing of an injured person. Medical management begins as soon as possible after the onset of an injury or disease and continues until maximum medical improvement is achieved. Medical management can be particularly important in cases with no vocational prospects because although work may be an impossibility, medical costs must still be controlled. Medical management includes emergency care, inpatient care, and outpatient care.

Emergency Care. The injured person has his or her first major contact with an attending physician in an office or in an emergency room. This contact is significant and should be positive. It is best for the injured person to receive concrete information, that is, a formal diagnosis as opposed to the answer "a need for more evaluation." It is also best for the person to feel a sense of hope through a statement like "the condition will need treatment, but progress is expected."

There are delays to initiating medical management. The insurance company is not always aware of the initial office or emergency room visit until days or even weeks after it occurs. However, ideally, medical management should begin at the time of the emergency care. Medical management at this stage includes the following:

Diagnosis. A concrete diagnosis based on a complete medical history, thorough examination, and any testing should be secured. This is done through prompt personal contact between the rehabilitation professional and the attending physician.

Consulting Physician. If a diagnosis is not available, the services of a consulting physician should be secured to determine a diagnosis. This is done by referring the injured person to a specialist recommended by the attending physician or by the rehabilitation professional.

Selection of Proper Facility. If the injury is severe, a proper medical facility for initial inpatient care should be selected. For example, a person who sustains third degree burns may not be properly treated in a hospital that does not have a formal burn unit. The patient would be transferred at the request of the attending physician or rehabilitation professional.

Injured Person's Reaction. The rehabilitation professional

214—Medical Aspects of Claims

should meet with the injured person to personally assess the person's initial reaction to the injury.

Inpatient Care. Medical management is especially important when the injured person is hospitalized. The length of hospitalization varies from none to months. This aspect of medical management includes the following activities or issues.

Clarification of the Treatment Program Specifics and Length. The rehabilitation provider must answer the questions: Is surgery expected? Will conservative (nonsurgical) care suffice? If conservative care is the course of treatment, what specific therapies will be involved? Answers are obtained through the attending physician, consulting physicians, and other medical professionals at the hospital (such as nurses, therapists, or social workers).

Transfer. If the treatment plan does not seem to be resulting in progress within reasonable time limits, transfer to another medical facility may be indicated. This is accomplished by the rehabilitation professional, who negotiates with the attending physician, coordinates plans with consulting physicians, and evaluates alternative facilities. An example of a case that is a candidate for transfer would be a spinal cord injury treated in a local community hospital whose staff may not have the expertise to treat this challenging injury. There is a nationwide network of designated regional spinal cord rehabilitation centers that are better equipped to treat spinal cord patients. Transfer to this type of facility would provide more appropriate, higher quality treatment. There are similar networks for brain injury, burns, and cardiac care. Claim departments of reinsurers are usually a good source of referrals for locating these resources since the expense of these cases often involves reinsurance. The rehabilitation provider, however, should be a good resource for local or regional medical facilities.

Patient Reaction. The rehabilitation professional should assess the injured person's reaction to the treatment program. This is accomplished through personal contact with the person, spouse, family, and health care providers, if necessary. The assessment should include supporting the injured person through the various stages of disability, motivating and encouraging the person toward acceptance. This activity may also include the initial encouragement for a return to work.

Discharge. Plans for treatment upon discharge must be identified by the rehabilitation professional and confirmed with the attending physicians and other health care providers.

Outpatient Care. In this stage the person usually still needs medical treatment while adjusting to the activities of daily living, to the attitudes and reaction of spouse, family, society, and while planning for a return to work. Medical management at this stage consists of the following activities.

Clarification of Outpatient Treatment Program. This activity is similar to the one in the inpatient aspect of medical management. The rehabilitation professional must address such questions as: Is surgery anticipated? What therapies are being followed? Are these therapies resulting in progress? Is there a need for a consulting physician? To answer these questions, the rehabilitation professional would contact the attending and consulting physicians and the other medical professionals that may be involved at this stage.

This stage would also involve overseeing home modifications, equipment purchases, arrangements for attendants, or nursing care if there were a severe disability such as spinal cord or brain damage.

Alternative Treatment. If the treatment plan does not produce results, an alternative treatment plan must be developed. This is accomplished by negotiating with the attending physician and consulting physicians, and by identifying alternative treatment resources or programs. The injured person and his or her family must participate in the decision to begin alternative treatment.

An example of the need for alternative treatment might be a low back injury treated by a family physician. The treatment plan will typically involve bed rest and the use of medications for pain relief. However, medications can be narcotic, creating the potential for dependence. Such a treatment plan would be more disabling than helpful. In such a case, the rehabilitation provider should first identify alternatives that are designed for low back injuries, such as a physical therapy program, which emphasizes exercise rather than bed rest.

Medical management at this stage should also focus on how medication is used. Medication overuse and abuse is common. Medications must be reviewed and monitored to ensure that they are helping, not hurting, the person.

The provider should meet with the treating family physician not as an adversary, but to negotiate an alternative treatment plan. If negotiation fails, the provider can secure a second opinion from a consulting physician who could prescribe an alternative plan.

Injured Person's Reaction. An assessment of the injured person's reaction to the treatment program is again needed. The primary concern of the rehabilitation professional in the outpatient stage is to motivate and encourage the person to accept his or her limitations and to work toward maximizing the injured person's remaining abilities.

Return to Work. In order for the injured person to return to work, functional capacities must be determined and a release to work must be secured. This determination signifies the end of the healing period or the achievement of medical stability. Functional capacities are the residual physical abilities of the injured person. A *release to work* is a physician's approval for the person to return to some level of work. An assessment of functional capacities and the release to work are used to define the physical parameters for re-employment. This is a fundamental aspect of vocational rehabilitation. A release to work is needed before the person is actually ready to resume employment, although vocational rehabilitation can begin sooner. An assessment of functional capacities can also serve as a foundation for evaluating the patient's ability to handle the activities of daily living.

Vocational Rehabilitation

Vocational rehabilitation helps the injured person engage in suitable work as soon as possible after a disabling injury. The vocational rehabilitation process usually begins when the rehabilitation professional contacts the most recent employer and conducts a *job analysis*. As described in the preceding chapter, a job analysis is a formal assessment of the physical demands of a job determined through an on-site visit and guided by a comprehensive checklist of physical demands. These include lifting, standing, walking, sitting, reaching, climbing, and environmental demands. The job analysis is a fundamental means for determining the patient's potential to return to his or her former job, for determining the feasibility of modifying that job, and for obtaining a release to work from the attending physician.

The rehabilitation professional should want to return the person to his or her former employer. The employer already knows the value and skills of the employee, and the injured person should have less fear about a return to work in a familiar environment.

Return to Former Employer. If the injured person is unable to perform his or her original job, the first alternative would be a *job modification*, that is, a change in the physical demands, number of duties, emotional demands, and/or hours required in that job. In many cases these changes may be permanent. When the changes are temporary and the goal is to gradually resume full duty, job modifications are called *work hardening*. Work hardening is a technique that helps the injured party to gradually readjust to the physical demands of a job. The person practices job-related tasks using less weight, or for shorter periods of time, or at a slower pace than is required in the actual job. The rehabilitation professional assists the employer in identifying opportunities for job modification and coaches the worker during work hardening exercises.

The case in Exhibit 5-4 illustrates the use of a job analysis,

Exhibit 5-4
Job Analysis, Work Hardening, and Job Modification

> A records clerk who worked in an insurance company slipped on a tile floor where a coworker had spilled coffee and injured her lower back. She was treated by her family physician who had treated her high blood pressure for years. After four weeks of bed rest and medication, she still did not feel capable of returning to her job. Her supervisor described her job as "very easy" and could not understand why she did not return. The claim representative handling the case brought in rehabilitation services.
>
> The provider's first step was to meet with the supervisor and conduct a job analysis. She found that the supervisor was correct in that most of the record clerk's job was "easy" in terms of physical demands. The clerk sat 75 percent of the time, setting up new files, typing forms, and providing back-up at the switchboard. However, she stood for 25 percent of the time while sorting mail, pulling claim files, and delivering stacks of files to managers. The clerk also lifted plastic buckets of mail, which at times weighed over 40 pounds.
>
> With the job analysis in hand, the provider asked if the supervisor would allow the clerk to return to work only part time at first and to perform only the sit-down portion of her job. The supervisor agreed to this job modification. A schedule of increasing hours was then worked out so that after six weeks the clerk would be performing her regular duties. The work hardening plan was set. The rehabilitation provider then met with the clerk and her family physician to discuss the job analysis, temporary job modification, and work-hardening plan. All parties agreed to the plan.
>
> After only three weeks in the plan, the clerk began to resume her duties of lifting the plastic tubs of mail and delivering stacks of files. These duties resulted in a setback in her medical progress. A permanent job modification was negotiated whereby the mailroom brought smaller tubs weighing no more than 20 pounds when filled, and a cart was purchased to use in delivering the files. After six weeks, the clerk was back to her regular duties with the modifications noted.

followed by work hardening and a permanent but simple *job modification*.

It should be noted that a job analysis must neither always be performed for every job, nor always performed by a rehabilitation provider. Some employers list physical demands in their job descriptions. A claim representative can simply request a job description. Some jobs have previously been analyzed so that a copy of the job analysis may be obtained from the employer or a claim file.

If job modification is impossible, then a *transfer* to another position within the company should be explored as the next step in the vocational rehabilitation process. If this is not feasible, the possibility of

218—Medical Aspects of Claims

creating a *new position* with the employer should be explored by the rehabilitation professional.

Placement With a New Employer. If a return to work with the former employer is not feasible, then *job placement* would be the next step in vocational rehabilitation. Job placement can only be successful if specific *job goals* are identified by the rehabilitation professional. An unfocused "take what you can get" effort is rarely, if ever, successful. In fact, the latter approach is likely to lead only to a less than suitable and/or a temporary position, thus frustrating the injured person.

Job goals are usually identified through one of two methods. First, *transferable skills* can be identified by analyzing the skills a person has developed through work experience. For example, a foreman would be expected to have management skills that could be considered transferable to a management trainee position.

Once job goals are identified, the injured person must be trained in *job-seeking skills*, that is, instruction and practice in completing job applications and resumes, approaching a prospective employer, and interviewing. Next, a *labor market survey* must be completed. This is a formal exploration of job openings in the local community based on local employment service listings, newspaper ads, and direct employer contacts. Finally, the actual work of contacting prospective employers, sometimes called *job development*, and following up to secure a position would be conducted by both the injured person and the rehabilitation professional.

Vocational Evaluation. If transferable skills are neither evident nor extensive enough for suitable job placement, formal *vocational evaluation* or testing should be pursued. This testing should consist of an assessment of the person's IQ (intelligence), academic achievement levels, aptitudes, vocational interests, and personality. The assessment is usually made through a number of psychometric tests administered by a work evaluator or psychologist under the supervision of the rehabilitation professional.

Psychometric Tests. The following are psychometric tests frequently used in a vocational evaluation.

- Tests of Intelligence
  WAIS—Wechsler Adult Intelligence Scale—measures intelligence comprehensively, differentiating between verbal IQ (ability to learn by written or verbal expression or instruction) and performance IQ (ability to learn by demonstration, visual perceptual skill).
  BETA—measures intelligence on performance-oriented items. This examination was originally developed to test illiterate and foreign-speaking Army recruits.

- Tests of Educational Achievement
  WRAT—Wide Range Achievement Test—designed to measure reading (word recognition only), spelling, and mathematical performance levels.
  ABLE—Adult Basic Learning Examination—measures reading (vocabulary and comprehension), spelling, and mathematic performance levels.
- Tests of Aptitude
  GATB—General Aptitude Test Battery—measures six verbal-perceptual aptitudes (general learning ability, verbal aptitude, numerical aptitude, spatial aptitude, form perception, and clerical perception) and three physical aptitudes (finger dexterity, hand dexterity, and motor coordination).
  Bennett Mechanical Comprehension Test—measures understanding of mechanical principles or ability to learn skills such as complex machine operation and repair.
- Tests of Interest Patterns
  SCII—Strong-Campbell Interest Inventory—measures occupational interests in jobs requiring technical or college training.
  CAI—Career Assessment Inventory—measures occupational interests in jobs requiring less formal training.
- Tests of Personality
  MMPI—Minnesota Multiphasic Personality Inventory—measures over ten personality variables (such as introversion and extroversion) and is used primarily for differential diagnosis of psychological/emotional disorders. The MMPI has been used in the vocational evaluation process to assess the emotional stability of the injured person for occupations such as police officer and business manager where emotional stability is particularly important.
  EPPS—Edwards Personal Preference Schedule—measures sixteen needs or motives (such as autonomy versus dependence) that may influence suitability for an occupation.

Work Samples. A vocational evaluation may sometimes include the administration of *work samples*. Historically, this aspect of vocational evaluation was developed and performed in rehabilitation workshops. A work sample is a defined work activity that utilizes tasks, materials, tools, and equipment that are similar to those used in an actual job. For example, a soldering work sample may assess the injured person's ability to do electronics assembly without putting the person on the assembly line. A work sample is "normed"; that is, the time required by a normal industrial employee to perform a task and the accuracy with which that task is performed is known, and the injured person's performance is compared to that performance. The purpose of a work sample is to define skills, the person's interest in the job, physical capabilities, and work behaviors.

Work samples test more than psychometric tests because the person actually performs the task. Work samples are often better than a medical report for evaluating physical capacities because the person is concentrating on the tasks and "pushing" his or her limits, rather than concentrating on physical limitations. Work samples can assess whole body physical capacities such as lifting, standing, and bending. Finally, work samples can assess work behaviors such as the ability to complete a task once it is begun, to work around others, and to comply with work schedules.

Work samples typically take longer to administer and the results, longer to assess, than a one-hour analysis of transferable skills or a two- to six-hour psychometric test session. Work samples are usually administered over a period ranging from a minimum of one day to several weeks, depending on the variety of samples. Some evaluations require one to two days to allow the person to work through a battery of work samples. An example is the VALPAR System, which consists of thirteen work samples ranging from tasks that test whole body range of motion to money handling. Some evaluations involving a large battery require weeks to work through. Some providers have developed unique work samples to assess specific types of jobs such as auto parts counter work or wood lathe operation.

Special Training. If the preceding steps fail, the rehabilitation professional should consider some level of *training* that may involve remedial education, obtaining a high school diploma, vocational-technical institute courses (such as electronics), business school courses (such as accounting), a two-year program at a community college (associate's degree), or four years of college (bachelor's degree), though the latter is very rare. An *on-the-job training* (OJT) contract between a new employer and a funding source (such as a casualty insurance company) can provide the injured person with concurrent training and employment. The incentive for the new employer may be an arrangement such as a 50-50 agreement for wages paid during the training period.

Psychosocial Rehabilitation

Psychosocial rehabilitation is the third major component of the rehabilitation process and is performed primarily through counseling. Counseling focuses on the injured person's adjustment to his or her disability, pain, vocational change, and family support. For a complete approach to psychological and social adjustment to a disability, counseling should consider both the person and the family.

The success of counseling is often a prerequisite to the success of the rehabilitation process. Some injured people continue to feel totally disabled by their injury or disease despite the finest of medical management and vocational rehabilitation.

The rehabilitation professional is heavily involved in this counseling process. He or she must continually encourage the injured person to focus on ability rather than disability. A "carrot and stick" approach is used, with praise and support given for all positive efforts by the injured person to reach a goal (such as attendance at appointments, participation in therapy, and active job seeking). Nevertheless, the person is firmly confronted when he or she has been irresponsible (missed appointments, passive response to therapy, or failure to seek work).

The counseling needs of the injured person may sometimes be beyond the capability of the rehabilitation provider. For example, the injured person may continually demonstrate inappropriate or uncontrolled crying, irrational conversation, or extreme verbal hostility. In such complicated cases, a psychological evaluation and/or treatment by a psychologist or psychiatrist may be included as a part of the rehabilitation process. The financial liability for such an evaluation must be carefully considered before implementing the evaluation, weighing such factors as history of psychiatric disorders. This treatment should often be funded through health insurance rather than through the casualty insurer. An insurer will be reluctant to finance such treatment unless the accident in question clearly caused the psychological problem.

Counseling also presents the possibility of professional malpractice. Most rehabilitation providers are neither qualified nor licensed to perform psychotherapy. The rehabilitation provider can be legally liable if he or she does not recognize the need to refer the injured person to a licensed and qualified psychologist or psychiatrist, many of whom the rehabilitation provider should be familiar with. Providers of psychotherapy differ in their philosophies regarding the therapeutic value of work in the recovery process. Some believe it is therapeutic to return to productive work in the shortest possible time. Others believe it is harmful to subject the patient to the stress of the work environment. The rehabilitation provider or the claim representative should know the philosophy of any psychologist or psychiatrist who becomes involved in the care of an injured person.

Forensic Rehabilitation

Forensic rehabilitation was not identified as one of the major components in the rehabilitation process, but it is a growing aspect of

Exhibit 5-5
An Example of Forensic Rehabilitation

> A woman slipped on a wet floor at a major department store, fracturing her ankle. Her medical recovery progressed well, but she alleged total disability because of continued pain in her ankle. She terminated her usual employment at a local assembly plant because she could not tolerate the standing her job required. She changed doctors, deciding to consult a practitioner who ordered the use of a wheelchair and home health care. A general liability suit was filed against the department store for $1 million in damages based on extensive continued medical care, loss of future wage-earning capacity, and pain and suffering.
>
> The insurer offered rehabilitation services under a reservation of rights agreement, which were refused. A rehabilitation provider was asked to review the medical record and to conduct a job analysis at the prior employment site. The rehabilitation provider was a registered nurse who had also completed a master's degree in rehabilitation counseling, qualifying her as an expert witness in both medical and vocational matters. During discovery, the deposition of the rehabilitation provider was taken. She testified that the medical care of the original treating physician was appropriate and produced a statement from that physician that no future care was needed. She further testified that the job analysis revealed that the woman's job could be performed from a sitting position and produced a statement from the prior employer that an appropriate job opportunity existed. This woman's claim settled prior to trial for a very reasonable amount largely as a result of the impact of the rehabilitation provider's expert testimony.

rehabilitation. As illustrated in Exhibit 5-5, forensic rehabilitation is the use of rehabilitation expertise in a court or claims system. This chapter has thus far defined and discussed rehabilitation from a cooperative, perhaps even paternalistic, perspective. That is, it has been assumed that the injured person is basically cooperative and has voluntarily accepted rehabilitation services (although some states mandate rehabilitation in workers compensation claims). The process itself is based on the same assumption. In fact, experience and several studies of rehabilitation reveal that over 70 percent of the persons offered rehabilitation voluntarily accept and cooperate with the service. Nevertheless, the remaining 30 percent that do not accept rehabilitation[14] need to be addressed. Forensic rehabilitation is the response to this need.

The foundation for this application of rehabilitation was set in a landmark court of appeals case, *Kramer v. Flemming*.[15] The court ordered the use of a rehabilitation provider for expert testimony in a social security case. Since this case, the use of rehabilitation providers as expert witnesses has spread to hearings on workers compensation, general liability, auto liability, professional liability, and even ocean marine bodily injury claims.

To qualify as an expert witness, the rehabilitation provider must be shown to have qualifications relevant to the subject matter of his or her testimony. A provider testifying about treatment matters should be a registered nurse or an occupational or physical therapist. A provider testifying about vocational matters should likely be a certified rehabilitation counselor (CRC) or otherwise qualified in vocational matters.

Expert testimony in rehabilitation is generally given in answer to a "hypothetical question" concerning the injured person's rehabilitation potential. The freedom to give an opinion is extremely important as the provider may not have even met the injured person and may have to rely solely on employment and medical records as the basis of his or her testimony.

SUMMARY

Rehabilitation reduces the impact of injuries on the injured person, the family, the employer, the economy, and the insurance business. It can be of great value in certain cases, while other cases may not benefit from rehabilitation. Since rehabilitation can be expensive, claim representatives must be able to identify cases that are likely to benefit from rehabilitation; they must also recognize which rehabilitation services are suitable for a given case.

Professional rehabilitation providers are increasingly becoming part of the private for-profit sector. It is likely that they will have a formal education and recognized credentials in the field of rehabilitation. Numerous other professionals also play a role in rehabilitation. However, the key person in the process is probably the injured person. This person may have a variety of reactions to the disability that may help or hinder the rehabilitation process. The family and employer also play vital roles in the process. The claim representative must identify cases for rehabilitation, select the professional provider, and monitor the quality of the rehabilitation service.

Cases for rehabilitation may be identified by type of injury or through formal evaluation tools. Regardless of which is used, the claim representative must always exercise good judgment in identifying cases for rehabilitation. The rehabilitation process consists of various, often simultaneously performed services in the areas of medical management, vocational rehabilitation, and psychosocial rehabilitation. Rehabilitation professionals have been used increasingly to provide expert testimony in what is known as forensic rehabilitation.

224—Medical Aspects of Claims
Chapter Notes

1. As cited in "Vocational Rehabilitation in the Workers Compensation System," *Ark. Law Review*, vol. 33, pp. 742-743.
2. Minn. Stat. Annot. § 176.102.
3. Minn. Stat. Annot. § 65B.45.
4. A. Larson, *Workers Compensation*, Desk Edition (Albany, NY: Matthew Bender), § 61.20.
5. As cited in Chancy Croft, "Something More Important Than Money—Vocational Rehabilitation in Workers Compensation Cases," *Alaska Law Review*, vol. 3, 1986, p. 54.
6. A. Tebb, *Report to the Industry: Vocational Rehabilitation* (San Francisco: California Workers Compensation Institute, 1982).
7. J. Gardner, *Vocational Rehabilitation in Florida* (Cambridge, MA: Workers Compensation Research Institute, 1987).
8. D. Lengham, "Vocational Rehabilitation Cost Effectiveness Study," *Journal of Private Sector Rehabilitation*, vol. 3, 1988, pp. 15-25.
9. B. Zaidman, *Rehabilitation in the Minnesota Workers Compensation System* (St. Paul, MN: Minnesota Department of Labor and Industry, 1988).
10. J. Gice, "Return to Work Versus On-Going Disability," *Legal Insight*, 1988, pp. 13-16.
11. L. Nowak, *American Economist*, vol. 27, 1983, pp. 23-29.
12. R. Treitel, *Social Security Bulletin*, vol. 3-23, no. 4, 1979.
13. H. Hester et al., *Menninger RTW Scale* (Topeka, KS: Menninger Foundation, 1986).
14. J. Gardner, *Vocational Rehabilitation in Florida* (Cambridge, MA: Workers Compensation Research Institute, 1987).
15. 283 F.2d 916 (1960).

CHAPTER 6

Evaluation of Medical Treatment

A critical evaluation of a claimant's medical treatment is one of the most challenging tasks facing claim representatives. Claim representatives are not physicians, yet they must evaluate and judge the work of physicians and other trained medical personnel. In addition, they must usually do so alone—only a small minority of cases are significant enough to warrant expert assistance. This chapter explains how the claim representative performs the task of evaluating medical treatment.

As part of this evaluation, claim representatives must determine whether or not the claimant's injury or condition was caused by the insured event. Unlike health insurance that covers virtually all medical conditions regardless of cause, casualty insurance covers only injuries and conditions caused by a specific insured event, such as a work-related accident, an automobile accident, or an accident on certain premises. Having determined the cause of an injury or condition, the claim representative must evaluate necessity and appropriateness of treatment. Many claim representatives feel very inadequate for this task, yet they cannot abandon their responsibility by simply assuming that physicians will provide only the necessary treatment. Experience shows that physicians have incentives to overtreat. Claim representatives must also be satisfied that the suggested future course of treatment is appropriate and overall control of claimant's treatment is adequate.

To handle a case alone or to request assistance is one of the most crucial choices a claim representative must make. There are criteria that can be used to identify cases requiring additional or expert assistance. Nevertheless, because the claim representative does handle most cases alone, he or she must be knowledgeable about medicine and medical practices in order to be successful.

In all cases, the claim representative bases the evaluation on

226—Medical Aspects of Claims

medical bills, records, and reports. Claim representatives must therefore be familiar with the preparation, contents, maintenance, and significance of such documents. Selecting and procuring the documents essential to resolving a case is how the claim representative makes the best decisions in the most efficient manner.

The evaluation of certain cases does require additional or expert assistance. Experts can independently review medical records and examine the claimant. Claim representatives must understand the services offered by experts in order to hire the most appropriate expert service and to obtain the information needed to conclude the claim.

ISSUES IN MEDICAL TREATMENT

Any claimant is entitled to be compensated for *no more than* reasonable and necessary treatment for injuries and conditions caused by the insured event. Even when liability and coverage for the insured event are clear, claimants are not entitled to compensation for unnecessary treatment, unreasonable treatment (in amount or cost), or treatment for injuries and conditions not related to the insured event. The application of this concept of compensation to specific cases can be complex, and it is the claim representative's responsibility to ensure that compensation is appropriately provided. In order to do so, the claim representative must (1) verify the cause of the injury, (2) confirm the necessity of proposed treatment, (3) assess the need for further treatment, and (4) understand how to control treatment.

Verification of Cause

Casualty insurance, such as workers compensation, auto, or general liability, covers only those injuries or conditions caused by the insured event. However, it is common for claimants or their physicians to submit medical bills and reports for problems not caused by the insured event. This is generally not intentional, but the result of ignorance or thoughtlessness. Still, the claim representative should be aware that documents may be submitted for problems that are completely unrelated to the insured event, problems that are chronic, or problems that occur subsequent to problems caused by the insured event.

Unrelated Problems. At any given time, a significant number of people have some sort of medical problem. Some of these people become involved in accidents that are the subject of insurance claims. If they are injured in such accidents, they are likely to seek treatment for their accidental injuries and their pre-existing problems from the same physician. Because many physicians are indifferent about who pays them, all recent billings are likely to be directed to a casualty insurer if one "appears on the scene."

Because of the prevalence of pre-existing medical problems, claim representatives should always determine the nature of the patient's presenting complaint and the physician's treatment before paying bills for office visits. Similarly, claim representatives must understand the purpose of diagnostic and laboratory tests to know whether they are related to injuries suffered in the insured accident.

Chronic Problems. Chronic medical conditions, like unrelated pre-existing problems, are not usually caused by accidental injuries. Many claim representatives mistakenly believe that "chronic" and "acute" both mean bad or severe. In the context of medicine, however, chronic means ongoing or frequently recurring, and acute means sudden or recent.

Claim representatives must carefully investigate any condition described as, or known to be, chronic. Joint problems, especially in the spine, knees, or hips; osteoporosis; arteriosclerosis; diabetes; and arthritis are all common chronic problems. Indeed, claim representatives should suspect that chronic problems may be involved in any prolonged case unless the injuries are obviously caused by an accident.

It is frequently alleged that a chronic condition has been made worse by an accident. An exacerbation of a pre-existing problem is compensable, but with certain limitations. Once the condition has returned to its pre-injury status, it is no longer compensable. Likewise, an exacerbated chronic problem is no longer compensable if the natural course of that pre-existing condition would eventually have made it just as bad.

Intervening Problems. Some injured claimants begin to recover and then reinjure themselves. These injuries are known as intervening problems or injuries. The insurer responsible for the original injury should not pay for the new injury unless it was an unavoidable consequence of the first injury. This is an unusual event—intervening injuries are typically caused by independent accidents that are often a result of the claimant's negligence or some other uninsured cause. Treatment for an intervening injury will often be submitted for compensation along with treatment for the original injury. Unless the claimant admits that he or she has had a subsequent injury, such injuries can only be detected through careful reading of the medical records. Claimants are usually forthright about the cause of an injury with their treating physician.

Need for Correct Diagnosis. A correct diagnosis is critical to determining the cause of a claimant's injury. Unless the nature of a claimant's problem is known, its cause cannot be known.

Claim representatives should not accept a statement that refers only to symptoms, such as headache or back pain, as a diagnosis. An almost innumerable number of medical conditions can cause such symptoms.

While a diagnosis is critical, it is unnecessary for a physician to establish the diagnosis with one hundred percent certainty. Successful and appropriate medical treatment can be based on a presumptive, or working, diagnosis. A *presumptive* or *working diagnosis* is a condition believed by the physician to be the most likely cause of the patient's symptoms. Unless the failure to treat any other possible causes would endanger the patient, it is good medical practice to treat on the basis of a presumptive diagnosis. The alternative is to run expensive and nearly endless diagnostic tests.

Any physician who seems to be avoiding making a diagnosis should be required to provide a working diagnosis. Any physician who is providing treatment without at least a working diagnosis is operating outside the bounds of accepted medical practice.

Necessity of Treatment

Liability for treating injuries caused by an insured event is limited to necessary treatments. To be sure that treatments are necessary, the claim representative must be familiar with the usual treatments and treatment alternatives for various conditions.

Usual Treatment. Claim representatives handling injury claims become familiar with the usual treatment for injuries and conditions they see regularly. Most experienced claim representatives recognize the usual treatment for muscular strain and sprain, broken bones, lacerations, and joint problems. As a result, they can spot a course of treatment that appears unusual or excessive, such as the administration of drugs for conditions that might not be related to the drug, or treatment for muscle strain that lasts for months on end.

For injuries and conditions with which they are unfamiliar, claim representatives should consult the Merck manual or other similar treatment guide, or consult with an expert. Most experts can quickly determine whether the nature or extent of treatment in a given case seems at all unusual.

Redundancy of Treatment. Certain treatments essentially repeat other treatments. This problem is particularly common in chiropractic and physical therapy treatments (both of which are addressed at greater length in the next chapter).

Tests, like treatments, can be redundant. Imaging tests such as x-rays, CT scans, and MRIs serve a similar purpose. Multiple imaging tests may sometimes be necessary if it is difficult to identify the abnormality or structure in question. However, claim representatives are entitled to an explanation as to why the original imaging or other testing was not satisfactory.

As in determining the necessity of treatment, a claim representative's experience, certain reference works, and expert consultants can help to identify redundancy of treatment.

Alternative Treatment. In many cases, a claimant can be treated in an alternative manner that is much less expensive and equally medically sound. Patients and their physicians may not be motivated to consider alternative treatments when existing treatment is fully insured. For example, one medically sound alternative in many cases is to do nothing, or more precisely, to defer treatment while the physician simply follows the condition. The human body has a remarkable ability to heal itself. Much of the treatment provided by physicians does nothing more than relieve symptoms, the real cure coming from the body itself. While the alternative of doing nothing is often appropriate, claim representatives should only maintain that a particular treatment is unwarranted if they have solid expert support.

Because hospitalization is expensive, alternatives should be reviewed. Hospitalization should be avoided when possible. Many conditions that were once treated only in hospitals or that required long hospitalizations are now treated on an out-patient basis. Likewise, many forms of long-term treatment can be performed at home rather than in an institution. Utilization review and case management experts, discussed further in the next chapter, can provide excellent consultation services regarding alternative treatments.

Further Treatment

Unless a patient has fully recovered or reached a maximum level of medical improvement, further treatment should be expected. Claim representatives generally find that controlling future treatment is simpler and more successful than criticizing past treatment. However, controlling further treatment requires a clear statement of a treatment plan from the treating physician and careful analysis of any disability statements by the treating physician.

Treatment Plan. A physician should always have a plan for a patient's future treatment. Otherwise, the treatment will be largely haphazard and, as a result, may be ineffective. A claim representative should be aware of this plan. In making the claim representative aware of the plan, the physician reveals when he or she expects the treatment to conclude, what the expected results are, and when alternatives will be considered if the current treatment does not produce results. Making these statements also forces the physician to think through the course of treatment and to justify any treatment that in nature or duration goes beyond what was expected.

With certain medical conditions, it is likely that the physician can express future outcomes only in terms of probability. The claim representative cannot insist that the physician be more definite when it is impossible to do so. A physician who describes the expected outcome as uncertain should nevertheless be able to identify the possible outcomes and the treatments that would be expected with each.

Disability Statements. As explained in Chapter 4, a physician cannot make a meaningful statement about disability without knowing the physical demands of the patient's job. This is especially true for statements about future disability. Meaningful statements about future disability should include descriptions of specific impairments the patient is expected to suffer and the duration of such impairments.

Problems of Controlling Treatment

Claim representatives should neither assume that physicians will restrict treatment to only what is necessary nor that they will only treat injuries caused by the insured event. Physicians do have incentives to do otherwise. This does not imply deliberate dishonesty, only that physicians are not vigilant about the insurer's interests. In addition, claim representatives should not expect that claimants will question the nature and duration of treatment as prescribed by a physician. Like the physician, the claimant has something to gain from insured treatment.

The Physician's Disincentives to Control Treatment. Within the range of acceptable medical practice, physicians have a choice between conservative and aggressive treatment. There are powerful financial and legal incentives for physicians to be biased towards aggressive treatment. Obviously, the more a physician treats, the more he earns. In addition, the fear of malpractice suits causes many physicians to diagnose and treat to the maximum for their own protection. Finally, many physicians seem to choose an aggressive approach because some of their patients expect it. These patients expect action from their physicians, not mere reassurances that they will be fine.

When medical care is completely insured, physicians tend to justify putting their patients' expectations and their own interests above an insurer's. Indeed, some physicians go beyond aggressive treatment and knowingly abuse insurance. In light of his own and the patient's interests, it is easy for a physician to justify even outright abuse.

The Patient's Disincentives to Control Treatment. A patient whose treatment is fully insured will not usually second-guess a physician's orders for tests or a course of treatment. Most patients feel that money is no object when it comes to their health and someone else's money at stake.

As a result of this bias, many health insurers require copayment by the insured. The copayment provision is typically about 20 percent, forcing the patient to bear some expense of every treatment. However, casualty insurance, such as workers compensation or liability insurance, does not include copayment provisions. Thus, assuming that liability and coverage are clear, a patient with casualty insurance can expect every dollar of treatment expense to be paid. Claim representatives in casualty insurance cannot expect claimants to make suggestions about controlling treatment, but must expect to moderate treatment themselves.

Multiple Uncontrolled Treatment. In complicated cases, it is not unusual for a patient to visit several different physicians for consultation or treatment. In all such cases, the referrals to other physicians should be made by a single controlling physician familiar with the entire case. However, claimants often see numerous physicians, none of whom may know of or communicate with one another. In addition to being an abuse of the system, this is incorrect medical treatment. Such situations usually come about because the claimant or his or her attorney is "controlling" treatment. Claim representatives should always resist reimbursing such treatment until a single physician is controlling the case.

THE CLAIM REPRESENTATIVE'S ROLE

Claim representatives evaluate medical treatment for most cases on their own because most cases are too small to justify the expense of expert assistance. Furthermore, the medical treatment in most cases is legitimate and need not be analyzed by an expert. When the issues are relatively straightforward, in-house medical references may be enough to confirm payment for a claim. In many simple cases, payment can be made strictly on the basis of an itemized bill without supporting medical records. In more complicated cases, extensive medical records, including clinical and institutional records, are required before an informed decision as to what is payable can be made. In still other cases, a claim representative may need a medical consultant or an independent medical examiner to clarify the situation.

Numerous injury claims presented for reimbursement can be handled on the basis of a loss report and a standardized bill for services from the medical provider. A high percentage of injury claims, both "first party" and liability, involve minimal treatment over a brief period of time and are legitimate in every way. Given that the volume of injury claims handled by one claim representative can be very high, and given that most of these claims may be for small amounts, a claim representative must separate the cases requiring extensive investigation from ones that can be handled with minimal investigation and documentation. One of the "occupational hazards" of claim handling is the tendency to become cynical about the legitimacy of injury claims. Cynicism may be well-founded in a few cases, but the vast majority of claims presented for reimbursement are simple, straightforward cases that can be resolved quickly by appropriate payment.

Many serious injuries speak for themselves. For example, a loss report may indicate that the injured person sustained a fracture of the femur. During an interview, the claimant indicates he was taken to the hospital where a surgical procedure was performed to repair the fracture. The claimant is currently casted and walking with crutches. Physician and hospital billings substantiate the claim and extent of the injury. The only issues not yet resolved may be the probabilities for a functional impairment and whether these functional limitations create a disability for the patient. A request of the attending physician to address this issue and to provide support for his findings with documentation from the medical record might complete the investigation.

One of the most critical functions of a claim representative is to identify cases that must be evaluated with additional assistance. Such cases typically involve serious or complex injuries and a significant financial exposure for the insurer. Early involvement of experts is essential to effective medical management. Thus, claim representatives must be thoroughly familiar with the criteria used by their insurers to identify serious cases.

For cases handled solely by the claim representative, the claim representative must rely on his or her knowledge of medicine, medical practices, and medical cost containment. Many claim representatives receive no special training in these areas and must educate themselves or accept the claimant's case at face value.

As an insurance professional, the claim representative's role is to investigate and verify injury claims and to learn to ask the right medical questions. A claim representative is not a physician or a medical expert, but an insurance expert whose role is to develop adequate information in a reasonable period of time in order to make timely payment of bona fide claims and to resolve all others.

Identification of Serious Cases

The typical criteria used to identify serious cases are type of injury, dollar amount, and medical complexity. In addition, claim representatives must also be aware of cases that may be serious because of potential exaggeration. In well-run claim operations, supervisors and managers play a significant role in screening cases.

In addition to the serious cases identified below, which typically require careful investigation and documentation, claim representatives should develop a means of identifying claims whose causes and treatments may be dubious. However, the claim representative should not limit the review and verification to one physician or medical facility. Doing so could be construed as harassment by the physician or facility and could result in litigation against the insurer for any claim denials.

Identification by Type of Injury. Certain types of injuries are known to be serious or troublesome to insurers. Some insurers consider all injuries of a certain type to be serious and require them to be brought to the attention of supervisors, managers, or outside experts. Some examples follow:

- Quadriplegia or paraplegia
- Amputation (other than fingers and toes)
- Loss of sight or hearing
- Third degree burns over more than 15 percent of the body
- Brain trauma
- Joint replacements

The advantage of using type of injury as a criterion for identifying serious cases is that it is not ambiguous. Claim representatives will always know whether or not to handle a case on their own as soon as they know the nature of the injury. The disadvantage of this criterion is that certain serious cases may not be listed and might therefore be overlooked until it is too late. For example, cases of low back pain are usually not serious, but some can develop into claims for permanent total disability.

Identification by Dollar Amount or Length of Disability. Some claim departments require claim representatives to involve supervisors, managers, or experts whenever the case appears to be worth more than a certain dollar amount. A variation of this procedure is to require all cases expected to involve a certain length of disability to be referred. That is, cases involving more than four weeks of disability, for example, or cases involving any disability at all may have to be referred. Identifying serious cases by dollar amount or length of disability is the most common criterion used in claim departments. Most cases that would be identified by type of injury would also be identified as serious on the basis of dollar amount or length of disability.

To be effective, this identification criterion must be applied early in the case. Claim representatives must be able to accurately and diligently project dollar exposures. Claim representatives using this

234—Medical Aspects of Claims

criterion go through the same mental process as is used in reserving a claim. The reserve should represent the amount expected to be spent on the case. Accurate reserves should result in accurate identification of cases needing more assistance. The advantage of this approach to identifying serious cases is that it does not exclude seemingly ordinary injuries with a significant dollar exposure.

Identification by Medical Complexity. Some insurers require claim representatives to refer any case in which the claim representative is not familiar with the nature of the injury or treatment. Identification by medical complexity is advantageous because it provides a standard that "flexes" from one claim representative to another depending on the knowledge of each claim representative. Ideally, this system would help to identify only those cases needing referral.

The drawback of this criterion is that it requires claim representatives to recognize what they do not know. In addition, there are many cases in which the claim representative understands almost all of the case, but not everything. There is great danger that such cases should be, but are not, referred.

Indicators of Exaggerated Claims. Experience demonstrates there are certain common characteristics of claims that indicate the need for additional medical investigation. The presence of one or more of these characteristics in a given claim is not conclusive proof that the injury claim is exaggerated. The more there are of these characteristics, the more thorough the investigation should be.

- An aggravated pre-existing condition that under normal circumstances requires long-term continuing medical care (diabetes or arthritis, for example).
- The injury or the severity of the injury seems inconsistent with the facts of the loss or the physical evidence. For example, a serious neck injury allegedly caused by an automobile accident with little or no damage to either vehicle.
- Problems characterized only by subjective reports. Injuries such as strain or sprain, anxiety or depression, or an ill-defined syndrome (a collection of symptoms) require the claim representative to request extensive records of the physician's findings in order to help identify the extent of the medical problem.
- Certain personality types who view trauma and especially minor injuries as a way of drawing attention to themselves and receiving care from a medical provider. The personality disorders, discussed in Chapter 3, represent most of these types. The needs of these individuals are almost impossible to meet, and their claims are often characterized by long letters, daily phone calls about minor details, and an exaggerated willing-

6 • Evaluation of Medical Treatment—235

ness to discuss all aspects of the injury and treatment.
- The use of unusual or controversial medical treatment such as acupuncture, rolfing, or deep massage, or treatment coupled with prescriptions for medical appliances that appear excessive for the injury involved, such as at-home whirlpool baths, T.E.N.S. units, or special support beds and mattresses for routine back or neck sprains.
- Involvement of legal representation.
- Redundant diagnostic testing as in the use of x-rays, followed by a CT scan, thermograms, and eventually an MRI, each with negative results and often associated with extensive laboratory tests and electronic testing such as EEGs and EKGs.
- The presence of certain injuries such as sprains or strains, especially of the neck and back, or other soft tissue injuries that seem resistant to healing; the presence of conditions such as TMJ (temporo-mandibular joint syndrome), thoracic outlet syndrome, post-traumatic stress disorder, carpal tunnel syndrome, or any psychological or psychiatric disorder that appears to be inconsistent with the severity of the injury.
- Accidents involving injuries to multiple parties who have identical injuries, the same medical provider, and the same attorney.
- Legal liability. In general, claimants who are not negligent might profit most by exaggerating their claim in order to increase the amount of recovery.
- Individuals who may be subject to seasonal layoffs, such as construction workers or farm laborers, may tend to exaggerate injury claims when the time of year at which they expect to be laid off approaches.

Claim representatives must remember that these circumstances are simply indicators. No action to deny or compromise an injury claim should be made simply because of the presence of one or all of these indicators. These indicators simply mean that additional medical investigation is needed before the claim can be concluded.

Involvement of Supervisors and Managers. In any well run claim operation, claim representatives are not the only personnel involved in deciding which cases require additional assistance. Supervisors regularly review files and should spot cases claim representatives should not be handling alone. A supervisor should know each claim representative's level of expertise and is responsible if the claim representative continues handling a serious case.

Managers are responsible for establishing criteria for case referral and for selecting outside experts for the claim department. The experts should be interviewed to determine their skills, staffing, claims philosophy, and fees. Managers are responsible for communicating the claim department's needs to each expert service.

Cases Handled by the Claim Representative

As mentioned, claim representatives handle most claims on their own. They do so with the medical records and reports of the claimant and their own knowledge of medicine, medical practices, and medical cost control.

Medical Records. Claim representatives cannot rely on claimants to give accurate accounts of their treatment since so many claimants do not pay attention to, or do not understand, their treatment. As a result, medical records are the primary acceptable evidence of medical treatment. Medical records are fully discussed in the next major section.

The Claim Representative's Medical Knowledge. Claim representatives must continually improve and expand their medical knowledge. There is no limit on the amount of knowledge to be learned. One of the most effective means to learn is to concentrate on unfamiliar material encountered in actual claims. The need to understand the material for an actual claim provides a strong incentive to learn.

Failure by claim representatives to educate themselves in medical matters is a failure to fulfill an essential part of their responsibilities. Claim representatives must evaluate coverage, liability, and damages in every case. In injury claims, the damages are determined by medical matters.

MEDICAL RECORDS

Medical records are fundamental to the investigation and documentation of medical and injury claims. The claims process for injury cases has a beginning (the report of loss) and an ending (payment, denial, or compromise), but the intermediate steps vary depending on the type and complexity of the claim. As indicated in Exhibit 6-1, the claim representative must at each step judge the adequacy of documentation. If the medical documentation is adequate, the claim can be concluded. If it is not, the claim representative should continue to bring in medical evidence until all questions have been answered.

The types of medical records described in this section are the basic tools used to determine the validity of an injury claim and what is owed on the claim. Medical bills and records can also guide the investigation. These records may clarify whether there is coverage for the loss and can provide information concerning how the loss occurred. These

Exhibit 6-1
Claim Verification Process

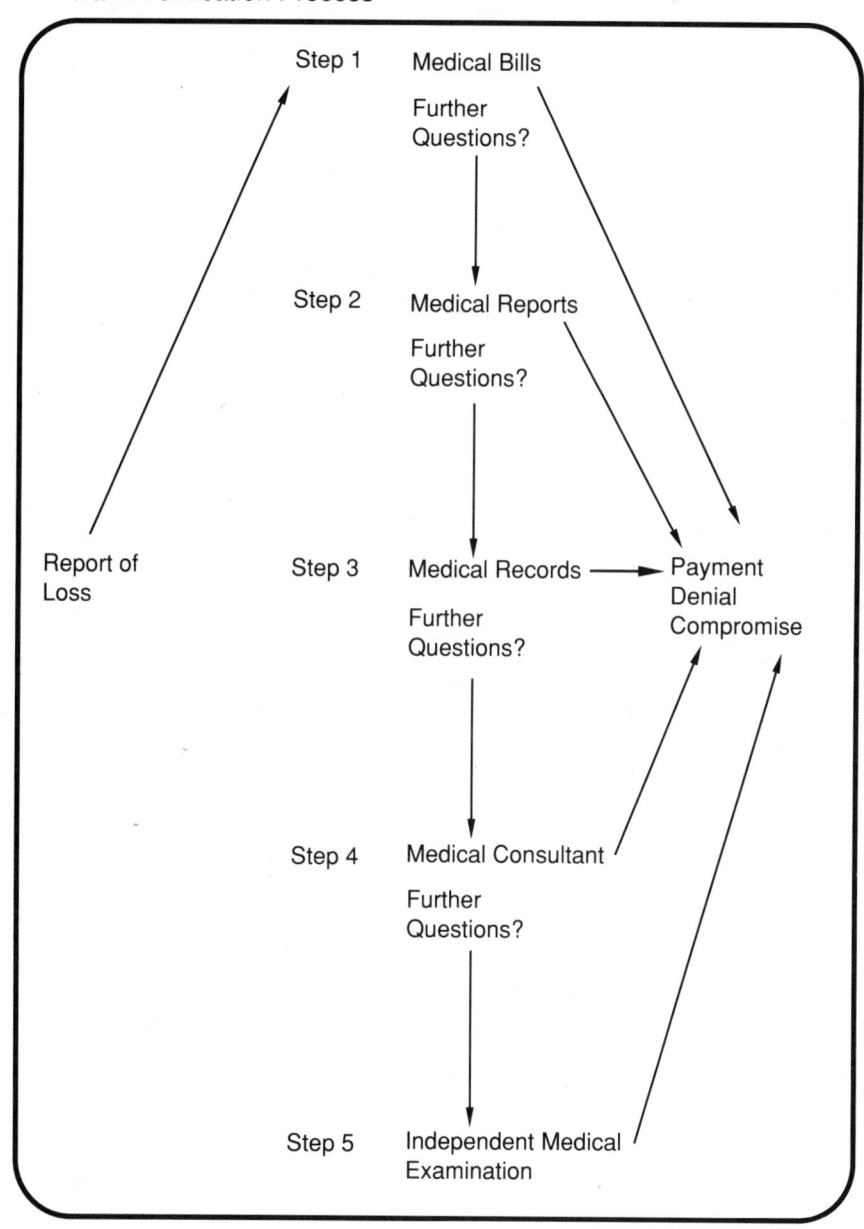

```
                Step 1    Medical Bills
                          Further
                          Questions?
                            ↓
                Step 2    Medical Reports
                          Further
                          Questions?
                            ↓
Report of       Step 3    Medical Records  →  Payment
Loss                                           Denial
                          Further              Compromise
                          Questions?
                            ↓
                Step 4    Medical Consultant
                          Further
                          Questions?
                            ↓
                Step 5    Independent Medical
                          Examination
```

documents often include a statement from the victim about how the injury occurred, and the claim representative can rely fairly heavily on the truth of these statements since they are made shortly after the injury while memories are still fresh and for the purpose of obtaining treatment.

Medical records can provide clues to unrelated or pre-existing conditions, and they can indicate prior admissions to the same treating facility. Blood alcohol levels and the presence of other substances in the body are also often documented in these records. This section explains the purpose of and standards for medical records, identifies and describes the types of medical records used in a claims investigation, and explains the importance of and considerations related to obtaining these records.

Purpose of and Standards for Medical Records

Medical records, medical reports, clinical notes, and medicolegal reports offer different types of information for a claim review. These records are prepared by professionals from different medical disciplines, and each type of document has a unique role in the care and treatment of an injured patient. To understand the relevance of these documents in the claim review process, the claim representative must recognize that these documents offer objective as well as subjective information. Claim representatives can better understand the contents and organization of medical records when they understand the purpose of and standards for preparation of such records.

Nature and Purpose of Medical Records. A *medical record* is any document that identifies the patient and the health care and services provided to this individual. It is a collection of information written by the health care professional responsible for the patient's care, pertaining to the patient's health including past and present personal and familial histories and past and present illnesses or injuries and treatments. A medical record is legally viewed as official proof that specific patient services were provided.[1] The term "record," as defined for purposes of the Federal Privacy Act of 1974, means tangible or documentary record (as opposed to a record contained in someone's memory).[2] The purpose of this record is to document and plan current patient care. The kind and amount of information to be included is dictated by what is essential to resolve a medical problem or to prevent future problems.

Medical records are the health care provider's means of communicating to other health care professionals. They also help the health care provider to organize his or her own thoughts and observations. The information in a medical record should be objective and concise. "The medical record must be the natural extension of the basic science training of the physician; in short, it must be a scientific manuscript."[3]

Health care providers must follow numerous requirements in preparing a medical record. The record must document the course of care and treatment and demonstrate appropriateness of care, provide sufficient information to establish a fair fee for service, and provide data needed to protect the legal interests of the patient, the medical provider, and any health care facility wherein the medical services were provided. The records may also help to educate other health care professionals, provide data to expand the body of medical research and development, and possibly identify diseases that are a threat to public health.

Standards for Preparation of Medical Records. Health care professionals should learn the scope, necessity, and value of accurate record keeping and report writing in their undergraduate and graduate education. A technician, whether involved in laboratory research or in the taking of x-rays, is taught to record the procedure and identify when it was done and by whom, and to describe the steps followed to ensure the quality of the procedure. Nurses are taught to document their observations, the treatment they provide, and the patient's response to that treatment. They also document information reported to other attending health care providers concerning patient progress or problems.

Textbooks explain the administration of medical records; the value and use of medical records; the development, content, and maintenance of medical records in various institutional settings; the forms and designs of authorizations for disclosure of information; the nomenclature and classification systems; and the legal aspects of medical records.[4] In graduate and postgraduate training, the student is further educated in recording and reporting information specific to the needs of a given discipline or specialty. Medical education stresses the need for detail in reporting the treatment provided and as proof of service rendered.

Health care professionals are state-licensed and have a responsibility to work within their scope of practice as determined by state statute or code. The scope of practice describes the areas of treatment a professional is licensed to provide; it also requires each provider to bear the responsibility for maintaining records.

Types of Medical Records

The most common medical records are bills, clinical notes, reports, hospital records, and records from other institutions.

Medical Bills. Once an injury claim has been presented, a standard coded, itemized medical bill provided by the health care facility or medical provider is the first document required for verification of the claim. There are various forms of bills, ranging from handwritten notations on a physician's prescription pad to fairly refined

240—Medical Aspects of Claims

and standardized formats in which each procedure or treatment is given a code specifying the diagnosis and itemizing the services rendered.

Many health insurers, Medicare, Medicaid systems, and workers compensation insurers require standardized billing on a UB-82 (hospital billing form) or HCFA 1500 (physician billing form). Examples of both billing forms are shown in Exhibits 6-2 and 6-3. These two forms were developed by the Health Care Financing Administration to provide details of medical services provided for insurance reimbursement purposes. Coded and itemized bills in a standardized format should be obtained for all injury claims as a first step in a logical system of proper claim verification. The information contained in standardized bills may be sufficient to conclude a claim.

Clinical Notes. Clinical notes are a collection of the health care provider's observations, examination, work-up, and treatment. This record should include an extensive review from the initial visit, the findings of any outside diagnostic services, and a detailed description of the plan of treatment. As such, the notes should provide data that can be used to verify the cause or severity of an injury or illness. The clinical notes also refresh the provider's memory on subsequent visits. The provider can rely on previous notes to decide what questions to ask the patient, what symptoms to observe, and to plan for any possible changes in the treatment. This type of record keeping helps the provider to control the treatment.

Medical Reports. A medical report may be a part of the total medical record or a summary of the information within the medical record. As part of the medical record, a report summarizes one aspect of treatment. For example, it may detail a surgical procedure, describe a specimen sent to the lab for a pathology evaluation, or state the progress of a patient in a physical therapy session.

Medicolegal reports are prepared by the health care provider for an attorney, claim representative, or industrial commission. They describe the injury, the current physical and mental condition, and the expected outcome of the patient's treatment. The report is used in negotiating a settlement, and it may also be the basis for further medical and legal research in a malpractice case. Such reports also recap a case for health care providers before deposition or trial. These reports are not intended to provide all details of a case, but should summarize a case, concluding with the provider's opinion. Even with a medicolegal report, it may be necessary to review the complete medical records to verify details in a report.

A *narrative report* is similar in nature to a medicolegal report in that the provider summarizes the course of treatment and states a diagnosis. Narrative reports are generally written for other health care providers and are usually accompanied by supporting documentation from the medical record. A narrative report may also be written for an insurer in support of a claim of injury, a claim by the provider for a fee for service, or to substantiate the need for services provided.

To complete any of these reports, the provider's signature and date of review and approval must be included. Completing a report with a statement that reads "dictated but not read" indicates that the provider may or may not agree with the report content. A signature, on the other hand, makes the provider accountable.

Exhibit 6-4 is a summary of the types of information in medical reports. Because all medical reports are essentially written from memory by the attending medical provider, it is important that all elements of a report (illustrated in Exhibit 6-4) be included in the body of the report. If elements are missing, the claim representative should continue to investigate the case by securing the clinical or hospital records and clarifying any questionable areas in the medical reports.

Hospital Records. Hospital records detail the care and treatment of the patient while in the hospital. Such records are "visible evidence of what the hospital is accomplishing."[5] Licensure and accreditation requirements mandate that hospitals maintain records at a specified level of completeness and accuracy. Hospitals are also required to control the dissemination of such information. These requirements and guidelines are established by the Department of Health and Human Services, the Joint Commission on Accreditation of Hospitals, and state law and/or regulations.

The Joint Commission on Accreditation of Hospitals (JCAH) is a voluntary organization. Although voluntary, JCAH standards are as influential with hospitals as are state and federal regulations. The JCAH has specific standards regarding the contents and maintenance of medical records. The JCAH requires records to be maintained for all patients, that the records are detailed enough for physicians to provide continuing care or consultations or to assume the care of the patient, and to permit utilization review and quality assessment activities.[6] The JCAH also specifically requires all medical records to contain the following information:

- Identification data
- Medical history
- Report of physical examination
- Diagnostic and therapeutic orders
- Evidence of informed consent
- Clinical observations, including progress notes, consultations, and opinions
- Reports of procedures and tests
- Conclusion at end of hospitalization or treatment[7]

The flow of medical information in hospital records begins in the

242—Medical Aspects of Claims

Exhibit 6-2
UB-82 Hospital Billing Form

6 • Evaluation of Medical Treatment—243

Exhibit 6-3
HCFA 1500, Physician Billing Form

HEALTH INSURANCE CLAIM FORM
READ INSTRUCTIONS BEFORE COMPLETING OR SIGNING THIS FORM

☐ MEDICAID ☐ MEDICARE ☐ CHAMPUS ☐ OTHER

PATIENT & INSURED SUBSCRIBER INFORMATION

1. PATIENT'S NAME *First name Middle Initial Last Name*
2. PATIENT'S DATE OF BIRTH
3. INSURED'S NAME *First name Middle Initial Last Name*
4. PATIENT'S ADDRESS *Street City State ZIP Code*
5. PATIENT'S SEX ☐ MALE ☐ FEMALE
6. INSURED'S MEDICARE AND/OR MEDICAID NO. *(include any letters)*
7. PATIENT'S RELATIONSHIP TO INSURED ☐ SELF ☐ SPOUSE ☐ CHILD ☐ OTHER
8. INSURED'S GROUPING *(Or Group Name)*
9. OTHER HEALTH INSURANCE COVERAGE Enter Name of Policyholder and Plan Name and Address and Policy or Medical Assistance Number
10. WAS CONDITION RELATED TO
    A. PATIENT'S EMPLOYMENT ☐ YES ☐ NO
    B. ACCIDENT ☐ AUTO ☐ OTHER
11. INSURED'S ADDRESS *Street City State ZIP Code*
12. PATIENT'S OR AUTHORIZED PERSON'S SIGNATURE *(Read back before signing)* I authorize the Release of any Medical Information Necessary to Process this Claim and Request Payment or MEDICARE Benefits Either to Myself or to the Party Who Accepts Assignment Below
    SIGNED _____ DATE _____
13. I AUTHORIZE PAYMENT OF MEDICAL BENEFITS TO UNDERSIGNED PHYSICIAN OR SUPPLIER FOR SERVICE DESCRIBED BELOW
    SIGNED *(Insured or Authorized Person)*

PHYSICIAN OR SUPPLIER INFORMATION

14. DATE OF ▸ ILLNESS/FIRST SYMPTOM OR INJURY/ACCIDENT OR PREGNANCY (LMP)
15. DATE FIRST CONSULTED YOU FOR THIS CONDITION
16. HAS PATIENT EVER HAD SAME OR SIMILAR SYMPTOMS? ☐ YES ☐ NO
16A. IF AN EMERGENCY CHECK HERE ☐
17. DATE PATIENT ABLE TO RETURN TO WORK
18. DATES OF TOTAL DISABILITY FROM _____ THROUGH _____
    DATES OF PARTIAL DISABILITY FROM _____ THROUGH _____
18. NAME OF REFERRING PHYSICIAN OR OTHER SOURCE *(e.g., public health agency)*
20. FOR SERVICES RELATED TO HOSPITALIZATION GIVE HOSPITALIZATION DATES ADMITTED _____ DISCHARGED _____
21. NAME & ADDRESS OF FACILITY WHERE SERVICES RENDERED *(if other than home or office)*
22. WAS LABORATORY WORK PERFORMED OUTSIDE YOUR OFFICE? ☐ Yes ☐ No CHARGES

6 • Evaluation of Medical Treatment—245

Exhibit 6-4
Information in a Medical Report

> Summary Report Form
> Patient Name
> Address
> Age
> Date of Injury
> Facts of the Accident
> Past Medical History
> Current Medical History
> Laboratory/X-Ray Findings
> Physical Examination
>   Height Weight
>   Body System Review
> Description of Injury
> Current Medical Treatment
> Consultations
> Level of Functional Impairment/Restrictions
> Prognosis

admissions office of the hospital. When a patient is admitted, the first and most essential forms are completed. This part of the process provides the administrative data needed to identify the patient and assigns a patient identification number or hospital number that will be used on all medical records for this patient throughout the hospital stay.

The nursing service develops and maintains a chart on which all pertinent medical information is recorded. The chart is kept at the nursing station on the floor where the patient is staying. The admitting physician is responsible for compiling the history and performing the physical examination. Other physicians may be called in for consultation or additional care and treatment. All health care providers involved in the case record on the chart their findings and services provided. This system provides easy access to pertinent information for all health care providers involved with the patient.

When the patient is discharged, the file is forwarded to the medical records department for storage. Any subsequent reports are forwarded to the medical records department to be combined with the existing record. Exhibit 6-5 illustrates the flow of medical information within the hospital system.

The claim representatives should know what records may be in-

Exhibit 6-5
Flow of Medical Information in the Hospital System

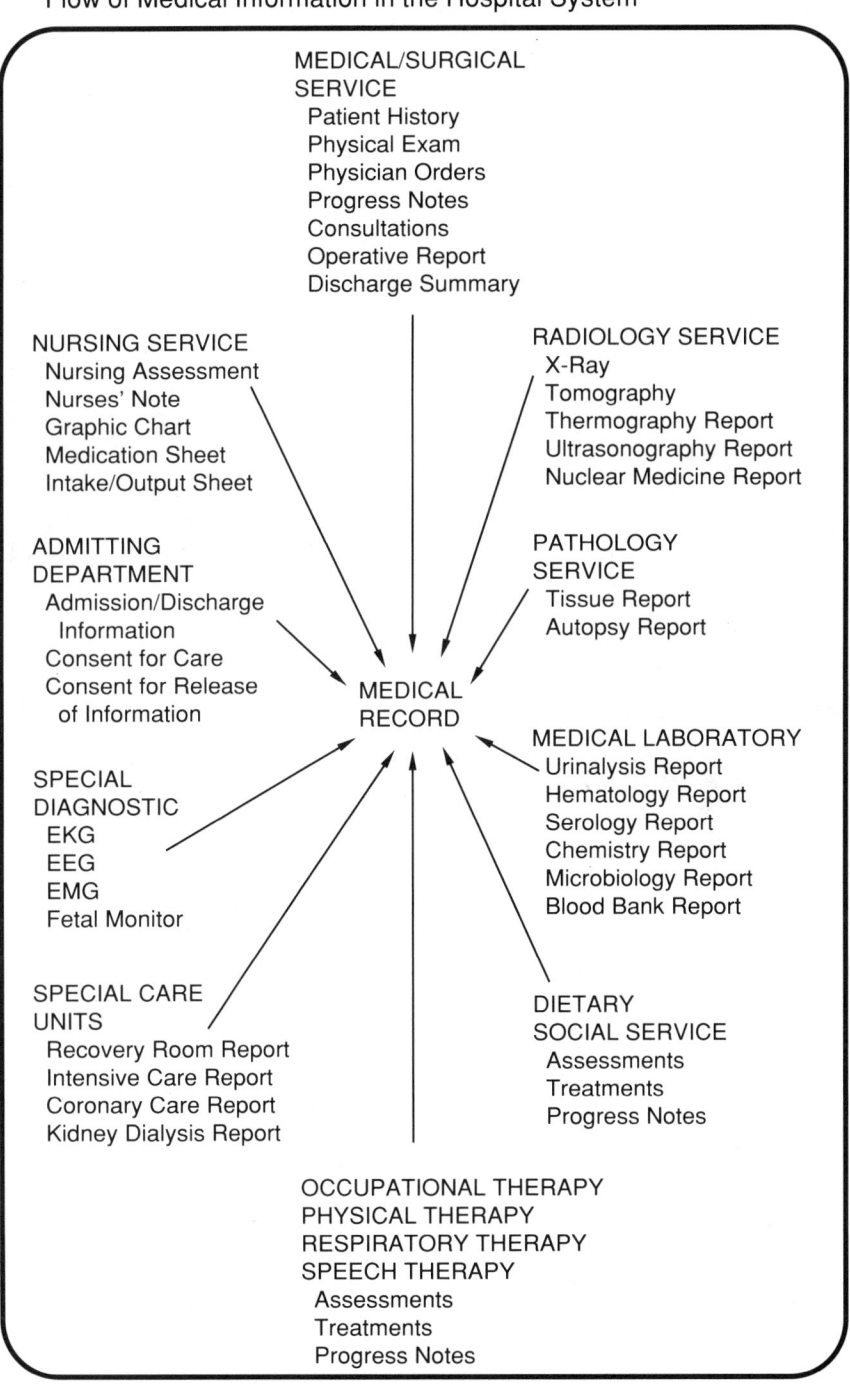

MEDICAL/SURGICAL SERVICE
 Patient History
 Physical Exam
 Physician Orders
 Progress Notes
 Consultations
 Operative Report
 Discharge Summary

NURSING SERVICE
 Nursing Assessment
 Nurses' Note
 Graphic Chart
 Medication Sheet
 Intake/Output Sheet

ADMITTING DEPARTMENT
 Admission/Discharge Information
 Consent for Care
 Consent for Release of Information

SPECIAL DIAGNOSTIC
 EKG
 EEG
 EMG
 Fetal Monitor

SPECIAL CARE UNITS
 Recovery Room Report
 Intensive Care Report
 Coronary Care Report
 Kidney Dialysis Report

MEDICAL RECORD

RADIOLOGY SERVICE
 X-Ray
 Tomography
 Thermography Report
 Ultrasonography Report
 Nuclear Medicine Report

PATHOLOGY SERVICE
 Tissue Report
 Autopsy Report

MEDICAL LABORATORY
 Urinalysis Report
 Hematology Report
 Serology Report
 Chemistry Report
 Microbiology Report
 Blood Bank Report

DIETARY SOCIAL SERVICE
 Assessments
 Treatments
 Progress Notes

OCCUPATIONAL THERAPY
PHYSICAL THERAPY
RESPIRATORY THERAPY
SPEECH THERAPY
 Assessments
 Treatments
 Progress Notes

248—Medical Aspects of Claims

cluded in a patient's chart so that relevant information can be obtained for the claim review process. The claim representatives should clarify which records he or she needs because if the entire record is requested, unnecessary information will be received. In addition, there will be a delay in receiving information because of the time required to reproduce an entire file. Furthermore, copy charges for records by a hospital are usually by the page.

Exhibit 6-6 lists the records and reports that may be available from a medical chart along with the information contained in each.

Other Medical Records. The *emergency room* is considered an outpatient facility. Emergency care records are therefore not included in the inpatient hospital chart. Nevertheless, like in-hospital records, these records must meet JCAH and other legal standards. Therefore, the information in the emergency room record should be concise and objective, documenting the need for services provided. The source of any information in the emergency room record should always be identified.

The emergency room record includes patient identification, time and means of arrival, pertinent history of illness or injury, physical findings, and vital signs. Also documented is emergency care given to the patient prior to arrival, such as that provided by the ambulance service, as well as the diagnosis and therapeutic orders given by the attending physician, and whether any orders are declined by the patient. Clinical observations, the disposition of the patient, and results of treatment are also reported. Any instructions given to the patient or family for follow-up care should be noted.

Ambulatory care records must meet JCAH standards for content and maintenance. Ambulatory care centers provide for outpatient surgical and diagnostic treatment requiring short-term care. Highly skilled medical providers can treat and monitor the patient on a same-day basis. Information for this record should include patient identification data; relevant history of illness or injury; physical findings; diagnostic and therapeutic orders; clinical observations, including results of treatment; reports of procedures and tests and their results; disposition of the patient; and the pertinent instructions to the patient and family for follow-up care. With changes in the health care delivery system, more services are now being provided in these settings, and claim reviews will more frequently include services provided by these facilities.

All licensed medical facilities providing inpatient housing are required to maintain concurrent patient records. Rehabilitation centers, psychiatric facilities, and long-term care or nursing home facilities fall into this category. These facilities often maintain their records in a chronological diary system rather than by department, as is done

Exhibit 6-6
Medical Chart Records

Admission Record	Data required to accurately identify the patient; to include name, address, age, religious preference, marital status, next of kin, attending physician, payment source, admitting diagnosis, type of admission.
Admission History & Physical	
	Chief complaint, history of present illness, personal and familiar history, body system review, physical examination, admitting impressions/diagnosis.
Discharge Summary	Concise summary of the course of hospital stay to include significant findings, procedures performed, condition of patient at discharge, instructions given to patient and/or family.
Physicians Orders	Diagnostic and therapeutic orders dated and signed by the attending physician and/or any other physician in attendance during the course of stay.
Physicians Progress Notes	
	Brief note written by any physician in attendance following an assessment of the patient or treatment of the patient to note findings and/or results.
Nursing Record/Nurses Notes	
	Consist of information on patient care assessment, planning, intervention, and evaluation.
Short Stay Record	A condensed record may be kept for patients who require less than 48 hours of hospitalization. Patient identification information, description of the condition, physician's findings, treatment given, and other data to justify diagnosis and treatment. No discharge summary is required.

Other Reports

Consultation Reports	Attending physician requests an evaluation by another provider stating the purpose and the nature of the consultation desired. The report in return is a narrative description to the attending physician of findings and recommendations. Signed and dated.
Pathology and Clinical Laboratory Reports	
	Reports of clinical findings following pathology examinations and laboratory tests. Signed and dated.

Radiological and Other Diagnostic

Laboratory Reports	Physician impressions following a review of the diagnostic procedure results per film video, scope, tracing, etc. Signed and dated.

(continued)

250—Medical Aspects of Claims

Social Services — Such reports may contain intimate details of the patient's life. Some of the information obtained may also be considered hearsay. For this reason many hospitals require a summary of such records be made to include the information considered to be of value to the physician and other health care personnel providing care.

Other Areas:
Intensive Care Units
Labor and Delivery
Dietary
Therapy
- Psychotherapy
- Speech Therapy
- Occupational Therapy
- Respiratory Therapy
- Physical Therapy

---

in hospital records. It is therefore often necessary for the claim representative to obtain the entire record to thoroughly review a case.

Emergency medical technicians and paramedics may provide emergency medical care under the supervision of a physician who monitors the case from a local trauma center. Any services must be recorded and maintained for legal purposes and for an attending physician to review in the emergency room. These records are important in establishing the facts of an accident and the nature of the trauma. The emergency service system that responds to the accident maintains a permanent file of these records.

Notes recorded by private duty nurses document the care and treatment provided to the patient and the patient's response. These records can establish whether the patient requires licensed nursing services or a nursing aid or attendant. They can also establish the dates and times of nursing care and treatment. These details may be needed when the claim representative is considering reimbursement for hourly services billed by these medical professionals.

Obtaining Medical Records

Obtaining medical records is usually a straightforward procedure. In any injury case, the claimant has made his or her medical condition an issue. Therefore, the claimant must produce evidence supporting the claim and will usually cooperate with a claim representative seeking medical records. The claim representative must obtain medical records with due regard for privacy rights and state law and must organize the records in a useful manner.

Privacy. Privacy is the degree of control individuals have over the distribution of information about themselves; "it is the right to a reasonable expectation of confidentiality."[8]

When under the care of a medical provider, patients share intimate details of their life hoping to give the provider the best foundation for making a diagnosis and prescribing treatment. The medical provider must record this information, which must be protected and released only when it is deemed relevant to do so.

The medical provider and/or the institution and patient own the *medical records*. The provider or institution owns the *physical records*. The patient owns and has a right to the information contained within the record. The patient has a right of access to his or her medical information at any time.

The Federal Privacy Act of 1974[9] was passed to safeguard individuals against invasions of privacy by federal agencies. It requires such agencies, except as otherwise provided by law, to do the following:

1. Permit an individual to determine what records pertaining to him are collected, maintained, used, or disseminated by such agencies;
2. Permit an individual to prevent records pertaining to him, obtained by such agencies for a particular purpose, from being used or made available for another purpose without his consent;
3. Permit an individual to gain access to information pertaining to him in federal agency records, to have a copy made of all or any portion thereof, and to correct or amend such records;
4. Collect, maintain, use, or disseminate any record of identifiable personal information in a manner that assures that such action is for a necessary and lawful purpose, that the information is current and accurate for its intended use, and that adequate safeguards are provided to prevent misuse of such information;
5. Permit exemptions from the requirements with respect to records provided in this act, only in those cases where there is an important public policy need for such exemption, as has been determined by specific statutory authorities;
6. Be subject to civil suit for any damages which occur as a result of willful or intentional action, which violates any "individual's rights" under this act.[10]

This law affects the claim review process whenever information must be obtained through the Medicare or Medicaid systems, military health records, federally owned and operated health care institutions such as Veterans Administration hospitals, or federal programs estab-

252—Medical Aspects of Claims

lished and governed under the Federal Drug and Alcohol Abuse Act.

State Requirements. Each state's requirements for obtaining medical records vary. Claim representatives must know their own state or local requirements. For example, Alabama requires the express consent of a patient or representative in order to obtain records;[11] Tennessee requires that state hospital records may be obtained only with a *subpoena duces tecum*.[12]

Medical Authorization. The patient has the right to approve a release of information to any party. This approval is known as a medical authorization, an *authorization for release of medical information*, or *authorization for disclosure*. A written release for disclosure of information gives the health care provider authority to release the material contained in the medical record. The authorization for disclosure should clearly state the intent of the release.

An authorization should include the following information:

1. Name of the health care provider or institution to which the authorization is addressed.
2. The names of those persons, firms, corporations, or public body to which such information is to be released.
3. An adequate description of the information to be disclosed.
4. The signature of the patient whose health record is requested, or of the individual legally authorized to act on the patient's behalf.
5. The specific expiration date of the authorization. A patient may revoke an authorization at any time, although not retroactively.
6. Any prohibitions on disclosure of specific information.
7. Any prohibition of proposed new use of information without additional consent of the patient.[13]

Organization of Medical Information. Once medical documentation has been received and the supporting claim file information, such as the loss report, statements, and bills, is in place, the information should be organized on the basis of *data* and *opinion*, then placed in chronological order.

Medical *data* is objective information that can be seen or measured by the health care provider. Opinions are the provider's conclusions based on a review of the data, the patient's complaints, and often pure supposition. The claim reviewer can reasonably expect to find a mixture of data and opinion. For instance, a file might include the following information: an x-ray showing a displaced shoulder (data), patient complaints of pain when rotating the shoulder (subjective information), and a physician's statement, "There was a displacement of the right shoulder sustained when the patient was thrown to the ground and landed on that shoulder," (opinion). In this case, it would be reasonable to accept the physician's opinion since it is supported by objective and subjective evidence.

Findings based on subjective evidence and supposition on the part of the medical provider require further investigation. For example, a patient may present with headache and nausea, but x-rays of the head may be negative. Because the patient states he did not have headaches prior to his recent accident, the medical provider might conclude that the headaches result from the accident. This situation should be further investigated in order to discover any pre-existing medical problems that might be contributing to the patient's discomfort. Additional information could also be provided by further diagnostic evaluation in the form of other tests or an independent medical exam.

When extensive medical services have been provided, or when multiple providers have been involved in the care and treatment of a patient, it is important to chronologically organize the bills and records. This recreates the course of treatment and enables the claim representative to understand the relevance of various services and to identify medical problems that may not be associated with the reported accident. Gaps in the treatment plan that require additional investigation may be noted. A chronological review defines when, where, and how the initial diagnosis was made; it also illustrates the patient's progress during the course of care and treatment as well as any complications that arose during that process. Claim representatives should determine whether the various health care providers appear to agree on the cause and treatment of the medical condition.

EXPERT ASSISTANCE

In certain cases, claim representatives need expert assistance to address medical issues. The two most commonly used expert services are retrospective review and independent medical examinations. Another type of expert service, utilization review, is discussed in the next chapter.

Retrospective Review

If a review of all records and bills fails to resolve questions as to cause of injury and appropriateness of treatment, a review by an independent medical consultant should be considered. Frequently, the claim representative may have questions about the type and frequency of treatment. In this situation, a medical consultant may be asked to provide an opinion. This process is called a retrospective review.

254—Medical Aspects of Claims

Nature and Purpose. A *retrospective review*, sometimes called a records review, is a review of a claimant's medical records by another physician. The retrospective review physician does not usually see the claimant. A retrospective review is a "peer review" (review of one medical provider by a medical provider practicing in a like discipline) to consider any of the following:

- The relationship between the injury and the known facts of the accident
- The relationship between the treatment and the injury claimed
- The necessity of ongoing medical treatment

The consultant must submit a written report giving an opinion about the medical questions asked. The conclusions should be based as much as possible on objective evidence. A copy is usually given to the patient. If the reviewing physician cannot reach a conclusion within a reasonable degree of medical certainty, he should explain why he cannot support or dispute the claim.

Preparation. A retrospective review is ordinarily performed by a medical provider who specializes in the same discipline as the treating physician, or in the area of medicine that most directly relates to the medical issue in the case. For example, if the treating physician indicates that the injured party has a thyroid imbalance that was traumatically induced by the accident, an endocrinologist (a specialist in the treatment of thyroid and other endocrine disorders) may be the physician of choice for the retrospective review.

The steps listed below should be followed in preparing for a retrospective review:

1. The claim representative should introduce the reviewing physician to the facts of the accident.
2. The claim representative should explain what issues should be included in the reviewing physician's report.
3. The claim representative must send to the reviewing physician all documentation, including clinical notes, hospital records, reports and x-ray films, and any supporting materials from other attending health care providers. Failure to provide the complete medical record may completely discredit the reviewing physician's report.
4. The claim representative should ask the reviewing physician if it seems that information may be missing from the records. A claim representative may not be aware that certain reports are available.
5. The claim representative must give the reviewing physician a deadline. In the claim review process, turnaround time is vital to an equitable decision. Various statutes require a decision on a claim within a specific period of time, typically thirty days.

Independent Medical Examination

Most medical insurance policies provide, as a condition of the contract, that the insurer may obtain a medical examination of the injured party as many times as it deems necessary. In third-party tort claims that become the subject of a lawsuit, at least one independent medical examination can be secured as part of the discovery procedure. Even before suit is filed, many plaintiff attorneys will allow the insurer an independent medical examination if doing so helps to conclude the claim.

Role of the Independent Medical Examination. An independent medical examination (IME) has a limited and specific definition in the medical community. It includes a brief review of the patient history and treatment to date and a physical examination of the patient. The purpose of the examination is to help the physician make a medical determination as to causation, current physical impairment, and the need for present or future treatment.

For example, in a claim involving scarring, the issue of scar revision may arise. The treating physician may indicate that the revision is needed but may be far from definitive in his recommendation. In this situation, an IME may be helpful both for resolving the claim and for helping the patient plan his or her future medical care. The IME is essentially a second medical opinion.

In many cases, however, claim representatives need an IME as well as a retrospective review to resolve a claim. For example, a claim might involve a soft tissue injury with what appears to be unnecessary or unreasonable treatment, or treatment at a greater frequency than would be expected for the injury. This condition along with an allegation of continuing disability and need for treatment may require an IME with retrospective review.

Nevertheless, an IME has benefits not available from a retrospective review alone. The most obvious is that the independent examiner has an opportunity to actually examine the injured person. This provides information that may be the basis for a prognosis and determining the necessity of future treatment. The independent medical examiner also has an opportunity to evaluate the injured party as a witness if the case goes to litigation. This aspect of the independent medical examination is critical because an experienced medical examiner can provide good insight as to whether the injured party is overreacting or exaggerating and how this will come across to a jury.

Arranging an Independent Medical Examination. The timing of an independent medical exam and retrospective review can be very critical in liability claims, especially when court rules allow only one such examination prior to trial. Under these rules, it is best to schedule the examination only when the claimant has reached maximum recovery. If the independent medical examination is conducted while the claimant is still actively treating, the medical examiner can only attest to the fact that an injury was sustained, and that at the time of the examination recovery was in progress. The examiner will not be able to attest that a *full* recovery has been made. If partial or permanent disability is alleged at the time of trial, such a report would not provide a defense to this allegation. It is generally premature to request an independent medical examination prior to securing and reviewing the available medical records of the treating physician.

As with a retrospective review by a medical consultant, claim representatives must communicate fully to the independent medical examiner, must outline their medical questions, and must include all medical records and other pertinent file materials. The failure to forward complete medical records may completely discredit the exam.

The determination as to the type of medical professional to be used for an independent medical examination depends on the type of injury. If the injury involves a fracture, an orthopedic surgeon is generally chosen. If the condition involves scarring, the obvious choice would be a board certified plastic surgeon. The selection process becomes a little more complex when the existence of the injury is based on subjective evidence only. If it is alleged that the head or neck were injured and that the injured party was unconscious for any period of time, a neurologist or neurosurgeon would probably be chosen. If the injury involves a strain, sprain, or disc herniation of the thoracic or lumbar spine, or if pain radiates to the legs, an orthopedist or orthopedic surgeon and possibly a neurosurgeon should be selected. Nerve involvement would normally indicate the need for a neurologist. General surgeons or internists might be chosen if there were very extensive injuries to numerous organs. A careful review of the treatment records along with some research by the claim representative should help to determine the type of medical professional best able to answer the claim representative's questions. In very complicated cases, it may be helpful for the claim representative to consult with a local physician or defense attorney.

Problems With Expert Reviews and Examinations

While expert reviews and examinations can provide valuable assistance to claim representatives, they do have drawbacks. They are expensive and difficult to arrange and may not affect the claimant's case at all.

Cost and Difficulty in Making Arrangements. These problems are related. Only a small minority of physicians are willing and able to perform these services: it has been estimated that there are forty to fifty patient care physicians for every one performing independent medical exams.[14] The best IME physicians are scheduled long in advance because they are generally not available on short notice. As a result of their scarcity and the demand for their services, good IME physicians charge several hundred to a thousand dollars for their services.

Noneffect on Claimant's Case. Despite their cost, reviews and exams frequently fail to diminish a claimant's case. Independent reviews and exams often confirm the claimant's case. This is only a problem in that the review or exam and its expense prove to be unnecessary. Otherwise, it is valuable to learn that claimant's case is confirmed. Claim representatives should regard it as their responsibility to pay what is due on a case, not to pay the least possible.

More problematic are independent reviews and exams that are inconclusive. These cost as much as any other review or exam, but provide little or no useful information toward concluding the claim. Reviews or exams can be inconclusive for a number of reasons. The reviewing physician may not be the right kind of specialist. For example, an orthopedist may review a case in which the main issues are psychiatric. The reviewing physician may not wish to be critical of a colleague, thus giving every benefit of the doubt to the treating physician. The case may involve issues that are on the frontier of medical knowledge, and the reviewing physician may not be fully acquainted with the scientific literature. Finally, like the treating physician, reviewing physicians must rely on the claimant for information about medical history and the accident in question. An IME may therefore fail to prove or disprove an injury.

SUMMARY

In every claim for bodily injury, a claim representative must answer several questions related to a claimant's medical treatment. First, did the insured accident cause the injuries or conditions from which the claimant suffers? This may not be so if the claimant has pre-existing problems, chronic problems, or intervening problems not related to the insured event. Second, was the treatment the claimant received necessary? Unusual and redundant treatment should not be reimbursed. Finally, what future treatment will be needed? The claim representative carries the burden of answering these questions because patients and physicians have strong incentives to overtreat.

One of the claim representative's key responsibilities is to identify cases for which the claim representative must get additional help from supervisors, managers, or outside experts. Serious cases can be iden-

258—Medical Aspects of Claims

tified by type of injury, dollar amount, length of disability, or medical complexity.

For the vast majority of cases handled by the claim representative alone, the claimant's medical records are the essential evidence. Claim representatives must understand what information is contained in different records, how these records are created and maintained, the type of institutions from which records may be obtained, and how records should be obtained.

For certain cases, claim representatives use outside experts to evaluate medical issues. Consulting physicians might only review records in a retrospective review, they might examine the claimant in an independent medical examination, or they might do both. Reviews and exams can be expensive and difficult to arrange, and there is no guarantee that they will affect a claimant's case.

6 • Evaluation of Medical Treatment—259
Chapter Notes

1. Kathleen A. Waters and Gretchen Frederick Murphy, *Medical References in Health Information* (Rockville, MD: Aspen Publishing, 1979), p. 257.
2. 66 Am Jur 2d, Records, §46.5.
3. Lawrence Weed, M.D., *Medical Record, Medical Education, and Patient Care* (Chicago: Year Book Medical Pubs., Inc., 1970), p. 5.
4. See for example, Edna K. Huffman, *Medical Record Management*, 8th ed. (Berwyn, IL: Physicians' Record Co., 1985).
5. JoAnne C. Bruce, *Privacy and Confidentiality of Health Care Information* (Chicago: AHPI, 1984), p. 13.
6. *Accreditation Manual for Hospitals* (Chicago: Joint Commission on Accreditation of Hospitals, 1986), pp. 79-80.
7. *Accreditation Manual*, p. 80.
8. Arthur F. Southwick, *The Law of Hospital and Health Care Administration*, 2d ed. (Ann Arbor, MI: Health Administration Press, 1988), p. 322.
9. 5 U.S.C. §552a.
10. Bruce, p. 57.
11. Ala. Code §27-21A-25.
12. Tenn. Code §10-7-504.
13. Adapted from Pennsylvania Bar Institute, *Analyzing Medical Records* (Harrisburg, PA, 1988), pp. 21-23.
14. Ronald E. Gots, M.D., "Medical Claims Flay Casualty Insurers," *National Underwriter*, September 18, 1989, p. 86.

CHAPTER 7

Medical Cost Control

The value of a bodily injury liability or workers compensation claim is determined to a great extent by the medical expenses incurred by the claimant. As a result, liability and workers compensation claim representatives are faced with the challenge of evaluating and controlling the medical cost of a claim. This task is complicated by many factors:

- The incentives for over-treatment, which can result from an absence of treatment plans and can abuse the system.
- The dynamic nature of the field of medicine often makes today's standard of care obsolete tomorrow and can cause disagreements among medical experts on the necessity and proper method of treatment.
- The legal powers of claim representatives handling casualty claims are limited.
- The significant rise in the past several years in the cost of medical treatment generally.

To deal with the issues of medical cost management, the claim representative can use a number of cost management/containment techniques. Most of these techniques originated in the health care industry. They are important to casualty claims because of their indirect effects on casualty costs and because many of them can be directly adopted in casualty claims handling.

This chapter has two main sections. The first deals with the general escalation of medical costs and the resulting effect on claims. The second describes the techniques to control these costs, including audits, alternative fee arrangements, and utilization review. Also discussed is the application of certain utilization guidelines to chiropractic and physical therapy treatments.

THE ESCALATING COST OF MEDICAL TREATMENT

General increases in medical costs have become a major economic, social, and political issue in the United States. In turn, these cost increases have been the chief cause of increases in the medical costs of casualty claims. They have also caused the cost of insurance covering injuries, such as workers compensation and general liability, to increase faster than other lines of the property-casualty insurance industry. This section identifies the causes for rising medical costs and discusses the effect of these increases on casualty claims costs.

Historical Perspective

National health expenditures have grown enormously in the past two decades. In 1989, spending for health care reached $604.1 billion or 11.6 percent of the Gross National Product (GNP).[1] This compares to 7.4 percent of GNP spent on health care in 1970.[2] It has been projected that health care spending will continue to rise and will consume 15 percent of GNP by the year 2000.[3]

The U.S. currently has the highest level of health expenditures, as measured by percentage of GNP, of the industrialized nations. Since 1960, increases in national health expenditures have consistently outpaced the annual increases in the Consumer Price Index (CPI), as shown in Exhibit 7-1.

Sources and Uses of United States Health Care Dollars. The sources and uses of health care dollars are presented in Exhibit 7-2. The exhibit shows the dollar amounts (in billions) and how the percentages of each dollar are accounted.

Notice that many sources contribute to the total expenditure for health and that even the largest, private health insurance accounts for less than one-third of the total. One effect of this diversity of sources is that no one source has complete power over the system. Each source may have limited control over how money is spent, but none has the power to control medical spending generally. Indeed, the categories "patient payments" and "private insurance" represent thousands of payors. Medicare is the largest single payor and accordingly has considerable voice in how money is spent. In contrast, workers compensation sources collectively account for only a minor percentage of health dollars and, as might be expected, have a limited voice in how money is spent.

Hospitals and physicians account for most of the use of health dollars. Accordingly, most medical cost control efforts are directed at

7 • Medical Cost Control—263

Exhibit 7-1
Annual Increases in National Health Expenditures Versus CPI

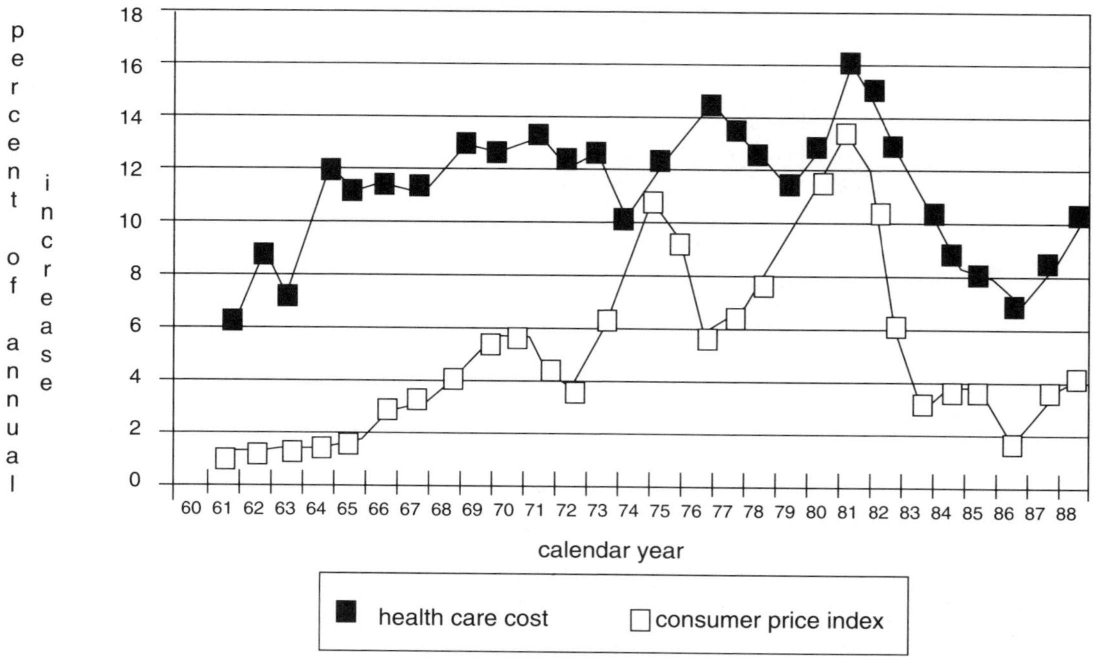

percent increase of annual

■ health care cost   □ consumer price index

Source: Health Care Financing Administration. Data on CPI from U.S. Department of Labor.

Exhibit 7-2
U.S. Health Care Dollars

Sources of Health Care Dollars (1987)
(For health services and supplies only)

	Billions of Dollars	% of Total
Direct patient payment	$123.0	25.4
Private insurance	157.8	32.7
Other private sources	5.9	1.2
Medicare	$ 83.0	17.2
Public assistance (mostly Medicaid)	54.2	11.2
Other public sources	48.4	10.1
Workers compensation (private and public)	$ 10.9	2.2
	$483.2	100.0

Uses of Health Care Dollars (1987)
(For health services and supplies only)

	Billions of Dollars	% of Total
Hospitals	$194.7	40.3
Physicians	102.7	21.3
Dentists	32.8	6.8
Drugs and sundries	34.0	7.0
Nursing home care	40.6	8.4
All other uses	78.4	16.2
	$483.2	100.0

Source: *Statistical Abstract of the United States 1990*, U.S. Department of Commerce, p. 93.

hospitalizations and surgeries. However, the other uses of health dollars are not insignificant and have drawn greater attention from insurers and other payors.

Shortcomings of the United States Health Care System. The fact that the U.S. health care system is the most costly does not mean that it is the most effective. In fact, the effectiveness of the U.S. health care system is questioned by many. There is enormous waste that takes the form of unnecessary procedures, duplicate services, and poor case management. At the same time, large numbers of Americans remain uninsured and cannot afford health care. Many believe the system needs fundamental changes.

Despite the serious problems of the U.S. health care system, it is doubtful that radical change, such as a nationalized health care system, will occur in the near future. Physicians, hospitals, insurers, and attorneys all have a substantial interest in the current system and substantial political power to prevent change. In addition, other than as voters, patients have little control over the health care system.

Causes of the Rise in Medical Costs

Aside from inflation, the rise in health care costs can be attributed to several factors: innovations in medical technology; hospital capacity; population changes; a surplus of physicians (and resulting demand creation); lack of cost control and sharing; the nature of health care; and, to a certain degree, the recent medical malpractice insurance crisis.

Innovations in and Spread of Medical Technology. Every year advances are made in medical diagnostic and therapeutic equipment. Largely because of extraordinary advances in miniaturization and computer technology, medical services are now delivered on a highly sophisticated technological level. The use of diagnostic techniques such as magnetic resonance imaging (MRI), CT scan, and ultrasound has become routine. While patients undeniably benefit greatly from these new technologies, these benefits have been expensive.

When the high cost of the equipment is borne by a physician as part of his or her private office overhead, the physician wants to make greater use of the equipment in order to realize a return on his or her investment. New technology is therefore expensive in two ways. First, the equipment itself is costly. Second, the physician's attempt to recoup his or her purchase cost through increased utilization passes the cost on to the patient. In this way, the technology essentially increases the cost of medical services by generating treatment where none may be needed.

Despite the physician's use of advanced technology, its cost is demonstrated mainly by increased hospital costs. Hospitals are the typical owners and operators of high technology equipment. It is common for all hospitals in a given area to acquire any available new technology without careful analysis of the rate at which it will be utilized. Thus, all hospitals in a given geographic area may own and operate the same new equipment, and all of them may be underutilizing the equipment. The cost of the excess unused capacity must be factored into the per patient charge or into the hospital's general overhead.

Hospital Capacity. The plant and equipment of a hospital represent an enormous investment. This cost must be recovered through the charges to each patient. The overhead costs of a hospital are relatively fixed. Thus, the more patients a hospital serves, the less the per patient overhead cost. Conversely, hospitals that are not fully utilized must spread their overhead among existing patients, increasing the per patient cost. Unfortunately for the sake of hospital rates, hospital utilization declined during the 1970s and 1980s, especially in private for-profit hospitals whose occupancy rates fell from 72.2 percent in 1970 to 51.0 percent in 1987.[4]

Population Changes. As the postwar baby-boom generation ages, and as life expectancy increases, the U.S. population has experienced an upward shift in its age composition. The portion of the population over age 65—when health care use rises significantly—continues to grow faster than other age groups. The impact of this shift on medical costs has so far been modest, but it will become greater in the next century.

A Surplus of Physicians and Demand Creation. The number of physicians has been growing faster than the general population. The rate of physicians per 100,000 population grew from 168 in 1970 to 252 in 1987, and the trend points to further growth.[5] The Graduate Medical Education National Advisory Committee (GMENAC) conservatively predicted that there will be a surplus of about 145,000 physicians by the year 2000.

Because of the technical nature of medical services, an increase in the supply of physicians tends to cause a simultaneous increase in demand for services. In most markets, suppliers have no control over demand, and an increase in supply leads to a reduction in price as a result of competition. This is not so with medical services. Doctors have substantial control over the amount of treatment patients receive. If there are fewer patients per physician, the physician will not necessarily lose revenue if more revenue per patient can be generated. There is pressure from the supply side to increase utilization. Physicians, rather than patients, generally determine how many follow-up visits a patient makes, whether the patient must undergo surgery, and whether the patient is to be cared for in a hospital rather than at home.

Lack of Cost Control or Cost Sharing. Insurance has undoubtedly contributed to medical inflation by taking away both the health care provider's and the patient's incentive to exercise cost control. Payments for medical services have traditionally been made retrospectively (after services had been provided) on an itemized fee-for-service basis. An expectation of 100 percent reimbursement provided little incentive for the supplier to practice cost control.

In addition, medical services have traditionally been viewed as different from other consumer products and services for which the consumer is able and willing to exercise bargaining power. Society, for the most part, views health care as a right rather than a commodity. Cost of service, therefore, has not been of primary concern.

Lack of medical knowledge by the patient also causes indifference to cost control. The highly technical nature of health care restricts patient participation in the decision-making process. After the initial decision to seek a physician's help, the average person relies almost completely on the physician's judgment to determine and to order appropriate types of service.

However, since the early 1980s, attitudes have begun to change. Both government and private industry have implemented cost control strategies, including incentives for patients to moderate use of the health care system by sharing part of the costs. Becoming more common are health insurance plans offered by private employers who require employees to share the cost in two ways. First, the employee must pay a portion of the health insurance cost, typically 10 to 20 percent. Second, the insurance itself covers only after the employee pays a deductible, typically $100 per year, and co-pays the provider's bill, usually paying 20 percent up to some maximum per year.

The Nature of Health Care. The fact that health care is a service contributes to the difficulty in achieving economic efficiency in the health care system. Health care is delivered by physicians, nurses, technicians, and related health workers. Improving efficiency in service industries is not as easy or as measurable as in manufacturing industries. This is especially so in health care because the "output" of the industry is difficult to identify. Crude measures of output, such as numbers of patients treated or number of cases of a certain illness treated, do not reflect anything about the quality of service or the extent of illness and disability avoided.

The Medical Malpractice Insurance Crisis. A large increase in medical malpractice lawsuits and award amounts occurred in the mid-1970s. Medical malpractice insurance premiums increased accordingly, even to the point of driving some physicians away from high-risk practices, such as obstetrics and gynecology. Medical malpractice insurance became a significant addition to the cost of providing medical care. This additional cost is passed on to the consumer through higher fees.

More importantly, the threat of a medical malpractice lawsuit has altered the way physicians provide services, encouraging them to order more diagnostic tests and perform more costly procedures. Such practices are called *defensive medicine* because they are performed as much to protect the physician as to cure the patient. Such defensive medical practice causes unnecessary utilization throughout the medical system. It is impossible to quantify exactly how much treatment is unnecessary and defensive in nature. This cost of the malpractice threat may be greater than the direct costs of malpractice insurance and payments.

Effect on Casualty Claim Costs

Rising medical costs have greatly affected the costs of casualty claims. The costs of bodily injury claims have increased at a faster rate than the costs of property damage claims. From 1980 to 1988, the cost of automobile bodily injury claims increased 158 percent compared to a 98 percent increase in automobile property damage claims.[6]

Liability Claims. The exact effects of the increase in medical costs on the cost of liability claims cannot be measured. In the past twenty years, many other factors have also played a role in increasing liability claim costs; they include the medical malpractice crisis, changes in society's perceptions of legal liability, changes in tort laws, and experiments with the no-fault concept. Nevertheless, it follows that as the value of medical specials increases, so does the value of a liability claim. Therefore, it is not surprising that the cost of liability claims, like the cost of health care, has been increasing faster than inflation in general. Furthermore, an increase in medical specials is likely to make it easier for tort thresholds to be exceeded, thus reducing whatever effectiveness the no-fault system might have provided.

Workers Compensation Claims. While the effects of increased medical costs on liability claim costs cannot be exactly measured, such effects are apparent and measurable in workers compensation costs. From 1981 to 1988, payments for workers compensation medical benefits increased 161 percent compared with only an 81 percent increase for indemnity benefits, as shown in Exhibit 7-3.

It should be noted that the increase in workers compensation medical benefits has been even greater than the increase in health costs in general. In the same period (1981 to 1988) national health expenditures rose by about 90 percent. Exhibit 7-4 shows the relationship between workers compensation benefits and national health care costs. The relative increase in workers compensation suggests that cost containment practices in workers compensation are deficient in comparison with those of other payment sources, such as health insurance or Medicare. Both medical providers and consumers may be looking more toward casualty claims as an alternative source of payments for health services.

Limitations on Cost Control. The casualty claims system has several limitations on effective cost control including limited options, limitations on insurer legal powers, lack of incentives, and fear of adverse reactions.

Exhibit 7-3
Rate of Increase in Workers Compensation Benefits—
Medical Versus Indemnity

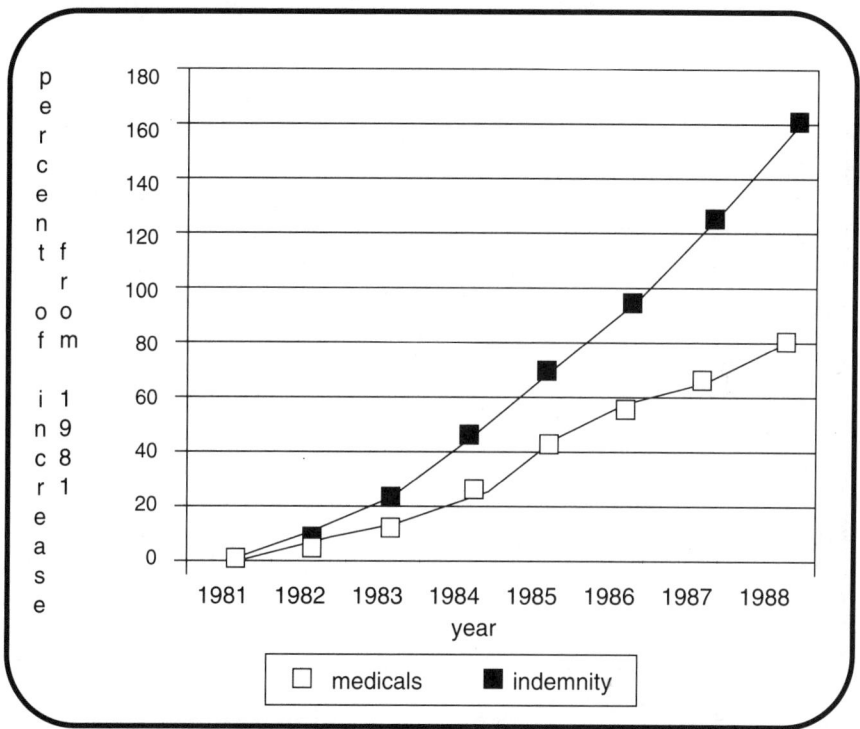

percent increase from 1981 — y-axis (0 to 180)
x-axis: year (1981–1988)
Legend: □ medicals ■ indemnity

Source: Social Security Administration

Limited Options. Any cost containment option that would shift part of the cost to the claimant, such as deductibles or co-payments, is not applicable to casualty claims. This kind of option would be contrary to the tort principle that the wrongdoer should fully compensate the victim, and to the workers compensation principle that the employer, and ultimately the consumer, should pay all costs of work-related injuries.

Limitations on Insurer Legal Powers. Workers compensation benefits are closely regulated by state governments. Each state has certain rules with respect to the rights of employers and employees in the securing and payment of medical services. For example, the employee has the right to make the first choice of the treating physician in many states, although in some cases, the selection must be made from a list provided by the employer. In all states, the employer or its insurer must make payment promptly upon receipt of adequate documentation.

Liability claims are not as highly regulated as workers compensa-

Exhibit 7-4
Rate of Increase in Medical Costs—Workers Compensation Versus National Health Expenditures

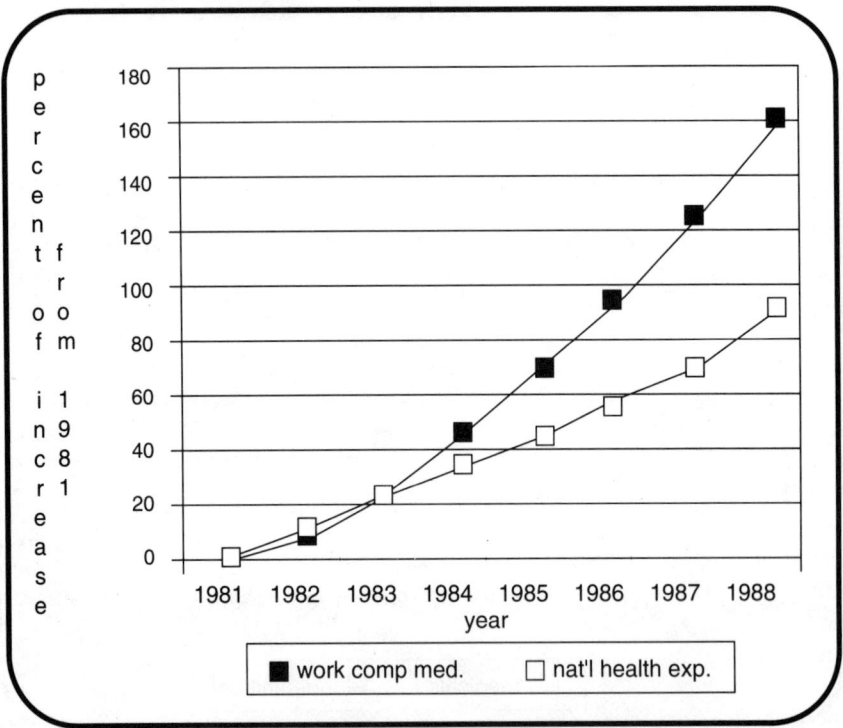

Source: Social Security Administration

tion claims. The absence of regulations in general, and of well-defined regulations in particular, does not mean that the payor has more control. On the contrary, the degree of control is much more uncertain. It is extremely difficult, if not impossible, for a claim representative to dictate to an injured third party how and where to seek treatment. Thus, medical cost control is largely an after-the-fact exercise.

Lack of Incentives. Because the settlement value of a claim is determined largely by the cost of medical treatments, there is no incentive for a claimant to keep these costs at a minimum. On the contrary, there is an incentive to inflate medical expenses in hope of a larger settlement.

Because claim representatives handling casualty claims lack first-party contractual powers, they usually cannot concentrate on cost control as effectively as health insurance claim representatives. Furthermore, the claim representative's incentive to scrutinize medical bills is even weaker in liability claims than in workers compensation. A liability claim representative is often faced with a variety of issues, such as property damage and negligence determination. Typically, workers compensation claim representatives can focus much more on the medical aspects of a case. In workers compensation, any reduction in medical expenses can be immediately measured, whereas in a liability claim, the existence of other factors, such as general damages (pain and suffering) and comparative negligence, make it less possible to identify medical cost savings.

Fear of Adverse Reactions. By nature, the relationship between parties involved in a third-party liability claim or workers compensation claim is more adversarial than in first-party insurance. This adversarial relationship can be exacerbated by the introduction of cost containment efforts. Some claim representatives fear that cost containment efforts will be perceived by the claimant as a limitation on the right to receive medical treatment, therefore making it more likely that the claimant will retain an attorney and drive up the cost of a claim.

MEDICAL COST CONTAINMENT METHODS

Numerous systems and strategies to contain health costs have evolved in recent years. Some of these techniques have more relevance than others to casualty claims. Nevertheless, claim representatives must learn about all such techniques to understand current practices of the medical community and the cost problems facing casualty insurers, and to anticipate trends in casualty claims.

Audits of health care provider bills provide a certain degree of protection. Improper, redundant, or excessive charges can be identified and eliminated through audits. Alternate fee arrangements hold considerable promise as a cost containment technique. Such arrangements can shift to the medical community the burden of policing the appropriateness and extent of treatment. Utilization review is the most promising cost containment method for casualty claims. It includes a number of specific techniques, all of which involve analysis of the necessity of treatment. A proper analysis of the necessity of treatment requires an expert knowledge of medicine and medical practices.

Chiropractic and physical therapy treatments are frequently abused by claimants to build their cases, yet both types of treatment play a legitimate role in recovery from traumatic injuries. Claim representatives must develop guidelines for the use of these treatments in order to identify cases needing cost control.

Importance of Cost Containment Methods

Most cost containment methods described below originated in the health insurance business or in government health programs. Some of these methods are applicable to casualty claims; others are not. Nevertheless, all cost containment techniques are important because of their indirect and potential effects on casualty claims.

In addition, claim representatives must understand all cost containment methods in order to apply the appropriate method to a given case. This is so even when the case has been referred to an outside expert for cost control assistance because claim representatives are responsible for overall management of a case and for claimant control.

Cost Shifting

As noted above, the vast majority of health costs are paid by health insurers, government programs, or directly by the patient. Only a small percentage are paid by casualty insurers. As a result, payment sources other than casualty insurers have been much more sensitive to increasing costs and have been far ahead of casualty insurers in the use of cost containment techniques. Their success in containing costs has resulted in the shifting of some costs to casualty insurers.

Cost shifting is the charging of higher fees to payment sources that impose few controls. Payment sources that impose substantial controls and regulations will not accept whatever costs the medical provider happens to generate. Costs not covered by a regulated payment source may be shifted to a relatively unregulated source, such as workers compensation and liability insurance. As more and more payment sources become regulated, health care providers are increasingly pressured to shift costs to the few remaining unrestricted payment sources. For example, as inpatient hospital costs are increasingly controlled, hospitals have shifted costs to outpatient and ancillary services that are less closely controlled.[7]

Hospitals and physicians have been increasingly diligent in searching for a connection between their treatments and a work-related or other kind of accident.[8] To the extent that such a connection exists, it is perfectly legitimate for charges to be directed to the applicable insurer. Whenever an insured is treated for accidental injuries, health insurers now routinely specifically ask their insureds about any connection to auto or work-related accidents. In some cases, they make such inquiries for any type of treatment at all. Before such inquiries became routine, health insurers were undoubtedly paying for a great number of accidents that could have been covered by casualty insurance.

Unfortunately, pressure from regulated payment sources may have led many physicians and hospitals to exaggerate the connection between their treatment and a work-related or other kind of accident.[9] One of the chief ways in which health insurance cost controls are significant for casualty claim representatives is the possibility that physicians and hospitals might overstate a work or accident connection. Casualty claim representatives must realize that because of the cost control pressures from health insurers, physicians and hospitals have great incentive to impose increasing costs on casualty insurers, thus making cost containment methods even more important for casualty insurers.

Changes in the Legal Environment. Claim representatives must also be familiar with cost containment strategies because the law governing casualty claims is unlikely to remain fixed, especially workers compensation law. The legal authority to impose certain cost controls may soon exist where it is now absent. For example, the Workers Compensation Research Institute reports that as of 1990, twenty-six states employ medical fee schedules, compared to only thirteen in 1983; eleven states review medical bills, compared to four in 1983; and nine states run utilization review programs, up from four in 1983. In addition, twenty-one states limit the employee's initial selection of physician, and to protect against doctor-shopping, as many as thirty-nine states limit change of physician by the employee.[10]

Although it is a highly effective strategy for health insurers, cost sharing is likely to remain politically unacceptable in casualty insurance. However, it is foreseeable that many of the techniques of utilization review, discussed below, will be authorized for use by casualty insurers. Most of these techniques impose no cost on the claimant and have proven effective in controlling medical costs without compromising the quality of service. As utilization review techniques are increasingly recognized as part of health insurance and medical practice, it is more likely that they will be authorized for use in casualty claims. Casualty claim representatives should anticipate increasingly widespread use of utilization review.

The Role of the Claim Representative. The claim representative is not a medical expert. Therefore, the claim representative's job is not usually to apply the various cost containment techniques described in this chapter, but to recognize which techniques can be applied and when they should be considered. The specifics of cost containment analysis should be left to medical experts. The claim representative is responsible for the overall management of a claim. While the claim representative need not be knowledgeable in all technical details of cost control, he or she must have an understanding that is adequate enough to coordinate, intervene in, and direct all cost containment activities similar to the way in which a claim representative controls a claim while a defense attorney handles litigation.

A claim representative must be familiar with the laws in his or her jurisdiction with respect to the various cost containment techniques.

274—Medical Aspects of Claims

Not all cost containment techniques are applicable in all states or to all types of cases. Certain cost control techniques can be implemented after the fact, such as audits and utilization review. Such an approach cannot prevent any unnecessary treatment from occurring, but can arm the claim representative with arguments against paying for it.

The claim representative is responsible for conveying to the claimant the necessity and objective of cost containment. On one hand, it should be made clear that the insurer is responsible only for necessary and reasonable treatment. On the other hand, the claimant should be advised that cost containment efforts are not used to limit the claimant's right to seek treatment, but to ensure the quality of treatment in a way that is most economical for the insurer.

Despite such efforts, many claimants do not cooperate with cost containment efforts unless required to do so by law.

Fee Audits

Fee audits are a fundamental tool of medical cost containment. In a fee audit, bills from health care providers are analyzed to ensure that proper items of service are being billed and that the charges for such service are appropriate. Fee audits can detect services not provided, those not provided in the manner or scope indicated, and can also detect redundant services. Fee audits can also identify improper charges by comparing charges to rates that are considered proper. Fee audits can be performed through the use of state fee schedules and hospital bill audits.

State Fee Schedules. About half the states use some form of fee schedules in workers compensation cases to limit the fees charged by physicians and, sometimes, hospitals.

Fee schedules are a form of price control. They were first introduced by the federal government in the early 1970s. These schedules, as adopted by Medicare, allowed fees to rise with a cost index. Thereafter, the states developed fee schedules in workers compensation. Most state fee schedules are based on a relative value scale. Services are measured in terms of number of units, with a predetermined price per unit. The effect of a fee schedule is to establish fixed relative values for various medical service and treatments. A few states use a modification of Medicare or Medicaid schedules. Massachusetts' fee schedules, for example, are set at 150 percent of Medicaid rates. Some state schedules use a combination of these approaches. While generally not overly restrictive, state fee schedules somewhat limit the amount health care providers could otherwise charge in an unrestricted market.

Health care providers' compliance with fee schedules is of some advantage to insurers. In addition, various studies have reported that bills audited against state fee schedules can result in savings, ranging from 10 percent to 15 percent, that would not be realized if health care providers did not comply with fee schedules.[11]

The use of fee schedules has become increasingly routine in workers compensation claims handling. Insurers can easily train their personnel to audit bills against fee schedules or can refer the work to outside bill auditing firms. These firms can usually review bills by computers that "know" the fee schedules of every state and locale.

The effectiveness of fee schedules can be limited. Alone, they do not control the degree of utilization. Medical providers can theoretically make up any lost revenue caused by fee schedules by increasing the amount of services because the fee schedule concept does not address the necessity of treatments. Nonetheless, not using fee schedules means that a company may be paying for both excessive charges and excessive utilization. Fee schedules should be used as a first step in any cost containment program. Increasingly, bill auditing services will also analyze the frequency and duration of treatment in addition to comparing charges to fee schedules.

Usual, Customary, and Reasonable Charge. A common criterion for fee schedules is the usual, customary, and reasonable charge (UCR). Among other limitations, health insurance contracts almost invariably limit reimbursement to the UCR, which limits fees to the local prevailing rates that are reasonable. Usual, customary, but unreasonable charges should be rejected. The UCR standard is not written into casualty insurance contracts, but it is still important in casualty claims. The law itself provides that reimbursement for medical services should be limited to UCR amounts. Casualty claim representatives can refuse to pay unusual or unreasonable charges. Independent fee auditing services can provide advice about UCR amounts.

Hospital Bill Audits. Hospital bill audits are likewise performed to ensure the appropriateness of charges. The services billed by the hospital are compared to what the physician ordered and to what was actually performed. The objective of these audits is to identify billing errors such as duplicate charges and charges for services not rendered.

Hospital bill audits are performed by firms specializing in cost containment. Nurses at these firms use computers to review billing charges against hospital records, often conducting on-site audits at the hospitals. Audit services may be charged at a fixed fee, at a percentage of the bill, at a percentage of savings, or per line on a bill. Hospital bill audits typically produce savings of about 5 percent.[12] Larger savings usually come from larger bills in which there is a greater potential of billing errors.

276—Medical Aspects of Claims

Hospital bills should be selectively audited. The decision to audit is based on criteria established by insurers and may include the dollar amount of bills (such as those above $5,000), length of stay (such as three days or more), and hospital reputation. Bills showing disproportionate charges from certain departments may be audited, with the focus only on the department in question. Most cost containment service firms provide a free preliminary screening of bills considered for audit to assess whether an audit is likely to yield savings.

Like fee schedules, hospital bill audits do not address the issue of necessity of treatment. As hospitals continue to improve their billing procedures to prevent errors, hospital bill audits can be expected to become less necessary. In response, bill auditing services have adopted and begun to offer utilization review services, described later in this section.

Alternative Fee Arrangements

A very different approach to medical cost containment is the move away from the traditional fee-for-service (FFS) mode of payment to some forms of alternative fee arrangement. Under the traditional FFS system, the health care provider sets its fee, and the insurer or patient pays it after the service is rendered.

In the 1970s, the concept of alternative fee arrangements was introduced by the formation of preferred provider organizations (PPOs), health maintenance organizations (HMOs), and diagnostic related groups (DRGs). Because these alternative arrangements provide incentives for medical providers to manage the degree of utilization, they are commonly referred to as managed care.

Preferred Provider Organizations. A preferred provider organization (PPO) is a medical provider or a group of medical providers organized to offer services at a discount in exchange for a high volume of referrals. The primary advantage of PPOs is their willingness to negotiate fixed fees at a discount for all types of services. The discounts usually exceed 20 percent off the fee schedules or UCR amounts.[13] PPOs typically have utilization control measures within their network to control costs and help realize a profit. Large employers that can generate a large volume of referrals from employees and their dependents have been especially able to utilize PPOs. The term "preferred provider" reflects the status the health care organization enjoys with its source of referrals.

PPOs can be formed by physicians, hospitals, joint ventures of physicians and hospitals, insurance companies, or cost containment firms. Insurers (and self-insurers that are large enough) and other producers of health care can enter into PPO arrangements directly or through a third-party cost containment service firm.

The typical PPO arrangement includes four types of important parties: the health care providers who offer a service to PPO participants; the PPO organization that creates the PPO arrangement; the employer or insurer that refers participants to the PPO health care providers; and employees or insureds and their dependents who obtain health services through the PPO. In many PPO arrangements, the health care providers, the employer, or the employer's insurer own and control the PPO organization. In other cases, the PPO is a separate for-profit organization.

PPOs, or employers and insurers using PPOs, negotiate various sorts of fee discounts. The most common arrangement for hospital services is to establish a fixed per-diem charge at a rate below that paid by indemnity-type insurance plans. For other health services, especially physician services, PPOs arrange a percentage discount from the fee usually paid by indemnity insurance plans. *Percentage discount arrangements* offer less certainty of savings. The "usual" fee, from which discounts are calculated, may be fictional in the sense that it is rarely, if ever, paid by any party. Thus, the "discount" fee may be as high as any other. A more certain form of discount is a fixed fee per "diagnostic related group" or DRG. DRGs, discussed below, are a popular arrangement for complete surgical fees, including all pre- and post-operative care.

The crucial distinction between PPOs and health maintenance organizations is that PPOs do not bear the risk that the health care needs of its users will be greater than expected. PPOs arrange discounts with health care providers, but pass along to employers and their insurers all actual costs based on the discounted fees. Employers or their insurers must create incentives for employees and their dependents to use the PPO. These incentives are usually reduced deductibles or reduced co-payments. Without incentives, employees and their dependents are free to use the PPO or not as they wish.

PPOs have become increasingly popular arrangements for workers compensation in states where the employer has the right to select the treating physician. Without the right to select the physician, the employer and its insurer cannot guarantee any particular volume of claims, and PPOs become impractical.

Health Maintenance Organizations. Health maintenance organizations (HMOs) are an arrangement whereby the medical providers are paid a fixed fee per patient for all services provided in a specified period, typically a year. HMOs are popular with health insurers because their costs are predictable. However, despite this fact, the cost of HMOs to insurers and employers has continued to climb as underlying medical costs rise. While HMOs are less expensive than

278—Medical Aspects of Claims

indemnity plans, their annual increase in cost has paralleled that of indemnity plans.

Physicians working for HMOs are typically on a fixed salary, regardless of the number of procedures performed, with provision for a share of the profits. Alternatively, HMO organizations contract with independent physicians or physician groups that may also treat non-HMO patients. In either case, the HMO bears the risk that participants may need more health care than expected. The HMO commits to provide all care needed by its participants in exchange for a fixed fee per year.

HMOs create a strong incentive for medical providers to control utilization. Over-utilization affects the HMO's profitability. In an HMO, a *primary physician* acts as a "gatekeeper" in controlling utilization. Participants who join an HMO obligate themselves to go through the gatekeeper physician when seeking care. HMOs emphasize preventive medicine based on the premise that early detection of health problems will result in treatment that is briefer and less costly. Thus, HMOs "manage" health care.

Certain PPOs have become more active in health care management through arrangements such as "gatekeeper" physicians and restrictions on which physicians may be seen. Furthermore, certain HMOs allow participants to choose their own primary physician by paying an additional fee. As PPOs respond to employer pressures and accept some financial risks of excessive treatment, and as HMOs allow a wider choice of physicians, the distinction between HMOs and PPOs may become less clear.

The HMO concept is not applied as easily as the PPO concept to casualty claims. HMOs would limit a claimant's choice of physician and ability to seek further treatment. Patients can only be subjected to the rules and limitations of an HMO with their consent.

Diagnostic Related Groups. Diagnostic related groups (DRGs) are an arrangement in which payments are based on the diagnosis of the illness or injury. Therefore, a fixed fee is paid for a given diagnosis regardless of whether the actual services provided were more or less than usual. The most important use of DRGs is in the Medicare system.

DRGs are also used in the insurance industry. A good example is the predetermined "packaged" cost of prenatal care and delivery charged by obstetricians and gynecologists. The providers' incentive to control utilization is similar to that created by HMOs. However, the primary application of DRGs is payments to institutions, such as hospitals and nursing homes rather than to physicians. DRGs work best when the illness, injury, or treatment has an easily identifiable beginning and end, such as hospital admission and discharge.

The effectiveness of DRGs depends on the appropriateness of the diagnosis and the fees. An incorrect diagnosis can result in unnecessary treatments, which in turn create unnecessary fees. For example, someone who is burned on 5 percent of the skin surface but is diagnosed as having been burned on 15 percent of the skin surface will receive much more extensive and expensive treatment than may be necessary. DRGs must also work on another level. Despite the correctness of a diagnosis, the fees must still be correctly set when the DRG is initially arranged. Otherwise, inequitably high fees can lead to unnecessarily rising costs. On the other hand, inequitably low fees can create a shortage of care. An example of a fee set too low would be $20 applied to one session of kidney dialysis. At this rate, given the total cost of the treatment, no hospital would be willing to provide the service.

The DRG concept is compatible with liability or workers compensation claim situations (where the beginning and end of treatments is relatively easy to determine), but its application is still extremely limited because providers and payors are unwilling to accept the concept. Neither providers nor payors are yet comfortable with the idea of a fixed fee per injury in liability or workers compensation claims.

Utilization Review

Utilization review (UR) includes all cost containment techniques that evaluate the appropriateness of treatment with respect to necessity, frequency, and cost. An objective of UR is to identify unnecessary care and to encourage alternative treatments. UR services are provided by about 150 utilization review organizations (UROs). Most UROs are owned by insurance companies, third-party administrators, or health care organizations. Many UROs also provide bill auditing services and reviews of physical therapy and chiropractic treatments.

UR is a respected specialty in medicine. The American Board of Quality Assurance and Utilization Review Physicians (which has about 3,000 members) gives an annual board certification program. The Joint Commission on Accreditation of Hospitals (JCAH) requires hospitals to have UR committees for self-review before they can be accredited. The reported savings from UR have been estimated at approximately 8 percent.[14]

Ronald E. Gots, M.D., Ph.D., has stated the basis of utilization review:

> The basic two underlying principles of medical utilization review are that the providers of care cannot be the sole arbiters of what care is to be provided and that modern medical practice is predicated upon sound principles. In regard to the former, those who pay must have

a say. Pertaining to the latter, there are right and wrong ways to evaluate and manage patients. In a similar vein, there are also expensive and less expensive ways to provide medical care and expensive does not always mean better. As one would expect, there is ample room for the exercise of medical judgment. The parameters of that judgment are delineated by sound scientific and broad-based experiential principles. If this were not so, there would not be any reason for a medical education, or the publication of medical texts or scientific literature. Physicians would practice by feel without regard for the body of knowledge that underlies these feelings.[15]

Consistent with Dr. Gots' second principle, the American Medical Association (AMA) has advocated uniform criteria for UR. The variation in standards and procedures used by the hundreds of UROs has been a burden to physicians and has undermined the credibility of UR in the minds of affected physicians. The AMA therefore advocates uniform, consistent, and publicly available standards that should be created solely by physicians. In a similar effort, the American Managed Care and Review Association (AMCRA), a professional organization of UROs, has advocated uniform standards for UR procedures.

Creating uniform standards on which to base UR decisions and procedures would improve the efficiency and credibility of UR, but the process of establishing these criteria may be delayed by differences among the involved parties. In addition to members of the AMA and AMCRA, hospitals, Blue Cross/Blue Shield, third-party insurers, and federal and state health programs would be affected. Each of these organizations has a slightly different interest in UR. For example, hospitals conduct internal UR to satisfy the Joint Commission on Accreditation of Hospitals, while third-party payors conduct UR to determine responsibility for health care costs. This difference in interest may make it more difficult for the parties to agree on standards. In addition to these different interests, standardization of UR may be delayed by private UROs that consider their decision criteria a valuable proprietary asset.

UROs make decisions about the care to be provided using two general approaches, statistical and case specific. Ideally, a combination of these approaches would be used. Statistical decision-making involves comparing the diagnosis and treatment of a given case to the statistically typical treatment for that diagnosis. This approach requires a knowledge of treatment protocols that are medically and scientifically valid and acceptable. It also depends on a vast amount of data on treatment types and amounts. Cases reviewed by comparison to statistical models are identified for further review whenever the treatment appears to be inappropriate or excessive. Most UROs review the cases so identified with case-specific analysis. Case-specific analysis is the only type of UR done by many UROs. In this analysis, a nurse or doctor employed by the URO reviews the records of the case in question and gives a clinical opinion on the appropriateness of treatment.

The results of statistical analysis may be more consistent than those of case-specific analysis. The process can also be more intellectually rigorous if the expert system (a high level computer used for decision making) in use incorporates the latest scholarly work. Nevertheless, case-specific analysis is probably essential in order to account for each factor in a case and to accommodate clinical judgment.

UR can be relatively easily applied to casualty claims handling. The key to the success of UR is clear communication with treating physicians and hospitals, which increases the likelihood that they will accept the UR service's recommendations. This kind of cooperation is essential to the success of UR. The most successful UR programs have a high level of involvement from the URO's physicians. The concept of UR as applied to casualty claims is illustrated in the case study set forth in Exhibit 7-5.

UR can include any of the following:
- Preadmission certification
- Concurrent reviews
- Catastrophic care management
- Psychiatric and substance abuse reviews
- Retrospective reviews
- Peer reviews

Preadmission Certification. Preadmission certification is a prospective review. It is also referred to as preadmission review or preadmission screening. Preadmission certification is a process of establishing preapproval for hospital admission or surgery. Preadmission certification can prevent unnecessary treatment and suggest alternative treatment. As noted earlier in this chapter, more money is spent on hospital care than on any other element of health care spending. Many hospitalizations are unnecessary—in some cases because the treatment is unnecessary, and in other cases because the treatment, although necessary, can be provided on an out-patient basis.

Second opinions are common in preadmission certification. Preapprovals of surgeries and requests for second opinions have long been practiced by claims personnel in workers compensation. Second opinion consultations often cause the patient to reconsider the proposed surgery. Frequently, the need for surgery depends on how painful or disabling the condition is to the patient. In these cases, the patient must decide whether the problems caused by the condition are sufficient to justify the risks of surgery. For example, back surgery for disc problems or degenerative conditions is usually optional. The patient can choose to live with the symptoms or to have surgery, which

Exhibit 7-5
Case Study—How to Use UR for Management
of Workers Compensation Claims

A claimant with a serious back injury did not respond well to two months of conservative chiropractic treatments. The claimant was re-examined by a physician who diagnosed a herniated disc and suggested back surgery.

The insurance company involved in the claim dealt with two cost containment service firms. Firm A provided hospital bill audit services and medical rehabilitation services using only nurses. Firm B, which had higher fees, provided a full range of UR services and employed physicians with different specialties.

The claim representative referred the case to Firm B because of the need for an appropriate specialist who could talk to the treating doctor and hospital, and the likelihood that surgery and follow-up treatment would cost in excess of $15,000. The claim representative then wrote to Firm B summarizing the facts of the case and treatments to date, and enclosed the claimant's medical records with the letter.

After reviewing the case, a representative of Firm B suggested the following:

- Obtain a second opinion on the need for back surgery.
- If back surgery is necessary, have a medical specialist of Firm B work with the treating physician, the surgeon, and the hospital to monitor the claimant's condition, determine the length of hospital stay, and oversee all other services during this period.
- Monitor the treatment plan with the treating physician after the claimant is discharged from the hospital.

The claim representative suggested that a physician of Firm B should review the medical records to determine if the physician could confirm the need for back surgery without a full examination of the claimant. Such a review proved to be sufficient to confirm the need for surgery, and the claimant was admitted to a hospital.

A medical specialist of Firm B consulted with the treating physician and the hospital and worked out a plan for discharge. Originally, the claimant was scheduled to be hospitalized for eight days. However, continuous monitoring showed that the claimant was ready to be discharged after five days. During this period, Firm B reviewed and suggested some changes in ancillary services, and recommended the use of generic drugs, resulting in additional savings.

Upon the claimant's discharge, the treating physician prescribed physical therapy. The claim representative agreed that a physical therapist employed by Firm B would review the initial evaluation of the claimant's physical therapist and would follow up if necessary.

The claimant wanted to return to the chiropractor for more treatments. Upon review of the treatment plan, Firm B suggested to the claimant's treating physician and the chiropractor that the chiropractor's plan for treatments would essentially duplicate services provided by the physical therapist. The claimant's physician and the chiropractor agreed. Physical therapy only was authorized for one month, at the end of which the need for therapy was re-evaluated.

includes such risks as surgical scars and adhesions that can cause the problem to be as bad as ever. Often through the process of obtaining a second opinion, the patient decides how bearable or unbearable his or her problems are.

Concurrent Reviews. The purpose of concurrent review is to monitor the appropriateness of services and length of hospital stay. Concurrent review can also help to determine whether or not a doctor's orders are being followed. As with precertification, concurrent reviews can provide information about alternative treatments. For example, concurrent reviews might show that the type or amount of physical therapy is inappropriate or that generic drugs could be used instead of brand name drugs.

Discharge planning, usually part of concurrent reviews, is the process of establishing a program for the type and amount of treatment after the patient is discharged from the hospital. Patients discharged from hospitals frequently need nursing home care, intravenous drug therapy, physical therapy, oxygen, antibiotics, or follow-up doctor services, all of which should be planned.

Determining the need, and by extension, the length of stay is one of the most valuable aspects of concurrent review. Patients should not be hospitalized unless they cannot practically receive appropriate care outside a hospital. They should not be hospitalized merely for the doctor's convenience—many patients are admitted and discharged on dates that suit the doctor's schedule rather than as indicated by medical necessity. Analyzing the length of stay has resulted in substantially shorter periods of hospitalization than were common fifteen to twenty years ago.

Catastrophic Case Management. Case management is a UR technique that early on identifies potentially long-term claims and ensures that the case is managed properly. Long-term and catastrophic claims result in the highest level of waste in the form of duplicate testing and unnecessary services, and as a result, in the highest costs. Good planning can prevent wasteful and unnecessarily costly procedures.

Serious disabling injuries can require medical care that costs tens of thousands of dollars per year and continues for the life of the patient, often thirty or forty years. The total expected cost of such cases can often exceed one million dollars. It is therefore essential that the patient receive necessary and appropriate care in the most cost-effective manner. Case managers are experts in coordinating such care. With a high level of commitment to the patient, they do not settle for inadequate or inferior care, but work to ensure that patients receive the best appropriate care.

A case manager's most important function is to determine in what setting a patient can best receive care. If practical, the patient's home is the most desirable location. Most patients are much more physically and psychologically comfortable at home than at other locations. However, the patient's home is not a feasible place for care if the patient's needs create too great a burden for the patient's family. Case managers interview the patient, the patient's family, and the doctors to determine if home care is feasible.

When a patient must be institutionalized, case managers are experts at selecting the most appropriate facility. For example, certain rehabilitation centers specialize in serving victims of brain trauma.

Psychiatric and Substance Abuse Reviews. Psychiatric and substance abuse treatments are often the focus of specialized utilization review. Because the employee benefit cost of psychiatric services has risen much faster than medical costs generally, UROs that specialize in psychiatric care have developed. These UROs apply the usual techniques of preadmission review, concurrent review, and discharge planning. Case management is also practiced with an emphasis on the appropriateness of the type and setting of psychiatric services.

Psychiatric treatment can be a lengthy process both because the need for treatment and the extent of progress are subjectively determined. Because hospitalizations for psychiatric conditions last much longer and thus are much more expensive than other hospitalizations, psychiatric utilization review tries especially to curb unnecessary hospitalization. Fortunately, there are numerous effective out-patient alternatives to hospitalization, including individual and group therapy and treatment in residential settings.

Psychiatric UROs are usually applicable to substance abuse programs. Substance abuse treatment serves an essential health need and can reduce other medical costs and increase productivity. Those addicted to drugs and alcohol frequently have a great deal of other medical problems and a high incidence of accidents. Although alcohol and substance abuse is rarely alleged to be a result of an accident, it is often part of the picture in an accident claim.

Retrospective Reviews. Retrospective reviews, conducted after services have been performed, can identify unnecessary or excessive treatment. Services are evaluated against the same criteria as in prospective or concurrent reviews. Retrospective reviews are also conducted to gather data for future use rather than to determine alternatives for the case in review. In a casualty claim in which the parties are in an adversarial relationship, a retrospective review may be the only UR tool available. It cannot stop unnecessary treatment, but it can identify it.

Peer Reviews. Peer reviews have been mandated for health care providers for Medicare patients since 1982. Peer review organizations

(PROs) are sponsored by public and private entities to review care for both Medicare and other patients. Typically conducted by a panel of medical professionals, reviews are based on accepted guidelines. PROs are separate from UROs, and the information they generate is generally not available or useful for critiques of individual cases by a casualty insurer.

Guidelines for the Use of Chiropractic Treatments

Claim representatives are frequently faced with claims for chiropractic treatment. To control the costs of these claims, claim representatives must be familiar with chiropractic as a form of medical care and with guidelines for the use of chiropractic treatments.

Status of Chiropractic. Chiropractic is a form of medical care that emphasizes the manipulation and adjustment of the spine and adjacent tissues to promote the well-being of the nerves. Chiropractors believe that an accident can jolt a vertebra out of place, which exerts pressure on nerve roots, thereby causing pain and affecting circulation. Treatment consists mainly of manipulations of the spinal column to correct any such misalignment.

The traditional problem in chiropractic care is that it was not recognized by many in the medical community as a legitimate practice. Twenty years ago, the American Medical Association (AMA) warned physicians against referring patients to chiropractors. (The AMA withdrew this warning by the end of the 1970s.) Today, more and more doctors and chiropractors are working together. Hospitals have begun to use chiropractors on staff. Chiropractors are now licensed to practice in all fifty states. While this is partly attributable to strong lobbying efforts by chiropractors, the field of chiropractic has also come a long way from its beginning when services were performed by practitioners who had no formal training and all illnesses were believed to stem from subluxations of the spine.

As a result of these changes, claim representatives must realize that chiropractic is now an accepted method of care. Nevertheless, they should also realize that chiropractic care has limited application. Different states have different guidelines and regulations for chiropractic treatments. Very few states allow chiropractors to perform surgery or prescribe drugs. Back or neck pain resulting from fractures or diseases must be referred to a medical doctor. In many cases, chiropractic can complement, but not replace, other medical care.

Chiropractic Review. Chiropractic care can be one of the most problematic aspects of a claim because it can be by nature frequent and continuous. As a result, it is easily abused by those who want to build up their medical expenses.

Many cost containment service firms offer the review of chiropractic treatment as a specialized service. They can evaluate the necessity, reasonableness, and cost of the various chiropractic treatments. Cost containment techniques for chiropractic care include fee schedules, bill audits, and utilization review. Claim representatives with any question about chiropractic care should use these firms.

There is no universal set of guidelines that applies to the use of chiropractic care. Insurance companies and cost containment firms usually develop their own. However, the guidelines below should be followed in the review of any case involving chiropractic care.

- There should be a clear diagnosis of the problem, documented by the clinical evaluation (neck or back pain is not an acceptable diagnosis).
- There should be a well-established plan of treatment with specific functional goals, description of procedures, and estimates of frequency and duration of treatments.
- The usual chiropractic treatment consists of manipulation of the spine and one or two other "modalities." The usual other modalities are hot packs; cold packs; diathermy; ultrasound; traction; massage; and electrotherapy (such as T.E.N.S. treatment). Other modalities may be acceptable, but should be investigated because they may be unusual, unnecessary, or unrelated to the injury.
- There should be relevant diagnostic tests. (This is a very difficult area for nonmedical experts to assess, but redundant tests and/or tests not directly related to the injured body parts should be rejected.)
- Frequency of care should be decreasing. For a typical back injury claim, the reduction should occur *at least* every four weeks.
- There should be noted improvements as treatment progresses. Lack of improvement indicates that other problems may be making the claimant unresponsive to treatments.
- "Maintenance" care is beyond the stage of maximum improvement and should be minimal. Such care may not be the responsibility of the workers compensation or liability insurer.
- Chronic problems should be recognized because they can neither be cured by intense treatments nor should they be treated as frequently as acute problems.

In addition to these guidelines, the following "red flags" should signal the claim representative to refer the case to an outside review firm:

- More than three modalities per visit
- Treatments beginning long after the accident
- Patient was treated prior to accident
- Thermographic charges (thermography is a controversial procedure that is generally not accepted) or charges for unknown and unusual modalities
- Separate billings for diagnostic tests and treatments for different but related body parts, for example, the arm and the shoulder
- Multiple diagnoses for the same condition

Guidelines for office visit frequency are listed in Exhibit 7-6. They apply to ordinary lumbosacral strain and sprain. Complications such as intervertebral disc disease, facet joint syndrome, or degenerative joint disease can cause the treatment patterns to vary. Any questionable case should be referred to a UR firm specializing in chiropractic review for an informed evaluation.

Guidelines for the Use of Physical Therapy

Like chiropractic care, physical therapy may be received frequently and continuously and is therefore subject to abuse. Unlike chiropractic, however, physical therapy has an entirely different origin, employs different techniques, and has always been accepted by the medical profession as legitimate treatment. Claim representatives must be familiar with the status of physical therapy as a treatment and with the guidelines against which the use of physical therapy is reviewed.

Status of Physical Therapy. "Physical therapy is a form of health care that prevents, identifies, corrects, and alleviates acute or prolonged movement dysfunction of anatomic or physiologic origin."[16] Physical therapists evaluate patients' functional limitations, select goals for improvement, and establish a treatment program to achieve those goals. Physical therapy programs include treatments that apply elements such as light, heat, water, electricity, and mechanical agents. Hands-on techniques, training, and education are also used.

All fifty states require physical therapists to be licensed. They must complete an education program accredited by the American Physical Therapy Association and pass a licensure exam. The license in each state prescribes the scope of physical therapy practice and the manner in which physical therapists can obtain patients.

Physical therapy is generally prescribed by a physician. Most states allow osteopaths to refer patients, but only a few allow chiropractors to do so. The prescription may or may not include specification of certain modalities or procedures. At the beginning of treatment,

Exhibit 7-6
Office Visit Frequency Guidelines

The following guidelines relate to the frequency of visits for chiropractic conditions; e.g., lumbosacral strain. Diagnosis may dictate a different treatment program. Supplemental information, such as the monthly status report, should be requested if:

- Visits exceed one per day (for chronic conditions)
- Visits exceed two per day (for more than two days for acute conditions)
- One visit per day exceeding one week's duration
- Three visits per week exceeding one month's duration
- Visits exceed twelve to fifteen in the first month of care
- Visits exceed twenty-four for two consecutive months of treatment
- Visits exceed one per month for maintenance care unless justified by a special set of circumstances
- Three modalities/procedures are used in addition to manipulation

For purposes of these guidelines, start a new count of office visits if the patient has been free of treatment for sixty days or if there is a new diagnosis. If there is validation of a new diagnosis, cases of alleged exacerbation should quickly respond to the treatment program.

Reprinted with permission from *Medi-Call Moments, Chiropractic Guidelines for Claims Handling*, Aetna Commercial Insurance Divisions.

a physical therapist assesses the patient to determine the appropriate type of care, to set realistic goals and objectives, and to determine an appropriate length of time in which the treatment will produce the expected outcome.

Physical Therapy Review. In a physical therapy review, a claim representative should look for patient improvement relative to specific "functional" goals and for a reduction in treatment frequency over time. Many UR firms provide cost containment services for physical therapy cases. Some of these firms specialize in physical therapy review.

Exhibit 7-7 lists the guidelines or red flags against which the use of physical therapy should be reviewed. If the case being reviewed shows evidence that the elements listed in the exhibit are present, this should be a signal to the claim representative that the case may require further review. However, the "red flags" should not become the only criteria upon which the claim representative should base a decision to deny payment for treatment. A claim representative should get a professional UR before rejecting any bills for a course of treatment. Likewise, when in doubt about the validity of treatment, claim representatives should feel free to consult a physical therapy UR specialist.

Exhibit 7-7
Physical Therapy: Use of "Red Flags" for Utilization Review Activities

The listed items represent "*red flags*" or guidelines which enable the claim representative to identify those cases which may require utilization review/peer review. These red flags should *not* be confused with screens or practice standards. Evidence of red flags in a case *should not* result in outright denial of claims. Decisions regarding nonreimbursement should only result after a thorough UR/review process.

Red flags are divided into five categories as follows:
- The referral process
- Treatment records
- Physical therapy modalities/procedures/techniques
- Provider's credentials
- Billing statements

The Referral Process
- No evidence of patient referral for physical therapy
- Patient is treated concurrently by more than one provider (i.e., DC, DO)
- Extensive treatment (more than one month) without evidence of referral renewal/update
- Physical therapy treatment course not projected (i.e., 4-6 weeks)

Treatment Records
- Paucity of physical therapy documentation
- Tests performed without report submission
- Lack of established goal (short/long term)
- Physical therapy treatment log inconsistent with billing statement

Physical Therapy Modalities
- Local modalities (i.e., ultrasound, electrical stimulation) continued unmodified for more than two weeks without evidence of improvement of condition
- "Palliative" modalities extended beyond the normal tissue healing period (6-8 weeks)
- Daily use of more than three modalities
- Continued use of palliative modalities without exercises
- Lack of fading schedule of treatment

Provider's Credentials
- Services entitled "physical therapy" or "physiotherapy" without evidence of a licensed physical therapist's involvement
- Nonsupervision of "supportive personnel" (i.e., aides or assistants) by a licensed physical therapist or physician
- Absence of professional ensignias/initials/titles
- Nonauthentication of clinical records (i.e., no signatures or treatment notes)

Billing Statements
- Fees appear to be high for geographic area
- Billing dates do not correspond to treatment notes
- Incomprehensible treatment codes, abbreviations and descriptions
- "Stacked modalities" (i.e., more than three local modalities per session)

This listing is not intended to be definitive or an all-inclusive red flag listing. However, involvement of two or more of these red flags may signal the need for further case review.

Reprinted with permission from Physical Therapy Review Services, Inc.

Effectiveness of Cost Containment

The results of cost containment efforts are mixed. Cost containment practices that emphasize the reasonableness of charges like fee schedules and hospital bill audits were probably more useful when they were first introduced because medical providers have since increasingly improved their billing process. In fact, there is anecdotal evidence to suggest that these techniques have become less effective by encouraging medical providers to increase utilization in order to recoup lost revenues.

Alternative payment systems such as PPOs, HMOs, and DRGs are quickly replacing the traditional FFS system in the health insurance field. These managed care arrangements create incentives for medical providers to control costs and utilization. There is ample evidence that the concept is working. For example, the hospital utilization rate actually is much lower for HMOs than for FFS plans. However, it has been argued that HMOs only appear to be more effective because its users tend to be younger and healthier than other client populations.

All health care plans include some elements of UR. UR is also the most effective cost-containment practice available to casualty insurance payors. UR firms have begun to offer their services in the workers compensation area. Virtually all UR programs report savings. However, the degree of documented savings varies from program to program and depends on the method of identifying the amount saved.

The most notable impact of cost containment is a shift in care from inpatient to outpatient settings. From 1965 to 1988, the total number of outpatient visits has increased 167 percent, yet the number of hospital admissions has actually declined since the early 1980s, as shown in Exhibit 7-8. The average length of hospital stays has also declined from 8.0 days in 1970 to 6.4 days in 1989.[17] This is a direct result of cost-containment programs designed to reduce hospitalization through alternative outpatient services.

Despite these favorable trends, hospital costs themselves continue to increase and still account for the largest share of health spending. However, these recent cost increases have come at a slower rate than that of other health care services.

While cost containment is theoretically acceptable as a necessary means to control cost increases and excessive utilization, it can be difficult to apply. Unlike the standards for a physical product, it is very difficult to develop and universally apply standards for health services. Furthermore, each "fix" can in turn create its own set of problems. For example, fee schedules can unnecessarily increase utilization. DRG rates are difficult to set properly and might thus distort treatment decisions.

There is evidence that cost containment has been somewhat suc-

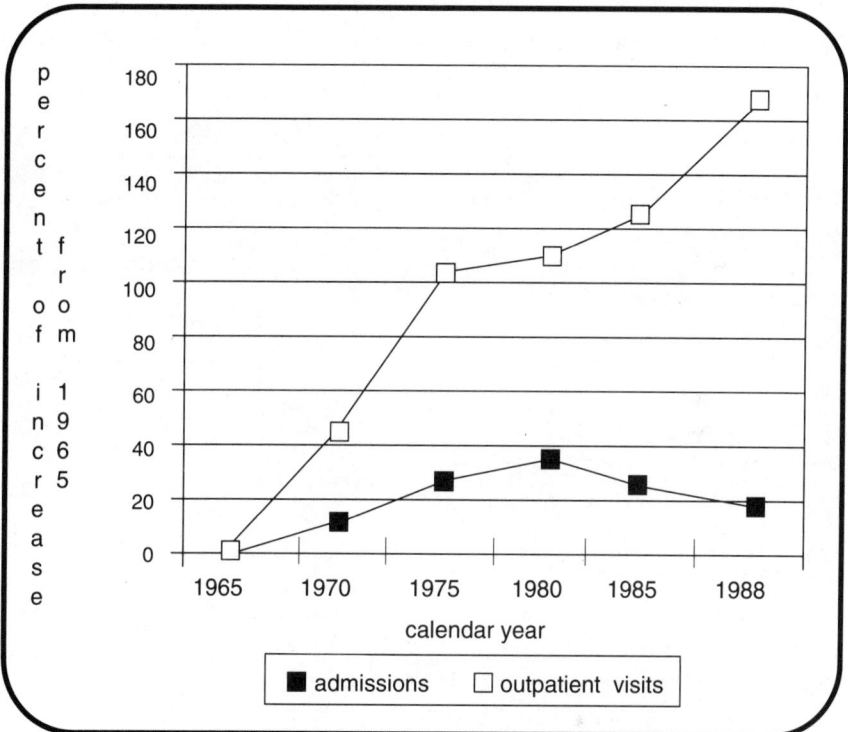

Exhibit 7-8
Rate of Increase in Outpatient Visits Versus Hospital Admissions

percent of increase from 1965
(y-axis: 0 to 180)

calendar year: 1965, 1970, 1975, 1980, 1985, 1988

■ admissions   □ outpatient visits

Source: American Hospital Association, Chicago IL. Hospital Statistics.

cessful in slowing the increase of medical costs. On the other hand, the field of cost containment is still evolving and thus cannot be seen as a complete solution to the problem of rising health costs.

SUMMARY

As health care costs continue to rise, medical cost containment is becoming integrated into the claims handling process. The technical nature of medicine requires that most cost containment efforts be carried out by medical professionals, but it requires a claim representative to be knowledgeable about, and devote effort to, the medical aspects of claims.

The cost containment methods discussed in this chapter originated in the health care field and are relatively less often used in liability and workers compensation claims handling. The application of cost containment in casualty claims is further complicated by legal limitations peculiar to casualty claims. However, the concept of cost control has

292—Medical Aspects of Claims

always been part of the claims handling process. The challenge to claim representatives is to keep up with its dynamic nature.

Chapter Notes

1. Adrienne C. Locke, "Health Care Cost Hikes Won't Moderate: Agency," *Business Insurance*, January 7, 1991, p. 3.
2. *Statistical Abstract of the United States 1990*, U.S. Department of Commerce, p. 92.
3. *Issues Report, 1990* (New York: National Council on Compensation Insurance), p. 11.
4. *Statistical Abstract of the United States 1990*, U.S. Department of Commerce, p. 105.
5. *Statistical Abstract of the United States 1990*, U.S. Department of Commerce, p. 101.
6. Adapted from *Best's Aggregates and Averages, Property-Casualty* (Oldwick, NJ: A.M. Best Co., 1989), p. 98.
7. Jerry Geisel, "Insurers, UR Firms Target Rising Outpatient Claims," *Business Insurance*, February 20, 1989, p. 10.
8. Jeffrey S. Harris, et al., "Workers Compensation: Business as Usual May Mean Going Out of Business." *NCCI Digest*, Vol. IV, No. III, October 1989, p. 35.
9. Ronald E. Gots, M.D., Ph.D., "Workers Compensation: The Last Bastion of the Open Medical Checkbook," *Journal of the International Association of Industrial Accident Boards and Commissions*, Summer 1987, p. 36.
10. Christine Woolsey, "Workers Compensation: States Embrace Tools to Control Medical Costs," *Business Insurance*, December 31, 1990, p. 46.
11. Gots, p. 37.
12. Gots, p. 37.
13. Meg Fletcher, "Benefit Cost Controls Can Cut Comp Expenses," *Business Insurance*, February 27, 1989, p. 16.
14. Paul J. Feldstein, Ph.D., et al., *The New England Journal of Medicine*, May 19, 1988, as reported in *Medi-Claim*, Vol. 9, No. 3, State Farm Insurance Companies, p. 11.
15. Gots, p. 37.
16. Fact Sheet, *Physical Therapy and the Physical Therapist*, American Physical Therapy Association, p. 1.
17. *Statistical Abstract of the United States 1990*, U.S. Department of Commerce, p. 108.

Bibliography

Accident Facts 1989 Edition. Chicago, IL: National Safety Council, 1989.

Accreditation Manual for Hospitals. Chicago, IL: Joint Commission on Accreditation of Hospitals, 1986.

Best's Aggregates and Averages, Property-Casualty. Oldwick, NJ: A.M. Best Co., 1989.

American Psychiatric Association. *Diagnostic and Statistical Manual of Mental Disorders.* 3rd ed., revised. Washington, DC, 1987.

Bruce, JoAnne C. *Privacy and Confidentiality of Health Care Information.* Chicago, IL: American Hospital Publishing, Inc., 1984.

Calliet, Rene. *Soft Tissue Pain and Disability.* Philadelphia, PA: F.A. Davis Co., 1988.

The Center for Defense Case Analysis, Inc. *The Personal Injury Law Defense Bulletin*, no. 6, May 1989.

Cooper, Robert J. and Repko, Glen. *The Disability Due to Personality Disorder.* Reprinted in Herbert J. Lasky, *Guidelines for Handling Psychiatric Issues in Workers Compensation Cases.* Rancho Palos Verdes, CA: Lex-Com Enterprises, 1988.

Croft, Chancy. "Something More Important Than Money—Vocational Rehabilitation in Workers Compensation Cases." *Alaska Law Review* 3 (1986): 54.

Feldstein, Paul J. et al. *The New England Journal of Medicine* 19 May 1988, as reported in *Medi-Claim*, vol. 9, no. 3, State Farm Insurance Companies, p. 11.

Fletcher, Meg. "Benefit Cost Controls Can Cut Comp Expenses." *Business Insurance*, 27 February 1989, p. 16.

296—Bibliography

Gardner, J. *Vocational Rehabilitation in Florida.* Cambridge, MA: Workers Compensation Research Institute, 1987.

Geisel, Jerry. "Insurers, UR Firms Target Rising Outpatient Claims." *Business Insurance,* 20 February 1989, p. 10.

Gice, J. "Return to Work Versus On-Going Disability." *Legal Insight* (1988):13-16.

Gots, Ronald E. "Medical Claims Flay Casualty Insurers." *National Underwriter,* 18 September 1989.

_____. "Workers Compensation: The Last Bastion of the Open Medical Checkbook." *Journal of the International Association of Industrial Accident Boards and Commissions,* Summer 1987, p. 36.

Guide to the Evaluation of Permanent Impairment. Chicago, IL: American Medical Association, 1984.

Harris, Jeffrey S.; Iskowe, David S.; Goldstein, Stuart R.; Sawyer, George P.; and Warren, Stryker, Jr. "Workers Compensation: Business as Usual May Mean Going Out of Business." *NCCI Digest,* vol. IV, no. III, October 1989, p. 35.

Hester, H., et al. *Menninger RTW Scale.* Topeka, KS: Menninger Foundation, 1986.

Huffman, Edna K. *Medical Record Management.* 8th ed. Berwyn, IL: Physicians' Record Co., 1985.

Issues Report, 1990. New York, NY: National Council on Compensation Insurance, 1990.

Kubler-Ross, Elizabeth. *Death: The Final Stage of Growth.* New York, NY: Simon and Schuster, 1986.

Larson, Arthur. *Workers Compensation,* Desk Edition. Albany, NY: Matthew Bender.

Leavitt, F. and Sweet, J.J. "Characteristics and Frequency of Malingering Among Patients with Low Back Pain." *Pain* 25 (1986):357.

Lees-Haley, Paul R. "A Checklist for Defending Psychological Testing Claims." *Claims,* December 1989, p. 49.

_____. "Confronting Neuropsychological Testing." *For The Defense,* May 1990, p. 27.

Leigh, Hoyle and Reiser, Morton F. *The Patient: Biological, Psychological, and Social Dimensions of Medical Practice.* 2nd ed. New York, NY: Plenum Medical Book Co., 1985.

Lengham, D. "Vocational Rehabilitation Cost Effectiveness Study." *Journal of Private Sector Rehabilitation* 3 (1988): 15-25.

Locke, Adrienne C. "Health Care Cost Hikes Won't Moderate: Agency." *Business Insurance*, 7 January 1991, p. 3.

Matkin, Ralph E. *Insurance Rehabilitation: Service Applications in Disability Compensation Systems*. Austin, TX: Pro-Ed, 1985.

Pennsylvania Bar Institute. *Analyzing Medical Records*. Harrisburg, PA, 1988.

Physical Therapy and the Physical Therapist (Fact Sheet). Fairfax, VA: American Physical Therapy Association.

Nowak, L. *American Economist* 27(1983): 23-29.

Rubin, Stanford E. and Roessler, Richard T. *Foundations of the Vocational Rehabilitation Process*. Baltimore, MD: University Park Press, 1978.

Schretlen, David J. "The Use of Psychological Tests to Identify Malingered Symptoms of Mental Disorder." *Clinical Psychology Review* 8 (1988):451.

Shuman, Daniel W. *Psychiatric and Psychological Evidence*. Colorado Springs, CO: Shepards/McGraw-Hill, 1986.

Southwick, Arthur F. *The Law of Hospital and Health Care Administration*. 2nd ed. Ann Arbor, MI: Health Administration Press, 1988.

Statistical Abstract of the United States 1990. U.S. Department of Commerce, 1990.

Tebb, A. *Report to the Industry: Vocational Rehabilitation*. San Francisco: California Workers Compensation Institute, 1982.

Treitel, R. *Social Security Bulletin*, vol. 3-23, no. 4 (1979).

U.S. Department of Labor. *Selected Characteristics of Occupations Defined in the Dictionary of Occupational Titles*, 1981.

U.S. Department of Transportation. *Major Vehicle Crash Losses and Their Compensation in the United States, A Report to the Congress and the President*. Washington, DC: Government Printing Office, 1971.

"Vocational Rehabilitation in the Workers Compensation System." *Ark. Law Review* 33:742-743.

Waters, Kathleen A. and Murphy, Gretchen Frederick. *Medical References in Health Information*. Rockville, MD: Aspen Publishing, 1979.

Weed, Lawrence. *Medical Record, Medical Education, and Patient Care*. Chicago, IL: Year Book Medical Pubs., Inc., 1970.

Woolsey, Christine. "Workers Compensation: States Embrace Tools to Control Medical Costs." *Business Insurance*, 31 December 1990, p. 46.

Zaidman, B. *Rehabilitation in the Minnesota Workers Compensation System*. St. Paul, MN: Minnesota Department of Labor and Industry, 1988.

Index

A

Abscess, 62
Abdomen, injuries to the, 83
Abducens nerves, 27
ABLE (Adult Basic Learning Examination), 219
Abrasion, 63
Acceptance, 203
Acceptance of disability, 160
Accessory nerves, 27
Acetabulum, 13
Achievement and aptitude tests, 53
Achilles tendon, 21
Acromioclavicular joint, 11
Acromion process, 11
Acting out, 108
Adjustment disorder, 135
Affect, 121
Age, effect of on length of disability, 175
Agoraphobia, 122
Alternative fee arrangements, 276
Alternative treatment, 229
Alveoli, 39
AMA Guide to the Evaluation of Permanent Impairment, 164
Ambulatory care records, 248
American Psychiatric Association, 149
Americans with Disabilities Act, 163
Amnesia and fugue, 123
Amnestic syndrome, 119
Amputations other than fingers and toes, 208
Anatomy and medical terminology, 1
Aneurysm, 37
Anger, 203
Ankle jerk reflex, 101
Anterior, 2
Anterior chamber, 34
Anterior rami, 28
Antisocial personality disorder, 127
Anvil, 36
Anxiety, 107
Anxiety disorder, generalized, 132
Anxiety disorders, 122
Aortic rupture, 82
Aqueous humor, 34
Arachnoid layer, 28
Arachnoid membrane, 25
Arm, bones of the, 12
Arteries, 36
Arteriosclerosis, 37
Arthritis, 69
Arthroplasty, 70
Ascending colon, 40
Atlas, 4, 9
Atrophy, 20
Attending physician, 198
Attitudes toward and myths about disability, 158
Audiologist, 200
Auditory canal, 34
Auricle, 34
Authorization, medical, 252

Authorization for disclosure, *252*
  for release of medical information, *252*
Auto liability case study in rehabilitation, *195*
Avoidant personality disorder, *128*
Avulsion wounds, *65*

B

Ball and socket joint, *13*
Bargaining stage, *161*
Basal skull fracture, *79*
Behavior modification, *149*
Bertolotti's syndrome, *95*
BETA, *218*
Biceps reflex, *102*
Bile, *40*
Bills, medical, *239*
Bipolar mood, *121*
Bizarre delusion, *120*
Bladder, *45*
Body dismorphic disorder, *136*
Bones of the face, *6*
Bony spur, *97*
Borderline personality disorder, *128*
Brachial plexus, *29*
Brachioradialis reflex, *102*
Brain, *22*
Brain damage, suspected, head injury or, *208*
Broca's area, *24*
Broken hip, *16*
Bronchioles, *38*
Bronchus, *38*
Burns, *67*
Bursa, *70*
Bursae, *21*
Bursitis, *70*
Bursting compression fractures, *89*

C

CAI (Career Assessment Inventory), *219*

Calcaneus, *19*
Callus, *77*
Capillaries, *38*
Cardiac muscle, *19*
Carpal bones, *13*
Carpal tunnel syndrome, *71*
Cartilage, *70*
Case studies as evidence of costs/benefits of rehabilitation, *195*
Cases handled by the claim representative, *236*
Casualty claim costs, effects of medical costs on, *268*
CAT scan, *101*
Catastrophic case management, *283*
Catatonic behavior, *121*
Causation, establishing in review of psychological claims, *144*
Causation in fact, *111*
Causes of rise in medical costs, *265*
Central, *3*
Cerebellum, *25*
Cerebral cortex, *23*
Cerebrospinal fluid, *22, 25*
Cerebrum, *22*
Certified insurance rehabilitation specialist (CIRS), *197*
Certified orthotist, *200*
Certified rehabilitation counselor (CRC), *197, 223*
Cerumen, *34*
Cervical plexus, *29*
Cervical spine, degenerative and traumatic problems in, *99*
Cervical vertebrae, *9*
Chiropractic review, *285*
Chiropractic treatment, guidelines for the use of, *285*
Chondrophyte, *97*
Choroid portion, *34*
Chronic problems, *227*
Circulatory system, *36*
Claim representative, cases handled by, *236*
  role in determining temporary

Index—301

disability, *173*
    in evaluating medical treatment, *231*
    in medical cost control, *273*
    in rehabilitation, *204*
Claim representative's medical knowledge, *236*
Claim representative's responsibility, rehabilitation services and the, *196*
Claim verification process, *237*
Claims, effect of disability on the value of, *157*
    exaggerated, indicators of, *234*
    problem psychological conditions in, *129*
    for psychological conditions, evaluation of, *140*
    stress, *131*
Clavicle, *9, 11*
Clinical dependence, *120*
Clinical notes, *240*
Closed reduction, *77*
Coccyx, *6*
Cochlea, *36*
Collapsed lung, *82*
Colles fracture, *13*
Colon, *40*
Comminuted fracture, *76*
Complications, effect of on length of disability, *179*
Compound fractures, *75*
Compression fracture, *89*
Concurrent review, *283*
Concussion, *80*
Conductive deafness, *36*
Condyles, *4*
    medial and lateral, *16*
Congenital problems, *94*
Conjunctiva, *33*
Constriction of awareness, *108*
Consulting physician, *198, 213*
Contusions, *62, 80*
Conversion disorder, *136*
Convolutions, *23*

Cooperative physician, *174*
Coping mechanisms, *159*
Cornea, *34*
Corpus callosum, *23*
Cortex, *23*
Cost containment, effectiveness of, *290*
Cost containment methods, importance of, *271*
    medical, *271*
Cost control, limitations on in the casualty claims system, *268*
Cost control and cost sharing, lack of, *266*
Cost shifting, *272*
Costs/benefits of rehabilitation, *193*
Costs of disability, *163*
Counseling, *221*
Counter-phobic measures, *108*
Cranial nerves, *25*
Cranial venous sinuses, *25*
Cranium, *3*
Criteria, impairment, in the *AMA Guide*, *165*
Cuboid bone, *19*

D

Damages, general, *112, 158*
    special, *158*
Data, *252*
Deafness, conductive, *36*
    nerve, *36*
Decubitus, *22*
Defense mechanisms, *108*
Defensive medicine, *267*
Degenerative disc disease, *97*
Degenerative disease in the cervical spine, *99*
Degenerative disorders, *96*
Delirium, *118*
Delusional disorder, *121*
Delusions, *120*

Dementia, *119*
Denial, *108, 161, 202*
Dependence on and abuse of psychoactive substances, *120*
Dependent personality disorder, *128*
Depersonalization disorder, *123*
Depressed fracture, *79*
Depression, *110, 203*
   disability and, *161*
Depressive episode, *121*
Dermabrasion, *67*
Dermis, *22*
Descending colon, *40*
Determination of disability, *164*
Determination of loss of earning capacity, *186*
Diabetes mellitis, *42*
Diagnosis, *213*
   differential, *118*
   of distinct psychological disorders, *113*
   importance of, *141*
   need for correct, *227*
   of personality disorders, *126*
   of spinal problems, *100*
Diagnostic related group (DRG), *277*
The Diagnostic and Statistical Manual of Mental Disorders (DSM), *113*
Diagnostic testing, *48*
Diaphragm injuries, *83*
Dicephalon, *24*
Dictionary of Occupational Titles (DOT), *169*
Differential diagnosis, *118*
Digestive system, *40*
Disabilities, acceptance of, *159*
   debunking myths about, *159*
   effects of on the disabled person, *160*
Disability, acceptance of, *160*
   attitudes toward and myths about, *158*
   costs of, *163*
   definition of, *156*
   determination of, *164*
   effect of on the employer of the disabled, *163*
   effect of on the value of claims, *157*
   nature of, *155*
   overcoming, *174*
   physician's basis for determining, *167*
   psychological disorders and, *144*
   simulated, *162*
   stages experienced as a result of, *161*
   temporary, determining, *173*
      factors affecting the length of, *175*
   workers compensation definition of, *156*
Disability statements, *230*
Disc bulging and herniation, *90*
Disc herniation, *90*
Disc problems, treatment of, *93*
Disc protrusions, *90*
Discharge, *214*
Dislocation, *70*
Disorders, anxiety, *122*
   degenerative, *96*
   dissociative, *123*
   impulse control, *125*
   mental, *114*
   mood, *121*
   personality, *125*
   sexual, *123*
   sleep, *124*
   somatoform, *135*
   stress, *131*
Displaced fractures, *77*
Displacement, *109*
Dissociative disorders, *123*
Distal, *3*
Distinct psychological disorders, diagnosis of, *113*
Dollar amount or length of disability, identification of serious

cases by, *233*
Dream anxiety disorder, *124*
DRG, *277*
Drug use, psychological claims and, *146*
DSM, *113*
Duodenum, *40*
Dura mater, *25, 28*
Dyssomnias, *124*

E

Ear, *34*
Electromyelogram, *101*
Emergency care, *213*
Emergency room record, *248*
EMG, *101*
Employer, effects of disability on, *163*
　former, return to, *216*
　new, placement with a, *218*
　role of in rehabilitation, *203*
Epicondyles, medial and lateral, *13*
Epidermis, *22, 62*
Epidural hematoma, *79*
Epidural space, *28*
Epiglottis, *38*
Epiphysis, *78*
EPPS (Edwards Personal Preference Schedule), *219*
Esophagus, *40*
Ethmoid bone, *4*
Eustachian tube, *36*
Evaluation of claims for psychological conditions, *140*
Evaluation of medical treatment, *225*
Exhibitionism, *124*
Expert assistance, need for in addressing medical issues in claims, *253*
Expert reviews and examination, problems with, *256*
External, *3*

Extradural space, *28*
Eye, *33*

F

Fabere's sign, *101*
Face, bones of the, *6*
Facet joint impingement, *97*
Facet joint sprain, *97*
Facet tropism, *95*
Facial nerves, *27*
Facsia, *21*
Facsitis, *21*
Factitious disorder, *137*
False ribs, *9*
Family, role of in rehabilitation, *203*
Fantasy, *109*
Fear, *203*
Federal Drug and Alcohol Abuse Act, *252*
Federal Privacy Act of 1974, *238, 251*
Fee audits, *274*
Fee schedules, state, *274*
Female reproductive system, *46*
Femur, *13, 16*
Fetishism, *124*
Fiber optics, scopes and, *52*
Fibrous union, *78*
Finger jerk reflex, *102*
First and second degree burns, *67*
Flail chest, *82*
Foot, bones of the, *19*
Foramen magnum, *4*
Forensic rehabilitation, *221*
Formal evaluation tools, identification of rehabilitation candidate through, *208*
Formal studies, rehabilitation in liability claims and, *194*
Fracture, colles, *13*
Fractures, adverse results of, *78*
　in children, *78*
　and head injuries, *75*

healing of, 77
skull, types of, 79
spinal, 89
types of, 75
wedge and compression, 89
Fragmentation of the disc substance, 90
Frontal bone, 3
Frontal lobe, 23
Fugue, amnesia and, 123
Function or performance, tests of, 50
Functional pain, 107

G

Gallbladder, 40
Gatekeeper physician, 278
General damages, 112, 158
Generalized anxiety disorder, 132
Glenoid cavity, 12
Glossopharyngeal nerves, 27
Glossopharyngeal neuralgia, 74
Glove anesthesia, 31
Goniometry, 165
Graduate Medical Education National Advisory Committee, (GMENAC), 266
Greater trochanter, 16
Greater tubercle, 13
Greenstick fracture, 76
Guidelines for use of chiropractic treatments, 285
Guidelines for the use of physical therapy, 287

H

Hallucinations, 121
Hammer, 36
Handicap, 156
Head injuries, 75, 79
Head injury or suspected brain damage, 208

Health care, nature of, 267
Health care dollars, sources and uses of, 262
Health care expenditures, 262
Health care system, shortcomings of, 264
Health maintenance organizations (HMO), 277
Hearing loss, 208
Heel bone fracture, 208
Hematoma, 62, 80
Hemothorax, 82
Hepatic artery, 40
Herniation, disc, 90, 97
Hip, broken, 16
Hipbone, 13
Histrionic personality disorder, 128
HMO, 277
Hospital-based nurse, 199
Hospital bill audits, 275
Hospital capacity, medical costs and, 265
Hospital records, 241
Hospitalization, 149
Humerus, 12
Hypersomnia, 124
Hypertrophic scar, 65
Hypertrophy, 20
Hypochondriasis, 136
Hypoglossal nerves, 28
Hypothalamus, 24

I

Identification, 109
of the rehabilitation candidate, 207
of serious medical cases, 232
Ileocecal valve, 40
Ileum, 40
Ilium, 15
IME (independent medical examination), 255

Impairment, *156*
  permanent, overcoming, *180*
  reports of, *167*
Impairment criteria, in the *AMA Guide*, *165*
  comparison of patient data with, *168*
Impulse control disorders, *125*
Incision, *64*
Incus, *36*
Indemnity payments and disability, *158*
Independent medical examination (IME), *255*
Indicators of exaggerated claims, *234*
Infection, *64*
Inferior, *2*
Injured person, *202*
  reactions of the, *203, 213, 215*
Injuries, abdominal, *83*
  caused by rib fractures, *82*
  diaphragm, *83*
  head, *79*
    fractures and, *75*
  internal, *81*
  kidney, *87*
  liver, *83*
  to muscles and joints, *68*
  pancreas, *86*
  psychological, *105*
  skin, *61*
  spleen, *85*
  trauma and other, *61*
Injury, identification of serious cases by, *233*
  type of, identification of rehabilitation candidate by, *208*
Injury to brachial plexus, *208*
  to nerves, *32*
Inpatient care, *214*
Insomnia, *124*
Insulin, *42*
Intellectualization, *109*
Intelligence tests, *53, 218*
Intentionally created symptoms, *137*

Interbrain, *24*
Intercostal spaces, *9*
Interest patterns, tests of, *219*
Interest tests, *53*
Interior conchae, *6*
Intermittent explosive disorder, *125*
Internal, *3*
Internal injuries, *81*
Intervening problems, *227*
Iris, *34*
Ischium, *15*
Islands of Langerhans, *42*
Isolation, *19*
Issues in medical treatment, *226*

J

Jaundice, *42*
Jejunum, *40*
Job analysis, *181, 216*
Job demands, determining, *168*
Job development, *218*
Job goals, *218*
Job modification, *216*
Job placement, *218*
Job placement specialist, *202*
Job-seeking skills, *218*
Joint, definition of, *3*
Joint Commission on Accreditation of Hospitals (JCAH), *241*
Joints, injuries to, *68*
Judgment, in identifying cases for rehabilitation, *212*

K

Keloid scar, *65*
Kidney injuries, *87*
Kidneys, *42*
Kleptomania, *125*
Knee jerk reflex, *101*
Kneecap, *16*
Kramer v. Flemming, *222*
Kyphosis, *9*

L

Labor market survey, *218*
Laceration, *64, 80*
Lacrimal bones, *6*
Laminae, *8*
Langers lines, *65*
Large intestine, *40*
Larynx, *38*
Laseque's sign, *101*
Lateral, *3*
Lateral and medial epicondyles, *13*
Leg, bones of the, *16*
Legal environment, changes in as related to medical cost containment, *273*
Lesser trochanter, *16*
Lesser tubercle, *13*
Liability cases, tools to identify rehabilitation candidates in, *209*
Liability claims, effect of disability on, *158*
  effect of medical costs on, *268*
Ligaments, *21, 68*
Ligation, *62*
Limitations on cost control in the casualty claims system, *269*
Linear fracture, *75*
Liver, *40*
Liver injuries, *83*
Longitudinal arch, *19*
Longitudinal fissure, *23*
Longitudinal fracture, *77*
Lordosis, *9*
Loss of earning capacity, determination of, *186*
Lower extremities, *16*
Lumbar plexus, *31*
Lumbar vertebrae, *6*
Lumbarization, *95*
Lung, collapsed, *82*
Lymphocytes, *42*

M

Magnetic resonance imaging (MRI), *101*
Maladjustment of the sick role, *111*
Male reproductive system, *45*
Malingering, *139*
Malleolus, medial, *16*
Malleus, *36*
Mal-union, *78*
Mandible, *6*
Manic episode, *121*
Manual dexterity and mechanical tests, *53*
Masochism, *124*
Maxilla, *6*
Medial, *3*
Medial and lateral condyles, *16*
Medial malleolus, *16*
Medical authorization, *252*
Medical bills, *239*
Medical causes, relationship of to psychological disorders and claims, *146*
Medical chart records, *249*
Medical complexity, identification of serious cases by, *234*
Medical cost containment methods, *271*
Medical cost control, *261*
Medical costs, causes of the rise in, *265*
Medical evaluation, *167*
Medical examination, independent, *255*
Medical information, authorization for release of, *252*
  organization of, *252*
Medical knowledge, claim representative's, *236*
Medical malpractice case study in rehabilitation, *196*
Medical malpractice insurance crisis, *267*

Medical management, *190, 213*
Medical record, *238*
Medical records, *236*
  nature and purpose of, *238*
  obtaining, *250*
  other, *248*
  purpose of and standards for, *238*
  standards for preparation of, *239*
  types of, *239*
Medical reports, *240*
Medical technology, innovations and spread of, *265*
Medical terminology, anatomy and, *1*
  roots in and definitions of, *55*
Medical treatment, claim representative's role in controlling, *231*
  escalating cost of, *262*
  evaluation of, *225*
  issues in, *226*
Medical treatment costs, historical perspective, *262*
Medications, *149*
Medicine, defensive, *267*
Medicolegal reports, *240*
Medulla, *24*
Meninges, *25, 28*
Menisci, medial and lateral, *16*
Mental disorders, *114*
  major categories of, *118*
Mesentery, *40*
Metacarpal bones, *13*
Metatarsal arch, *19*
Metatarsal bones, *19*
Midbrain, *24*
Middle ear, *34*
Minnesota Multiphasic Personality Inventory (MMPI), *142, 219*
Moderate or major burns, *208*
Mood disorders, *121*
Motivation, effect of on length of disability, *179*

MRI (magnetic resonance imaging), *265*
Multi-axial system, *115*
Multiple fractures or any crushing type of injury, *208*
Multiple personality disorder, *123*
Multiple uncontrolled treatment, *231*
Muscles, *19*
  classification of, *21*
  injuries to, *68*
Myelogram, *101*
Myocardial infarction, *208*
Myths about disabilities, debunking, *159*

N

Narcissistic personality disorder, *128*
Narrative report, *240*
Nasal cavities, *38*
Navicular bone, *19*
Necessity of treatment, *228*
Neck problems, *99*
Need for correct diagnosis, *227*
Nerve deafness, *36*
Nerves, cranial, *25*
  injury to, *32*
Nervous system, *22*
Neurilemma sheath, *32*
Neurologist, *198*
Nonstriated muscle, *19*
Non-union, *78*
Nurse, hospital-based, *199*
  registered, *199*

O

Oblique fracture, *77*
Obsessive compulsive disorder, *122*
Obsessive compulsive personality

Index—307

disorder, 129
Occipital bone, 3
Occupation, 169
   effect of on the length of disability, 178
Occupation code, 169
Occupational therapist, 199
Oculomotor nerves, 26
Odontoid process, 9
Olecranon process, 13
Olfactory nerves, 25
Open reduction, 77
Opinion, 252
Optic nerve, 26
Organic anxiety syndrome, 119
Organic delusional syndrome, 119
Organic hallucinosis, 119
Organic mental syndromes and disorders, 118
Organic mood syndrome, 119
Organic personality syndrome, 119
Organic psychoactive substance disorders, 119
Organs and systems, 32
Orthopedist, 198
Orthotist, certified, 200
Osteoarthritis, 69, 97
Osteomyelitis, 79
Osteophyte, 97
Osteoporosis, 78
OTR, 199
Outpatient care, 214
Outpatient treatment program, clarification of, 215
Overcoming disability, 174

P

Pain, 106
Palatine bones, 6
Pancreas, 42
Pancreas injuries, 86
Panic disorder, 122
Paralysis, suspected, spinal cord injury or, 208
Paranoid personality disorder, 127
Paraphilias, 123
Parasomnias, 124
Parietal bones, 3
Partial union, 78
Parties to the rehabilitation process, 196
Passive aggressive personality disorder, 129
Patella, 16
Pathological gambling, 125
Patient reaction, 214
Patient's disincentives to control treatment, 230
Pedicles, 8
Peer review, 284
Pelvis, 13
Percentage discount arrangements, 277
Peripheral, 3
Peristaltic waves, 40
Permanent impairment, overcoming, 180
Permanent-partial, 157
Permanent-total, 157
Personality, 125
Personality disorders, 125
Personality tests, 53
Phalanges, 13, 19
Pharynx, 38
Phobia, social, 122
Phobias, 122
Phrenic nerve, 29
Physiatrist, 198
Physical capacities, determining and restoring, 182
Physical capacities test, 182
Physical records, 251
Physical therapist, 199
Physical therapy, guidelines for the use of, 287
Physical therapy review, 288
Physician, attending, 198
   consulting, 198, 213

Physician cooperative, *174*
Physician's disincentives to control treatment, *230*
Pia mater, *25, 28*
Pinna, *34*
Placebo, *107*
Placement with a new employer, *218*
Pleura, *38*
Pleural cavity, *38*
Plexus, *28*
Pneumothorax, *82*
Pons varolii, *24*
Population changes, medical costs and, *266*
Portal vein, *40*
Positional terms, *2*
Posterior, *2*
Posterior chamber, *34*
Posterior protrusion, *90*
Posterior rami, *28*
Posterolateral protrusion, *90*
Post-traumatic stress disorder, *132*
Pott's fracture, *19*
PPO, *276*
Preadmission certification, *281*
Preadmission review, *281*
Pre-existing conditions, *144*
    effect of on disability, *178*
Preferred provider organizations (PPO), *276*
Pressures from outside the industry, rehabilitation and, *192*
Primary physician, *278*
Privacy, *251*
Private rehabilitation services, *197*
Problem psychological conditions in claims, *129*
Problems, chronic, *227*
    intervening, *227*
    unrelated, to insured event, *226*
Problems of controlling treatments, *230*
Professional rehabilitation provider, *196*

qualifications of, *197*
Projection, *110*
Prosthetist, *200*
Proximal, *3*
Psychiatric and substance abuse review, *284*
Psychiatrist, *201*
Psychoactive substances, dependence on and abuse of, *120*
Psychoanalysis, *148*
Psychoanalyst, *148*
Psychogenic pain, *107*
Psychological conditions, problem, in claims, *129*
Psychological disorders, distinct, diagnosis of, *113*
    establishing the existence of in claims evaluation, *140*
    treatment of, *148*
Psychological injuries and conditions, *105*
Psychological pain, *107*
Psychological response to physical injury, *106*
Psychological symptoms, evaluation of, *111*
Psychological testing and its problems, *142*
Psychological tests, *52*
Psychological treatment, focus of, *112*
Psychologist, *201*
Psychometric tests, *218*
Psychosocial adjustment, *191*
Psychosocial rehabilitation, *220*
Psychosocial stressors, *108*
Psychosomatic pain, *107*
Psychotherapy, *148*
Ptosis, *26*
Pubis, *15*
Pudendal nerve, *32*
Pudendal plexus, *32*
Puncture wounds, *64*
Pyloric valve, *40*
Pyromania, *125*

Q

Qualifications of the professional rehabilitation provider, *197*
Quality assurance, *204*

R

Radial nerve, *31*
Radiographic tests, *51*
Radius, *13*
Rage and anger, roles of for the disabled, *161*
Rationalization, *110*
Reaction formation, *110*
Reading tests, *53*
Reasonable accommodation, *163*
Reconstructive surgery, *67*
Record, medical, *238*
Records, ambulatory care, *248*
　emergency room, *248*
　hospital, *241*
　medical, obtaining, *250*
　medical chart, *249*
　physical, *251*
　review, *254*
Recreational therapist, *201*
Red flags, *286, 288*
Redundancy of treatment, *228*
Referred pain, *32*
Reflex sympathetic dystrophy, *212*
Reflex tests, *50*
Registered nurse, *199*
Rehabilitation, claim representative's responsibility in deciding on, *196*
　costs/benefits of, *193*
　　case studies for, *195*
　definition of, *190*
　forensic, *221*
　formal studies for the use of in liability claims, *194*
　nature of, *189*
　need for, *192*
　psychosocial, *220*
　statutory references to, *190*
　vocational, *191, 216*
　　and counseling, role of, *185*
Rehabilitation candidate, identification of, *207*
Rehabilitation engineer, *200*
Rehabilitation physical therapist, *199*
Rehabilitation process, *190, 205*
　other key parties in, *202*
　parties to, *196*
Rehabilitation professionals, other, *198*
Rehabilitation provider, professional, *196*
Rehabilitation services, private, *197*
Report, medical, *240*
　medicolegal, *240*
　narrative, *240*
Reports of impairment, *167*
Repression, *110*
Reproductive system, female, *46*
　male, *45*
Respiratory system, *38*
Retina, *34*
Retrospective review, *253, 284*
Return to former employer, *216*
Return to work, *215*
Review, chiropractic, *285*
　concurrent, *283*
　peer, *284*
Review, physical therapy, *288*
　preadmission, *281*
　psychiatric and substance abuse, *284*
　retrospective, *253, 284*
　utilization, *279*
Rheumatoid arthritis, *69*
Rib fractures, injuries caused by, *82*
Roots in and definitions of common medical terms, *55*

Rorschach Inkblot Test, *142*
RPT, *199*
Ruff, *100*
Rupture of the annulus fibrosis, *90*

S

Sacral plexus, *31*
Sacralization, *95*
Sacroiliac joint, *16*
Sacrum, *6, 9*
Sadism, *124*
Sampling tests, *48*
Scapula, *11, 12*
Scar, treatment of, *66*
Scars, *65*
Schizoid personality disorder, *127*
Schizophrenia, *120*
Schizotypal personality disorder, *125*
Sciatica, *93*
SCII (Strong Campbell Interest Inventory), *219*
Sclera, *34*
Scoliosis, *9, 95*
Scopes and fiber optics, *52*
Selected Characteristics Companion Volume, *170*
Selected Characteristics of Occupations Defined in the DOT, *170*
Selection of proper facility, *213*
Semicircular canals, *36*
Sexual disorders, *123*
Sexual dysfunctions, *124*
Sick role, adopting, *161*
   maladjustment to, *111*
Sigmoid colon, *40*
Simple fractures, *75*
Simulated disability, *162*
Skeleton, *3*
Skills, job-seeking, *218*
   transferable, *185, 218*
Skin, *22*

Skin grafting, *67*
Skin injuries, *61*
Skull fractures, types of, *79*
Sleep disorders, *124*
Sleep terror disorder, *124*
Sleep-wake schedule disorder, *124*
Sleepwalking disorder, *124*
Small intestine, *40*
Social phobia, *122*
Social worker, *201*
Soft tissues, *19*
Somatization disorder, *136*
Somatoform disorders, *135*
Somatoform pain disorder, *137*
Spasm, *19*
Special damages, *158*
Speech pathologist, *200*
Sphenoid bone, *4*
Spina bifida, *8, 95*
Spinal cord, *28*
Spinal cord injury or suspected paralysis, *208*
Spinal fractures, *89*
Spinal fusion, *93*
Spinal nerves, *28*
Spinal problems, *88*
   diagnosis of, *100*
Spinal stenosis, *97*
Spine, *6*
Spinous processes, *8*
Spiral fracture, *77*
Spleen, *42*
Spleen injuries, *85*
Spondylolisthesis, *89*
Spondylolysis, *89*
Spondylosis, *96*
Sprain, *88*
Sprains, *68*
Standards for preparation of medical records, *239*
Stapes, *36*
State fee schedules, *274*
Sternum, *9*
Stirrup, *36*

Strain, *88*
Strains, *68*
Stress, *107*
   maladaptive reaction to, *135*
   other types of in psychological claims, *146*
Stress claims, *131*
Stress disorders, *131*
Stress fractures, *78*
Stressors, psychosocial, *108*
Striated muscles, *19*
Styloid process, *13*
Subarachnoid space, *28*
Subcutaneous tissue, *22*
Subdural hematoma, *79*
Subdural space, *28*
Subluxation, *70*
Substance abuse, *120*
Superficial wounds, *62*
Superior, *2*
Supervisors and managers, involvement of in claim operations, *235*
Support from the insurance business, rehabilitation and, *193*
Surgery, reconstructive, *67*
Surplus of physicians and demand creation, medical costs, and, *266*
Symphysis pubis, *16*
Symptoms, intentionally created, *137*
Synovial fluid, *13*
Systems, organs and, *32*

T

Talus, *19*
TAT, *142*
Tatooing, *63*
Temporal arteritis, *75*
Temporal bones, *3*
Temporary disability, determining, *173*
   factors affecting the length of, *175*

Temporary-partial, *157*
Temporary-total, *157*
Temporomandibular joint, *6*
Temporomandibular joint syndrome, *73*
Tendons, *21, 68*
Testing, diagnostic, *48*
Testing problems, *143*
Tests, in diagnosing spinal problems, *101*
   psychological, types of, *142*
   radiographic, *51*
   sampling, *48*
Tests of function or performance, *50*
Tests of intelligence, *218*
Tests of interest patterns, *219*
Thalamus, *24*
Thematic Apperception Test (TAT), *142*
Therapist, occupational, *199*
   physical, *199*
   recreational, *201*
Therapist bias, *141*
Thermography, *101*
Third degree burns, *68*
Thoracic vertebrae, *6, 9*
Thorax, *9*
   injuries to the, *82*
Thyroid cartilage, *38*
Tibia, *16*
TMJ, *73*
Trachea, *38*
Training, special, for rehabilitation, *220*
Transfer, *214, 217*
Transferable skills, *185, 218*
Transverse arch, *19*
Transverse colon, *40*
Transverse fracture, *76*
Transverse processes, *8*
Transvestic fetishism, *124*
Trauma and other injuries, *61*
Traumatic problems in the cervical spine, *99*

Treatment, alternative, *229*
  further, *229*
  identifying serious cases that require, *232*
  multiple uncontrolled, *231*
  necessity of, *228*
  patient's disincentives to control, *230*
  physician's disincentives to control, *230*
  problems of controlling, *230*
  redundancy of, *228*
  usual, *228*
Treatment of disc problems, *93*
Treatment plan, *229*
Treatment program, clarification of outpatient, *215*
Treatment program specifics and length, clarification of, *214*
Treatment of Psychiatric Disorders, *149*
Treatment of psychological disorders, *148*
Treatment of psychological systems, *140*
Trichotillomania, *125*
Trigeminal nerves, *27*
Trochlear nerves, *27*
Turbinate bones, *6*
Tympanic cavity, *34*
Tympanic membrane, *34*
Type of injury, identification of serious cases by, *233*

U

Ulna, *13*
Ulnar nerve, *31*
Undifferentiated somatoform disorder, *137*
Undoing, *110*
Unrelated problems, *226*
Upper extremities, *12*
Ureters, *45*

Urinary tract, *42*
URO, *279*
Usual, customary, and reasonable (UCR) charge, *275*
Usual treatment, *228*
Utilization review, *279*
Utilization review organization, *279*
Utilization review services, *150*

V

Vagus nerve, *27, 40*
VALPAR system, *220*
Vascular layer, *34*
Veins, *36*
Verification of cause, *226*
Vertebra, construction of, *6*
Vertebral column, *6*
Vertebral foramen, *8*
Vestibule, *36*
Vestibulocochlear nerves, *27*
Visceral, *3*
Vision loss, *208*
Vitreous humor, *34*
Vocational evaluation, *218*
Vocational rehabilitation, *191, 216*
Vocational rehabilitation and counseling, role of, *185*
Vomer, *6*
Voyeurism, *124*

W

WAIS—Wechsler Adult Intelligence Scale, *218*
WAIS-R, *142*
Wechsler Adult Intelligence Scale-Revised (WAIS-R), *142*
Wedge compression fracture, *89*
Wedge fracture, *89*
Whiplash, *69, 97*
Work evaluator, *202*

Work hardening, *182, 216*
Work sample, *219*
Work tolerance, *182*
Workers compensation case study on rehabilitation, *195*
Workers compensation cases, tools to identify rehabilitation candidate in, *209*
Workers compensation claims, effect of disability on, *157*
  effects of medical costs on, *268*
Workers compensation definitions of disability, *156*
Wounds, avulsion, *65*
  puncture, *64*
  superficial, *62*
WRAT (Wide Range Achievement Test), *219*
Wrist, *13*

X

X-ray tests, *51*

Z

Z-plasty, *65*
Zygomatic bones, *6*